Dietrich Bonhoeffer
THEOLOGIAN OF REALITY

Other books by André Dumas

Der Krieg in Algerien, Zürich 1959
Le contrôle des naissances. Opinions protestantes, Paris 1965
Ideologia e Fé, Rio de Janeiro, 1968
Les mots qui nous font croire et douter, Paris 1971
Éthique, église et société industrielle, Paris 1971
Éthique, église et sexualité, Paris 1971

André Dumas has also contributed to
Technology and Social Justice, London 1971

Dietrich Bonhoeffer
Theologian of Reality

ANDRÉ DUMAS

TRANSLATED BY
Robert McAfee Brown

The Macmillan Company, New York, New York
Collier-Macmillan Limited, London

CONTENTS

INTRODUCTION

At the conclusion of his *Concluding Unscientific Postscript*, Søren Kierkegaard penned the words, "And oh, that no half-learned man would lay a dialectical hand upon this work, but would let it stand as it now stands!" Kierkegaard almost got his wish. He remained unknown and his work uninterpreted for many years, but he was finally discovered, and many scholars as well as "half-learned men" ("piddling pedants" is perhaps a better translation) have laid hands, some "dialectical" and some not, upon his work.

Something of the same sort happened to Dietrich Bonhoeffer, though in his case the time span was considerably compressed. As M. Dumas points out, it was on toward two decades after his death before serious studies on Bonhoeffer began to appear. But in recent years the rate has accelerated, and Bonhoeffer has been subjected to such a variety of interpretations – from being a repristinated Lutheran to being an incipient atheist who lost his earlier faith – that he might also be presumed to wish with Kierkegaard that interpreters would leave his writing alone and let it speak for itself.

There is an important difference, however, between Kierkegaard and Bonhoeffer. Kierkegaard's entire literary production was carefully conceived and meticulously carried out, each book thought out in relation to the others, the whole orchestrated with incredible artistic as well as theological foresight and ingenuity. Not so with Bonhoeffer, whom circumstances denied the life of careful and scholarly output that might otherwise have been his. Save for his first two books, both of which were university dissertations done in the typically thorough pattern of solid German theological research, Bonhoeffer's literary output was sporadic, hasty and frequently incomplete. Only one book, *The Cost of Discipleship*, got any significant attention during his lifetime, and his three most important writings – *Christ the Center*, *Ethics* and *Letters and Papers from Prison* – are not really "books" at all, the first being a compilation of notes

taken by students at one of Bonhoeffer's early lecture courses at
the University of Berlin, the second being a series of drafts and
fragments for a book that was far from ready for publication
when Bonhoeffer was arrested, and the third being a grab bag
of letters, poems, essays and aphorisms produced under very
trying circumstances and obviously not intended for publication.

The result is that Bonhoeffer's literary output *does* need an
interpretive, if not "dialectical," hand laid upon it, since so
many of the ideas that have subsequently been associated with
his name have been sloganized into theological catch-phrases
out of which whole systems have been spun that may or may not
have anything to do with what Dietrich Bonhoeffer himself was
trying to say and do. In a time when theology has been dominated by phrases like "religionless Christianity" (in itself a bad
translation of its German equivalent), or "the world come of
age," or "living in the world without God" (usually forgetting
that the context of the latter is the phrase "before God"), it is
not only useful but imperative to understand Bonhoeffer on his
own terms as clearly and as fully as possible.

As M. Dumas' survey shows, many interpreters have assumed
a radical break, an "epistemological shift," between the "early
Bonhoeffer" and the Bonhoeffer of the last letters from prison,
particularly those begun with the crucial letter of 30 April
1944. One of the great merits of the present work is to show the
continuities that must be understood if one is truly to understand
the developments and shifts of emphasis (but not of overall outlook) that are being explored in the final year of Bonhoeffer's
life. One discovers, for example, in the pages that follow, how
close in many ways Bonhoeffer was to Hegel, an influence on his
thought that has escaped the attention of most of the other
interpreters. The impact is not without its dangers, dangers that
M. Dumas duly notes, but it remains pervasive, and helps us
understand some of the key ideas in Bonhoeffer – the emphasis
on *structure*, for example – that would otherwise be difficult to
untangle.

This stress on the continuities also sets the groundwork for
pervasive ideas in Bonhoeffer's theology that are elaborated in
his early, and frequently neglected, writings, and that provide a
context for a further understanding of the later material in

Ethics and *Letters and Papers from Prison.* Thus to take only one
example, M. Dumas sees *Act and Being* – an extraordinarily
heavy, compact, dense and therefore neglected piece of writing
– as crucial for understanding Bonhoeffer's basic working out of
the relationship between God understood in the unique act of
his revelation ("the God of reality") and God understood as an
ontology of Being ("the reality of God") – a God who both
speaks *to* reality and is a part *of* reality. The first option seems
to lead to sheer transcendence (for how can that which is other
than the world really relate to it?) while the second seems to
lead to sheer immanence (for how can that which is within the
world be anything other than the world?). And it is his wrestling
with this problem that leads Bonhoeffer to ecclesiology and
Christology, the Church being the locus of the unity of act and
being, and being that locus precisely because it is where Jesus
Christ, who himself is the word of God to reality and also the
structure of reality, is found. For Bonhoeffer God is found within reality, not somewhere else, particularly not in "metaphysics" or "inwardness," those two deceptions that Bonhoeffer
described in the prison letters as the characteristics of "religion,"
his pejorative terms for the evasions of reality that are sought
either in a dualistic otherworldliness or an immanentistic pious
inner self.

So the key word in all of this, as the subtitle and text of M.
Dumas' book make clear, is "reality" (*Wirklichkeit*). As Bonhoeffer uses it, it is an extraordinarily rich word, most of the
nuances of which are lost by the frequency with which the word
is employed in ordinary English conversation. Throughout his
book M. Dumas contrasts the French equivalent of *Wirklichkeit*, *la réalité*, with *le réel*, a contrast that has been impossible
to render consistently in English. *Le réel* refers to the everyday,
empirical, here-and-now world around us, the world of "facticity" to use Heidegger's word, and it is rendered by such
terms in the English translation. *La réalité*, always translated
"reality," has a very different meaning: it is the world that has
been re-structured by the presence of God within it in Jesus
Christ, a *new* world that can not only be seen by eyes of faith
but can be entered into and lived by lives of faith.

Bonhoeffer's most extensive discussion of "reality" is found
in *Ethics*, Part One, Section V, on "Christ, Reality and Good,"

and the following excerpts may be useful pointers as the word crops up in the pages that follow:

When we say that God is the ultimate reality, this ... is not the religious rounding off of a profane conception of the universe. It is the acceptance in faith of God's showing forth of Himself, the acceptance of his revelation ... In Jesus Christ the reality of God entered into the reality of this world ... In Christ we are offered the possibility of partaking in the reality of God and in the reality of the world, but not in the one without the other. The reality of God discloses itself only by setting me entirely in the reality of the world, and when I encounter the reality of the world it is always already sustained, accepted and reconciled in the reality of God ... Participation in the reality of God and of the world in Jesus Christ today ... must be such that I never experience the reality of God without the reality of the world or the reality of the world without the reality of God (*Ethics*, pp. 189, 194f.).

Thus the apparently innocent-sounding phrase, "in the midst of reality," is telling us that God is found neither in some "other" world nor in our own inwardness, but at that point where man's life and experience have been transformed and re-structured by the divine action, so that there is *now* a new situation in terms of which man can live.

This is not a cheap and easy transformation, for the new structure has the content of *deputyship*, another key word, or the life lived vicariously for others, a theme present as early as *Christ the Center* (1933) even though it captures the theological imagination more acutely in Bonhoeffer's phrase a decade later of Jesus as "the man for others." The seal of the thought is the life and death of the thinker, and Bonhoeffer's own martyrdom shows how fully he embodied not only the conviction that if Jesus is the man for others, this is a pattern his followers must embrace in what Bonhoeffer had earlier called "the *cost* of discipleship" or following-after, but since the Church is "Christ existing in the form of community" (so defined in Bonhoeffer's earliest work, *The Communion of Saints*), it must also be the church that "is there for others" (so defined in Bonhoeffer's last work, *Letters and Papers from Prison*). Bonhoeffer's ideas do not deserve to be uncritically accepted simply because he died for them (good men have often died for wrong causes), but when there is such a remarkable consistency between what a man believes, how he lives, and why he dies, then we are all forced to take a second and searching look at that unity of thought, life and death, no matter how disturbing to our comfortable modes of thinking and living such a look might be.

Any translator lets go of a work with fear and trembling, since he has taken responsibility not only for his own renderings but for those of another. I am conscious of many imperfections in the pages that follow, but a great many of those that were originally present have been caught and excised thanks to the extended help I have received from M. Dumas himself, who has been extraordinarily generous with his time. During the final months of revision, circumstances enabled us to have two full days together in New York and also two days in Paris going over the translation together. And while I cannot, of course, make him responsible for my English, I can credit him with showing me many nuances in his French that might otherwise have gone undetected. I have been given equally generous help by the staff of secretaries in the office of Humanities Special Programs at Stanford University, and by my son Peter, who did much typing, editing and checking of references. Whenever possible, existing translations of works in French or German have been used, and where the latter were unavailable, translations from German sources have been made by Mrs Elisabeth Herrmann. In only a few cases has it been impossible to trace a quotation back to its original location. When Bonhoeffer materials are quoted from *No Rusty Swords* or *The Way to Freedom*, the original reference in *Gesammelte Schriften* has also been given. Since there are so many editions of *Letters and Papers from Prison*, the *date* of the letter being quoted is always provided, followed by the page number of the 1967 third and enlarged revised hardcover edition, published by SCM Press and Macmillan. Except for *Letters and Papers from Prison*, rendered in footnotes as *LPP*, and *Gesammelte Schriften*, rendered as *GS*, the full titles of Bonhoeffer's works have been used in the footnotes to save the reader from a forest of *CS*'s, *CD*'s, *AB*'s, and so forth. Finally, English readers should remember that the frequent contrast of the terms "resistance" and "submission" represent a word-play on both the German and French title given to Bonhoeffer's prison letters, *Widerstand und Ergebung*, and *Résistance et Soumission*.

Close work with M. Dumas' text for over a year, in France, Switzerland, Massachusetts and California, has left me increasingly impressed with the incisiveness of his analysis and the depth of his interpretive ability. I hope that readers will credit him with whatever new insights they discover in the following pages, and hold me responsible for any places that still seem opaque. Even more, I hope that they will have the same experience I have had – that a book like this is not only a theological joy in its own right, but that it also leads beyond itself to a new and richer acquaintance with its subject, Dietrich Bonhoeffer, "theologian of the God of reality and of the reality of God."

New Year's Day 1971   Robert McAfee Brown

I

The Context
of Bonhoeffer's Theology

1. The task of theology

Theology is an attempt to speak about God in such a way that one is really speaking about *God*, and really *speaking* about him. Dogmatics deals with the Word of God and hermeneutics with our words about that Word. Theology thus walks a tightrope between two risks – the risks that its God will vanish or that its speech will become inaudible – in moving toward a single promise, the hope that the Word of God and our words about that Word will mutually enrich one another, and that the reality of God will cast light on the reality of man. That promise informs the task of theology, even though in working it out more attention is often devoted to the two risks that threaten it.

First of all, does theology's speech really describe God, or, to put the matter negatively, does it not waste its time on repetitions that may sound beautiful but only elaborate or eternalize something that is merely human? If that is so, it would be wrong to use any other word than "anthropology" to describe a kind of speech that had man as its source, man as its task and man as its boundary. It was the Greeks rather than the Hebrews who coined the word "theology," and they were well aware of the difficulty of speaking of a god separated from man,[1] or even more, separated from a world that was understood as the meeting place of men and gods. In this regard, Plato exercised

---

[1] "Separated" (*chōristos* in Greek) indicates both what is differentiated from matter and what exists by itself. For Plato, the two meanings coincided, but not for Aristotle. Cf. Pierre Aubenque, *Le Problème de l'Être chez Aristote*, Presses Universitaires de France, Paris 1962, p. 36.

remarkable modesty, the modesty of a rational dialectic that used myths to describe an ascent toward the unconditioned motivated by love, and the even greater modesty of a mythic theology that criticized the gods of current literary and popular mythology, and which particularly avoided using the word "god" in a positive sense, preferring the term "divine" (meaning the divine part of man, when he discovers his true home outside the world of sense experience).

With Aristotle, the problem of the separation of god from existence was more complicated. On the level of cosmology, Aristotle distinguished more clearly than Plato between a remote heaven, the dwelling-place of the divine, and an earth involved in the day-to-day stuff of human history. But in a very pointed way Aristotle raised the problem of the relationship between ontology and theology, even if he did not clearly resolve it. He did not distinguish clearly between a "divine being" who would be the first cause and prime mover of reality so that we could understand reality on its own terms, and a "god" who would be separate from that reality – free from "generation and corruption" – a god who would truly be god precisely because of his difference from what we understand about the world on its own terms. Out of this background, theology slowly took shape as speech about a separate god, which for Greek thought was obviously a principle and not a person. But we must never forget that in Greek thought this separation of god from the world stayed at the level of an exercise of thought, without developing into a formal confession of faith. The Greeks felt too strongly that man belonged to the cosmos not to recognize that the gods must also belong to it. These, then, are ways of relating nature and the cosmos – ways that are interrelated, remarkable, enigmatic and ruled by necessity.

For a Greek, to raise the problem of the creation of the world by God would be to start from the wrong end, for it is always the world that creates. The gods are born when man knows how to perceive their birth. The creation of gods is thus the time when the deepest meanings of reality are explored.[2] To affirm that

[2] Men are those "to whom the immortals appeared (*antephanēsan*) fully visible" (Hesiod, fragment 165, line 5 [Oxford Classical Texts, 1970, p. 165], cited by Jean Beauffret, "L'Athéisme et la Question de l'Être," *Études philosophiques*, Paris, July–September 1966).

reality was created by God would be to render it absurd, for then instead of God being understood in terms of the world, the world would have to be understood in terms of God. This would mean abandoning what we can discover by reflection and poetry to enter what can only be understood through obedience and confession. It would mean turning from manifestation (in which the meaning comes from below) to revelation (in which the meaning is given from above), from hermeneutics to exegesis, from astonishment and wonder to faith – and one simply cannot imagine a Greek mind being willing to put up with such things. Consequently theology, as the Greeks elaborated it, remains ambiguous about the Platonic outer edges and the Aristotelian depths of the world and man, which it interprets without ever going beyond them. In terms of the etymology of the word *theo-logy*, *logos* wins out over *theos*. It is reflection about speech itself that provides the norms for deciding what such speech can designate as fixed and immutable. To speak of "god" is to ponder the very basis of Being for man's being, since man is the creature for whom Being is both presence and withdrawal.

In biblical thought, however, the perspectives are reversed. There is no word for "theology" for there is no *a priori* assurance that human thought can give an account of the "beginnings," if the latter word means not only foundation but creation as well. However, "God" exists, with a degree of consistency that is never given to him by Greek thought. Before man can speak of a god separated from the world, God himself is already at work creating the world and man. His separation is obvious; it is called "holiness," with all the ontological and ethical implications of the word. One thing alone is sure, namely that God is found neither in the spatial boundaries of the world, nor in its mythic depths, for God calls that world into being, and the One who thus calls forth is not included in what is called. We must therefore turn to another path than reflection and poetry if we are going to speak of the One who is the basis of all that is, a path that is more independent of the cosmic process but also more concrete.

History provides such a path. It starts things and keeps them going. It is thus a useful analogy for man as he tries to think about the unthinkable act of creation, the calling into being of the world which no man witnessed. Thanks to history, stripped of the Greek sense of contingency but filled with a personal meaning from the image of the One who gets it under way, biblical thought can conceive of God as separate, the One who not only causes everything to rise up, but involves himself in the uprising. The problem is not, as it is with the Greeks, to be able to conceive of a god who is separate from the world, but rather to believe that the holy God continues to intervene in what he has created, and that he continues to act with man who hereafter becomes, within the world, "the image and likeness of God,"[3] the partner in a covenant made not only with nature as in the case of Noah, but also with history as in the case of Abraham.

In choosing to call himself the Word, and in describing his creative work as speech, God indicates that he depends on man, not as the spectator who is overwhelmed by his miracles, nor as the anxious investigator of his silence, but as a trusted friend who shares in his undertaking. *Logos*, speech, is the mode of being through which God chooses to make himself known as the God of man. In becoming the Word, God does not diminish himself to the level of a human experiment of thought, in the morass and the tomb of words. Rather, he defines himself as an accessible presence, and he defines world history as the dialogue between the revelation of the Word and faith in that Word. By becoming historicized in this way, the cosmos seems to be more humanized than is the case in Greek thought, where the cosmos remains the silent mother of all that is, a mother who does not mediate any word beyond a word about man. According to biblical thought, therefore, there is a God "high and lifted up," who creates man along with the universe, but who, in the same act by which he makes all things appear, makes clear that creation is purposive rather than at the mercy of fate. Man is the recipient of this purposiveness and the cosmos is the theatre in which the drama is enacted. If we may schematize the triangular relationship between God, man and the world a bit too antithetically, we see that in Greek thought man attempts to select out of the world an immutable principle that he can call god, while in biblical thought God offers man an opportunity to

---

[3] Cf. Gen. 1.26. Cf. Karl Löwith, *Gott, Mensch und Welt in der Metaphysik von Descartes bis zu Nietzsche*, Vandenhoeck, Göttingen 1967, pp. 7–23.

think about the world and experience it as both a duty and a promise.

Each perspective has a "theology" – a word hesitantly developed by the Greeks and appropriated somewhat too eagerly by the Christian tradition – that we must now define more carefully. Actually the word is hard to deal with, since it combines the biblical belief in the prevenient and sovereign presence of God with the Greek attempt to use human language to describe what will remain meaningful within the structure of its speech. It is a word, to use Sartre's famous notion of a "useless passion,"[4] which implies that there has been a reconciliation between the *en-soi* (the being in-itself) of God, and the *pour-soi* (the being for-itself) of man. It says two things: (1) "God is" and (2) "I can speak of him," and it implies that the conjunction "and" does not create a gulf but an equivalence, or at least a correlation. It makes this assumption in two ways that are intertwined throughout the long history of the word: *either* that the transcendence of the world by a god illustrates an ongoing yearning in human thought for the unchangeable, *or* that the incarnation (which is a way of talking about the creator God as the Word) gives an historical basis for human speech to describe the One who is the Word become flesh. Needless to say, this second way is more demanding than the first. Its assurance is based on the affirmation of a reality in time and space, while the first claims a transcendence over time and space. We know, of course, that *any* claim runs the danger of removing truth into the realm of unreality. However, theology, whose foundation is the God who has actually become the Word revealed to man and incarnate in man, is itself a faith-claim, particularly since it believes that specific events can communicate truth, and since it confers on a specific history an extra-anthropological and extra-cosmic language to describe the gift of God's presence. If such a theology of the Word of God were unwilling to be described as a claim, it would do better in that case to call itself a theophany. But in so doing it would deny the very problem on which it is based, namely that God remains God even when man speaks of him. It would then be dealing with an obscure presence and would lose all sense of a

---

[4] Sartre, *Being and Nothingness*, Philosophical Library, New York 1956, and Methuen, London 1957, p. 615.

presence that was understood and believed. In fact, it would return God to the anonymous depths of the world out of a desire to minimize the mediation that is expressed by God in his decision to offer himself as the Word, and by man in his willingness to have access to understanding only by faith in a word. Thus theology, even when it is created by the biblical events, does not escape from the difficulty that was acknowledged even by those who created the word itself: when I speak of God can I speak of a truly "Other," of one who does not merely intensify the hopes and fears of men, and the wonders and enigmas of the universe? Can I speak of God otherwise than as One who transcends or engulfs what I already know? Can I, in other words, cease to be a Greek? But just as importantly, when I speak of God, can I speak of him from my human stance, in human language, according to my honest understanding and my own possibilities for authentic life? Can I speak of Him as other than a supernatural object or an imposing unreality? Can I stop thinking in terms of a theophany, i.e. in terms of a meaningless miracle?

Throughout its history, theology has lived by the promise that the dogmatic claim of the creative Word must be and can be expressed in man's own language, that God does not die but communicates himself through words, that for God speaking and doing are inseparable, and that that bond is the hope of all speech. Without words, reality totters between unfathomable mystery and sheer givenness, whether one is dealing with human statements or with God's covenant with men. That promise remains as theology walks on the narrow ridge between two possible deceptions, and only by doing so can it find a way out of the impasse. The history of theology is thus an unceasing struggle on the double front of the objectivity of the word directed toward God, and the existential reality of man's language.

2. *Objective revelation and existential interpretation*

Contemporary Protestant theology offers a particularly clear example of the problem that is inherent in every attempt to speak about God in human language. Indeed, our present situation does not have a single dominant characteristic, but is composed of two poles that correspond to the double fear already expressed, either (1) that speech about God, whether shamefaced or modest, can only be a subjective monologue within man's heart in all of his ups and downs, or (2) that such speech, whether barren or proud, can never become more than a declarative monologue about an objectified God, lacking authentic relationship to human understanding and decision. In the first instance we have the situation of subjectivism, and in the second instance deliberate objectification. The work of Karl Barth and his struggle against the elevation of nineteenth-century liberal subjectivism is a grappling with the first attitude, while the work of Rudolf Bultmann and his denunciation of the rational emphasis in orthodoxy contends with the second. Their double presence, coming at the same time (even though the impact of Barth's dogmatic affirmations was slightly earlier than Bultmann's questions about hermeneutical methodology), occupies the theological front, where they have carried on a kind of trench warfare. Their various offensives against each other have done little to refresh their vocabularies, and it seems difficult for either side to effect a decisive breakthrough. But before dealing with this relative immobility and locating the originality of Bonhoeffer's contribution in relation to it, let us recall briefly the Barthian impulse toward the God who is "totally other," and the Bultmannian reflection about the kind of language men can use to express their faith.

As a preacher of the Word of *God*, Barth rebelled against the reductionist effect of the liberal exegesis of nineteenth-century theology. He felt that it put so much emphasis on endless introductions to the historical authenticity of texts, on their conditioning by the culture of their age, on their composite development and their irrelevance to contemporary issues, that the only things left after such dissection were a few pious and moralistic generalities – the tiny mouse of religious individualism brought forth by the mountain of scientific investigation.[5] The God of prophetic and apostolic proclamation was thus transformed into the God who was known within the depths of man's inner consciousness.

As Kant had maintained in a faithful formulation of this

---

[5] Cf. Barth, *The Epistle to the Romans*, Oxford University Press, London 1933, pp. 6–10.

religion limited to moral demands by the "narrow gate"[6] of reason, the "God within ourselves" is the authentic interpreter of all revelation. Objective speech about God is thus impossible, or at any rate confused, when theology forgets to distinguish methodologically between (a) the objects of *understanding*, which belong to the empirical world of experimentation, but among which neither God nor freedom nor the soul nor eternity can be affirmed; and (b) the objects of *transcendental reason*, which, according to Kant, can have regulative importance as moral postulates and final assurances for the non-temporal reconciliation of Kantian metaphysics, but which can claim no constitutive reality. If theology wants to be taken seriously, without falling into idolatrous anthropomorphism, it will therefore take care not to objectify God. A God whose ultimacy is sacrificed for the sake of his objectivity is a God who has become illusory. God must always remain in a transcendent other-worldly realm. As Hegel put it, with quaint and malicious irony in discussing Kant: the one thing most important for Kant, to know the absolute, God, is the one thing absolutely unknowable.

Liberal theology had accepted these limitations imposed by Kantian methodology. Out of loyalty to the new critical emphasis of human reason, it had conceded that knowledge of God was rooted solely in the religious experience of individual duty. This acknowledgement was all the more sincere since the Bible (re-read without dependence on a Greek metaphysics of being that had obscured its essential message) seemed indeed to center around a similar ethic of the infinite worth of the human being loved by God. Nineteenth-century theological liberalism thus felt itself doubly faithful: both to the scientific straight-

---

[6] "*Meta*-physics," i.e. what lies "beyond physics," becomes paradoxically for Kant "the science of the *limits* of human reason" (*Opus Postumum*, cited in Jean Lacroix, *Kant*, Presses Universitaires de France, Paris 1966, p. 119). Kant particularly liked Matt. 7.13: "Enter by the narrow gate: for the gate is wide and the way is easy, that leads to destruction, and those who enter by it are many." In his own Bible he underlined "wide is the gate," and wrote in the margin, "the Church!" Cf. his own commentary on the passage: "The *strait gate* and the narrow way, which leads to life, is that of good life-conduct; the *wide gate* and the broad way, found by many, is the *church*. Not that the church and its doctrines are responsible for men being lost, but that the *entrance* into it and the knowledge of its statutes or celebration of its rites are regarded as the manner in which God really wishes to be served" (*Religion Within the Limits of Reason Alone*, Open Court Publishing Co., Chicago 1934, p. 148).

forwardness of a world that demanded critical proof of any faith wishing to be distinguished from obscurantism; and to the inner spirituality of a God who was the legislator of man's soul. It was perfectly acceptable to argue that man needed God, but it was assumed that speaking of his objective reality could be no more than a verbal trick, and something moreover that biblical religion ruled out.[7]

In his forceful revindication of objectivity for theological understanding, Barth had stormed the "narrow gate" of Kantian reason. From one aspect, Barth had embraced the Platonic heritage of Kant at many points, but particularly Kant's basic distinction, reinforced by Kierkegaard, between the temporal and the eternal, this world and the beyond, earth and heaven, the flesh and the spirit. But from another aspect, he methodically swept away the objections of Kantian idealism. He decided not to start from the human possibilities that we have of knowing, but from the realization that makes it possible for us to know the One by whom we are already known. In other words, Barth reversed the idealist orientation of the Kantian and Cartesian systems. *Cogitor, ergo sum*[8] became Barth's battle-cry, by which he meant: I am involved as obedient subject to a God who does not remain perpetually beyond my reach, as Kant felt, since I am already within his reach. God once again becomes the object who structures man, and man once again becomes the subject who is directed by the recognition of faith in the objective reality of God.[9] By thus reversing the meaning of the two words "subject" and "object," Barth rediscovers the assurance that dogmatic understanding is possible, without being threatened by Kant's criticism of the emptiness of the ontological argument.

---

[7] Cf. Helmut Gollwitzer, *The Existence of God as Confessed by Faith*, SCM Press, London, and Westminster Press, Philadelphia 1965, "Existentializing of the Talk of God since Kant," pp. 67–78.

[8] Cf. Karl Barth, *Der Römerbrief*, Berne 1919: "An objective knowledge, and not one based on experiences, events, sentiments" (p. 2 [cf. *Romans*, Eng. trans. of 6th ed., Oxford University Press, London, p. 28]). "If we do not find ourselves in the peace of the reality of God, we are obliged to find ourselves in the discord of his ideality" (*Römerbrief*, p. 182).

[9] But according to Barth, God is also the *subject* who is revealed, hidden and communicated. Cf. the helpful analysis of Barth's use of subject-object terminology as applied to God in James Brown, *Subject and Object in Modern Theology*, SCM Press London 1955, Ch. VI.

God gave himself as the object of [Anselm's] knowledge and God illumined him that he might know him as object. Apart from this event there is no proof of the existence, that is of the reality of God. But in the power of this event there is a proof which is worthy of gratitude. It is truth that has spoken, and not man in search of faith ... Truth has spoken – in a way that cannot be ignored, refuted or forgotten, and in such a way that man is forbidden and to that extent is unable not to recognize it ... That Anselm's Proof of the Existence of God has repeatedly been called the "Ontological" Proof of God, that commentators have refused to see that it is a different book altogether from the well-known teaching of Descartes and Leibniz, that anyone could seriously think that it is even remotely affected by what Kant put forward against these doctrines – all that is so much nonsense on which no more words ought to be wasted.[10]

The whole Barthian thrust is contained in this initial affirmation: objective knowledge of God through revelation is possible, since revelation has actually taken place. God's action is self-authenticating. What he has done gives us the right to speak of him. After that, the "narrow gates," which Kant had taken so seriously, can be reopened with a certain flourish, thanks to which one can understand Barth's tremendous attraction to Hegel. The realism of knowledge broadens out from inwardness to outwardness, from the private world of consciousness to the public world of corporate humanity and cosmic purpose. The Trinity, just as with Hegel, again becomes the most adequate way to think theologically about the world, which is both God's gift and his concern. Without ceasing to be a human activity, theology already shares fully in the eschatological vision which is centered in Jesus Christ. Thus there is no real break between the early Barth's critical preaching of God as "wholly Other," and the unfolding of christological knowledge in the mature Barth's *Church Dogmatics*. In both cases God's objective reality stands as much for his otherness as for his communicability. From the moment that this objectivity takes possession of us we are no longer sidetracked by problems of method. Once we have described the basic fact, the given, "the thing," the creative object to whom we can relate (*die Sache*),[11] we will

---

[10] Barth, *Anselm: Fides Quaerens Intellectum*, SCM Press, London 1960, John Knox Press, Richmond 1961, p. 171.

[11] Barth, *Der Römerbrief*, Berne 1919, pp. 6–11. Note that Barth uses the term *die Sache* and not *das Ding* (an impersonal object).

receive, in our situation as servants of the Word, a kind of childlike *naïveté* which is like God himself, since God (and following him, theology) fears neither competition nor failure. In the reality of God's name are included his necessity, his rationality and his beauty, which are both the tasks and the fruits of theology.

Having come to the point where we can speak of *God*, which is also the starting point for the whole Barthian thrust, the question of how we can *speak* of God is raised again. For we may have the misfortune to say the name of the "wholly Other," to engage in a full christological and trinitarian understanding of the whole of reality, and still ignore the man to whom all of this is addressed. In saying "God," we may lead man to believe that his own existence is destroyed. In confessing our faith in objective revelation, we may make it impervious to human understanding and decision. Such is undoubtedly the threat that hangs over any comprehensive theological (not to mention philosophical) speech. It establishes a speculative understanding that provides a sufficient place, from its own point of view, for every concrete reality. But these realities, by reason of being so precisely understood and located, lose their own originality. They cease being partners and become mere analogies, secondary reflections of a truth already fully available without them. There is a danger that God's otherness will become mere strangeness, and his plenitude a mere matter of size. Man's questions run the risk of being stifled by the assurance of exact theological answers. When speech slides too quickly over the preliminary problems of method and the possibilities of knowledge, it becomes unreflective declaration. It assumes that its words are identical with what it is talking about. As a result it empties theological affirmations of their power to encounter and to change human lives. God is no longer the inner voice of conscience, but there is a danger that he will become an outer voice that is objectively cut off from human existence.

As we turn to Bultmann, I should make clear once more that I have no intention of trying to characterize fully either the work of Barth or that of Bultmann, but only to compare their influence briefly, to set the stage for Bonhoeffer's particular contribution. In 1922, Bultmann, in the same way as Barth, wanted to expound the epistle to Romans, going beyond the preliminary questions of historical criticism and the general truths of inner consciousness, by establishing "an inner relationship to the matter [also *Sache!*] with which the text deals."[12] But it was just this "matter" that he found it impossible to recover as an object that could be objectively known. A reality was discoverable, to be sure, pointed to by the text, but a text that was itself influenced by the point of view and style of an author immersed in the historical process himself. As Bultmann put it, "criticism can never be radical enough," for it will try precisely to stress the transcendence to which the text witnesses by its *rapport* both with the text and its author. Thus all of the critical and methodological questions are reintroduced, not in order to submit the "incredibility" of revelation to a rationalistic tribunal or to reduce the message of God to the subjective needs of men, but to *interpret* the transcendence of a saving event that comes to us through statements that either express it in a context that has become part of the dead past, or (what is worse) distort it by transforming transcendence into a religious object discernible in the world.

"Demythologization," which became Bultmann's theological crusade twenty years later, was the vehicle for such interpretation. The word itself is unfortunate, since it is hard to distinguish between a *critique* of myth as the rational vehicle of a pre-scientific humanity, and a *rejection* of myth as an irreducible pointer to a basic message. In relation to the first of these two meanings, one can understand Bultmann's honesty in seeking to locate the true scandal of faith elsewhere than in the perpetuation of beliefs (such as a certain kind of cosmology) that we look upon as false, even though they were acceptable to men of biblical times. But in relation to the second of these meanings, the matter is more complex: how can the saving event of Jesus Christ still be kerygmatic, i.e. a proclamation and a reality, if it has nothing in common with a positive "mythic" significance that faith has attached to the historic signs of the cross and resurrection? While we must destroy mythologies that are false explanations of the intrusion of the "beyond" into "this world," we must not let such destruction cover up the "mythic" state-

---

[12] A fuller treatment can be found in Bultmann's review of Barth's *Epistle to the Romans*, available in English in J. M. Robinson, ed., *The Beginnings of Dialectical Theology*, Vol. I, John Knox Press, Richmond 1968, pp. 100-20, esp. pp. 118-20.

ments (in the second meaning of one thing referring symbolically to something else) that proclaim the call to faith based on significant events.[13]

This uncertainty over the use of the word "myth" makes it preferable, in describing Bultmann's task, to speak about his goal (existential interpretation) rather than his means of reaching that goal (demythologization). It is not a matter of eliminating outmoded or false mythological remnants, but of interpreting the biblical speech of God so that it can be understood as a word addressed to man.

Myth should be interpreted not cosmologically, but anthropologically, or better still, existentially.[14]

It is clear that Bultmann means by this an understanding of existence, and that Heidegger, in *Being and Time*, had provided a description that is exact, universal, concrete and formal enough not to prejudge the existential decisions by which every man is called to choose, through action, the true possibility of his being.

Existential interpretation stresses this possibility – the possibility that the divine speech may challenge man to understand and to live in a new way. It seeks to give God back his role as the one who questions man's obedient freedom, without existentialist analysis (which is the task of theological interpretation) ever being relieved from the necessity of existential decision (which is the act of the believer). The act of thinking and the act of living are thus separated only in order to be more firmly joined together, for even theological thought is content to theorize, so long as its own structures do not demand a clear-cut choice.

Of course Bultmann does his thinking out of the background of Heidegger's ontology, with its availability of being for Being, and not out of Kant's critical philosophy, with the preciseness of its abstract limits. But Heidegger himself had given a profound

[13] "Theology must decide whether it wants to be mythology or philosophy. There is no middle ground. The existential interpretation of mythology is itself already a philosophical criticism of theology" (Helmut Haug, "Offenbarungstheologie und philosophische Daseinanalyse bei Bultmann," *Zeitschrift für Theologie und Kirche* 55, 1958, p. 253).

[14] Bultmann, in H.-W. Bartsch, ed., *Kerygma and Myth* I, SPCK, London 1953, p. 10.

interpretation of Kantianism as an attempt to base ontology on man's finitude.[15] Furthermore in Kant, as Heidegger pointed out, the human subject is receptive. His understanding is dependent rather than independent. Respect is the supreme mark of his obedience to the unconditional demand. While for Heidegger temporality and death are the chief marks of human finitude, for Kant man's acknowledgement of a sense of ought is crucial. Thus there is an existentialism in Kant which, with all its differences of vocabulary and content, is not far from Bultmann's concern for existential interpretation. By forbidding a thoughtless use of the word "objective" to designate God, Kant laid the foundations for a metaphysic of ethics that is attainable by man, who shares both in the finitude of a world cut off from being and in the openness of that world to being. Understood in this way, Kantianism is neither a step toward positivism, with its non-speculative and non-transcendent moral demands, nor the initial stage of absolute idealism, in which the human subject becomes supreme. It is rather the modern form of a possible ontology in which man no longer tries to put himself in the midst of being but submits himself to the claims of being.

By making the necessary adjustments we see how existential interpretation can likewise help to de-objectify God, for to describe God as an "object" (whether of the world or in the world) would be either meaningless superstition or an attack on his Lordship.[16] And it is in order to re-establish human understanding and obligation that Bultmann, like Kant, develops a new set of methodological presuppositions and a fresh vocabulary. Barth had swept all these away, so that he might understand objectively how God gave himself to man's understanding, but Bultmann multiplied them, so that man might know that God is neither the prisoner of man's fears nor beyond his obedient hearing.

We can conclude, in the light of this brief picture of the recent theological scene, that objective revelation, by placing itself, as in Anselm, on the side of a God whose reality is given in his

---

[15] Cf. M. Heidegger, *Kant and the Problem of Metaphysics*, Indiana University Press, Bloomington 1962.

[16] Cf. André Malet, *La Pensée de Rudolf Bultmann*, Labor et Fides, Geneva 1962, pp. 5-21.

name, runs the risk of speculative metaphysics, in which man contemplates something done outside himself; while existential interpretation, by placing itself, as in Kant and the early Heidegger, on man's side, runs the risk of describing nothing more than a human approach to a kind of understanding and decision that are only transcendent possibilities. But we can also record that there has hardly ever been a theological era that has felt more strongly the necessity (with Barth) of a *God* who is more than the mere repetition of man's inner yearnings, and the necessity (with Bultmann) of being able to *speak* about a God who is more than a religious "object" far removed from man's ability to understand and his very ability to be. This, then, has been the double theological concern of our time – on the one hand really to speak about *God*, against all reductive subjectivism, and on the other hand really to *speak* about him, against all objectification of self-contained supernatural truths.

In this situation of trench-warfare, where everything that is objective tends to seem non-existential and vice versa, the creative independence of Bonhoeffer's theological contribution is impressive.

3. *Bonhoeffer's theological method*

Bonhoeffer's work is fragmentary. It is influenced by the various events that stimulated, colored, and diversified it. It changes in feeling, according to urgency and moods. It invites interpretation. It tests out various limited hypotheses that are apparently contradictory. It is polyphonic, for it refuses to ignore things that cannot be reduced to systematic harmony or monotonous repetition. As we will see, Bonhoeffer's legacy is similar to such treasures; everyone works the vein that enriches his own understanding of issues.

Nevertheless, his books are tightly reasoned. They are not catch-alls for constantly shifting convictions, even when one trail is unexpectedly abandoned in order to explore a new one. Heidegger has written: "Thinking means reduction to one thought which will some day remain in the sky of the world like a star."[17] And Giradoux offers the following description of

---

[17] Heidegger, *Aus der Erfahrung des Denkens*, Neske, Pfullingen 1954, p. 7, cited in Heinrich Ott, *Wirklichkeit und Glaube* I, 1966, p. 81.

the slow ascent of the new star through the glimmers of light
that announce its coming:

The most poignant path of all is the one that leads a writer toward
his masterpiece. Among all the encounters that occur between beings,
plants and lights, which taken together uphold our world, the most
exalted and yet the most uncertain and most threatened encounter
is the one that takes place through mutual silence and ignorance,
between the poet and a dark shadow which even he cannot identify
clearly ... This crucial encounter is preceded by a thousand little
encounters with certain words, certain inflections, certain glimmers
of light, certain odors, that mark the proper route. It was by certain
words that illumined the way, by certain expressions that caught fire,
that Racine was led slowly but surely to *Bérénice*, and Shakespeare to
Troilus and Cressida.[18]

I would make the same wager that Bonhoeffer, for whom things
were so discontinuous and chopped up and whose theological
life extended through the unbelievably quick changes in Germany between 1906 and 1945, "from idealism to the democracy
of the masses," as Karl Kupisch has put it,[19] had only one
concern: to hold onto the world around him, since God is
found in the concrete. This means making christological reality
the center of one's very being, the place where God and the
world are no longer strangers, in order to display that relationship "without [metaphysical] separation or [immanentist]
confusion," which is simply the application of the Chalcedonian
formula about the person of Christ to reality. It means maintaining the full range of thought, action and meditation about
the mystery of the incarnation that saves confession from being a
series of worn-out platitudes, life from a barely-endured pragmatism, and piety from inner smugness. It means finally a
willingness to savor the everyday world as the salt of faith – if
we may thus reverse the meaning of Matt. 5.13 – for if there is
no more faith *on earth*, "how shall its saltness be restored? It is no
longer good for anything except to be thrown out and trodden
under foot by man."

There are two ways of denying the incarnation: either by
returning God to heaven, isolating him from the world by

[18] Jean Giraudoux, *Les Cinq Tentations de La Fontaine*, Grasset, Paris 1938.
[19] Cf. Karl Kupisch, *Zwischen Idealismus und Massendemokratie*, Lettner, Berlin
1959.

metaphysical speculation, dogmatism, inwardness and religion; or by failing to see that he is already mysteriously present in reality,[20] which is what men did in the case of Jesus of Nazareth by their shortsightedness, their comfortable optimism or their sceptical pessimism. The reality of which Bonhoeffer speaks consists of a world already inhabited by the incarnate Christ. As he sees it, positivism and idealism are only abstract understandings of that specific reality. From the standpoint of his realism, Bonhoeffer works out a christological analysis of the concrete, which is neither superimposing God's work on man's failure, nor letting man take over once God retires, but rather the way in which God as man in Jesus Christ takes the world upon himself, and the way in which man yields to that responsibility in such a way that it is an act of submission but not surrender. It is a realism that is full of tension, for the world of men is a very battlefield from the moment that God commits himself to the recovery of its lost unity. But this realism is also serene, for if man takes risks by his thought and action, if he calculates the stakes and pays the price, he does not have to worry about the outcome, which is in God's hands.

Before describing Bonhoeffer's particular method any further, let us try to locate him in relation to Barth's objective revelation and Bultmann's existential interpretation. At first glance, Bonhoeffer seems to have moved gradually from the former to the latter. Whereas Barth begins as a preacher and ends as a systematic theologian, Bonhoeffer begins as a dogmatist and becomes more and more concerned to make his preaching understandable to his contemporaries. He is thus a convinced and grateful follower of Barth who, when confronted by the fact that humanity no longer felt the need for God, looked for new ways of interpreting how God speaks to man, thereby aligning himself with Bultmann's concern if not his perspective.

Bultmann is aware of the scientific dishonesty involved in demanding that modern man believe not only in "salvation by faith" but also in the mythological world-view that the biblical authors used to express that belief. Consequently he proposes to "demythologize" the biblical terminology in order to liberate its underlying purpose, which is to proclaim that salvation

---

[20] "The factual is not truly the real, but an abstraction from its fulness" (Ott, *Wirklichkeit und Glaube* I, p. 154).

comes to men who give up believing in themselves, who turn away from their self-sufficiency to grace, and who believe in the reality of the forgiveness accomplished on the cross.

In similar fashion, Bonhoeffer is aware of the unreality represented by the demand that in addition to inhabiting the earth where God became incarnate, modern man must also inhabit another "religious" world that has always been part of the traditional Christian message. Consequently he proposes to free Christian preaching and existence from this religious aura that distorts the truth of faith. God is always involved in reality. Consequently if religion retreats to unreality, God will be found in what is *non*-religious. God is where men are. He is ultimate reality in the midst of penultimate realities, in "this-worldly transcendence."[21]

Non-religious interpretation means that God wants to be believed in, in Jesus Christ, without any worldly or other-worldly, religious or non-religious, end in view. It is not religious words about the greatness of God but non-religious words of his abasement that have conquered the world ... The condescension of God is the real assumption of his transcendence.[22]

Interpreted in this way, Bonhoeffer would be a Barthian as far as dogmatics and preaching were concerned, but as far as hermeneutics and methodology were concerned, he would subsequently have pursued a course parallel to Bultmann's – with this difference however: Bultmann, deeply concerned with scientific rationality, did not want to require a false *sacrificium intellectus* in the name of faith, whereas Bonhoeffer, deeply committed to the radical this-worldliness of Christianity, did not want to equate the obedience of faith with the evasion of formal belief, or the inclusiveness of Jesus Christ with the provincialism of religion. Bultmann is more an intellectual, Bonhoeffer more a man of action in both a spiritual and political sense. Bultmann, very much a traditional Lutheran, emphasizes the acceptance of the free gift of salvation. Bonhoeffer, more concerned with the problem of worldly responsibility than simply with the justification of the sinner, speaks of Jesus Christ

[21] R. Gregor Smith, "Diesseitige Transzendenz," in *Die Mündige Welt* II, 1956 pp. 104–16. Cf. Stephen Neill, *Men of Unity*, SCM Press, London 1960, Ch. 9, "Bonhoeffer and Worldly Christianity."

[22] Hanfried Müller, *Von der Kirche zur Welt*, pp. 418, 421.

and of the life of the Christian who follows him in a more political, cosmological and ontological way. Bultmann is more concerned with hermeneutics, Bonhoeffer with ethics.

This quick attempt to locate Bonhoeffer, as one combining Barthian scholarship with an interpretive task paralleling Bultmann's, is not false. I am willing to defend it, even though I must later point out that it underplays Bonhoeffer's independence of thought and creative originality – not, to be sure, as one who must discover everything for himself and submit to no influences, but rather as one who thinks things through on his own terms.

The theological relationship between Bonhoeffer and Barth was very deep, even though they met only a few times. The human relationship was cordial and the spiritual relationship was trusting and close.[23] Bonhoeffer never studied under Barth. He only heard him lecture during a two-week session at Bonn in July 1931, after he had already published *Communion of Saints* and defended his second dissertation on *Act and Being*. From this distance, Bonhoeffer with his scientific upbringing feared that dialectical theology was neglecting the critical questions posed by liberal exegesis. He was afraid that its emphasis on the transcendent act of God made it impossible to ground an ontology in Christ, to provide a dogmatic base for the empirical church, or to develop a concrete ethic. He therefore saw Barth as a theologian whose epistemology was based on Kant, and whose understanding of Christian existence came from Kierkegaard, while Bonhoeffer viewed himself as schooled in a neo-Lutheranism that wanted to reconcile the critical demands of the modern mind with the realism of sacramental thought. In the eyes of the young Bonhoeffer, Barth's preaching of God as

---

[23] Here are some indications of the sources of the Bonhoeffer-Barth relationship. Bonhoeffer texts: *The Communion of Saints*, pp. 165, 207, 223, 226–7, 238–40; *Act and Being*, pp. 11, 81f., 90, 93–4, 98n., 101ff., 129n., 135ff., 175–6; *No Rusty Swords*, pp. 12, 19, 27, 32–3, 49, 62–3, 76, 90, 115–16, 119, 120ff., 140f., 204–7, 219, 230–1, 234, 237; *The Way to Freedom*, 16, 25, 43, 102, 104f., 115, 119ff., 122, 198, 269, 275. Some texts from Karl Barth: *Church Dogmatics* III/1, pp. 194ff., 240, 245; III/4, pp. 4, 10, 14f., 21f., 404, 406, 449, 548, 653; IV/1, p. 70; IV/2, pp. 505, 533ff., 540ff., 553, 557, 599, 641. Interpretations of the relationship: Regin Prenter, "Dietrich Bonhoeffer and Karl Barth's Positivism of Revelation," in R. Gregor Smith, ed., *World Come of Age*, pp. 93–130; Heinrich Ott, *Wirklichkeit und Glaube* I, pp. 50–4, 106–25.

the "totally Other" ran the risk of metaphysical dualism by placing God's claim outside the world, and ontological inconsistency by underestimating the being of God in the church.[24]

Nevertheless, Bonhoeffer defended the Barthian dogmatic enterprise as early as 1931 in a lecture on "The Theology of Crisis and its Attitude with Respect to Philosophy and Science,"[25] given to the American students at Union Theological Seminary. In it he accepts the view that theology should concentrate on its own domain, without worrying too much about its relationship to the philosophical culture surrounding it. God speaks to us in his revelation about the new reality that we are, and not about the new ideal that we ought to be. It is the fact that God truly enters into history that makes him invisible to our human eyes, as distinct from idealism's claim that the new values Jesus brought to earth are clearly discernible. Pseudo-revelations can be seen, whereas true revelation is hidden, and is simply foolishness to those whom God has not freely chosen to receive the secret by faith. God is unconditioned and free. "God's coming in Christ is the proof by God himself that man cannot come to God."[26] This is why God does not complete man's moral or religious activity. He limits it in a single act of judgment and grace. The same man who is limited and judged, is also the man who is justified. He has no "reasons" for believing. The theological premise that cannot be proved but must be accepted is the premise that God speaks.

All that has been summarized up to this point is fully Barthian, indeed early Barthian! Bonhoeffer is an intrepid transcendental and dialectical Daniel cast into the lion's den of American reliance on religious experience . . .

However, Bonhoeffer does not evade the methodological problems inherent in a position that never portrays God as an object approachable through formal or cognitive presuppositions. He calls attention to

the great antithesis of the Word of God and the word of man, of grace and religion, of a pure Christian category and a general religious category of reality and interpretation.[27]

[24] Cf. "Das Wesen der Kirche" (The Nature of the Church), Appendix A in Bethge, *Dietrich Bonhoeffer*, German edition, pp. 1057ff.

[25] Printed as Appendix II, *No Rusty Swords*, pp. 361–72, cf. *GS* III, pp. 110–26.

[26] Bonhoeffer, *No Rusty Swords*, p. 365.

[27] Bonhoeffer, *No Rusty Swords*, p. 366; cf. *GS* III, pp. 116f.

However, he goes on, we are not able to dispense with some philosophical formulation, however inadequate, in order to describe revelation. Barth himself uses the vocabulary of the neo-Kantians of the Marburg school. Thus one must at all costs avoid using "naïve realism" as an interpretive tool. In order to speak of God, Barth adopts the terminology of the Kantian transcendental Ego. Bonhoeffer puts to Barth the question raised by Griesebach (which is also from another side, he adds, Heidegger's question): in limiting itself, i.e. in setting its own limits, is not this way of thinking egocentric? Does it not do violence to reality? For here is the philosophical circle (and also the theological circle, as Bonhoeffer recognizes) *par excellence*: how can one think comprehensively and yet in thinking comprehensively not finally lose touch with concrete reality, which is yet another limit to thought that thought itself cannot establish? Moreover Barth sees in this fatal egocentricity of philosophic thought a clear proof of man's sin. What is necessary to break the circle therefore is God's unique act of revelation. This does not hinder Barth, in an effort to describe this act of revelation, from finding usable elements for theology even in "Idealism [which] sees God as eternal subject, [and in] realism which sees reality as transcendent object"[28] – an approach that allows him to speak of God simultaneously as essential subjectivity and as the most objective of realities.

So ends Bonhoeffer's 1931 lecture. It is of great interest, for it shows an adherence to Barthian dogmatics that is never repudiated. But it also manifests Bonhoeffer's concern that speech about God must be able to cope with philosophical questions about the terms of the intelligibility of *all* human speech. The lecture thus underlines the fact that even with his eclecticism, which is sometimes humorous (in order not to yield to the momentary fascination of philosophical "armor" and "eurekas") and sometimes deliberate (in order not to let himself be diverted from the proper object of theology by the formulations of human reason), Barth himself makes use of the vocabulary of the philosophers.

Theology's contribution to philosophy is to use the reality of revelation to break the circle of egocentric understanding, the chief shortcoming of which is the weakness of abstraction,

[28] Bonhoeffer, *No Rusty Swords*, p. 371; cf. *GS* III, p. 123.

whatever precautions it takes toward better self-understanding and self-limitation. Philosophy's contribution to theology is to use the reality of the world to break the circle of an over-inclusive affirmation and claim that is the weakness of a "positivistic" supernaturalism, whatever precautions it takes to speak kerygmatically rather than speculatively. The adjective is particularly appropriate for it is the one chosen by Bonhoeffer thirty years later in 1944, to describe his fear that Barth's dogmatics would end only in a restoration of orthodoxy – a "positivism of revelation."[29] Naturally it would be wrong to claim that in 1931 Bonhoeffer already understood the question that still remained fragmentary and enigmatic when he posed it in 1944. But only the subterranean course of an idea enables one to verify its importance and clarify its scope. It seems clear that from the beginning Bonhoeffer feared that Barth's dogmatics (which Bonhoeffer accepted) might end in speculative abstraction because of its lack of verification in reality – an abstraction in which the subject would exert its power of knowing from a unique transcendent standpoint located in a "beyond" that would be normative for everything else. God would be the subject-object from which I could understand the world by detached theological speculation.

In thinking comprehensively (whether starting from Kant's transcendental ego or Barth's trinitarian revelation and "christological concentration") is not systematic thought so self-contained that reality remains exterior to it and that it thus becomes abstract? Theology can fall into the egocentricity of objective revelation, just as philosophy can fall into the egocentricity of transcendental reflection. Bonhoeffer finds the safeguard against these dangers in his concept of reality (*Wirklichkeit*). He never uses the old liberal word "experience," which he considers too individualistic and interiorized. It is reality that always obligates theology and philosophy to test themselves by limits they do not control. Reality helps theology maintain its dialogical truth. Bonhoeffer's question about Barth in the prison letters becomes all the more important as in the same passages he gives credit to Barth and to Barth alone for having initiated the discussion of the difference between faith and

---

[29] Bonhoeffer, *Letters and Papers from Prison*, letters of 30 April 1944, p. 153; 5 May 1944, p. 157; 8 June 1944, p. 181 (hereafter cited as *LPP*).

religion in the *Epistle to the Romans*, a discussion about reality that disappears, Bonhoeffer avers, in the later *Church Dogmatics*, in which the world of objective revelation becomes all-inclusive, and in which every biblical passage has its own self-evident worth without any critical reality to limit it, so that human reality therefore has only to be silent in the face of the givenness of revelation laid down as a fact in itself. When revelation always understands reality better than reality can understand itself, the influence of reality on theological speech is destroyed by a theological explanation of the whole of reality. The restoration of "orthodoxy" (which Bonhoeffer feels Barth's *Church Dogmatics* comes dangerously close to supporting) would mean the establishment of a system of affirmation that might be true enough, but without any grasp of the everyday world. And as Bonhoeffer wrote to Bethge on 30 April 1944, "For the religionless working man (or any other man), nothing decisive is gained by this 'positivism of revelation.' "[30]

As one might suspect, this critique of Barth's position has brought forth all kinds of reactions. It comes from one of Barth's closest friends – one who received constant theological stimulation from Barth's *Church Dogmatics*, who appreciated the man even more than his books, and who in prison described the reception of a cigar from Barth as something "really indescribable," a kind of sacrament of friendship and mutual trust.[31] It is thus in any case impossible to make Bonhoeffer into an opponent of Barth. But all thought needs to be understood, or at the very least interpreted. After Bonhoeffer's death Barth minimized the importance of the expression "positivism of revelation," concerning which he hoped, as he said good-humoredly, "that in heaven at least he has not reported about me to *all* the angels (and the fathers of the church too) with just this expression." Barth saw in the phrase, as in the whole project of non-religious language, only a warning against the non-reflective and lazy chatter that goes on "under thousands of Christmas trees" where the world in fact finds nothing to think about, because the speaker himself thinks about nothing.[32]

Helmut Gollwitzer thinks instead that Bonhoeffer is criticizing

[30] Bonhoeffer, *LPP*, 30 April 1944, p. 153.
[31] Bonhoeffer, *LPP*, 26 November 1943, p. 98.
[32] Cf. R. Gregor Smith, ed., *World Come of Age*, pp. 90f.

a certain kind of biblical fundamentalism and allegorizing, which was the consequence of the Barthian reaction against the liberal and rationalistic presuppositions of the previous theological generation. But Gollwitzer adds that in this case Bonhoeffer ought to have criticized himself rather than Barth, since Bonhoeffer's own commentary on Ezra and Nehemiah gives an extreme Christian interpretation of those Old Testament books that is unwarranted by the facts of history. Here, Gollwitzer insists, Bonhoeffer is more guilty of a "positivism of revelation" than Barth himself.[33]

Regin Prenter takes Bonhoeffer's critique more seriously. He sees it as central to the non-religious proposals of the later Bonhoeffer. To him "positivism" means understanding faith-claims as factual propositions in a literalistic sense without any living relationship between God's gift and the world. In this situation faith becomes a set of rules about what must be believed. Revelation remains other-worldly. It locates God in his objective being, no matter what happens to the world in relation to him. As a Lutheran, Prenter also fears what he calls a grandiose "supralapsarian speculation"[34] in Barth's theology, by which he means a focussing of all theological thought on the intertrinitarian love of God and on predestination before the fall, leaving the world as no more than the echo and analogy of that love, and salvation as the inevitable consequence of predestination. If that is so, says Prenter, Barth has made too little of the event of the world as creation, and Bonhoeffer would have had every right to raise a serious question about his speculative leanings toward gnosticism (Prenter clearly rejects the word, but only after having suggested it), and to set up over against such leanings his own emphasis on this-worldliness. Prenter concludes that the ontic element in Bonhoeffer's thought fortunately corrects those elements in Barth's thought that are too purely cognitive.

Heinrich Ott has dealt at great length with the question of Bonhoeffer's relationship to Barth.[35] According to him, Bon-

---

[33] In Zimmerman and Smith, eds., *I Knew Dietrich Bonhoeffer*, p. 140. Martin Storch shares Gollwitzer's point of view, and finds more traces of a "restoration of orthodoxy" in the theology of the Confessing Church than in Barth's work.

[34] In *World Come of Age*, p. 126.

[35] Ott, *Wirklichkeit und Glaube I, Zum theologischen Erbe Bonhoeffers*, 1966, pp. 50–4, 106–25.

hoeffer was always close to Barth in building a theology not from the anthropological possibilities of "religious" man but from the reality of the God who acts by coming to man and speaking to him. On the other hand, Barth, along with the Confessing Church, conceived of theology too much in terms of ongoing proclamation, without giving enough attention to real questioning.[36] In this sense, Barth imposed a now-dated confessional situation on the whole theological task. This situation of a Barthian confessionalism had a twofold origin: (*a*) its *initial* origin, which grew out of its antithesis to liberal theology, which the young Barth saw in Roman Catholic teaching, as well as in liberal Protestantism's emphasis on religious "experience," and (*b*) its *historic* origin, which grew out of the struggle of the Confessing Church against heresy in Nazi Germany. But according to Ott, this confessional style renders Barth's thought – no matter what its genius, culture and warmth may be – unfit for true dialogue. It tends to become unilateral, simply making declarations in monologue form, with a kind of "impressive closed-mindedness."[37] Ott writes: "For Barth, theology is understood as a system, not as a method."[38] Barth's theology puts all biblical passages too uncritically on the same level of importance. It transforms faith into law. It tears apart the unity which the gift of the incarnation had established between the church and the world, for on the one hand faith becomes unbelievable, and on the other hand the world is left to its own devices. Its procedure is too deductive, as for example when it moves from christology to anthropology. It lacks the step-by-step method that Ott recommends (following Bonhoeffer, he insists), and that he calls a dialogical incarnational method, in which each assertion must submit to the process of *verification*.[39] According to this method, the claim that it is *God* who speaks, and the claim that one can *speak* of God, come together again in a kind of testing that is more a matter of

[36] Ott, *op. cit.*, p. 121.

[37] Ott, *op.cit.*, p.47. Ott states that Barth, with his method of extended essays in fine print, is less dialogical than St Thomas, with his method of questions and answers.

[38] Ott, *op. cit.*, p. 387.

[39] The term is taken from Ebeling: "If we began before by asking whether the subject of which theology speaks can be verified as reality, we now ask whether the subject of which theology speaks itself verifies reality" ("Theology and Reality," in Ebeling, *Word and Faith*, SCM Press, London, and Fortress Press, Philadelphia 1963, p. 195).

showing than of speaking, so that the concrete nature of the incarnation is exemplified in the theological method itself. In place of the orthodoxy without dialogue that threatens Barth's whole system, Ott indicates that he prefers dialogical realism.

We will examine Ott's assertions when we deal with various interpretations of Bonhoeffer in Chapter IX. They appear to set dialogical method in opposition to the need for systematic presentation, in which case they would fail to do justice to the power that Bonhoeffer always acknowledged in systematization. It is surely the proper task of theology to think everything through systematically from where God is to be found, and no situation of dialogue can exempt theology from this task. On the other hand, Ott really appears to understand Bonhoeffer's question: "But where *is* God to be found?" Is he in some other-worldly objective revelation, or is he in the agony and victory that he experiences in the midst of the everyday world that has become non-religious and has no inclination for either meta-physics or inwardness? Certainly such a question does not create mutually exclusive alternatives, for revelation teaches the world about its true reality. But it points up the line of division between an orthodox way of speaking on the one hand, in which objective correctness is made up of an impersonal and alienating impenetrability, and, on the other hand, a word that is always threatened, that can speak of the everyday world only by par-ticipating in its contradictions – which was the initial concern of dialectical theology. If Ott is right, then the very success of the Barthian system constitutes its failure, just as the successes of Kantian criticism or Hegelian ontology constitute their failure. But did Barth ever think he could succeed in deducing everything positively from christological and trinitarian revela-tion? Bonhoeffer's question, because he was the most creative of Barth's friends, thus remains the same sort of question as the one Barth had asked about the limits that save philosophy from its egocentricity.

The relationships between Bonhoeffer and Bultmann are not nearly as close,[40] and they occur at a less central point. Bon-

[40] Cf. Ebeling, "The Non-Religious Interpretation of Biblical Concepts," in *Word and Faith*, pp. 98–161, esp. pp. 138–41, and G. Harbsmeier, "Die nicht-religiöse Interpretation biblischer Begriffe bei Bonhoeffer und die Entmytholo-gisierung," in *Die Mündige Welt* II, pp. 74–92. Cf. also Gerhard Krause, "Dietrich

hoeffer approves of Bultmann's attempt to speak of God in terms of contemporary reality. In this sense, he places himself among those who have recognized Barth's "limitations."[41] He appreciates the fact that Bultmann does not stifle the critical questions of liberal theology. The two of them share a love for the nineteenth century, a refusal to engage in any *sacrificium intellectus*, and a fear that dogmatic theology will no longer be heard because of its objectivizing or positivistic tendencies. When he refers to Bultmann's famous 1941 essay on "The New Testament and Mythology," it is not for the purpose of criticizing (in Barthian fashion) its latent anthropology, or the musty odor of natural theology in its stress on "pre-understanding" (*Vortverständnis*), or even its philosophical dependence on Heidegger's terminology, but rather to point out that the enterprise was really not radical enough.[42] At first glance, therefore, Ebeling seems justified in placing Bonhoeffer and Bultmann close to one another, and in reducing the criticisms that Bonhoeffer addresses to Bultmann to the level of a misunderstanding about the alleged "liberal" intention of demythologizing (just as Barth had reduced the question of the "positivism of revelation" to the level of a misunderstanding), and to Bonhoeffer's failure to notice the degree of identity between Bultmann's attack on myth and his own condemnation of religion.[43] In the light of this, it is not surprising that in *Honest to God*, Bishop Robinson should have equated the concerns of Bonhoeffer and Bultmann (and Tillich), suggesting that all three were aiming to speak of God in a way that was non-traditional, non-metaphysical, non-religious, non-mythological, non-supernaturalistic – a God neither "up there" nor "out there."[44]

Such generalizations, however, only confuse matters. They promote false agreements under the pretext that these theologians, so profoundly different, all wanted to create a way of

Bonhoeffer und Rudolf Bultmann," pp. 439–61, and Heinrich Ott, "Existentiale Interpretation und anonyme Christlichkeit," pp. 367–81, in *Zeit und Geschichte: Dankgabe an Bultmann Zum 80. Geburtstag*, Tübingen 1964.

[41] Bonhoeffer, *LPP*, 8 June 1944, p. 181.

[42] Cf. Bonhoeffer, *LPP*, 5 May 1944, p. 156. Barth's critique is found in Bartsch, ed., *Kerygma and Myth* II, SPCK, London 1962, "Rudolf Bultmann – An Attempt to Understand Him," pp. 83–132.

[43] Ebeling, *Word and Faith*, pp. 139f.

[44] J. A. T. Robinson, *Honest to God*, SCM Press, London, and Westminster Press, Philadelphia 1963, esp. Ch. 2, "The End of Theism."

speaking about a God who has become "unbelievable" to modern secularized man. Actually Bonhoeffer's opposition to Bultmann runs deep, for it arises both out of Bonhoeffer's Barthianism and out of the specifics of his anti-Barthianism. Like Barth, Bonhoeffer is afraid that demythologization is only an existentialist version of the "typical liberal process of reduction – the 'mythological' elements of Christianity are dropped and Christianity is reduced to its 'essence.' "[45] Like Barth, he objects to Bultmann's minimizing of the positive worth of the Old Testament, to the individualism of the act of faith, and to the stress on existential interpretation without enough concrete historicity. And above all, Bonhoeffer sees in Bultmann an exaggerated version of the lack of realism that he believed was already betraying Barth's system. Bonhoeffer is worried not because Bultmann runs the danger of too much speculative and deductive systematizing, but because, even more than Barth, he is in danger of locating God at the far end of a leap of faith outside the world. Bultmannian eschatology involves a denial of the world of the believer, who is thrust into the "moment," *à la* Kierkegaard, outside all his securities, toward the transcendent assurance of faith. This is utterly different from "discipleship," from following Jesus Christ in the world, which Bonhoeffer claims is an affirmation of the world by the Christian who shares in the sufferings and the victory of God in this world. Bonhoeffer fears that Barth's objectivity will turn into speculative positivism, but he fears even more that Bultmann's existentialism will result in an idealism of possibility rather than reality. Quite typical in this connection is a comment in *Act and Being* – which Gerhard Krause curiously describes as the strongest criticism ever made of Barth – in which Bonhoeffer, after having placed Barth and Bultmann side by side as theologians of the act, still prefers Barth to Bultmann because, as he puts it, Bultmann is too dependent on the category of "possibility" to characterize the being of man in general, quite apart from the reality of the encounter with revelation.[46]

[45] Bonhoeffer, *LPP*, 8 June 1944, p. 181. "Bultmann's approach is fundamentally still a liberal one (i.e. abridging the gospel), whereas I am trying to think theologically. What does it mean to 'interpret in a religious sense'?" (5 May 1944, p. 156).
[46] Bonhoeffer, *Act and Being*, p. 98 n.3.

Thus although Bonhoeffer's non-religious interpretation and Bultmann's existential interpretation share a common methodological concern, i.e. to *speak* of God from the perspective of contemporary man, they remain very different. For Bultmann, it is the non-scientific cosmology of the biblical mentality that creates the problem. For Bonhoeffer, it is in a larger sense the metaphysical dualism of a Platonized Christianity that obstructs man's ability to listen. To push the point, it is the specific realism of the miracles that deters Bultmann, while it is the vague idealism of the *kerygma* that deters Bonhoeffer. For Bultmann "mythology" stands for an unacceptable pseudo-rationality. For Bonhoeffer "religion" is trying to speak about an unlivable pseudo-reality. Harbsmeier has developed this contrast best in saying that for Bultmann the central problem is the problem of how man is to *understand* God, whereas for Bonhoeffer it is the question of *the presence or absence* of God in men's lives.[47] When Bultmann ponders, Bonhoeffer is undergoing temptation. Although very close to Barth, Bonhoeffer protects himself against orthodox positivism. Although further removed from Bultmann, Bonhoeffer also demonstrates the need for interpretation, in order that God can be spoken to man where he really is, and not only affirmed above or beyond him.

We have looked in considerable detail at this three-cornered debate between Barth, Bonhoeffer and Bultmann, for it is at the heart of the current theological situation. Barth speaks of the Word of *God*, running the risk of overpowering transcendence, inclusion and recapitulation. Prenter uses three equivalent words to describe how Barth's theology can become external to the concrete world of creation: actualism, analogism and universalism.[48] In this view the world in its concrete reality is ignored, even though its theological significance is fully explained. Bultmann wants to be able to *speak* about God in the language of man, running the risk of existentialism, voluntarism and individualism in the language of faith, in which God always remains the inexpressible appellant and giver of human openness.

[47] In *Die Mündige Welt* II, pp. 74–80. ·
[48] Cf. "Bonhoeffer and Barth's Positivism of Revelation," in R. Gregor Smith, ed., *World Come of Age*, esp. pp. 106–22.

Bonhoeffer, as sensitive to the reality of the Word as to the reality of language, might be the one who could reconcile the two perspectives, objective and existential, without succumbing to their dangers.

That is one possible line of interpretation. But Bonhoeffer's situation is seen much more clearly if we look at him by himself, in the acknowledged "distance" that was characteristic of him both as a person and as a thinker.[49] Neither a student of Barth nor a disciple of Bultmann, coming neither from Bonn nor Marburg but from Berlin and in this sense "isolated" and being his own master, Bonhoeffer belonged to the currents that preceded dialectical theology and he indicated those that would follow it. He never used the characteristic vocabulary of early Barthian transcendentalism (God as "totally Other," the infinitely qualitative distinction between God and man, crisis, the *actus purus*, the impossible possibility), or the vocabulary of Barth's *Church Dogmatics* in its fully developed form (the analogy of faith, election, justification, sanctification, Jesus as victor). Nor did he use the vocabulary of Bultmannian existentialism (historicity, possibility, understanding, conceptuality, decision, and, of course, the contrasts between ontological and ontic, between existential and existentialist). He likewise avoided the vocabulary of nineteenth-century liberalism (experience, personality, inwardness, essence and values).

So Bonhoeffer's theology was neither transcendental, existential, nor liberal. It can best be described as structural. From his earliest works through the *Ethics*, we find a remarkable continuity in his expression of Christian faith, not as the beyond that is self-authenticating, nor as an encounter that takes place, but as a structuring that combines self-knowledge with self-realization. Before God, Jesus Christ is the center and the responsible structure of reality. He is neither beyond the world nor in the depths of being, but at the center of the empirical world, which is no longer understood pragmatically but as having an ontological structure understood in christological terms. Such vocabulary, it must be understood, is based on the categories of space, logic, physics and geography, more than

---

[49] Cf. Chapter II below, "A Biographical Sketch," where an attempt will be made to introduce Bonhoeffer as a person, after this rather abstract initial chapter.

on those of time, events, personality and history.[50] The analysis of creaturely-existence (*Dasein*) aims at demonstrating its reality by grasping its hidden and active structure, rather than by opening it to a message that would transform it from beyond itself. Hegel's influence in this seems undeniable (an influence continually present in *Communion of Saints*, *Act and Being* and *Christ the Center*), but it is a Hegel less concerned to describe the logic of history, or to conceptualize the spirit of an age and a people, than to describe subjective experience in objective terms, in brief, a Hegel who is a logician and an anti-Kantian, more than a philosopher of becoming. Bonhoeffer had been able to subscribe to such Hegelian formulas as the following:

Only that which is not true is inaccessible ... The real subject matter is not exhausted in its purpose, but in working the matter out ... The force of mind is only as great as its expression ... Only the spiritual is the actual, the real ... Spirit consists, not in being a meaning, not in being the inner, but in being the actual, the real.[51]

To be sure, Bonhoeffer also saw in Hegel the triumph of human autonomy and of the anonymity of the spirit. In one of his prison letters he even accused Hegel of pantheism.[52] But it is important to insist here on the ontology of the everyday world that Bonhoeffer drew from Hegel as the formal model for his christology, ecclesiology and ethics, whereas Barth, as we have seen (and Bultmann even more than Barth), started from the transcendentalism of Kant and Kierkegaard. To offer a broad generalization, one could say that Barth and Bultmann began as Kierkegaardians; Bultmann remained one, while Barth became a Hegelian – which is what Bonhoeffer always was!

The two key-words in Bonhoeffer's thought, what might be called his formal principle and his substantive principle, are structuring (*Gestaltung*) and deputyship (*Stellvertretung*).[53]

[50] On the spatial rather than historical emphasis in Bonhoeffer's thought, cf. the pertinent comments by Christoph von Hase, "Begriff und Wirklichkeit in der Theologie Bonhoeffers," in *Die Mündige Welt* I, p. 33.

[51] Hegel, *The Phenomenology of Mind*, Macmillan, New York 1931, pp. 69, 74, 766.

[52] Bonhoeffer, *LPP*, 16 July 1944, p. 195: "In the last resort, Kant is a deist, and Fichte and Hegel are pantheists."

[53] *Gestaltung* comes from *Gestalt*, which can be translated as "structure," "form," "figure," or "shape." In interpreting Bonhoeffer, a logical emphasis is preferable to a personalistic one, in order to emphasize the concrete and real, and not only intentional and ideal, character of the structuring of the world in Jesus Christ.

1. Jesus Christ is the one who *structures* the world by representing its true reality before God until the end. When biblical words like "redemption" and "salvation" (which Bonhoeffer seldom employs) are used today, they imply that God saves us by extricating us from reality, blissfully removing us from any contact with it. This is both gnostic and anti-biblical. In the same way the word "fall," which is neo-Platonic and non-biblical,[54] leaves us with the impression of being cast out of a paradisial state. However, true biblical preaching does not say that man falls into terrestrial darkness, or that God plucks him out of the world in order to install him in heaven. Rather it says that God recreates his good creation in Jesus Christ, proclaiming to faith's expectation that there are new heavens *and* a new earth, just as Genesis had told how the heaven and earth of the first Adam were described, the first heavens having been created like the earth itself and in no way constituting an eternal copy of a transient earth. Therefore, instead of being called "savior" by Bonhoeffer, Jesus Christ is described by a series of non-religious words: he is a structure, a deputy, the one responsible for the world, he who restores their true "center" to all things.

In the light of this, it is interesting to note how Bonhoeffer's christology, so classical in its foundations, is formulated.[55] In Part One of *Christ the Center*, Bonhoeffer describes "The Present Christ – The 'Pro Me,' " before speaking in Part Two about "The Historical Christ," where he deals with various types of christology. At first glance, this arrangement seems very Bultmannian and existentialist: I come to who Christ is "in himself" through the Christ who exists "for me"; I understand his nature through his work. This sounds remarkably like Bultmann's

---

Bonhoeffer speaks of Jesus Christ as the central structure of the world, of the church as the concrete structure of Christ, and of the world as the structuring of reality in Jesus Christ. Cf. *Communion of Saints*, especially pp. 103–55; *Act and Being*, pp. 117–26; *Christ the Center*, pp. 41–67, and *Ethics*, pp. 224–62. In his early lectures on the nature of the church Bonhoeffer characterizes the structure which is from God as both unity and wholeness, in contrast to the composite and synthetic structures that men create artificially (cf. Bethge, *Dietrich Bonhoeffer*, Appendix A, "Das Wesen der Kirche," in German edition, p. 1060).

[54] Cf. Paul Ricoeur, *The Symbolism of Evil*, Beacon Press, Boston, Mass. 1968, p. 233.

[55] Bonhoeffer, *Christ the Center*, Harper and Row, New York (= *Christology*, Collins, London) 1966, 236pp.

contention that it is not because Christ is Christ that he transforms believers, but that it is because he transforms them that he is Christ.

The saving efficacy of the cross is not derived from the fact that it is the cross of Christ; it is the cross of Christ because it has this saving efficacy.[56]

But a more careful reading reveals a totally different direction in Bonhoeffer's thought that can be clarified by examining the German terms he uses in *Christ the Center*. Part Two is called "The Historical Christ," and Bonhoeffer uses the adjective *geschichtliche* (an interpreted event), instead of *historisch* (a neutral fact) which in terms of Bultmann's existentialist contrasts we might have expected. Part One, on the other hand, is called "The Present Christ," and here Bonhoeffer uses *gegenwärtige* (presence in the here and now), rather than *geschichtliche* (an interpreted event) which once again in the light of a Bultmannian approach we might have expected. What this brief linguistic exercise shows us is that Bonhoeffer is *not* saying, as Bultmann does, that we first come to know the Christ of existential interpretation and only then the Christ of concrete history. Rather, he is saying that we begin with the concrete present in order after that to reflect on various ways of conceptualizing it. The approach is ontological and Hegelian, not existentialist.

Part One of *Christ the Center* is striking. It describes the structure *(Gestalt)*[57] of Christ as Word, Sacrament and Community, and then speaks of the place of Christ as center *(Mitte)* of human existence, of history, and finally as the mediator (also *Mitte*) between God and nature. Thus it is a christology employing the categories of structure and space. *Ethics*, written ten years later, is simply the concrete unfolding of this approach.[58] The Church is the concrete place where the human existence receives its form and structure in Christ, where the everyday world rediscovers its true reality, and where nature becomes redirected toward the One who is neither at its far reaches, nor its negation, but is its hidden center. This is why to

[56] Bultmann in H.-W. Bartsch, ed., *Kerygma and Myth* I, p. 41.
[57] In the English translation of *Christ the Center*, *Gestalt* is translated "figure."
[58] Cf., for example, *Ethics*, p. 193: "Participation in the indivisible whole of the divine reality – this is the sense and purpose of the Christian enquiry concerning good."

be a Christian is to become true man once more. In this way, Bonhoeffer hopes to overcome the fatal divorce between objective meaning outside of man and an existential meaning confined to man, between a transcendent object and an individualistic subject, between objective nature and subjective history, between speculation focussed on another world and speculation reduced simply to a consideration of man. His formal principle, which I have called "structural" (or, if one prefers, "structuralist"),[59] is a third way, along with Barth's objective revelation and Bultmann's existential interpretation, to speak of *God* while *speaking* about the reality in which God is already present.[60]

Actually, Bonhoeffer never described this method. He employed it in an ongoing relationship with Barth's theology, and in accord with a similar desire for a liveable reality that Bultmann displays toward the *"croyable disponible,"*[61] but always with his own independence. It is by this method, in my judgment, that Bonhoeffer provides a fresh way for contemporary theology. He applied it successively to the established church, the Confessing Church, and the "non-religious" church, relating it to each new situation, but with Jesus Christ always at the center.

It should be clear that "non-religious interpretation" has no particular worth in and of itself. It is simply taking the method of seeing Jesus Christ as the structure and center of reality and applying it to a new situation whose novelty and consistency Bonhoeffer discovered very powerfully while in prison. He did not "adjust" Christianity to a world gradually come of age, a

[59] Concerning "structuralism," let us borrow the simplest definition: "'Structuralism' is an attempt to discover, beneath the observed facts, the hidden reason for their appearance, to bring to light this underlying shape, which can therefore be called a structure . . . Structure is both a reality – that shape which analysis uncovers – and an intellectual tool – the law of its variability . . . 'Structural' refers to structure both as syntax, and as reality" (Jean Pouillon, "Un Essai de Definition du Structuralisme," *Les Temps Modernes*, November 1966, pp. 779f.).

[60] How a theology of the Word is maintained in the midst of an ontological analysis, is a question that has not yet been answered.

[61] The expression is Paul Ricoeur's and is virtually untranslatable. It suggests an attempt to express one's beliefs in terms related to one's own cultural situation, terms that are "available" for use in such a way as to gain cultural credibility. It characterizes helpfully the Bultmannian concern to destroy the false conceptual scandals for the sake of the only real scandal – that of the cross, grace and faith.

modern world that would thereby have become a determining norm for him. Bonhoeffer was not so entranced as some have said by the philosophy of history nor by its aiways-debatable evaluations, and indeed we must ask whether man has truly come of age and become non-religious. Bonhoeffer simply maintained at the end of his life his initial affirmation that God can only be found in the midst of the world, even if it is now a "godless" world. Just as Bultmann put demythologizing at the service of existential interpretation, Bonhoeffer puts the "non-religious interpretation of Christianity" at the service of his theological method, which is to speak of God in the midst of man's everyday life in the world. If the terms are reversed, one runs the risk of making Bonhoeffer only an adapter of Christianity to the secularization of the world,[62] thereby missing the power of his theological conviction:

When we say that God is the ultimate reality, this is not an idea through which the world as we have it is to be sublimated. It is not the religious rounding-off of a profane conception of the universe . . . Its purpose is, therefore, participation in the reality of God and of the world in Jesus Christ today, and this participation must be such that I never experience the reality of God without the reality of the world or the reality of the world without the reality of God.[63]

2. Bonhoeffer's second key-word, along with structuring, is *deputyship (Stellvertretung)*, in the strongest meaning of the word.[64] Jesus Christ structures the world at its center because, having been conformed to reality, he becomes responsible for it before God. His responsibility rests upon his deputyship, not in the sense that he replaces man to relieve him of the burden of costly grace, but in the sense that he takes on the selfhood of all men, and invites us in our turn to carry his cross, as an act not of resignation, but of faithfulness in our situation, the acceptance of struggle and responsibility.

---

[62] Bethge rightly comments that Bonhoeffer did not use the term "secularization," which suggested to him the church's nostalgia for a golden age in the past. (Cf. *Die Mündige Welt* I, p. 21.)

[63] Bonhoeffer, *Ethics*, pp. 189, 195.

[64] The word suggests taking someone else's place in order to fulfill his responsibility, i.e. to engage in vicarious action. Bonhoeffer speaks of the deputyship of Christ, of the church and of the Christian in *Communion of Saints*, pp. 82–5, 103–44; *Act and Being*, pp. 153–84; and *Ethics*, pp. 224–7.

Deputyship, and therefore also responsibility, lies only in the complete surrender of one's own life to the other man.[65]

Here again we see Bonhoeffer utilizing a non-religious vocabulary to describe the fundamental meaning of redemption in contemporary terms, in which Jesus Christ saves men only by becoming man, submits to God only by resisting as man, and makes freedom possible in the world only by actually expressing that freedom in the midst of reality. So the structure of responsible life is marked by four things: holding ourselves responsible for our fellow human beings (deputyship), acting in a manner conformable to reality ("correspondence with reality"), accepting guilt and freedom, and taking the risk of concrete decisions.[66] This is the non-religious way of describing the work of Jesus Christ as neighbor, incarnate, burdened and committed. Thus Bonhoeffer is able to speak about the reality of man without ignoring the reality of Christ, and vice versa.

Apart from this responsible deputyship of the world before God, the structuring of the world in Christ would remain a verbal pretension, either enigmatic or pure formal logic. But with this concrete deputyship, which involves obedience even to the point of the cross, structuring receives a content, and structuralism acquires a logical meaning lived in accordance with fulfilled reality. Structure indicates the place that is never vacated, while deputyship indicates the meaning of what is lived there. The two words come together to express, in non-religious language, the extent and reality of salvation achieved in Jesus Christ.

Bonhoeffer's theology is a theology of reality. It was Ebeling who first made the point,[67] stressing in a remarkable way that this insistence on reality, even more than on truth or freedom, had in some respects a medieval emphasis.

The basic structure of "religion" is supplementing reality by God, and the basic structure of "non-religiousness" is coping with reality

---

[65] Bonhoeffer, *Ethics*, p. 225. Cf. the entire section, pp. 224–7, where Bonhoeffer develops this theme compellingly.

[66] Cf. Bonhoeffer, *Ethics*, pp. 227–54.

[67] Subsequently, Heinrich Ott has written 394 pages on Bonhoeffer's theological heritage under the general title *Wirklichkeit und Glaube*, i.e. *Reality and Faith*, Fuchs entitled his speech to a gathering of pastors in Geneva, "Bonhoeffer, A Theology of Reality." And the present book, of course, is continuing the development of this theme.

without God ... The basic structure of faith [is] enduring reality before God. Thus defined, faith is concrete faith and finds "worldliness" at once both a necessity and a gift ... Being a Christian does not add anything to being a man but puts our humanity into force.[68]

To the alternatives, whether they be a dogmatic and unreal transcendence or a nihilistic and tragic denial of truth, Bonhoeffer responds not from the standpoint of naïve realism but on the basis of a christological ontology, insisting that the truth of God is hidden in the reality of the world, just as Jesus Christ even on the cross is the responsible man, the deputy hidden from the will of men. Nietzsche accused Christianity of being only a "Platonism for the people" – of imposing a false dualism on the world, of sacrificing the tragic beauty of the everyday world to the illusion of an ideal world because of resentment at its lack of power, of refusing to accept that what we call "truth" is only an expression of the "life force." Bonhoeffer quite simply believed that in Jesus Christ God and reality are creatively united in a struggle in which the everyday world is not destroyed, and God does not withdraw, but in which what is real for man takes place on the cross, and what is real for God takes place in the resurrection.

After, but only after, having tried to understand this way of thinking, let us now become acquainted with the man. For although the story of a man's life does not create his thought, his life will put it to the test.

[68] Ebeling, *Word and Faith*, p. 160.

II

A Biographical Sketch

1. *1906–1945*

Bonhoeffer's thought is too closely tied to the events of his life
to permit us to discuss his work without some knowledge of
those events. We will recall them briefly as a way of showing the
close connection between Bonhoeffer's theological themes and
the unfolding events of his life. This will also help us gain a
better understanding of Bonhoeffer's particular kind of subjectivity. In his writings, Bonhoeffer made a great effort not to
let his personal emotions cloud his ability to think clearly. In
terms of the vocabulary of *Life Together*, he felt that "psychological" (or human) pressures should not influence the sound-
ness or the "spiritual" (and intellectual) independence of one's
work. With the exception of the prison letters which were not of
course intended for publication, Bonhoeffer's writings, although
born in the midst of stirring events, are quite abstract and self-
effacing. Ideas must be able to stand on their own two feet
without being based on sentimentality or personality. Consequently we must become acquainted with the events of
Bonhoeffer's life, which are of fundamental importance for
understanding the development of his writings, but which never
appear directly in the texts themselves.[1]

1 The basic biographical source is the monumental work by Bonhoeffer's close
friend, Eberhard Bethge, *Dietrich Bonhoeffer: Theologian, Christian, Contemporary*
(1970), a slightly condensed version of the original German edition of 1967, which
contains many helpful appendices omitted from the English translation. Mary
Bosanquet, *The Life and Death of Dietrich Bonhoeffer* (1968), makes considerable use
of Bethge's material, and is the fullest biographical treatment apart from his.
Bethge's essay, "The Challenge of Dietrich Bonhoeffer's Life and Theology," in

Bonhoeffer was born on 4 February 1906, in Breslau, the same city where Friedrich Schleiermacher, the son of a Reformed pastor, had been born on 21 November 1768. Bonhoeffer's family was an upper-class family with a Lutheran heritage. He and his twin sister were the sixth and seventh children in a family of eight. His father was a well-known psychiatrist who became a professor at the University of Berlin in 1912. His mother, whose maiden name was Paula von Hase, was the granddaughter of the distinguished church historian, Karl von Hase, and the daughter of one of the emperor's chaplains. The latter had reproached William II for calling the working class "rabble," and had prevented William from preaching a sermon of his own in response. Consequently, when his irascible parishioner refused to attend further services, von Hase left the chaplaincy at Potsdam to become professor of theology at Breslau. When Bonhoeffer was in prison during the war, his mother's cousin, General Paul von Hase, was the commandant of Berlin, and made a significant visit to Bonhoeffer on 30 June 1944. A few weeks later, he was condemned to death by the People's Court, and executed before his nephew was.

In 1921 the family moved to Berlin and went to live in the attractive residential district of Grunewald. As a young man, Bonhoeffer appreciated all that his family provided in the way of balance, self-control, and respect for truth – a family that emphasized hard work and respect for each member's personality, but also a family that made music together, entered enthusiastically into sports and organized lively festivals among the neighbors.

R. Gregor Smith, ed., *World Come of Age* (1967), pp. 22–88, relates the events of Bonhoeffer's life directly to the development of his theology. W.-D. Zimmermann and R. Gregor Smith, eds., *I Knew Dietrich Bonhoeffer* (1966), is a collection of reminiscences by friends of Bonhoeffer. Theodore A. Gill, *Memo for a Movie: a Short Life of Dietrich Bonhoeffer* (1970), is a short but vivid presentation based on the works just mentioned.

Most of the books about Bonhoeffer's thought give some space to the events of his life. Cf. *inter alia* John D. Godsey, *The Theology of Dietrich Bonhoeffer* (1960), René Marlé, *Dietrich Bonhoeffer: the Man and his Work* (1968), William Kuhns, *In Pursuit of Dietrich Bonhoeffer* (1967), and Benjamin A. Reist, *The Promise of Bonhoeffer* (1969).

Two collections of translations from Bonhoeffer's *Gesammelte Schriften* also help to fill in many biographical details: *No Rusty Swords* (1965) and *The Way to Freedom* (1966).

Bonhoeffer himself was a sensitive and even chivalrous child, eager to win but knowing how to lose, friendly and yet reserved. He soon learned to weigh his words carefully. His sister-in-law, who was a childhood friend of the eight Bonhoeffers, wrote with a touch of humor:

Whereas we Delbrücks shrank from saying anything banal, the Bonhoeffers shrank from saying anything interesting for fear it might turn out to be not so interesting after all, and the inherent claim might be ironically smiled at.[2]

Bonhoeffer also knew how to listen, an ability that was characteristic of his whole life and theology:

He himself was one who asked questions. He could not stand empty talk. He sensed unfailingly whether the other person meant what he said.[3]

His twin sister remembers him as a boy who had no difficulty with his studies, was a very good companion although without close friends, was gay and friendly, but also experienced sudden moments of melancholy, as if, as she put it, he had been confronted by "the *eros* of far-away." She remembers with delight a kiss that he gave her at the time of her engagement, for, as she continues, this "was not a custom among us brothers and sisters." Later on, one of his students was astonished when Bonhoeffer told him that beside his relatives, there was only one person whom he had ever addressed as *Du* – an intimate form of German speech reserved for close friends. His sister-in-law summarizes her memories of him as follows:

To keep a distance in manners and spirit, without being cool, to be interested without curiosity – that was about his line.[4]

So Bonhoeffer's upbringing was "bourgeois," in a Berlin whose atmosphere was more liberal and university-oriented than it was military.

And the more his inner and outer life was uprooted from such a background, the more he expressed his gratitude for this nineteenth-century oasis extended into his own lifetime, for the "unashamed self-assurance" in which he had been so freely

---

[2] Emmi Bonhoeffer, in Zimmermann and Smith, eds., *op. cit.*, p. 36.
[3] *Ibid.*, p. 36.   [4] *Ibid.*, p. 36.

raised. When he was in prison he began to write a play, in which the son of a bourgeois doctor talks with a young proletarian. Their exchange helps to clarify what Bonhoeffer thought in 1943 of the "privileges" of his youth:

Christoph (the young bourgeois): I come from what they call a good home, that is from an old, respectable middle-class family, and I am not one of those who are ashamed to admit it. On the contrary, I know what strength there is in a good middle-class home. Nobody can know this who has not grown up in one. And it's hard to explain, but there's one thing you must know: we grew up to reverence what was created, what was given, and thus to respect every man. We regarded mistrust as mean and unworthy. The honest word and the honest deed is what we look for, and wish to accept without suspicion.

Heinrich (the young proletarian): You have a foundation, you have a ground beneath your feet, you have a place in the world, you have certainties for which you fight, and for which you may calmly let your head be battered in, because you know that your roots lie so deep, that they will grow up again ... This ground we do not have; so we are tossed to and fro, whichever way the storm blows; that's why we have nothing worth having our heads battered in for ...

Christoph (thoughtfully): Ground under your feet – it never struck me like that – I believe you are right – I understand, ground under your feet – to be able to live and die.

Heinrich: Is it their fault if they have been thrust into life without any firm support? Can you bypass them and talk to them about things that are irrelevant to them?[5]

There is an "aristocratic" accent here – if the word is not too strong – similar to that found in Simone Weil, in a statement likewise written in 1943.[6] Bonhoeffer never repudiated it. It is discernible in *Ethics*, and it comes back in the prison letters

[5] In Bethge, ed., *Die Mündige Welt* I, p. 13. The above translation, except for the last speech, is taken from Dress, "Remarks on the Theology of Dietrich Bonhoeffer," *Union Seminary Quarterly Review*, Winter, 1970, pp. 134f., translated by Professor and Mrs Reginald Fuller.

[6] "Security is an essential need of the soul. Security means that the soul is not under the weight of fear or terror, except as the result of an accidental conjunction of circumstances and for brief and exceptional periods. Fear and terror, as permanent states of the soul, are well-nigh mortal poisons, whether they be caused by the threat of unemployment, police persecution, the presence of a foreign conqueror, the probability of invasion, or any other calamity which seems too much for human strength to bear" (*The Need of Roots*, Routledge and Kegan Paul, London, and G. P. Putnam's Sons, New York 1952, p. 33).

with their reawakened affection for what his family meant to him, and the inner continuity of which he became aware:

I have certainly learnt a great deal, but I don't think I have changed very much ... except perhaps at the time of my first impressions abroad and under the first conscious influence of Father's personality. It was then that I turned from phraseology to reality.[7]

Bonhoeffer always retained this aristocratic nature, together with a tinge of melancholy and sudden decisions to act as he himself saw fit.

At the age of fourteen he decided to study theology, to the mild astonishment of his family, within which there was a fair amount of scientific scepticism in the midst of a long-standing Christian heritage. Bethge makes clear that Bonhoeffer's parents did not go to church regularly or take part in parish life. Instead, such religious observances as baptisms were celebrated at family gatherings, by calling upon a pastor who was a relative – a common upper-class practice of the time. It was acceptable to be a Christian, though scarcely a churchman. As is often true in similar situations, Bonhoeffer's mother, nourished in Moravian piety but without pietistic narrowness, put more stress on family worship than his father, who, while respectful and reserved on such matters, held to a scientifically-oriented "prudent agnosticism," which made him, for example, one of the German psychiatrists most hesitant to accept Freudianism because he found Freud too speculative, drawing conclusions far beyond what the evidence would bear. Bonhoeffer's decision to become a pastor therefore considerably surprised those who knew him. As Bethge puts it, "Because he was lonely, he became a theologian, and because he became a theologian he was lonely."[8]

Much later, in 1934, Bonhoeffer's father confided his thoughts about the decision to his son:

At the time when you decided to devote yourself to theology I sometimes thought to myself that a quiet, uneventful minister's life, as I knew it from that of my Swabian uncles and as Morike describes it, would really almost be a pity for you. So far as uneventfulness is

[7] Bonhoeffer, *LPP*, 22 April 1944, p. 149.
[8] Bethge, *Dietrich Bonhoeffer*, p. 23.

concerned, I was greatly mistaken. That such a crisis should still be possible in the ecclesiastical field seemed to me with my scientific background out of the question.[9]

Bonhoeffer himself almost never spoke of the reasons for his vocation, nor about the feelings he experienced at the time of his confirmation. As he saw it, curiosity about such personal matters always ran the risk of reducing a mystery to a commonplace. For his *abitur* (school-leaving examination) he wrote a strongly secular dissertation on "Catullus and Horace as Lyric Poets." He then set off for the faculty of theology, much better acquainted with the world than with the actual church.

He began his studies enthusiastically at Tübingen in 1923, where he was impressed by Adolf Schlatter's biblical realism and the emphasis he put on goodness, justice and nature in the study of the New Testament, Karl Heim's ability to help one feel solidarity with the doubt of unbelievers, and Karl Groos's grasp of Kantian logic.

The next year, after three months of travel in Rome and North Africa, Bonhoeffer settled in at the faculty of theology of the University of Berlin, where the great names in German theology taught: Adolf Deissmann, Ernst Sellin, Hans Lietzmann, Adolf von Harnack (the best known of all), and the two exponents of what was then called the "Luther renaissance," Karl Holl and Reinhold Seeberg. Wolf-Dieter Zimmermann, a theological student who did not become acquainted with Bonhoeffer until 1932, and who edited the personal reminiscences entitled *I Knew Dietrich Bonhoeffer*, paints a less attractive picture of the very academically-oriented teaching:

I studied theology because I came from a parsonage. But for two years I could not make head or tail of my studies ... What I heard in theology bored me infinitely. The pedantic juggling with Greek words and theological concepts seemed meaningless to me, and gave me no guidance. For Reinhold Seeberg we had to translate texts from the late middle ages, but what they meant, how they were related to God's actions, I never discovered. The same was true of Sellin's formalistic dealing with the book of Isaiah, and of Deissmann's elucidation of the New Testament. Only Lietzmann in his introduction to the New Testament and his exegesis of the Synoptic

[9] Letter of 2 February 1934, cited by Bethge, *op. cit.*, pp. 22f.

Gospels gave us a picture of what had happened at the time of Jesus, and its meaning for us.[10]

But Bonhoeffer gave his full attention to the tasks confronting him, with a taste for order, precision, rigor, and achievement that transformed him into a true revolutionary when he later came up against the great disorder of Nazism. He wrote a paper for Sellin on the various solutions to the problem of evil in Job, and two essays for Holl, one on "Luther's Feelings about his Work in the Last Years of his Life, according to his Correspondence of 1540–1546," and another on "Luther's Views of the Holy Spirit according to the Disputes of 1535–1545." The elderly Harnack wanted to make an historian out of Bonhoeffer. Indeed, it was Bonhoeffer who, speaking on behalf of the young theologians, gave the memorial address for Harnack on 15 June 1930, after the latter's death:

> Almost two generations separate us from him, whose closest pupils have in their turn already become our teachers . . . We knew him in his unswerving quest for truth and clarity . . . He was an ever ready listener and counsellor who was concerned with nothing but the truth of his answer. But it became clear to us through him that truth is born only of freedom . . . Because we knew that with him we were in good and solicitous hands, we saw in him as it were a bulwark against all shallowness and stagnation, against all the fossilization of intellectual life . . . He was a theologian, a conscious theologian . . . It was like him to say too little, or rather many words too few, than to say one word too many . . . But the little that he did say was enough for us. I end with a phrase which was a favorite of his: *Non potest non laetari, qui sperat in Dominum.* ["He cannot cease rejoicing, who hopes in the Lord."] [11]

Bonhoeffer worked particularly with Reinhold Seeberg in systematic theology, clearly picking up from him Ritschl's aversion to metaphysics, and continuing his academic endeavors with such essays as "Can a Distinction be Drawn between a Historical and a Pneumatological Interpretation of the Scriptures?", "Reason and Revelation in Early Lutheran Dogmatics," "The Teaching of Early Protestant Dogmatics on Life and Death and the Last Things," and "Church and

[10] Zimmermann and Smith, eds., *op. cit.*, p. 59.
[11] Bonhoeffer, *No Rusty Swords*, pp. 29–31 (*GS* III, pp. 59–61).

Eschatology." Under Seeberg's direction Bonhoeffer, then only twenty-one, defended his dissertation on 17 December 1927, on *The Communion of Saints, A Dogmatic Inquiry into the Sociology of the Church.*[12]

The theses which he defended the same day, against three opponents, in line with university custom, are interesting not only because of their broad cultural background, precise formulation and dogmatic stress, but also because they illustrate Bonhoeffer's fear that theology might become intellectually lazy. The following are typical:

2. The identification of "in Christ" and "in the community" in Paul (and his idea of Christ in heaven) are in unresolved contradiction.

3. Every evangelical Christian is a dogmatic theologian.

5. There is no sociological concept of the church which does not have a theological foundation.

8. Considered logically, faith rests not on psychical experiences, but on itself.

9. The dialectic of so-called dialectical theology has logical and not real character, and thus runs the risk of neglecting the historicity of Jesus.[13]

In this connection, it is worth recalling that during this period dialectical theology was developing far from Berlin. Karl Barth, who had published his *Epistle to the Romans* in 1919 at Berne, had been named Honorary Professor of Reformed Theology at Göttingen in 1922. He taught at Münster in Westphalia after 1926 and arrived in Bonn to teach in 1930. The first volume of his *Christian Dogmatics* (*Christliche Dogmatik*) appeared in 1927. In 1931, his theological method was clearly established with the publication of his book on Anselm's proof of the existence of God, *Anselm: Fides Quaerens Intellectum.* In 1932, the first volume of his completely rewritten dogmatics appeared, re-titled *Church Dogmatics* (*Kirchliche Dogmatik*). Bonhoeffer himself had no direct acquaintance with Barth until June 1931.

But we must return to the beginning of Bonhoeffer's own

[12] The first of the six books that constitute Bonhoeffer's life work, originally published in 1930, in a series edited by Seeberg, translated by Ronald Gregor Smith and others, 1963. Cf. Ch. III below, "Sociology and Ecclesiology."

[13] Cited in Bonhoeffer, *No Rusty Swords*, pp. 32f. (cf. *GS* III, p. 47).

career in 1928. After the successful defense of his thesis on the *Communion of Saints*, Bonhoeffer became assistant pastor of a German-speaking church in Barcelona. Here he sought for a unity between his intellectual concerns and the everyday life around him – a unity that is particularly difficult for a student to achieve. Here too he began the kind of travelling that "de-parochialized" him as a churchman and "de-nationalized" him as a German. For example, his whole Nordic temperament was challenged by discovering that in Spain the bullfight was the aristocratic mark of an ancient civilization.

Upon his return to Berlin in February 1929, he became assistant to Professor Wilhelm Lutgert in systematic theology, and on 18 July 1930, at the age of twenty-three, he defended his habilitation thesis (which qualified him for university teaching) entitled *Act and Being: Transcendental Philosophy and Ontology in Systematic Theology*.[14] On 31 July 1930 Bonhoeffer gave an inaugural lecture on the topic, "Man in Contemporary Philosophy and Theology."[15] However, he was given a year's leave of absence before beginning his teaching, a year he spent at Union Theological Seminary in New York City. His stay in America was a stimulating one, due to the many discussions and discoveries the year afforded. He had the chance to measure the effect of a practical Christianity with a strong communal stress but an uncertain confessional stance. He went through the sudden transition from vigorous theological dispute such as he had known in Europe to a more conciliatory type of Anglo-Saxon discussion.

After his second trip to the United States in June and July of 1939, Bonhoeffer worked out his reflections on the American scene in an essay of about thirty pages, entitled "Protestantism Without Reformation."[16] In it he offered an evaluation of the secularity of the state and its clear separation from the church, the vitality of the denominations, the church's sense of social responsibility, the openness of everyone to personal questions, the practical ecumenism on the American scene, and the agree-

[14] Bonhoeffer's second work, originally published in 1931 in a series edited by Lutgert and Schlatter, and republished in 1950 in Munich, by Kaiser. The English translation is *Act and Being*, 1961, 192pp. Cf. Ch. IV below, "Ontology without Metaphysics?"

[15] Text in Bonhoeffer, *No Rusty Swords*, pp. 50–69; cf. *GS* III, pp. 62–84.

[16] In Bonhoeffer, *No Rusty Swords*, pp. 92–118, cf. *GS* I, pp. 323–54.

ments that were possible on many issues without pompousness or bathos. But he also feared for the truth when it became so vague and sentimental, and for a church that could so easily be transformed into a social club and a family gathering place without theological rigor or even the need for any commitment of faith. Thus at many points American Christianity seemed to him the opposite of what he had known of German (and European) Christianity, where doctrinal precision was all-important, but where the experience of the "communion of saints" was losing ground.

To Bonhoeffer, as a privileged person, America above all represented one of the first occasions in which he could live a life of identification and deputyship, which, as we have already seen, is the basic concept of his christology and ethics. During the year he went to Cuba and to Mexico, and made frequent visits to Harlem. Paul Lehmann, a fellow student and close friend, recalls Bonhoeffer's relation to the black community:

What was so impressive was the way in which he pursued the understanding of the problem to its minutest detail through books and countless visits to Harlem, through participation in Negro youth work, but even more through a remarkable kind of identity with the Negro community, so that he was received by them as though he had never been an outsider at all.[17]

Bonhoeffer himself later told his students that he thought that in the piety, worship and theology of American Negroes he had encountered "the Christianity of the Reformation," whereas mainline American Protestantism seemed to him more like a social gathering.

On 1 August 1931 Bonhoeffer began teaching in the theological faculty of the University of Berlin, clearly destined for a brilliant theological career. During this period he took on many outside activities, thus betraying a certain indecision about how best to order his life. He accepted the post of youth secretary for an ecumenical organization, "The World Alliance for Promoting International Friendship Through the Churches," and was

[17] Cited in Bethge, *Bonhoeffer*, p. 114. Unfortunately, Bonhoeffer's eldest brother wrote him at this time, "The negro question is the central question in the United States. At all events, our Jewish question is a joke in comparison. There cannot be many people left who maintain they are oppressed here. At any rate, not in Frankfurt . . ." (Letter of 24 January 1931, cited in Bethge, *op. cit.*, p. 110).

a regular participant in its conferences, at Cambridge in 1931, in Czechoslovakia in July 1932, in Geneva and Gland in August 1932, and Sofia in September 1933. This ecumenical dimension – in the double sense of interconfessional and international – was thereafter one of the constant features of Bonhoeffer's life. It became increasingly important from the moment that Nazism began to isolate Germany and the German church from the rest of the world. In this round of ecumenical conferences, Bonhoeffer was a careful and hardworking secretary ("not easy to deal with" as Visser 't Hooft commented) whose constant desire was for the strong wine of theological reflection and clear-cut confessional faith to overcome the frequently insipid water of interconfessional toleration, international friendship and ecclesiastical bureaucracy. A brief episode will make the point: while a prince of the church was giving a long and rambling discourse, Bonhoeffer slipped a note to one of his friends on which he had written a quotation from Christian Morgenstern: "A fat cross on a fat belly – who would not feel the breath of the deity?"[18]

In addition to his ecumenical activities, Bonhoeffer became chaplain at the Technical University in Berlin, and tried without success to form a student parish. He also took charge of a confirmation class of difficult adolescents in a proletarian district of north Berlin, and moved into their part of the city, an act of identification not unlike his visits to Harlem during the preceding year. On 11 November 1931, he was ordained a pastor.

All this time he was teaching in the theological faculty at the University. During the winter semester of 1931–2, he gave a course on "The History of Systematic Theology in the Twentieth Century," and a seminar on "The Concept of Philosophy and Protestant Theology." During the summer semester his course was on "The Nature of the Church" and the seminar on the question, "Is There a Christian Ethic?" During the winter semester of 1932–3, his courses were on "Creation and Fall: A Theological Interpretation of Genesis 1–3" and on "Modern Theological Literature." Zimmermann, who became acquainted with him at this time, gives a vivid picture of the young professor in 1932:

[18] Zimmermann and Smith, eds., *op. cit.*, p. 90.

When I entered the lecture-room, there were about ten or fifteen students, a disheartening sight. For a moment I wondered whether I should retreat, but I stayed out of curiosity. A young lecturer stepped to the rostrum with a light, quick step, a man with very fair, rather thin hair, a broad face, rimless glasses, with a golden bridge. After a few words of welcome, he explained the meaning and structure of the lecture, in a firm, slightly throaty way of speaking. Then he opened his manuscript and started on his lecture. He pointed out that nowadays we often ask ourselves whether we still need the Church, whether we still need God. But this question, he said, is wrong. We are the ones who are questioned. The Church exists and God exists, and we are asked whether we are willing to be of service, for God needs us.[19]

Zimmermann continues:

What fascinated me in this man from the very beginning was the way he saw things; he "turned them around," away from where they were stored for everyday use, to the place God had ordained for them ... There was a lot of systematic theology in this lecture, as well as dogmatics and symbolics, but they served as occasions for dealing with the main question. And this was: What has God done? Where is he? How does he meet us and what does he expect from us? To answer these questions, the doctrine of the Church was necessary; it had no meaning in itself, it was part of the explanation of how God became man, and saved man.[20]

Bonhoeffer was worried about exerting too much influence over his students. He also talked in rather abstract terms during the many evenings he spent with students. Zimmermann reports

In the lecture room Bonhoeffer was very concentrated, quite unsentimental, almost dispassionate, clear as crystal, with a certain rational coldness, like a reporter. It was the same with his sermons.[21]

Another of his students recalls that Bonhoeffer's "formulations were laborious, not brilliant," but also quite "single-hearted."[22] In this connection, there is an interesting story about Bonhoeffer's offering himself as candidate for pastor of a country parish in 1933, when he wanted to leave his university post because of the pressure of the struggle of the Confessing Church. Bonhoeffer gave a simple, understandable and vivid sermon, and

[19] *Ibid.*, p. 60.   [20] *Ibid.*, pp. 6of.
[21] *Ibid.*, p. 62.   [22] Schönheer, *ibid.*, p. 126.

yet was turned down in favor of another candidate, because the church session considered him "too refined, too highfalutin, too grand."[23] As another of his students commented:

Bonhoeffer had an aesthetic and a logical side to his mind: he also knew how to enjoy life ... "near and far away at the same time, keeping a distinguished distance and yet ready and open."[24]

While Bonhoeffer was learning the tools of the professorial trade, Germany was going through its fateful turning from the Weimar Republic to the Nazi seizure of power, and German Protestantism was entering the crisis of totalitarian conformity and the whole struggle of the Confessing Church. A few dates will suffice to recall the events that were so crucial for the world, the church and theology – and, from the very beginning, for Bonhoeffer also. In the election of 14 September 1930, the Nazis increased the number of their deputies in the Reichstag from twelve to 107. In the election of 31 July 1932, they increased their numbers again by taking 230 seats, but they seemed to be losing ground when they won only 196 seats in the election of 6 November 1932. But the pace was quickly stepped up: on 30 January 1933 Hindenburg asked Hitler to become Chancellor of the Third German Reich, and on 27 February the Reichstag was burned. (Bonhoeffer's father was a psychiatric consultant when the presumed arsonist, Van der Lubbe, was brought to trial.)

In the church as well, event followed event with increasing speed. The "German Christians," who supported the "positive Christianity" and the anti-Jewish efforts recommended by Hitler,[25] almost gained a majority of seats in the November 1932 regional elections of the church to which Bonhoeffer belonged, winning 2,282 seats as opposed to 2,419. They easily won in the general election of 23 July 1933, getting 70 per cent of the vote. The "*Führer*-principle" was applied to the church in the person of the military chaplain Ludwig Müller, who on 26 April became Hitler's right-hand man in the Evangelical Church, was named Bishop of Prussia on 13 July, and was elected *Reichbischof* at the national Synod of Wittenberg on

---

[23] *Ibid.*, p. 67.   [24] *Ibid.*, p. 67.
[25] On 23 March 1933 Hitler made clear that he considered the confessional groups to be important factors in maintaining the *Volkstum*.

27 September. The concordat between Hitler and the Vatican was signed on 20 July 1933. Most important of all, the "Aryan clause," which forbade anyone who had Jewish blood or was married to a Jew to exercise a ministry in the church, was introduced at the Prussian general synod on 5 September. As Karl Kupisch points out, even though at that time there were only thirty-seven pastors of Jewish origin in the entire Evangelical Church of Germany, the question raised by the "Aryan clause" was crucial for the church's understanding of itself. Unfortunately, the faculty of theology at the University of Berlin did not take a clear position on the matter. Reinhold Seeberg, then seventy-five years old, considered it legitimate that "in good historical conscience one can believe there to be a German type of Christianity alongside of its Greek or Latin forms, without thereby falling into a narrow national fanaticism." His very affirmation that the "Aryan clause" did not involve a depreciation of non-Aryan Christianity was for all practical purposes an acceptance of it, for as he saw it the paragraph simply described "a lack of popularity (*Volkstümlichkeit*) and efficiency (*Wirkungsfähigkeit*) of non-Aryan Christians in relation to the present situation."[26] On 20 December 1933 Baldur von Schirach, with the help of Ludwig Müller, absorbed the Evangelical Youth movement into the Hitler Youth movement.

Nevertheless, however rapid were the political developments, and however widespread was the Nazi attempt to infiltrate to the very center of the government and doctrine of the church, the reaction that gave birth to the Confessing Church was no less vigorous. The pastors' confessional statement at Altoona (inspired by Hans Asmussen) dates from 11 January 1933; the letter of warning from Bishop Dibelius to his pastors from 8 March; the publication of Karl Barth's *Theological Existence Today* from 25 June; the clear condemnation of the "Aryan clause" by the Faculty of Theology at Marburg from 20 September; and the formation of the Pastors' Emergency League under Niemöller from 21 September, with the convening of its Council of Brethren on 20 October.[27]

---

[26] Cf. Karl Kupisch, *Zwischen Idealismus und Massendemokratie*, Lettner, Berlin 1959, pp. 216f.
[27] Cf. Godsey, *The Theology of Dietrich Bonhoeffer*, p. 85.

Bonhoeffer's family had always looked upon Nazism as the worst possible thing that could happen to the nation, the culture and the church. On the evening of 30 January 1933, the day of Hitler's seizure of power, Bonhoeffer's brother-in-law declared to the family gathering, with remarkable foresight, "This can only mean war!" Bonhoeffer himself, not particularly *au courant* on political matters in his youth, but sensitized to them by his international contacts and molded by the concrete clarity of his theological convictions, never had the slightest illusion about the disguises that Nazism adopted to capture, lull and mislead the German people. The most striking indication of his perception was the speech he wrote to be broadcast over the Berlin radio on 1 February 1933, the very day after Hitler had taken power. The broadcast was cut off the air before its conclusion, and the speech indicated from the start that Bonhoeffer was an avowed opponent of the regime. Speaking on the theme, "The Younger Generation's Changed Views of the Concept of *Führer*," Bonhoeffer raised questions about the meaning of the many appeals to youth at a time when technical culture demanded a great deal of experience. Do adults do this, he asked, because they are anxious, or because they like sensation? But the youth remain silent when they are approached out of curiosity, without being called upon to exercise responsibility themselves. One can therefore bypass the false question of a "generation gap," and look for ways to work together for the future all will share. At this point the text becomes transparently clear, and must be quoted directly:

The image of the *Führer* as it originally arose in the Youth Movement has been subject to significant changes during the last few years, but it is the one that exclusively influences young people in all their wishes and desires, and it has become the symbol of the young generation. The image of the *Führer* characterizes the political, philosophical and religious thought of the young generation ... Those among us who are in their forties can tell us that this way of speaking about the *Führer* was totally unknown in their youth. Are they calling for the *Führer* with the underlying conviction that things have acquired such large, destructive and chaotic power over humans that only a great personality can bring back the right order and unity? Or must we speak about the *Führer* like that every time we recognize the political necessity of giving up the ideal of the individual personality and are conscious of the use of human beings as masses? Is all that we have had to give up for ourselves being projected onto the ideal of a *Führer* where it can then be recovered in a greatly magnified and intensified way? How else can we account for the strange tension between the "cult of personality" and collectivism?

Or is the demand for a *Führer* the expression not only of our contemporary political situation, but also of a certain vital requirement of youth? That is to say, has it historical and psychological necessity? And in that case what are the limits of its significance? To what point is leading and being led healthy and genuine, and when does it become pathological and extreme? It is only when a man has answered these questions clearly in his own mind, that he can grasp something of the essence of "leadership." ... Ideals and illusions here lie cheek by jowl.[28]

Bonhoeffer developed the theme even more fully in a lecture given at the German High School for Politics in March 1933, in which we can already discern the idea of "mandate" that was later developed in *Ethics*:

The authority of the Leader or the authority of an office? ... The Leader has authority from below, from those whom he leads, while the office has authority from above; the authority of the Leader depends upon his person, the authority of an office is suprapersonal; authority from below is the self-justification of the people, authority of an office is a recognition of the appointed limits; authority from below is borrowed authority, authority of an office is original authority. The slogan of the authority of the Leader is "The Reich," the slogan of the authority of an office is "the state." ... The authority of an office implies the curbing of the individual in his freedom as an individual, his restriction, the need to be aware of other people, of reality ... The individual is responsible before God. And this solitude of man's position before God, this subjection to an ultimate authority, is destroyed when the authority of the Leader or of the office is seen as ultimate authority ... Alone before God, man becomes what he is, free and committed in responsibility at the same time. He becomes an individual ... Only the Leader who himself serves the penultimate and the ultimate authority can find faithfulness.[29]

---

[28] Bonhoeffer, *GS* II, pp. 20f., the last paragraph as translated in Bosanquet, *The Life and Death of Dietrich Bonhoeffer*, p. 112.

[29] Bonhoeffer, *No Rusty Swords*, pp. 195, 200, 203f. Cf. *GS* II, pp. 33, 37f. "The office of the state is neither Christian nor atheist, but responsible, and conforms to the facts." (Bethge, *Dietrich Bonhoeffer*, German edition, p. 117.)

These long quotations have been included for several reasons. For one thing, with their Hegelian overtones, they are typical of Bonhoeffer's thought, supportive both of the state and of the individual, against the crowd and against charismatic personalities who cease to be leaders (*Führer*) and become "misleaders" (*Verführer*, "seducers"), when they derive their authority from their person rather than their office. In political terms, the quotations are surely closer to Prussian conservatism than they are to democracy understood in French or Anglo-Saxon terms. Much of Bonhoeffer's *Ethics* is written from a similar point of view. And it is not altogether clear (Hanfried Müller to the contrary notwithstanding) that the Bonhoeffer of the prison letters ever thought otherwise. However, more important than any attempt to put Bonhoeffer into a political niche is the awareness these quotations offer us of Bonhoeffer's concrete involvement, his desire to be heard concerning what had really happened to Germany on 1 February 1933, and to indicate clearly before God, as a theologian, as a Christian, and as a contemporary man,[30] the limit that reality places around the totalitarianism of an inspired leader. The church has the office, the responsible mandate for the world, which the leader then seduces and organizes for his own purposes.

While all this was going on, Bonhoeffer continued his teaching. During the summer semester he offered a course on christology,[31] and a seminar on Hegel's Philosophy of Religion. In April he gave a speech on "The Church and the Jewish Question,"[32] and in August collaborated in drafting the Bethel Confession, which was published in November 1933, preceding the famous Barmen Confession of 29–31 May 1934. But he remained uneasy in a situation that gave the appearance of becoming stabilized once the initial conflicts were over. At the University of Berlin, and particularly in the faculty of theology, the academic tranquility seemed out of place to Bonhoeffer. He refused to take a parish in his own church, which had accepted the "Aryan clause" – the only pastor, according to Franz

[30] These are the three descriptive terms Bethge employs in the sub-title of his biography.

[31] Later published on the basis of students' notes as *Christology* (Collins, London) and *Christ the Center* (Harper and Row, New York), 1966, 126pp. Cf. *GS* III, pp. 166–242.

[32] Bonhoeffer, *No Rusty Swords*, pp. 221–9, cf. *GS* II, pp. 44–53.

Hildebrandt, to identify so fully with the non-Aryan pastors that he was unwilling to accept privileges denied to them.[33]

But it was in relation to the Confessing Church itself that Bonhoeffer experienced the greatest inner turmoil. Would it be satisfied with preserving itself against Nazi influence over its government and confession of faith? Would it be afraid to mix its theological opposition with a directly political opposition? Might not this fear then lead it to seek shelter along a path of inner retreat, where the purification of the church would have as its counterpart a type of doctrinal pietism that would forsake responsibility for the world? Specifically, could the church settle for refusing to accept the "Aryan clause" in its own life, unless it protested just as strongly against every discriminatory measure against the Jews in the entire nation? Bonhoeffer himself already knew what the answer must be: "Only he who cries out for the Jews has the right to sing Gregorian chant."[34] And as he said on another occasion:

If a madman drives his car on the sidewalk of the Kurfürstendamm [a large street in Berlin], I as a pastor cannot be content to bury the dead and console the families. I must, if I find myself at this place, leap up and prevent the driver from getting away.[35]

But in the spring of 1933 Bonhoeffer was in considerable torment. He was afraid that, out of respect for those weak in the faith, the church might yield to compromises of "patience" and "understanding" and become increasingly "liberal" like those who had doubts or preferred illusion to reality. In September 1934 he wrote his Swiss friend, Erwin Sutz, after the latter had suggested a dialogue between Hitler and Barth:

The Oxford Group movement has been naïve enough to try to convert Hitler – a ridiculous failure to understand what is going on – it is *we* who are to be converted, not Hitler ... Hitler must not and cannot hear us. He is obdurate and it is he who must compel us to hear – it's that way round.[36]

We must not forget that during this period Bonhoeffer was a lonely man. His first two books had attracted very few readers,

---

[33] Zimmermann and Smith, eds., *op. cit.*, p. 39.
[34] Bethge, ed., *Die Mündige Welt* I, p. 23.
[35] *Ibid.*, p. 14.
[36] Cited in Bethge, *Dietrich Bonhoeffer*, p. 285.

and until the publication of *The Cost of Discipleship* he was ignored by the public and by the authorities of the church in Germany, a man much as he had been in his youth, who was open yet reserved, able to make decisions but aware of the price entailed when one makes decisions, whether good or bad, without consulting others. To make a long story short, on 20 July 1933 he accepted a call to become pastor of a German parish in London. He remained there from October 1933 to April 1935. During these eighteen months in England, Bonhoeffer was extremely active in relating the German church and its suffering to the outside world, and in forcing the various ecumenical organizations to come to terms with the question of the Confessing Church. The Confessing Church was only an emergency organization without official standing, either national or international. But along with his friend George Bell (Anglican bishop of Chichester, head of the commission on "Life and Work," and thus responsible for the relations between the ecumenical movement and Germany) Bonhoeffer used the occasion of the Fanö Conference in Denmark in August 1934 to insist that the Confessing Church be able to express its viewpoint directly and that the ecumenical world clearly condemn the heresy of the "German Christians." During this English interlude he also investigated Gandhi's non-violence, and even envisaged a trip to India.

But reminders of reality and urgency came quickly. As early as 20 November 1933, Barth had urged Bonhoeffer to return as quickly as possible ("by the next boat") to his post on the church's firing line in Berlin. At the request of the Confessing Church Bonhoeffer did return in April 1935 to take charge of a seminary for preachers at Finkenwalde in Pomerania. From April 1935 until September 1937, when the Gestapo closed the seminary, Bonhoeffer lived at Finkenwalde with groups of twenty-five young ministers at a time, all of whom intended to serve parishes in the Confessing Church. At Finkenwalde he experimented with a spiritually disciplined community life with young pastors for whom, as one of them wrote, "pietism and enthusiasm were for almost all of us a form of Christianity which we rejected."[37] From Switzerland, Karl Barth expressed his concern about "an almost indefinable odour of a monastic

[37] Zimmermann and Smith, eds., *op. cit.*, p. 110.

eros and pathos,"[38] which he thought he detected in an invitation to biblical meditation that was being used at Finkenwalde.
Bonhoeffer listened to his critics and modified certain practices
as a result, but continued the life of brotherhood that left its
mark on all the participants. It was during this period that
Bonhoeffer became enthusiastic about the writings of Georges
Bernanos, whose novels, particularly *The Star of Satan, The
Renegade,* and *The Diary of a Country Priest,* impressed him deeply,
and which he urged his father to read.[39]

Life at Finkenwalde was divided between theological work,
spiritual discipline, enjoyment of nature, friendship, and service
to nearby parishes. During this period Bonhoeffer stressed two
things in particular: first, the concrete obedience of faith in
following Jesus Christ, and second, the importance of differentiating between spiritual community and psychological manipulation, so that others would not be unduly influenced by his
own personality. Thus he saw the need for a balance between
immediacy and reserve, between decisiveness and respect for
others. *The Cost of Discipleship*[40] is the fruit of the first conviction.
Bonhoeffer began it in 1935, and worked on it during the time
of his last seminar at the theological faculty in Berlin in February 1936. It appeared in November 1937, at a time when
twenty-seven pastors from Finkenwalde were already in prison.
Life Together[41] is the fruit of the second conviction. It was written
at Göttingen during September 1938 and appeared in 1939 on
the eve of the war. *The Cost of Discipleship* and *Life Together* are
two works of struggle and piety in the time of the Confessing
Church, just as *Communion of Saints* and *Act and Being* had been

---

[38] Letter to Bonhoeffer, 14 October 1936, in Bonhoeffer, *The Way to Freedom,*
p. 121, cf. *GS* II, p. 290.

[39] Cf. Bethge, *Dietrich Bonhoeffer,* pp. 103f.

[40] Bonhoeffer's third book (revised edition 1959, 285pp.). The German title is
simply *Nachfolge* ("discipleship" or "following after"). Cf. Ch. V below, "The
Immediacy of Obedience and the Mediation of the Word." *The Cost of Discipleship*
was published in 1937 by Chr. Kaiser Verlag in Munich, which published Barth's
works until 1933, and which since 1945 has published most of Bonhoeffer's.
The readers for the press initially turned down the manuscript of *The Cost of
Discipleship,* finding it too "enthusiastic" in relation to the Lutheran distinction
between law and faith, and also not clear-cut enough in its treatment of justification
by faith alone. Cf. Ernst Wolf, "Bonhoeffer and the Chr. Kaiser Verlag," in
Zimmermann, ed., *Almanach,* pp. 172–7, an essay omitted from the English translation, *I Knew Dietrich Bonhoeffer.*

[41] Bonhoeffer's fourth book (1954, 122pp.).

the two writings growing out of Bonhoeffer's period at the university. While at Finkenwalde he also wrote several other less important biblical studies: "King David" (1935); "The Reconstruction of Jerusalem according to Ezra and Nehemiah" (1936); "Timothy, the Servant in the House of God" (1936); and "Notes for Study in Reading the Pastoral Epistles" (1938).[42]

During these years he published only two articles in *Evangelische Theologie*, the journal which replaced *Zwischen den Zeiten* after the German church struggle got under way. However, both articles, and particularly the second, made a tremendous impact. In August 1935, "The Confessing Church and the Ecumenical Movement"[43] was published, and in June 1936, there appeared a controversial essay on "The Question of the Boundaries of the Church and Church Union."[44] The latter contained the famous phrase over which so much ink was spilled, "Whoever knowingly cuts himself off from the Confessing Church in Germany cuts himself off from Salvation,"[45] as well as a realistic assessment of the path that must be taken by the Church of Christ in Germany:

The Confessing Church takes its confident way between the Scylla of orthodoxy and the Charybdis of confessionlessness. It bears the burden of the responsibility of being the true Church of Jesus. It proclaims, "Here is the church!" "Come here!" In proclaiming this it comes up against both friends and enemies.[46]

This is how Bonhoeffer interpreted the role of the Confessing Church, a role that the official church authorities had a tendency to confine to the non-juridical (or perhaps overly-juridical) level of an "alliance among the confessional churches," i.e. churches in other respects defined by the great historic confessions of the sixteenth-century Reformation. Bonhoeffer wanted to make sure that traditional confessionalism did not become either a refuge from, or an evasion of, the need for contemporary confession; that support of church law did not

---

[42] These studies have not been translated; they are gathered together in *GS* IV, pp. 294–384.

[43] Bonhoeffer, *No Rusty Swords*, pp. 326–44, cf. *GS* I, pp. 240–61.

[44] Bonhoeffer, *The Way to Freedom*, pp. 75–96, with a response by Helmut Gollwitzer, pp. 97–106, and Bonhoeffer's response to the whole debate, pp. 106–14. Cf. *GS* II, pp. 217–63.

[45] Bonhoeffer, *The Way to Freedom*, pp. 93f.

[46] *Ibid.*, pp. 90f.

become a mere formality opposing obedience to the concrete demands of the moment; and that the safeguarding of the doctrinal integrity of the Reformation did not provide too easy an assurance that Jesus Christ was really being followed in the midst of Nazi Germany. Here also Bonhoeffer was doing battle against "Protestantism without Reformation," just as he had done during his time in America.

In August 1936 Bonhoeffer gave a lecture, his last public lecture, on "The Inner Life of the German Evangelical Church," one in a series designed to help foreign visitors who had come to Berlin for the Olympic Games understand the truth about the situation of the German church. During the same month he participated in a conference at Chambry in Switzerland, preparing for the ecumenical conference on Life and Work that was to be held at Oxford in July 1937. Two German delegations appeared at Chambry, one from the Confessing Church and the other from the official church. Both delegations were invited to Oxford but neither received authorization from the German government to attend. Two reports were sent to Oxford, one by the official church, signed by Eugen Gerstenmeier, who was later president of the German parliament, and the other in the name of the Confessing Church, signed by Hans Böhm and Dietrich Bonhoeffer. The latter contained a long discussion about the nature of the Confessing Church in Germany: was it simply an emergency organization, appealing to each person's individual conscience, or did it represent (in the light of the Synod of Barmen on right doctrine and the Synod of Dahlem on church government) the true church of Christ in Germany according to the Word of God?

Bonhoeffer gave considerable attention to these questions in 1937 and 1938. His Lutheranism ought to have satisfied him that God alone could recognize the true church. But his commitment to concrete obedience forced him to bring out into the open the radical choice that the Confessing Church faced. His opponents criticized what they continually called both his "Enthusiasm" (*Schwärmertum*) and his overly "Reformed" (i.e. Calvinist) emphasis on the visibility of the church, the ministry, discipline, the power of the keys and excommunication. For example, Hans Lietzmann wrote of Bonhoeffer on 17 August 1936:

... and recently Lic. Bonhoeffer, a highly-gifted but now altogether fanatical teacher, wrote *"extra ecclesiam nulla salus,"* meaning that whoever cooperates with the Reich Church Committee [e.g. in opposition to the Confessing Church] stands outside the Church of Salvation.[47]

And H. Sasse in his article "Against Enthusiasm" published in 1936 added:

The Confessing Church ... as distinct from the confessional movement, upheld by the Lutheran churches, is a sect, the worst sect, in fact, ever to have set foot on the soil of German Protestantism.[48]

Bonhoeffer gave no ground to his critics, however, when it came to sharpness of language:

Whoever looks on the Confessing Church as a movement or as the upholder of a cause is lost; ... he sees, in fact, nothing more than an undisciplined crowd without obedience, a non-church in fact. But he must not see us like that![49]

The Synod of Oeynhausen, on 17–22 February 1936, was actually the last general synod of the Confessing Church, following after Barmen (29–31 May 1934), Dahlem (19–21 October 1934), and Augsburg (4–6 June 1935). For a number of Lutherans criticized the Confessing Church for disobeying Paul's commandment in Romans 13 to be obedient to the governing authorities, and for interfering improperly with the ecclesiastical organization at Oeynhausen by refusing to recognize Kerrl, the minister of church affairs appointed by Hitler to replace Müller, the ineffective *Reichbischof*. According to these Lutherans, to avoid the risk of falling into "legalism" of the Calvinist variety, the Confessing Church ought to restrict itself to the defense of pure doctrine, without making a matter of church order into a matter of faith. Step by step, Bonhoeffer, making use of biblical texts and the Lutheran confessional statements themselves, defended the legitimacy of the Confessing Church at Oeynhausen. To the charge that the Confessing Church was repeating the Donatist heresy (and those so accused were called "Dahlemites" from the Synod of Dahlem), Bonhoeffer replied that the Donatists in St Augustine's time refused to admit that ministers guilty of

[47] Bethge, *op. cit.*, p. 431.   [48] *Ibid.*, p. 432.   [49] *Ibid.*, pp. 414–15.

mortal sin could validly administer the sacraments, while the Confessing Church contested the notion that false teachers, even if they proclaimed pure doctrine, could lead the church in the right direction. And he added, "But in this matter, the Confessing Church does not think more 'donatistically' than the whole Reformation."[50]

Today this relentless passion to defend the legitimacy of the Confessing Church and to attack the confessional illegitimacy of the authorities of the state church may appear to be no more than an unfortunate family quarrel, with Bonhoeffer rigidly flailing a dead horse, since the danger of the "German Christian" heresy had disappeared from the ranks of German Protestantism.[51] Without entering further into the traditional controversy between Lutherans and Calvinists over the visibility and boundaries of the church, there are two things that are striking in these events: on the one hand, the way Bonhoeffer committed himself to the empirical church in the form it had to take in order to follow Christ concretely; and on the other hand, the degree to which these internal church struggles absorbed energies that ought to have been available for issues outside the church, for other people, and for the world at large.

Although life in the seminary at Finkenwalde from 1935 to the outbreak of the war continued to bring clarity, friendship and real brotherhood to its participants, life in the Confessing Church itself was a troubling and disturbing existence. Each year added new problems. To attacks from without were added troubles from within, and it is appropriate that Bonhoeffer's last series of biblical studies at Finkenwalde on 20 June 1938 were on the theme of temptation.[52]

In the meantime, the pace of external events quickened. Niemöller was finally arrested on 1 July 1937. Finkenwalde

[50] *GS* II, p. 275.

[51] The "German Christians," as the bearers of an explicit heresy, had been discredited ever since the scandal of the mass meeting in the Sports Palace in Berlin on 13 November 1933. They continued only as a tiny remnant centered in Thuringia. Given these facts, it would appear that the church had won the struggle against the Nazi attempt to make it conform. But was the Confessing Church being responsible to the entire German people if it did no more than protect its own purity?

[52] Included in *Creation and Fall/Temptation*, pp. 95–128.

was closed in October 1937 by order of Himmler. The seminarians were divided into two groups and sent out to Kosslin and Gross-Schlönwitz. War got closer and the underground was formed. After February 1939, the time of the crisis brought about by General Fritsch, Bonhoeffer, thanks to his brother-in-law Hans von Dohnanyi, entered into close contact with the center of the resistance movement to which he belonged during the war, and particularly with Admiral Canaris and General Oster, the latter destined to be hanged the same day as Bonhoeffer six years later. The annexation of Austria, the *Anschluss*, took place on 12 March 1938. The Munich pact was signed on 30 September, and the invasion of Czechoslovakia occurred on 15 March 1939. In March 1939 Bonhoeffer returned to London to visit his former parish. There he renewed connections with several people in the ecumenical world, notably Bishop Bell, Leonard Hodgson of "Faith and Order," and Visser 't Hooft. The latter found him

... remarkably free from illusions, and sometimes almost clairvoyant... In the midst of the impenetrable world between "Munich" and "Warsaw," in which hardly anyone ventured to formulate the actual problems clearly, that questioning voice was a release.[53]

It was at this time that Bonhoeffer's Anglo-Saxon friends, Reinhold Niebuhr in particular, undertook to arrange a way out for him that would save him much difficulty. Bonhoeffer, due to be drafted for military service in July, had decided that although he was not in principle a pacifist, he would not accept conscription for a war in which, if his own country was victorious, Nazism would triumph throughout the world. His friends proposed that he come to the United States, where a great deal of pastoral work was needed among German refugees, and where he could also teach on various theological faculties. The Council of the Confessing Church at first hesitated to release him due to its manpower shortage, but finally agreed in order to maintain its ecumenical contacts outside of Germany. The invitation was for a two-year visit in America. It was tempting, for it included a combination of pastoral work, preaching and teaching. Bonhoeffer departed for London on 4 June, after having left a note on his desk at the seminary

[53] Bethge, *Dietrich Bonhoeffer*, p. 351.

expressing hope that his replacement would find joy in his post, "one of the finest pieces of work," he wrote, "in the Confessing Church," and urging him "to go for walks with the brethren" in the surrounding woods.[54]

Bonhoeffer set sail for New York on 7 June 1939, arrived there on 12 June, felt compelled to return on 7 July, and took one of the last ships for Germany, which he reached on 27 July. In New York he experienced an increasing anxiety which was accentuated by the security of being in America. He soon refused to become a pastor to refugees, in order to be free to return to Germany if the situation got worse. The loss of contact with what was going on in Germany upset him. He felt the need for identification with his suffering countrymen, and a prayer of intercession, offered for them in America, overwhelmed him with emotion and nostalgia. He made up his mind to return when a letter from Germany informed him that war would certainly come in September. He went back, leaving a letter of explanation for Reinhold Niebuhr:

Sitting here in Dr Coffin's garden I have had time to think and to pray about my situation and that of my nation, and to have God's will for me clarified. I have come to the conclusion that I have made a mistake in coming to America. I must live through this difficult period of our national history with the Christian people of Germany. I will have no right to participate in the reconstruction of Germany after the war if I do not share the trials of this time with my people. My brethren in the Confessing Church wanted me to go. They may have been right in urging me to do so; but I was wrong in going. Such a decision each man must make for himself. Christians in Germany will face the terrible alternative of either willing the defeat of their nation in order that Christian civilization may survive, or willing the victory of their nation and thereby destroying our civilization. I know which of these alternatives I must choose; but I cannot make that choice in security . . .[55]

Later he wrote from prison:

I want to assure you that I have not for a moment regretted coming back in 1939, nor any of the consequences either. I knew quite well what I was doing, and I acted with a clear conscience . . . And

---

[54] Bonhoeffer, *The Way to Freedom*, pp. 212f.
[55] Bonhoeffer, *The Way to Freedom*, p. 246, cf. *GS* I, p. 320.

I regard my being kept here . . . as being involved in the part that I had resolved to play in Germany's fate.[56]

These words should be compared to his statement in *Ethics*:

There is no glory in standing amid the ruins of one's native town in the consciousness that at least one has not oneself incurred any guilt.[57]

On the ship taking him back to Germany he wrote, "My inner uncertainty about the future has ceased."[58]

On the return trip he wrote a series of impressions about America to which reference has already been made, "Protestantism without Reformation." He himself left a certain kind of "Protestant" security to take on the insecurity and responsibility of the Reformation. As Bethge wrote in a striking summary:

The year 1932 had opened up the ecumenical movement to Bonhoeffer, and he became its passionate advocate as Germany increasingly isolated itself. When in 1939 he could have saved himself within that ecumenical movement, he shut himself out from it, confining his way deliberately to the separate and deadly fate of Germany.[59]

So on 27 July he was back in Berlin. On 23 August the German-Soviet Pact was signed. On 1 September came the invasion of Poland and the actual outbreak of war. Bonhoeffer was more and more cut off and isolated. He had not taught at the University of Berlin since 1936; indeed in August of the same year his accreditation had been withdrawn. On 17 March 1940 the seminary for preachers was finally and definitively forbidden by the Gestapo. On 9 September 1940 Bonhoeffer was forbidden to publish or to speak in Germany, and was ordered to keep the police informed of his place of residence. Shortly before these restrictions he was able to publish a little book on the psalms, *The Psalms: Prayer Book of the Bible*. But everything he wrote subsequently had to be published post-

---

[56] Bonhoeffer, *LPP*, letter of 22 December 1943, p. 115; cf. also the letter of 11 April 1944, p. 149.
[57] Bonhoeffer, *Ethics*, p. 340.
[58] Bonhoeffer, *The Way to Freedom*, p. 247, cf. *GS* I, p. 315.
[59] Bethge, *op. cit.*, p. 582.

humously. He no longer had any professional life since the seminary had been closed and all the young pastors mobilized. Twenty-five of them were killed at the front before Bonhoeffer entered prison.

Bonhoeffer now divided his life between political activity and intellectual work. He led a double life, without however being torn apart by it. Although he had virtually been a pacifist, he now saw that there was no escape into what could only be an irrelevant piety.

The patriot had to perform what in normal times is the action of a scoundrel. "Treason" had become true patriotism and what was normally patriotism had become treason.[60]

Thanks to his brother-in-law, Hans von Dohnanyi, who was working in the Military Intelligence Department (*Abwehr*) under Admiral Canaris, Bonhoeffer was given official documents that prevented his conscription and made it possible for him to visit Sweden and Switzerland and keep in contact with church authorities until his arrest. In August 1940 he had several conversations with General Oster. He used his ecumenical contacts, particularly his friendship with Bishop Bell, a member of the British House of Lords, to find out on behalf of the German resistance what would be the position of the Allies if the plot to remove Hitler from power were successful. From October 1940 on, Bonhoeffer was co-ordinated into the *Abwehr* in Munich for this purpose. He made three trips to Switzerland, from 24 February to 24 March, from 29 August to 26 September 1940, and again in May 1942; two trips to Norway and Sweden, from 10 to 18 April, and from 30 May to 2 June 1942. As we know, these contacts led to no tangible results. The Allies continued to insist on "unconditional surrender," as specified in the Atlantic Charter, and were not willing to listen to the muffled voices of the German opponents of Nazism.

For its own part, the German resistance was weak. It was worn out by isolation, long delays, and the difficulty of coping with the initial German victories and then the increasing setbacks. Above all, it had to contend with continuing suspicion and Nazi terrorism. In the end, it was finally divided in its

[60] Bethge, *op. cit.*, p. 579.

judgment about the moral obligation and the political consequences of the plot against Hitler, but went ahead with the
attempt, which nearly succeeded but failed to kill Hitler on
20 July 1944. This led to terrible reprisals: 7,000 arrests,
according to the Gestapo records; 4,980 deaths, according to
William Shirer, and 3,247 registered executions, according to
Pecher.[61]

Along with his political responsibility and his underground
activities in saving groups of Jews and helping them escape
from Germany, Bonhoeffer continued his theological study. He
finished part of the project that was most important to him,
his attempt to state the concrete and ultimate commandment of
God in the penultimate complexity of politics, culture and
morals. The conclusion of a course of lectures given as early as
1932 clearly described the direction of his research:

Luther could write both *De Servo Arbitrio* and about the tribute
money. Why cannot we do that? Who shall show us Luther?[62]

A work on ethics was a project Bonhoeffer had envisioned
since 1937. He worked on it piecemeal between 1940 and 1943,
sometimes in Berlin, sometimes on the estate of Frau von
Kleist in Pomerania, and sometimes in the Benedictine abbey
at Ettal in Upper Bavaria. The fragments written under these
trying circumstances constitute *Ethics*, published by his friend
Bethge in 1949.[63] In one of his prison letters Bonhoeffer wrote
of this project, "I sometimes feel as if my life were more or less
over, and as if all I had to do now were to finish my *Ethics*."[64]
Zimmermann recalls Bonhoeffer having said every now and then
that he did not expect to live into old age. He gave himself
thirty-eight years. "For him this was not a program or a

---

[61] There is a full account of the plot against Hitler and the attempt of 20 July,
in William Shirer, *The Rise and Fall of the Third Reich*, Simon and Schuster, New
York, and Secker and Warburg, London, 1960. He describes Bonhoeffer's participation and refers to him on pp. 374, 1017, 1024, 1072f. Bonhoeffer's brother-in-
law, Hans von Dohnanyi, is referred to on pp. 693, 904, 1019, 1024, 1026.

[62] Bethge, *op. cit.*, p. 140.

[63] The fifth of Bonhoeffer's major works, published with an introduction by
Bethge. The latest English edition is *Ethics*, Macmillan, New York 1965, and
Collins, London 1968, 382pp. The latter contains Bethge's important "Preface to
the newly-arranged Sixth German Edition," pp. i–iv. Cf. Ch. VI below, "The
Concrete Commandment."

[64] Bonhoeffer, *LPP*, letter of 15 December 1943, p. 107. Also cited in Bethge's
preface to *Ethics*, p. 14.

destiny that he was out to challenge. It was simply a given fact."[65] However, Bonhoeffer never gave up living for the future, either the world's future or his own. "To be irresponsible toward the future," he once wrote, "is nihilism; toward the present, enthusiasm." During the battle of Stalingrad, on 24 November 1942, he became engaged to Maria von Wedemeyer. He wrote his friend Bethge from prison on 17 December 1943:

We have been engaged now for nearly a year, and have never been alone together for one hour. Isn't it absurd? . . . And yet [Maria] goes through everything with a marvellous naturalness.[66]

Maria was the cousin of Fabian von Schlabrendorff, who took part in the attempt on Hitler's life at Smolensk in 1943 along with Colonel von Tresckow, and who was put into the concentration camp at Flossenburg the very day that Bonhoeffer was hanged there.

On 5 April 1943, Bonhoeffer was arrested by the Gestapo, shortly after his brother-in-law, on suspicion of involvement in the attempt at Smolensk. On 23 July, Keitel ordered that the charge of high treason against Bonhoeffer be dropped, and that he be indicted on the charge of "subversion of the armed forces." At the beginning of his imprisonment Bonhoeffer was inwardly troubled over the reasons for his confinement: were they political or confessional? Was he a conspirator or a witness? It was typical of Bonhoeffer's nature to reflect for a long time before drawing the concrete consequences of his thought. A pastor describes how he found Bonhoeffer very reserved and perplexed in the course of a discussion on the famous passage of St Paul in Romans 13 about being "subject to the governing authorities" of the state which "have been instituted by God."

Bonhoeffer seemed to me extraordinarily reserved, ready to consider every fresh problem put to him, taking even the remotest ideas into account. His conservative nature, his scholarly education and his thoroughness prevented any quick result.[67]

But once reflection had taken place, concrete action ought to

---

[65] Zimmermann, *Almanach*, p. 6 (not included in the English translation, *I Knew Dietrich Bonhoeffer*).

[66] Bethge, *op. cit.*, p. 740.

[67] Zimmermann and Smith, eds., *op. cit.*, p. 157.

follow immediately. "A historical decision cannot be entirely resolved into ethical terms: there remains a residuum, the venture of action."[68] His understanding of reality gave unity to his life, for he believed that in Jesus Christ there could be no divorce between God and the earth, or between faith and politics. As Gollwitzer wrote:

Since then our more intimate circle of friends has never again wavered in its clear affirmation that political resistance, under such a government of murderers, is a consequence of being a Christian, a fruit of faith, and a subject of pastoral counselling.[69]

Bonhoeffer was in the Tegel military prison for eighteen months, until 8 October 1944. From it were written all the letters to his parents and his friend Bethge, both censored and non-censored, that make up the book published under the title *Letters and Papers from Prison*.[70] These letters cover the period from 14 April 1943 to 23 August 1944. Several other items have been included in addition to the letters, among them a kind of balance-sheet written in 1942, in which Bonhoeffer, along the lines of the *Ethics* which he was then writing, reflects on the ten years just completed, as well as a "Report on Prison Life" after a year in Tegel, some prayers, "Thoughts on the Baptism of D.W.R. [Bethge]" his godson, a number of poems, two letters described as "Signs of Life" from the Prinz-Albrecht-Strasse prison, and an account by Bethge of Bonhoeffer's last days. These letters are the ones that made him so famous after the war, particularly those written from 30 April 1944 on, in which Bonhoeffer began to speculate about the future of the Lordship of Jesus Christ in a non-religious world come of age. Bethge emphasizes that after April 1944 Bonhoeffer gave up reading so many novels, immersed himself in the philosophy of knowledge, worked very hard to

[68] Bonhoeffer, *Ethics*, p. 344.

[69] Zimmermann and Smith, eds., *op. cit.*, p. 144.

[70] The sixth major work of Bonhoeffer, published in Munich in 1951. There have been many English editions. The most recent and the fullest is that of 1967 (240pp.). A few more prison letters can be found in Bethge, *Dietrich Bonhoeffer*, pp. 703–95. Bonhoeffer's letters to his fiancée are not included in *Letters and Papers from Prison*, but portions of them are available in Peter Vorkink, ed., *Bonhoeffer in a World Come of Age*, Fortress Press, Philadelphia 1968, Maria von Wedemeyer-Weller, "The Other Letters from Prison," pp. 103–13. Cf. Ch. VII below, "Christianity without 'Religion'?"

develop the new directions of his thought and undoubtedly wrote the draft of a book, completely lost, on which the well-known letters are only a commentary. These fragments from prison constitute the most conspicuous part of the heritage of a man who during his lifetime was scarcely known to his contemporaries, save for *The Cost of Discipleship* and his impetuousness as a young theologian who insisted on an uncompromising stand and a responsible widening of the concerns of the Confessing Church in Germany.

Von Stauffenberg's attempt on Hitler's life failed on 20 July 1944. On 22 September the Gestapo discovered the files at Zossen, which contained documents on the relationship between the *Abwehr* and the Allies. Up until this time, Bonhoeffer had had great hope that he could minimize his participation in the plot against Hitler, and his situation in prison had been one of relative comfort. On 8 October, however, he was transferred to Prinz-Albrecht-Strasse, the Gestapo prison. He was removed from it on 7 February 1945, and sent to the concentration camp at Buchenwald. Taken toward the Austrian stronghold with a convoy of deportees, he was overtaken on 6 April in the village of Schönberg, by emissaries of Hitler, who wanted to be assured from the depth of his Berlin bunker that the conspirators in the 20 July plot would pay to the bitter end, and had ordered Kaltenbrunner in a midday meeting on 5 April to see that Bonhoeffer and Dohnanyi, among others, did not survive. Brought back to the concentration camp at Flossenburg, Bonhoeffer was tried during the night by a court-martial of the S.S. He was hanged early on the morning of 9 April along with Admiral Canaris, General Oster, Judge Sack, Strünck and Gehre. His brother-in-law, Hans von Dohnanyi, was executed in the camp at Sachsenhausen the same day. His brother Klaus and another brother-in-law, Rüdiger Schleicher, were shot in Berlin on 23 April. Hitler committed suicide in his bunker exactly one week later.

2. *Continuity or discontinuity?*

Such was this brief life of thirty-nine years. It is usually divided into three periods, clearly differentiated by where Bonhoeffer was, what he was doing, how he was writing, and above all what he was thinking. These criteria give us the university period, from about 1927 to 1933, with *Communion of Saints* and *Act and Being*; the period of the Confessing Church from 1933 to 1940, with *The Cost of Discipleship* and *Life Together*; and the political period from 1940 to 1945, with *Ethics* and *Letters and Papers from Prison*.

This threefold division is not only convenient, but on the whole accurate. It is used by most of the commentators Bethge initially formulated it in a simple yet profound sequence

In his twenties Bonhoeffer said to the theologians, your theme is the church. In his thirties he said to the church, your theme is the world. And in his forties he said to the world, your theme, which is forsakenness, is God's own theme; with his theme he is not cheating you out of the fullness of life, but opening it up to you.[71]

A little more formally, John Godsey speaks of theological foundation, application and fragmentation.[72] The three subtitles which René Marlé has chosen to describe an "unusual man" with an "unusual destiny" approximate Godsey's evaluation: "A theologian of the church and of Christ," "One who taught others how to live," and "A man of disturbing vision."[73] Hanfried Müller has likewise worked out a remarkable if debatable interpretation around the same three periods, although his theme of progressive development forces him to minimize the value of *Life Together* in relation to *The Cost of Discipleship* and to stress a decisive break, a true "epistemological shift" – to use the expression which Althusser borrowed from Bachelard for his interpretation of Marx – between portions of the *Ethics* and *Letters and Papers from Prison*. Müller's title is a key to his interpretation: *From the Church to the World: A Contribution to the Relationship of the Word of God to Society in Dietrich Bonhoeffer's Theological Development*.[74] The three sections of his book are "The Word of God and the Community of the Church," "Life and Action in the Ecclesiastical Community," and "The Word of God and Human Society."

It is correct to say that Bonhoeffer encountered reality in three very different forms in living out the Word of God that

---

71 Bethge, in *Die Mündige Welt* I, p. 24.
72 J. D. Godsey, *The Theology of Dietrich Bonhoeffer*, 1960.
73 R. Marlé, *Dietrich Bonhoeffer, the Man and His Work*, 1968, 141pp.
74 Müller, *Von der Kirche zur Welt*, 1961, 579pp.

creates the church: first, the *established church*, the state church (*Volkskirche*), of which he was the ardent theological advocate against individualistic and existentialist temptations, whether of the old liberalism or the new dialectical theology; next, the *Confessing Church*, which rightly separated itself from the state church and represented a fighting and "monastic" purification of it, and of which Bonhoeffer was a passionate and partisan defender; and finally the *"non-religious" church*, the church hidden in the secular world, a church which was not an established church but a church on the march, not a confessing church but a listening church.

The world had changed between 1927 and 1945, and Bonhoeffer knew it. In 1927 "Christendom" still existed, even in the reduced, liberal and tattered form of the state church which no longer attracted the multitudes in a large industrial city such as Berlin then was. 1933 was the time of the catacombs of persecution – catacombs doubly hidden, since Nazism claimed to be the instrument of divine providence, and the helpless and fanatical masses along with the nationalistic and irresponsible middle class wanted the church to bless this instrument of providence. 1944 was already a time for anticipating the post-war period, when the church would be neither necessary to man come of age, nor persecuted by a totalitarian state. Bonhoeffer's realism consisted in a clear realization of these three periods, and Müller's work, even with its over-schematized treatment, is a remarkable organization of these three stages.[75]

As far as I am concerned, the aphorism by which Nietzsche summed up the progress of his own life and thought seems to me applicable to the three periods of Bonhoeffer's life:

Three metamorphoses of the spirit do I designate to you: how the spirit becometh a camel; the camel a lion, and the lion at last a child.[76]

---

[75] Müller thinks that Bonhoeffer expresses a certain understanding of the breaks in his own life in the successive stanzas of the poem, "Stages on the Road to Freedom," begun on 21 July 1944, after he had learned of the failure of the attempt on Hitler's life: Discipline (the period of *The Cost of Discipleship*), Action (the period of the *Ethics*), and Suffering (the period of *Letters and Papers from Prison*). Cf. Müller, *op. cit.*, p. 422 n.79. The poem is in *Letters and Papers from Prison* following the letter of 21 July 1944, pp. 202f., and at the beginning of *Ethics*.

[76] Nietzsche, *Thus Spake Zarathustra*, as cited in *The Philosophy of Nietzsche*, Modern Library, New York, p. 43.

The *camel* accumulates some weighty learning but he finally doubts that it will be of much use in the crucial moment of battle. This describes the first third of Bonhoeffer's life, the brilliant apprentice in systematic theology at the University of Berlin, who without ever denying his theological apprenticeship, realized nevertheless that this theological cargo might divert him from the struggling and suffering imitation of Jesus Christ. Consequently, Bonhoeffer became a *lion*. He took an active part in the struggle of the Confessing Church, passionately and despondently, enthusiastically and discouragedly. Last of all, the mysterious Bonhoeffer appeared, the lonely man of the final months in prison, Bonhoeffer the *child*, he who, according to Nietzsche, returns again, the man of ultimate vision. But there is this difference: in Nietzsche, the context of all this is the eternal return of the world, the sovereign and tragic game, the love of fate, the beginning of the ultimate madness, so that Nietzsche can sometimes sign his name as Dionysos and sometimes as Christ. In Bonhoeffer, the context is the discovery that in the godless world, God is present, that one must live *before* God the godlessness of the world, that one must live *with* God the God who is being "pushed out" of the world, and, in the companionship of Christ, the godforsakenness of the world.[77] Eric Fuchs picks up the image with sensitivity:

Perhaps we must relearn everything. We are undoubtedly more or less like Zarathustra's camel, too heavy, too encumbered by all of our culture, our theology, our piety. We also resemble the lion, and provided with our sharp and solid words we want to transform mankind and the world. Bonhoeffer reminds us, however, that those who enter the Kingdom of God are children.[78]

Fuchs quotes Nietzsche again:

But tell me, my brother, what the child can do, which even the lion could not do? Why hath the preying lion still to become a child?

Innocence is the child, and forgetfulness, a new beginning, a game, a self-rolling wheel, a first movement, a holy yea.

[77] Cf. A. Dumas, "Dietrich Bonhoeffer, une Église pour les Non-Religieux," in *Foi et Vie*, May–June 1966, p. 93.
[78] E. Fuchs, "Bonhoeffer, une Théologie de la Réalité," *Bulletin du Centre protestant d'études*, Geneva, July 1967, p. 33.

Aye, for the game of creating, my brethren, there is needed a holy yea unto life.[79]

The three periods in Bonhoeffer's life thus emphasize his capacity to approach problems anew, to speak in a fresh way, to take risks in thought as well as in action. He liked to say:

A proper sermon should be of the kind that holds out to a child a shining red apple or to a thirsty man a glass of fresh water and asks them, "Do you want it?"[80]

Zimmermann gives a good description of this freshness, in recalling the corrections of sermons which Bonhoeffer made privately with each pastor after he had preached at Finken-walde:

He taught us to accept a preached sermon as a word addressed to us, to which we had to bow. All the same he felt, as we did, that most sermons were too doctrinaire, too theoretical, too correct. In his opinion, "there should be a shot of heresy in every good sermon," meaning that it must drop the doctrinal evenness, must become one-sided, take sides, and dare to go beyond the boundaries of what is "permissible."[81]

The fact that Bonhoeffer went through so many different stages prevents the development of an imitative "Bonhoeffer-ian" theology. In Chapter IX we will discuss the various interpretations of his work, but even now we can be sure that the tone must remain polyphonic. It seems clear that his work was saved from systematic monotony by the events of his life. The speculative camel was torn apart by the pietistic lion, who in his turn was muzzled by the worldly child!

And yet as we trace the flow of Bonhoeffer's life, we can see how foolish it would be to cut his work into disconnected pieces. Bonhoeffer used what he had learned for creative new advances. Heidegger's words about the path of his youth can be applied equally well to Bonhoeffer:

To grow means to open oneself to the vastness of the sky and at the same time to root oneself in the darkness of the earth; man receives

[79] Nietzsche, *Thus Spake Zarathustra*, in *The Philosophy of Nietzsche*, Modern Library, New York, p. 44.

[80] *GS* II, p. 51, cited in Smith, ed., *World Come of Age*, p. 26.

[81] Zimmermann and Smith, eds., *op. cit.*, p. 190.

strength only when he is both submissive to the demands of the highest heavens and raised under the protection of the earth that sustains him.[82]

Bonhoeffer's *Letters and Papers from Prison*, which combines his reflections on the non-religious tomorrow that awaits the world with an appreciation of the nineteenth century and his parents, is a striking illustration of this openness toward tomorrow's sky and rootage in yesterday's earth. The most impressive thing about the man is finally the sense of continuity. Bonhoeffer himself was aware of this when he wrote from prison:

I have certainly learnt a great deal, but I don't think I have changed very much. There are people who change, and others who can hardly change at all . . . I don't think, in fact, that you yourself have changed much. Self-development is, of course, a different matter. Neither of us has really had a break in our [*sic*] lives. Of course, we have deliberately broken with a good deal, but that again is something quite different. Even our present experiences probably do not represent a break in the passive sense. I sometimes used to long for something of the kind, but today I think differently about it. Continuity with one's own past is a great gift, too. Paul wrote II Tim. 1.3a as well as I Tim. 1.13. I am often surprised how little (in contrast to nearly all the others here) I grub among my past mistakes and think how different one thing or another would be today if I had acted differently in the past; it does not worry me at all. Everything seems to have taken its natural course, and to be determined necessarily and straightforwardly by a higher providence.[83]

Even Helmut Gollwitzer felt that Bonhoeffer seemed "too phlegmatic,"[84] and Hammelsbeck writes:

I have learnt from my meeting and friendship with Bonhoeffer . . . to be worldly in an unworldly way, instead of falling in with the routine of the world; to be pious in a non-pious way, instead of

[82] M. Heidegger, *Der Feldweg*, Klostermann, Frankfurt-am-Main 1953, p. 3.

[83] Bonhoeffer, *LPP*, letter of 22 April 1944, p. 150. It is important to note that this was written only eight days before the famous letter of 30 April 1944, from which the appearance of the "totally new" Bonhoeffer is usually dated, the "man of disturbing visions," of "non-religious Christianity," and of the "godlessness" of atheistic christology. This would suggest that whatever discontinuity there is must be located between 22 and 30 April 1944!

[84] Zimmermann and Smith, eds., *op. cit.*, p. 141.

clericalizing the Church which is free in Christ, and the world in which Christ is freed and reconciled.[85]

Schleiermacher wrote in paragraph nine of his *Brief Outline of Theological Studies*:

If we envisage the union of religious interest and a scholarly mind, both of the highest degree, and distributed in as even a balance as possible over theory and practice: then this is the idea of a prince of the Church.[86]

Bonhoeffer would have laughed at this superb definition, for he himself wrote:

One must completely abandon any attempt to make something of oneself, whether it be a saint, or a converted sinner, or a churchman (a so-called priestly type!), a righteous man or an unrighteous one, a sick man or a healthy one. By this-worldliness I mean living unreservedly in life's duties, problems, successes and failures, experiences and perplexities. In so doing we throw ourselves completely into the arms of God, taking seriously, not our own sufferings, but those of God in the world – watching with Christ in Gethsemane. That, I think, is faith, that is *metanoia*: and that is how one becomes a man and a Christian.[87]

Schleiermacher and Bonhoeffer – two "children," one Reformed, the other Lutheran, born in Breslau, one hundred and fifty years apart. They seem to be utterly different: where Schleiermacher was romantic, emotional and religious, Bonhoeffer was realistic, reserved and scarcely religious at all. Schleiermacher died at the age of sixty-six, at the height of his glory, a true prince of the church, of learning, of piety and of his country. Bonhoeffer was killed when he was only thirty-nine, and after his death a number of good churchmen wondered whether he was still a believer when he wrote his prison letters, and whether he had not accidentally betrayed his country.[88]

[85] *Ibid.*, p. 187.   [86] *Op. cit.*, p. 130.
[87] Bonhoeffer, *Letters and Papers from Prison*, 21 July 1944, pp. 201f.
[88] Bonhoeffer's friend Bethge writes: "On four occasions, I have taken part in explosive discussions about Bonhoeffer's thought. The first was provoked by the famous phrase about salvation being found only in the Confessing Church; here Bonhoeffer was accused of being an 'enthusiast.' The second took place around the problem of costly grace; this time he was taken for an obscure pietist. Then there was the clamor over 'contacts with the enemy' during the war, and he was accused

Yet in spite of all the differences, Bonhoeffer's *Letters and Papers from Prison*, in an era of "atheistic" christology, technology and worldly realism, now evokes the same deep response that Schleiermacher's *Speeches on Religion to its Cultured Despisers* had elicited in 1799, in an era of non-christological theism, romanticism and pious idealism. A man is truly great when his words attempt to speak of God in the reality of his own time.

---

of high treason. And now the debate centers on non-religious interpretation of Christianity, and a well-meaning colleague conjectures at a pastors' conference that one should hope that at the very end of his life Bonhoeffer recovered his faith" (*Die Mündige Welt* I, pp. 18f.).

III

Sociology and Ecclesiology

Why the church? We know many unsatisfactory answers to this simple yet difficult question, but there are two answers that deserve serious consideration. One of them asserts that there is a church because it is of divine origin. God wants it that way. The church is the mediator of the means of grace. There is no way to reach God except through the church. The community of faith is like a canal or channel, and anyone who does not stay within its bounds gets lost in the desert of individualism and cannot reach either the source or the sea. This is an objective, positive type of response; its weakness is that it rules out the possibility of really serious self-examination.

The other answer asserts that there is a church because man, being a "social creature" as Calvin puts it, has need of such a community in which his faith is refreshed, his love sustained and his hope renewed. This is an existential, experiential type of response; its weakness lies in basing the church on its good deeds, with the danger that the church will melt away like snow in the sunshine, if it can be shown that its misdeeds outnumber its good ones. We are all aware today that it is at least as easy to make the case against the church as it used to be to glorify it: the church is guilty of pompous clericalism, rigid institutionalism, a stifling ghetto-mentality, obvious and parochial mediocrity, paternalistic misunderstandings, maternalistic inveigling – the list of charges can be extended indefinitely.

According to the first answer, the church is an authoritative fact; according to the second, a shaky ideal. So again the question is posed: why the church?

1. *Kant and Hegel on the reason for the church*

Kant and Hegel both engaged in extensive discussion about the church,[1] both as philosophers and as part of a culture that was basically Protestant. For our purposes they illustrate clearly the two types of response to which attention has just been called.

Kant adopts the second perspective: the church is a social necessity, at least in its visible form which Kant calls "statutory." If man remained isolated, he might indeed be able to overcome the radical evil which is just as inherent as the good will. However,

Envy, the lust for power, greed, and the malignant inclinations bound up with these, besiege his nature, contented within itself, *directly he is among men.*[2]

So the church is that ethical society in which men join forces in order not to fall once again under the spell of social evil. From this presupposition it is easy to see how the church is justified: it is to be the guardian of morality by imposing a legal framework from outside. It is also easy to see what threatens the church: it is always tempted to confuse itself with its own end and to absolutize itself, tendencies which Kant says provoke the stupidity of superstition or the folly of fanaticism. Kant is thus led logically to distinguish between two forms of the church, one pure, the other corrupt. The first of these is invisible, inward, and moral, for "the honest man is worth more than the elect." It distrusts all attempts to sanctify its own form, for every ecclesiastical form is tainted by the defects that arise out of its public responsibilities, whether the form be monarchial (here Kant mentions the pope and the eastern patriarchs), aristocratic (bishops and prelates) or democratic (the enthusiasts and the sectarians). The true church is a large family within which the invisible Father is honored in his Son, who represents him. Such a church is "a cordial,

---

[1] Kant, *Religion within the Limits of Reason Alone* (1793), Open Court Publishing Company, Chicago 1934, pp. 85–190; Hegel, *Begriff der Religion* (1825); *Die absolute Religion* (1829). Cf. Fackenheim, *The Religious Dimension in Hegel's Thought*, Beacon Press, Boston 1967.

[2] Kant, *op. cit.*, p. 85.

voluntary, universal and lasting association." This invisible church guarantees the stability of its structure and the freedom of its members. But we cannot help noticing that the church itself is continually falling into the same evil from which it is supposed to protect its members. It assumes that its own worship is the true end of man, whereas it is no more than a means to undergird morality. Its clergy, who should be no more than servants (*ministerium*) at the level of the invisible church, are transformed into the officials of a constraining holy institution.

In this way the church's faith (*Glaube*) becomes superstition (*Aberglaube*). Prayer, which ought to be a rekindling of moral initiative, degenerates into a means of grace, and Kant, long before Marx, denounced the forgiveness of sins as the opiate of the conscience. Such a degenerate church engages in a type of worship contrary to what God wills, for according to Kant's basic principle,

Whatever, over and above good life conduct, man fancies that he can do to become well-pleasing to God is mere religious illusion and pseudo-service of God.[3]

Kant's attitude therefore vacillates. He is not necessarily against the church when it "contains within itself something great, expanding the narrow, selfish, and unsociable cast of mind among men, especially in matters of religion, towards the idea of a cosmopolitan moral community; and it is a good means of enlivening a community to the moral disposition of brotherly love which it represents." But he is strongly against the church when the clergy have "usurped by dint of arrogating to themselves the prestige attached to exclusive possession of the means of grace."[4]

Hegel's ecclesiology is totally different, reflecting the ontological style of his philosophy in contrast to Kant's transcendental idealism. In Hegel's view, there is only one church, the church where the Spirit dwells, bringing about a union between the abstraction of the Father, the objectivity of the Son, and the subjectivity of man. The church is the logical fulfillment of faith, which begins with being, the initial indetermination (God the Father or the abstract universal),

---

[3] Kant, *op. cit.*, p. 158, italics in original.
[4] Kant, *op. cit.*, pp. 187f.

continues with reflection (the Christ in whom the abstract universal is individualized, objectified and externalized), in order to lead to the concept (the Holy Spirit, who enables us to grasp within ourselves, in both a universal and concrete way, the being who has been individualized in Christ). Thus the church ought to be a discernible reality to the degree that the Spirit is at work. The Trinity, which is fulfilled by the unification between the abstraction of God and the subjectivity of man, ought to lead to a concrete subjective church. In its ecclesiology, the church of the Spirit thus ought to reunite the infinite and the finite, the universal and the particular, in the same way that in the Trinity the Spirit reunites the Father and the Son. Thus the church's emphasis on Spirit never means, as it does in Kant, the church's invisibility, but rather its ability to effect a reconciliation between outer and inner, or (in Kant's terms) the phenomenal and the noumenal. Consequently Hegel is a strong supporter of worship and the sacraments. He sees them as the eternal repetition of the life, suffering and resurrection of Christ in the members of the church.

Hegel is therefore at the farthest remove from Kant's moralism, pietism and fideism, for he insists that what distinguishes God is that he becomes reality and does not remain simply a postulate, ideal or end. This makes it easy to understand why Hegel was happy to have one of his two sons become superintendent of the Prussian Church (a "statutory" church if there ever was one!) and was willing to give the oration at the three hundredth anniversary of the writing of the Augsburg Confession, whereas Kant was buried along the wall "outside" the church at Koenigsberg. In his anniversary speech Hegel equated the church with the Kingdom of God, and described it as the very life and power of the Spirit.

Out of such convictions, Hegel builds an unusual theory centering on four times when subsequent Christian history repudiated this union between God and reality that ought to be embodied in the church of the Spirit, as the completion of Christ's unique and objective work. The four periods are the following:

1. The medieval division of Catholicism, which was a division between the world and God. In this view, the world was devalued. God became far-removed and foreign to the

world. The church was no longer the place where God and reality were reconciled. As examples of this tendency, Hegel cites medieval sermons that put begging and the contemplative life above work, chastity above marriage and sexuality, and authority above freedom.

2. The division of the Protestant Reformation, which was a division between the soul and the world, particularly in the Lutheran doctrine of the two realms, the spiritual and the temporal, the interior and the exterior. This division was parallel to the medieval division and yet opposite to it. The church became the place for souls exiled from the world. If the Reformation achieved a real reconciliation with God, Hegel feels that its reconciliation with the world was only apparent.

3. The division of the Enlightenment and the age of reason, which put faith and reason in opposition to one another. The opposition was superficial both because reason was doing battle with a faith it did not believe in sufficiently to do true battle, and even more because it forgot that philosophy explains itself away when it explains religion away – it being Hegel's contention that philosophy deals abstractly with the same Absolute that religion proclaims concretely.

4. There is finally the division of fideism and Kantianism. In trying to counteract the dried-up rationalism of the Enlightenment, this new movement actually succumbed to it by creating a new division between empirical understanding and regulative reason, between knowledge and belief.

Now according to Hegel, all of these divisions ignored the fact that in Christianity, God and reality are united, and that the church is the place where this unity is realized and manifested. Consequently no philosopher has ever had a "higher" ecclesiology than Hegel's.[5]

[5] Due to the failure of the historic forms of the church, which are always falling into the divisions of "the unhappy consciousness" (cf. *The Phenomenology of Mind*, pp. 241–7) Hegel entrusted the task of achieving unity between God and the world to a rationally-ordered Christian state, thus escaping the danger of a time-bound Catholicism, which neglects the freedom of the Spirit, as well as the subjectivity of Protestantism, which neglects its universality. Hegel's doctrine of the state is actually a rational ecclesiology.

2. *The church as the structure of the world*

This long philosophical detour helps to show how Bonhoeffer's ecclesiology springs from a Hegelian orientation, whereas Barth's early views come from a Kantian transcendentalist perspective. According to Christoph von Hase, Bonhoeffer believes that

The Church is the place where the deputyship of Christ for humanity is fulfilled through the deputyship of believers toward one another and toward the world.[6]

The church is the world as it is meant to be in Jesus Christ, the space where the world is structured according to its true center. The church is the ongoing outworking of the incarnation.

Barth, on the contrary, insisting that the freedom of God's grace must not be captured or dispensed by any pious, religious or institutional organization of men, made clear in his *Epistle to the Romans* that the church is in opposition to the gospel understood as the incarnation of the ultimate human possibility on this side of the "impossible possibility" of God. Reflecting on the nature of the church at a later time, Barth commented in 1955 on Bonhoeffer's earliest work, *The Communion of Saints*:

This dissertation . . . not only awakens respects for the breadth and depth of its insight as we look back to the existing situation, but makes far more instructive and stimulating and illuminating and genuinely edifying reading today than many of the more famous works which have since been written on the problem of the Church . . . I openly confess that I have misgiving whether I can even maintain the high level reached by Bonhoeffer, saying no less in my own words and context, and saying it no less forcefully, than did this young man so many years ago.[7]

Barth thus followed Bonhoeffer's lead, even to the point of writing an appreciation of Hegel, something that would have been astonishing during the period of his *Epistle to the Romans*:

[6] von Hase, "Begriff und Wirklichkeit der Kirche in der Theologie Bonhoeffers," *Die Mündige Welt* I, p. 26.
[7] Barth, *Church Dogmatics* IV/2, p. 641.

Who knows whether it was not in fact the *genuinely* theological element in Hegel which made [theology] shrink back? ... Would modern man and the modern theologian have understood him better and accorded him a better reception, if there had not been these known theological objections to be raised against him? ... Many and great things would then have assumed a different aspect in the intellectual life of the nineteenth and twentieth centuries, and perhaps in their political and economic life too. But in that case Hegel would not have been Hegel, and we must therefore be content to understand him as the man he was: as a great problem and a great disappointment, but perhaps also a great promise.[8]

As I see it, Bonhoeffer's work is in many ways the fulfillment of the "great promise" to which Barth refers, namely that God and reality are united – not, as Hegel believed, by the progressive reign of the Spirit succeeding the abstraction of the Father and the objectification of the Son in order to be fulfilled by man's increasing self-awareness in the course of history's unfolding, but rather that God and reality are united in Jesus Christ through the incarnation, and that the church witnesses to this in the midst of the world by its faithful obedience to this real yet hidden mystery.

Let us now examine the circumstances in which Bonhoeffer had to think through the question of the church in 1927, how he responded at that time, and the degree to which that response remains fundamentally unchanged during the three periods Bonhoeffer had to confront: the state church, the Confessing Church and the "non-religious" church.

Why be concerned with the question of the church at all? Let us look first at Bonhoeffer's most elusive answer: because if God is really reconciled with the world, this reconciliation must be given tangible expression; it must have some "place," not as a higher (or lower!) platform leading to the world, or as a springboard from which to jump toward the world beyond (or within!), but as a structure within which this reconciliation is a daily reality. As Bonhoeffer wrote, "Only rationalism and mysticism deny God a 'place' [in the world]."[9]

The church is not removed from the world, for God is not removed from everyday life in Jesus Christ. But the church is

---

[8] Barth, *From Rousseau to Ritschl*, SCM Press, London (published as *Protestant Thought: from Rousseau to Ritschl* by Harper and Bros., New York) 1959, p. 305.

[9] Bethge, *Dietrich Bonhoeffer*, German edition, p. 1057.

not to be identified with the ordinary workaday world, for it is the reunified *structure* of that world. It is the pragmatic world understood in its true depth, as it is truly meant to be. It is the world formed in Christ, as Christ is already the church forming the world. The church displays the concrete and communal character of Christ, as Christ is himself a structuring, representative and "collective" person. Thus we see that from the very beginning Bonhoeffer's interest in the church grows out of christological realism far more than out of an attempt to make a "case for the church," or out of fears about the failures and shortcomings of existing empirical churches. For Bonhoeffer the church is Christ already present and at work, more than it is an institution either mediating Christ or ideally and insufficiently turned toward him.

Now in 1927 (as would also be true today) such a starting point was unusual, to say the least. Against Bonhoeffer were ranged philosophical liberalism, sociology of religion, the new dialectical theology of the transcendence of the Word, and the traditional doctrine of the institutional church as the means of grace. These were, a bit over-schematically, the four usual ways of justifying the existence of the church. Bonhoeffer studied each of them before stating his own point of view. He looked first at philosophical liberalism, which he felt grew out of individualistic idealism, and was closed to "sociality" by its concept of self-sufficient personality.

Next Bonhoeffer examined the sociology of religion, studying in detail the thought of Durkheim, Simmel, Weber and particularly Tönnies and Troeltsch. Sociology of religion had the tremendous advantage over idealism that it understood man as being basically open to others. But its viewpoint was culturally conditioned and lacked any theological base. Particularly when it dealt with the inner nature of Christianity, it reverted to idealistic individualism, supplemented by a typology of social forms which that individualism had assumed would persist. As Ernst Troeltsch, the open-minded and honest founder of the sociology of the Christian religion, wrote at the conclusion of his massive work on *The Social Teaching of the Christian Churches*:

The Gospel of Jesus was a free personal piety, with a strong impulse towards profound intimacy and spiritual fellowship and communion, but without any tendency towards the organization of a cult, or towards the creation of a religious community. Only when faith in Jesus, the Risen and Exalted Lord, became the central point of worship in a new religious community did the necessity for organization arise. From the very beginning there appeared the three main types of the sociological development of Christian thought: the Church, the sect, and mysticism.[10]

Troeltsch felt that the whole point of Christianity, as of idealism, was to lift man up to a transcendent ideal:

The Christian Ethos gives to all social life and aspiration a goal which lies far beyond all the relativities of this earthly life, compared with which, indeed, everything else represents merely approximate values. The idea of the future Kingdom of God, which is nothing less than faith in the final realization of the Absolute (in whatever way we may conceive this realization), does not, as short-sighted opponents imagine, render this world and life in this world meaningless and empty; on the contrary, it stimulates human energies, making the soul strong through its various stages of experience in the certainty of an ultimate, absolute meaning and aim for human labour.[11]

This is hardly distinguishable from Kant's kingdom of ends, and indeed one of Troeltsch's avowed purposes was "to reconcile Kant and Schleiermacher." Troeltsch points to several well-identified models in terms of which the church would become the vehicle for the social quickening of this striving toward the final absolute, the transcendent form of which has appeared on earth in the experience of the man Jesus:

The church-type itself, just because of this element of tension between pure Christianity and adjustment to the world which exists within it, has had a very changeful history, and is to-day becoming entirely transformed.[12]

[10] Troeltsch, *The Social Teaching of the Christian Churches*, Vol. II, George Allen and Unwin, London 1931, p. 993.

[11] Troeltsch, *op. cit.*, pp. 1005f.

[12] Troeltsch, *op. cit.*, p. 1007. Cf. the summary by Jean Séguy of Troeltsch's understanding of the essence of Christianity:

"Jesus did not found either a church or a sect. He preached communion with the Father, love among all men and unconcern for the world. He proposed no asceticism save the acceptance of the circumstances and conditions of life. At the heart of his preaching is a belief in the infinite worth of the individual, and a clear affirmation of the equality of all individuals before God. A community of brothers was created

Thus we find that while the sociology of the Christian religion did study the church, it viewed the church merely as something arising out of the needs of its members, far removed from what was assumed to be Jesus' purely individualistic outlook. The church illustrates the various forms that a movement of pure transcendence must assume as it becomes the indispensable cultural implementation of Jesus' individualism.

Bonhoeffer's intent was to write a *dogmatic* treatment in the light of the sociology of the church. But dogmatics itself was poorly equipped to relate the church to Christ. Neither neo-Lutheranism nor the early dialectical theology spoke of God save as an event of sheer grace – transcendent, tangential and vertical – in relation to which the church was a kind of "fall-out," or at best a recollection or memorial. In Christianity itself, Bonhoeffer once commented, an enemy cell of the church is hidden. Bonhoeffer wanted to respond to Troeltsch's personalistic sociology with Barth's transcendental theology, but was unable to do so convincingly. Indeed, the very opposite took place. For sociology became the door through which Bonhoeffer entered into a new dogmatic understanding of the true basis of the church. This happened in a roundabout way, through the long and intricate argument of *The Communion of Saints*.

Naturally one can avoid the bypaths if he adopts the basic Catholic position and equates the church with its own visible structure.[13] But Bonhoeffer makes clear that

No sociological structure is sacred in itself, and there is no structure capable of completely obstructing the Word in its course ... No church can claim to possess [pure doctrine] absolutely.[14]

He also acknowledges that he is ready to "recognize and

---

around Jesus. After his death it centered on the worship of his divinity, a conception born out of the need of the group to find cohesiveness" (*Archives de Sociologie des Religions*, 1961, No. II, p. 10).

Bonhoeffer's evaluation of Troeltsch was qualified: Troeltsch's work seemed to him to overemphasize the accidental forms that Christianity had historically taken, and to be too little based on the essential structures of the Christian world (cf. *The Communion of Saints*, pp. 16f.). Thus in his study of the church Bonhoeffer makes greater use of Tönnies' distinction between *Gesellschaft* (society) and *Gemeinschaft* (community) – sociological models which the Nazis unfortunately adopted – than of Troeltsch's distinctions between church, sect and mysticism.

[13] Cf. *The Communion of Saints*, p. 88.   [14] *Ibid.*, p. 187.

believe in principle, therefore, that the *sanctorum communio* is present both in the Roman Catholic Church and in the sect."[15] This openness to the Catholic position appears in many of Bonhoeffer's writings. For example, he describes the church as the ongoing presence of the structure of the incarnation in *The Communion of Saints*; ontology as counterbalancing a theology of "act" in *Act and Being*; "following after" Christ as a corrective to a purely externalized notion of justification by faith in *The Cost of Discipleship*; he advocates the restoration of confession in *Life Together*; the worth of the "natural" in *Ethics*; he stresses the "secret discipline" in *Letters and Papers from Prison*; and expresses a preference throughout for citations from the church fathers over those of the Reformers. This concern pervades all Bonhoeffer's writings and goes counter to the division between the visible and invisible church, or a purely individualistic type of religion that has often characterized Protestantism.

We must also remember that Bonhoeffer was deeply influenced by his trip to Rome in 1924. It was there that he discovered and learned to appreciate the universality of the Roman Catholic Church, its non-sectarianism, its appreciation of culture, its desire to relate its faith to public life, and its stress on the power of the confessional. At the same time he continued to warn against the dangers of legalism and casuistry, and to deplore the weakness of the traditional Catholic apologetic based on proofs for the existence of God that had not even taken Kant's challenge seriously. He was disappointed by the papal audience he attended, finding the pope impersonal, lifeless and cold, "lacking in everything papal, in all *grandezza*!"[16] But years later in his prison letters, Bonhoeffer could speak of Rome as "one of my favourite parts of the world."[17] There was nothing arrogant about Bonhoeffer's Protestantism.

However, whenever he dealt with Catholicism he explained why he could not accept the Catholic tendency to divinize the institution itself, with its implication that God had bound himself to that particular church and not to reality as a whole. For Bonhoeffer, Jesus Christ, and not a particular church,

---

[15] *Ibid.*, p. 187.   [16] Bethge, *Dietrich Bonhoeffer*, p. 40.
[17] Bonhoeffer, *LPP*, 24 March 1944, p. 143.

constituted the center of reality. Such, indeed, is the classical Protestant position. But none of this prevented Bonhoeffer from playing a significant ecumenical role in relation to the underlying problems he treated and reopened, particularly his doctrine of the church.

It is only by starting from reality, rather than from a claim by the church about its own foundation, that one can understand the question about the church of Christ. Bonhoeffer's own analysis deals first with human society. He wants, as he put it,

to understand the structure from the standpoint of social philosophy and sociology, of the reality of the church of Christ which is given in the revelation in Christ.[18]

In so doing, he follows his unvarying method of approach, e.g. to think about reality in relation to God and about God in relation to reality. We can see this more clearly by referring to a distinction Bonhoeffer later elaborated in *Ethics*: *ultimate reality*, which is the presence of the church overflowing from God's heart, must be verified in the *penultimate realities*, which *The Communion of Saints* identifies as the two human sciences of social philosophy (a non-empirical study of the foundations of society), and sociology (the science of the structure of empirical communities). Only such a "sociality," Bonhoeffer contends, can help us understand such major theological convictions as sin, salvation, revelation and particularly the "I-thou" relationship. Idealism, which is a community of spirits lacking "sociality," may be able to exist without these but Christian theology cannot. In theology, indeed, there is a recognition that the very existence of the reality of the "other" constitutes a barrier, and that reality cannot be understood without taking this barrier of the "other" into account. Idealism, on the other hand, fails to recognize this barrier, and moves on to the "you can" too soon after the "you ought." In idealism, the "thou" is covertly present in the "I" of the subject. But in theology (and sociology) the "thou" itself is truly a limitation, and sheer individuality is not a possibility. For the holiness of God is man's barrier and the sin of man is God's barrier. The person is never known in his totality; he is only understood and believed in. Thus in a very broad sense faith becomes the only possible base for a sociality determined to go beyond the individualistic domination of idealism.

In all this we can see how Bonhoeffer is moving constantly from sociology to theology and vice versa. Sociology opens up theological thinking, which is otherwise characterized by transcendental and individualistic idealism, to the *collective* categories that are indispensable in thinking through the meaning of its own affirmations. And theology, with its categories of dialogue, covenant and deputyship, provides sociology with a theoretical base that is stronger than the personalistic idealism on which it has built in the past. To put it another way, sociology's concreteness keeps theology from talking abstractly about the church, while theological reflection about the church provides sociology with a philosophic perspective it otherwise lacks. Culture encourages theology to understand its own resources, which alone can be the basis for culture. Sociality reopens in the direction of fundamental ecclesiology, which validates the fundamental meaning of sociality. Philosophy encourages theology to think about the structures that transform philosophy into an ontological analysis rather than arbitrary speculation. This is not a case of making theology and philosophy agree, but a way of looking at the same reality from two viewpoints – the social sciences and the givens of dogmatics.

It would be too much to claim that Bonhoeffer always succeeded in showing that the two viewpoints agree. In 1930, his cousin, Christoph von Hase, saw clearly what would happen to *The Communion of Saints*:

There will not be many who really understand it; the Barthians won't because of the sociology, and the sociologists won't because of Barth.[19]

This is because the typological interpretation of sociology sees reality at most as something to interpret, while confessional interpretation of dogmatics sees it as a present and hidden secret. It can always appear as though Bonhoeffer short-circuited mediation between the disciplines, and that the young man of twenty-one – a true "camel" in the field of academic science and rigorous investigation – affirmed more

[19] Bethge, *Dietrich Bonhoeffer*, pp. 58f.

than he could establish. But in any case his analysis is remarkable and above all the question about the church is clearly dealt with, not in conflict with reality, nor outside it, but at its very center.

The church is the concrete reminder that humanity was created one. In this sense the church is essential, for it is the "body" of society showing what society is meant to be – unbroken and undivided. Social philosophy (which Bonhoeffer defines as the science of the "origins" of human sociality) shows that man's consciousness is formed by his openness in reaching out beyond himself, with all the problems that entails, but also that this consciousness avoids absorption into collectivism by a legitimate kind of individualistic closedness. Sociology (which Bonhoeffer defines as the science of the structures of empirical communities) explains how a common will, and not simply outside pressures, creates community. Here also the individual resists surrendering his individual identity, for as Kant put it, "Man wants agreement, but nature knows better what is good for the spirit, and it wants debate." But it was Hegel who best described the reality of personal consciousness based on the otherness of the common will and its objectification in the state, and Bonhoeffer dared to quote his famous statement on the realization of the objective Mind: "It is mind that has reality, and individuals are its accidents."[20]

Sin is the breaking of this fundamental community. It is both ontological and social. It leads to "ethical atomism," the dividing of conscience against itself, and to infinite isolation. But sin is also the place where the closest solidarity is rediscovered. It is a kind of reverse realization of the church by the reality of the communion of sinners. It is collective guilt, which is the real meaning of "original sin" rather than some erroneous view of the biological transmission of sin. When he sins, each individual is also part of the human race. This is why the Bible never hesitates to speak of collective human sinners, such as nations, peoples and historical eras.

In this way we gain a better understanding of the question,

---

[20] Hegel, *Philosophy of Right*, par. 156; cited in Bonhoeffer, *The Communion of Saints*, p. 68. Cf. also Hegel's statement in *Reason in History*: "All the value man has, all spiritual reality, he has only through the state" (Liberal Arts Press, New York 1953, p. 52).

"Why the church?" The church is neither a religious society made up of individuals worried about "sociological self-affirmation," as Troeltsch puts it; nor is it simply a John the Baptist preaching the event of the Word, as the early Barth put it; nor, once again, is it the holy and infallible mediator of salvation, as Catholicism puts it. Rather, according to Bonhoeffer's now classic phrase, the church is the body of Christ as collective person, "Christ existing as the church."[21] Overflowing from the heart of God, the church is reality as restructured in Jesus Christ. Bonhoeffer shows exegetically that the problem of whether or not Jesus wanted to found a church is really a false problem,[22] for Jesus Christ *is himself* the church at the heart of reality, broken on the cross where the reality of every human disruption is objectively present, and then rebuilt at Easter where the universe is reconstituted. Thus Jesus Christ is not the founder of a church, as a religious community that lost sight of the truth when its founder died. Rather Jesus Christ is himself the foundation. The nature of the church is connected to the fulfillment of his revelation. Its necessity is found in that reality.

Only such a sequence provides a true foundation for the church, for every other way of adding the church onto revelation weakens it and casts doubt upon the pedagogical or apologetic justifications that are offered on its behalf. So Bonhoeffer's thesis emerges still full of the overtones of Hegelian assurance: "The Church is the presence of Christ, as Christ is the presence of God."[23] The New Testament knows one form of revelation: Christ existing as community.

Out of all this Bonhoeffer – who later became well known for having spoken of a "non-religious interpretation of Christianity" and an "anonymous Christianity" – went on to work out the strongest case imaginable for the empirical church. Does this mean that Bonhoeffer later did a complete about-face, moving *From the Church to the World* as the title of Hanfried Müller's book suggests? The opposite seems to be the case. Bonhoeffer

[21] Bonhoeffer, *The Communion of Saints*, p. 102. In his *Philosophy of Religion*, Hegel had spoken of "God existing as community." Cf. Ott, *Wirklichkeit und Glaube* I, p. 194 n.1.

[22] The exegetical problem is difficult, since the word *ekklēsia*, church, appears only twice in the gospels (Matt. 16.18 and 18.17).

[23] Bonhoeffer, *The Communion of Saints*, p. 101.

consistently saw the church as Christ not only entering into solidarity with the reality of the world, but becoming its deputy or representative[24] – whether that reality was the Prussian state church of his twenties, the independent Confessing Church of the Nazi Germany of his thirties, or the "non-religious" church witnessing through politics and prison as he approached his forties. At every stage along the way the church is allied with humanity, rediscovering its structures concretely. It attains its true end not by organizing its ministers in themselves, but by the creation of community, for the sake of which its ministers exist. It achieves both dimensions of the human sociality so well exemplified at Pentecost: collective humanity *and* the unwillingness to absorb individuals into an anonymous collectivity, symbolized by a common language *and* the separate tongues of fire. The unity of the church is the unity *of* the Spirit, not unity *in* the Spirit – a point at which Bonhoeffer clearly corrects the equivocal pantheism of certain of Hegel's phrases about the One who is eternally suprapersonal and immanent in humanity.[25] The empirical church has the advantage over Kant's (and sometimes also Luther's) invisible and interior church of reminding us that in theology reality precedes idealistic constructions. God makes it possible for us to understand him, and the church makes it possible for us to believe in him. So we must beware that in protesting the shortcomings of the state church we do not simply flee from the world about us, where God is, to some ideal realm, where man dreams, and we must not use Luther's painful break with the historic Roman Catholic Church as a continuing justification for fleeing from the concretization of Christ in the church. Toward the end of *The Communion of Saints* Bonhoeffer gives a pastoral explanation of why he prefers public worship to private worship in a "house-church," where there is a tendency to confuse the universal reality created by God with the "human" warmth of an intimate circle; and why he also prefers infant baptism and is against any confirmation service which suggests that the catechumens somehow create their

[24] "Not 'solidarity', which is never possible between Christ and man, but vicarious action [deputyship] is the life-principle of the new mankind" (*The Communion of Saints*, p. 107).

[25] Bonhoeffer also notes that the Church of the Spirit avoids identifying the Holy Spirit with the objective spirit of the community itself as Hegel does.

ideal of the church rather than recognizing that they are already part of the church.

In this realism about the church that is "realized" in Jesus Christ and "actualized" by the Holy Spirit,[26] Bonhoeffer pressed the point a little too far. His attempt, for example, to distinguish between the church of the *crowd* (the baptized), the *voluntary participants* (the considerably smaller number who worship and hear the sermon), and the *confessants* (the tiny group that receives communion), is an early version of later distinctions in religious sociology between various categories of church-goers, but it has no real theological significance. It is the ultimate expression of a very concrete ecclesiology, in which the Holy Spirit seeks social expression, since as Troeltsch put it, God is not an end who is beyond the relativities of temporal life, but the reality who unifies humanity without depersonalizing it. The church is the place where the deputy-ship of Jesus Christ extends to one and all. In the church one believes in the Holy Spirit, just as in the Holy Spirit one believes in the church. So it is through its identification with humanity that the church objectively becomes the church of the Spirit of God, who wants humanity to be fulfilled in the form of community.[27]

The church is thus at the heart of reality. It is not an intimate circle where people cultivate the memory of Jesus' personality (Troeltsch); it is not a scolding pulpit from which sin and salvation are proclaimed to the outside world (the early Barth); nor is it a sacred institution serving as a repository of the means of grace (Roman Catholicism). It is neither outside man's life nor the sacred object of his allegiance. It is the realization – fragmentary and hidden but also objective and empirical – of God's reunification of everyday life, of the human community, in Jesus Christ. A supra-personal and yet personal spirit is present in the church, a spirit who delivers men from the loneliness

[26] Cf. Bonhoeffer, *The Communion of Saints*, pp. 106–44, where the distinction is elaborated.

[27] One section of *The Communion of Saints* was rejected by Seeberg, the chairman of Bonhoeffer's thesis committee. It was called "Church and Proletariat." While Bonhoeffer refused to make an artificial identification between Tillich's "holiness of . . . the masses" and the "communion of saints," he did insist strongly that the proletariat was open to the call of the gospel, while the bourgeois did not understand that call. He also insisted that in becoming a bourgeois club, the church had lost touch with reality. Cf. *The Communion of Saints*, pp. 190–4.

of individualism without their being lost in the anonymity of the crowd. The church is certainly not the Kingdom of God, which will be the city of man without divisions either between men or between men and God, but the church moves toward that Kingdom, and is even now the foretaste of its coming.[28]

In his later writings Bonhoeffer puts less emphasis on transcendence than the early Barth, and is less existentialist and individualistic than Bultmann. John Godsey comments:

In Bonhoeffer we have a theologian whose thought is as Christocentric as that of Karl Barth, who raised the question of the communication of the gospel as sharply as Rudolf Bultmann, who was led to take the problem of our pragmatic, problem-solving technological world as seriously as Reinhold Niebuhr, but who, more than any of these men, thought from the perspective of the concrete church.[29]

Even if we take this statement with a grain of salt, it is still true that Bonhoeffer never fails to begin and end with the church. It is not a retreat he sometimes leaves in order to encounter society and the world, but the place where the world is brought to fulfillment in Christ. The church is that "space" where the world is formed in Christ and where Christ is formed in the world. It is the claim of Christ over the whole of reality, and it is the reality of his claim.

Surely few men have been as deeply aware as Bonhoeffer of the paralysis, isolation and religious unreality of the church Few men have been as pained as he at the bourgeois mediocrity of its architecture, its uninviting language and its bland activities, none of which suggest to the world that reality could be embodied within the church in a responsible and representative way. Let us not therefore imagine a Bonhoeffer who nursed illusions about the empirical church or who, disappointed by the state church, transferred his dream to the future of a "non-religious," non-parochial, non-institutional church, a kind of "incognito" church immersed in the world

[28] One of Hegel's shortcomings is the lack of any eschatological boundary between the rational State and the Kingdom of God. After his death history quickly placed severe limits around the realization of the Hegelian State. Honecker holds that Bonhoeffer likewise lacked any eschatological boundary in his "positivism of the church." (Cf. *Kirche als Gestalt und Ereignis. Die sichtbare Gestalt der Kirche als dogmatisches Problem*, 1963, p. 156.)

[29] Godsey, *The Theology of Dietrich Bonhoeffer*, p. 17.

and at last making common cause with it. Any reconstruction of a Bonhoeffer that makes him worldly because he has become anti-ecclesiastical, is just the opposite of the true Bonhoeffer, for in such a view God and reality would still be severed from one another. The church errs when it starts doubting the reality of God in proportion to a stronger belief in the reality of the world.

No – to the very end, Bonhoeffer's ecclesiology remained empirical, but his reality became the non-religious world. He did not abandon the church in order to rejoin the world, but following Hegel's great lesson (as corrected by a theocentric theology of grace) he believed that God brings the church to fulfillment *in* the world and the world to fulfillment *through* the church, that he brings faith to fulfillment in sociality, and sociality to fulfillment through faith. To be a member of Christ's church is, like Christ, to have the task of being the responsible servant and deputy of the whole world. Reinold von Thadden once summarized Bonhoeffer's point by suggesting that church members must first become more worldly if they are ever to become more spiritual. [30]

At the beginning of this chapter we raised the question, "Why the church?" There are many ways to elaborate the question. Is the church indispensable? Is it superfluous? Does it come after faith or before faith? Is it in the world or outside the world? Does it do good or evil? Must one be part of it or can one be free of it? Should one return to the church or should one participate in the exodus from the church to the world? Is our time one of rediscovery of the ecclesiastical community or of challenge to it? Is the church an institution or an event, or sometimes one and sometimes the other? Is it more important to assemble in the worshipping community or to be dispersed in the diaspora existence of mission? Are the boundaries of the church a sign of its power, or a frontier, or a source of self-preoccupation? Must one love the church or ought one to rebel against it? Is the church a reality helping to mould contemporary society, or is it on the fringes of society – a cozy ghetto, a captive of suburbia,[31] a rustic anachronism? If

[30] Cf. *Die Mündige Welt* I, p. 46.
[31] Cf. Gibson Winter, *The Suburban Captivity of the Churches*, Macmillan, New York, and SCM Press, London 1961.

the church is a sinking ship, should one try to plug the leak, jump into a lifeboat, or go down with the ship like a lonely captain making a futile yet honorable gesture?

We have been using the word "church" in the broadest possible sense, but if we were to use the more disputed word "parish," a whole host of further questions would have to be raised, for this is a time when the church has doubts – not about its glory (every Christian knows that glory is not self-glorification but deep understanding and love), but about what it is really accomplishing (since it is Christ's will that trees bring forth fruit and since he withered the sterile fig tree for failing to do so).

Bonhoeffer does not answer all these questions. A question receives its true answer only from the one who asks it. But he helps us deal with them, by basing the church on the reality of "Christ existing as community," so that the world not only may know but also experience – along with all the insults, brokenness and isolation that characterize the church – the reality of its reconciliation and reconciliation with its reality.

IV

Ontology without Metaphysics?

Bonhoeffer's second book, *Act and Being*,[1] was written as a
follow-up to the first, a kind of subordinate argument that
projects a light already examined in the main argument onto
a wholly new landscape. The new landscape is the theory of
knowledge in contemporary philosophy and theology, and the
light is the particular reality of the church that is described as
the revelatory "act" of God and also the "being" of his
revelation. The church is thus related to a transcendence that
comes *to* man and an ontology that is an ongoing part of his
experience. It is born out of God's freedom and expresses
God's faithfulness to his freely-given Word. The church acts
as a regulative principle to end the ongoing trench-warfare
between the beyond and the within – between advocates of *act*,
which Bonhoeffer characterizes as "outward reference, infinite
extensity, restriction to the conscious, extentiality and discontinuity" (or, as we would say, the event), and the advocates
of *being*, which Bonhoeffer characterizes as "self-confinement,
infinite intensity, transcendence of the conscious, and continuity" (or, as we would say, the institution).[2]

Bonhoeffer's professors gave him scant encouragement in
pursuing this line of investigation. Reinhold Seeberg proposed
instead that he limit himself to a more restricted historical
topic, such as the ethical inadequacies of a twelfth-century
treatise by John of Salisbury. Wilhelm Lütgert, to whom
Bonhoeffer was an assistant, was upset by the influence

---

[1] Bonhoeffer, *Act and Being*, 1961, 192pp.
[2] Cf. Bonhoeffer, *Act and Being*, pp. 13f.

Heidegger was having on Protestant theologians, for he considered Heidegger a neo-Thomist. But Bonhoeffer stuck to his guns
and went ahead with his ambitious project to test, in the field
of knowledge, the reality of the church as "Christ existing in
the form of community," and to verify at the level of human
understanding the fruitfulness of an ecclesiological reality
which he had already described as better equipped than
personalistic idealism to furnish a solid conceptual foundation
for sociology. So once again theology and philosophy are
dealt with together, but Bonhoeffer takes care not to mix
them. "God" and "being" refer to two different things. We
respond to them in different ways, and must avoid a dishonest
apologetic that sets up impasses on the one hand in order to
provide solutions and issues on the other. But speech about God
(which in being called "theology" already has a philosophical
name) and speech about reality (which is already directed
toward what gives being to things) cannot avoid comparing
their methods of approach because, quite rightly from the
point of view of Christian faith, God and reality have been and
remain indissolubly joined together in Jesus Christ.

In *The Communion of Saints*, the secular dimension of sociology
had reacquainted theology with a communal and representative understanding of Christ as the structural foundation and
not simply the religious founder of the church. In *Act and Being*
the opposite route is followed by posing the question: is the
church, as the real unity of God's act and being, able to shed
any light on secular discussion about contemporary theories
of knowledge?

Where Bonhoeffer fails in this brief work it is because he
tries to do too much. Where he succeeds, the success lies on
two levels: (*a*) to inform us, with a high degree of linguistic
precision, about the intellectual situation in 1929, shortly
after the publication of Heidegger's *Being and Time* in 1927
and on the eve of the growing theological divergence between
Barth's stress on objective act and Bultmann's stress on
existential act; and (*b*) to give us a better grasp of Bonhoeffer's
own way of confronting those two emphases. This way has
previously been described as "structuralism," but will here be
described as "ontology without metaphysics," if such diverse
terms are permissible. Shortly before his death, Bonhoeffer wrote:

The Church must come out of its stagnation. We must move out again into the open air of intellectual discussion with the world, and risk saying controversial things, if we are to get down to the serious problems of life. I feel obliged to tackle these questions as one who, although a "modern" [i.e. a Barthian] theologian, is still aware of the debt he owes to liberal theology. There will not be many of the younger men in whom these two trends are combined. How very useful your help would be! But even if we are prevented from clarifying our minds by talking things over, we can still pray, and it is only in the spirit of prayer that any such work can be begun and carried through.[3]

Thus during his time in prison Bonhoeffer once again became immersed in the problems of a theory of knowledge, something the circumstances of his life had scarcely permitted him to explore since he wrote *Act and Being*. This is why *Act and Being*, with its difficult and tightly-woven style, is as important for understanding Bonhoeffer's approach as Barth's *Anselm: Fides Quaerens Intellectum*[4] is for understanding Barth's approach, and Bultmann's "New Testament and Mythology" for understanding Bultmann's.[5]

1. *The intellectual situation in 1929*

The Communion of Saints was worked out between the non-dogmatic sociology of Troeltsch and Tönnies and Barth's vertical dogmatics of the event of the Word of God. *Act and Being* was developed between the transcendentalist perspective flowing from Kant and the ontological renewal set in motion by Heidegger.

First of all, Bonhoeffer characterizes *transcendentalism* as a desire to encounter man by limiting his rational apprehension of the transcendent, i.e. by limiting his ability to define an act which is actually the encounter with an "other," and not simply an extension of his own identity. According to Kantianism (interpreted as transcendentalism and in opposition to absolute idealism) man exists in relation to objects that confront his understanding and projections that are

---

[3] Bonhoeffer, *LPP*, 3 August 1944, p. 208.
[4] Barth, *Anselm: Fides Quaerens Intellectum*, SCM Press, London 1960, John Knox Press, Richmond 1961, 171pp.
[5] Cf. H.-W. Bartsch, ed., *Kerygma and Myth* I, SPCK, London 1953, pp. 1–44.

unattainable by his reason. The question of Being is dismissed as an unacceptable carry-over from earlier dogmatism. Man exists by virtue of these two acts of "grasping," which indicate that man is cut off from reality.[6] Reality is not in man's possession, but within reach and at a distance from his reach. Truth is the pure act of his entering into *rapport* with an objectively unknowable transcendence. Bonhoeffer thus radicalizes Kantianism as a philosophy of limitation and the unattainable, almost as much at the level of understanding (against phenomenalism) as at the level of reason (against idealism). From this position, which Bonhoeffer believed was Kant's original position, Fichte's monistic idealism seemed to Bonhoeffer a disastrous caricature. In it, the self is unlimited and unconditioned. Thought is still defined through the act of "grasping," but in fact the triumph of the knowing and acting self destroys the transcendent through encounter with it, so that this act, without real transcendentalism, introduces in a hidden way a being who does not have to express itself as being. This is why, according to Bonhoeffer, Hegel knew better than Fichte how Fichte had already betrayed Kant – the same Hegel who would have been so close to Spinoza, if only the latter had spoken of subjectivity rather than substance.[7] In neo-Kantianism, finally, we see the total reversal of Kant's original position, since in it thought becomes the basis of the transcendental without always having this transcendental as its unattainable and irreducible background.

The young Bonhoeffer's theological attraction to Kant's transcendentalism is as clear as his rejection of the absolute idealism he feels was wrongly derived from Kant. In the first case God remains the functional correlate of the act of the mind, whereas in the second God gradually becomes identical with the self-understanding of the transcendental self, and human personality becomes the only true and unconditioned reality. This being so we must ask: if the worm entered the fruit so quickly, was not the fruit already rotten from the

---

[6] "Grasping" is used in this discussion as a way of describing man's reaching out for something because he is cut off. It is a way, in other words, of describing "act" rather than "being."

[7] Hegel, Bonhoeffer states, should be the perfect example of an absolute reconciliation between act and being. But he adds, "Hegel wrote a philosophy of angels, but not of human existence" (*Act and Being*, p. 27).

start? So Bonhoeffer turns the question back to Kant himself, and asks whether the elimination of every category of being in the act of knowing does not pave the way for the fatal transformation of transcendentalism into idealism. If the fundamental nature of being lies in the act of its being thought, such an act must be correlative to a being independent of the act. If trancendental actualism wants to avoid transforming the realities that create it into ideas that it creates itself, if it wants to retain the notion of reality as a limit, as the creator of acts of "grasping," can it ignore the category of being as fully as it says it does, and what would be the dangers arising from the uncritical use of this category?

Bonhoeffer next moves from a discussion of transcendentalism to a second and *ontological* approach to a theory of knowledge. Here he examines the positions of Hegel, Husserl, Scheler, Heidegger and the neo-Thomist Przywara. As far as *Hegel* is concerned, it seems clear that being is preordained to the realm of reason and that the Kantian thing-in-itself is transformed into the supra-personal substance of mind. In *Husserl's* position we discover the hesitation of a strongly idealist phenomenology moving toward an ontology of essences as they are sought by consciousness. But the *noema* remain immanent within consciousness, and science cannot determine the transition from intentionality to reality. According to Bonhoeffer, Husserl thus vacillates between an "eidetic" anti-empirical reductionism tending toward essentialism, and an accentuation of the role of consciousness as constituting reality, in the manner of neo-Kantian idealism. The latter emphasis finally carries the day, and the spontaneity of consciousness derived from existence prevails over the vision of the original givenness of being.[8] In *Scheler's* analysis, ethical and religious values constitute the true predicates of being. Being known precedes the knowledge of being. But Scheler's conclusions do not move beyond idealism: from the side of God (or of values) the essences really never become existences. Furthermore:

[8] Bonhoeffer's analysis in 1929 calls to mind Merleau-Ponty's famous preface to *The Phenomenology of Perception*: "What is phenomenology? It may seem strange that this question still has to be asked half a century after the first works of Husserl. Phenomenology is the study of essences ... But it is also a philosophy which puts essences back into existence" (The Humanities Press, New York 1962, p. vii).

The envisioning I is endowed with the capacity to take into itself the whole world, the fulness of life, the good and the very deity.[9]

In *Heidegger's* willingness to take time seriously (something almost totally ignored by Husserl and Scheler,) we come at last to a theory of knowledge that places existence and being face to face. The starting point is no longer the Kantian transcendental consciousness, but an ontological interpretation of creaturely-existence ("a hermeneutics of *Dasein*," as Bonhoeffer describes it).[10] This creaturely-existence moves toward its own final end, i.e. death, in order to attain its original wholeness. It understands itself as "thrown" into the world, a fact that produces an anxiety the self must assume. This provides a correction for the Cartesian error of failing to put the question of being to the *sum* in *Cogito ergo sum*. This would provide a true ontology for creaturely-existence for which thought is only one characteristic. However, Bonhoeffer comments, this structure of the being of consciousness remains within the confines of idealism, in the sense that being remains limited to the being of *human* consciousness. Moreover, such restraint is perhaps only a necessary precaution in his thought, and Heidegger actually offers a sound anthropological balance between the act of decision and the being of the self's re-appropriation in the finitude and mortality of human creaturely-existence. Even so, Bonhoeffer concludes, this understanding is of no use to theology, for the identification of being and the world is so strong here that such an understanding of being cannot possibly be applied to God, who cannot be "incapsulated" within the finitude of either being or creaturely-existence, since this very finitude itself is created by him. There is no room left for the idea of revelation.

So we come finally to neo-Thomism, which seems to occupy the far right ontologically on the spectrum Bonhoeffer offers us. During this period, the Catholic theologian *Przywara* had developed the distinction between God and man in the following manner: Essence and existence coincide in God, a coincidence that constitutes the very nature of Being. In man, existence always differs from essence, for man is always in

---

[9] Bonhoeffer, *Act and Being*, p. 57.

[10] *Ibid.*, pp. 59f. In conformity with the English translation of *Act and Being*, *Dasein* is here rendered "creaturely-existence."

process of becoming. The analogy between being and becoming consists in the openness of the finitude of creaturely existence to the timelessness of being, an openness that Przywara rightly defends against Heidegger. In formal terms, this "analogy of being" makes an interesting metaphysics possible, in that it particularizes the consciousness of man and the being of God, without isolating the first in subjective idealism or the second in a closed ontology. But questions crowd in, and out of his Lutheran heritage Bonhoeffer raises several: Can such a formal metaphysics really result in a concrete theology? Does not the fall of man damage the possibility of using the all-inclusive category of being for both God *and* man? How is it possible, in such a formalistic perspective, to take sufficient account of the personality of God as well as the contingency of law and gospel? Paradoxically, does not this position also leave us with a transcendence that is merely apparent, in which man projects his own power of being toward Being, rather than actually encountering the otherness of the being of God?

2. *Theologies of act and being*

This brief survey of the philosophical situation in 1929, during which it has only been possible to emphasize the highlights, leaves us with a double inadequacy: in idealism God is absorbed into the human self, and in ontologism he is absorbed into formal being. However, the survey also convinces Bonhoeffer that the two categories of act and being are necessary in order to speak about how God touches our lives and sustains them; since the church has already been described as the structure of "Christ existing in the form of community," i.e. the church as the recipient *to* which Christ gives himself and also as the place *in* which the gift is given, a valid transcendentalism is needed to express the relationship *to*, and a valid ontology is likewise needed to express the dwelling *in*.

Before going on to the theological section of his work, Bonhoeffer again takes the precaution of denying creaturely-existence any possibility of gaining access to being, even in a formal or an existential-ontological (as distinct from ontic) sense. In so doing, he lines up with Barth and explicitly rejects the path taken by Bultmann and Tillich, a path that he sees as contrary to the determining principle of theology, i.e. that all speech is based on reality rather than on possibility. Thus philosophy's boundary is not defined by something that finally completes it, but by the action of Jesus Christ that precedes it.

However, in order to speak about the non-philosophical reality that sustains them, theologians have no option but to use human language, and that means philosophical language. Thus almost all that can be said in this situation has been said once we have properly located the conceptual perspectives by which theologians go on to speak of what has not yet been referred to – the reality of God himself. Or, to make the point from another perspective, and one that surely describes Bonhoeffer's position in *Act and Being*, the philosophical prologue about act and being becomes concretized when it provides perspective on the theological scene in 1929. Let us examine how Bonhoeffer applies each category to the theme of revelation.

1. Revelation interpreted by the category of *act* stresses the contingency of the freedom of God, who gives himself to man's understanding in whatever way he chooses, without even being bound to the " 'entity' of his historic Word."[11] It is the existence of God and his purposes that establishes the existence of man as God's partner. God is like manna in the wilderness, available for man to use but not able to be stored away for the future; he is understood as "pure act," precisely in the instability of his availability. The contingency of revelation is thus interpreted as the proper mark of his transcendence, compared with the non-contingency of human reason.

Bonhoeffer takes exception to this overly nominalistic and occasionalistic approach of early Barthianism for, as he says, it is based on a description of the revealed reality of God that is too formalistic and lacking in concreteness. God becomes the pure claim of the absolute "Thou" upon the human "I," and this formalistic "Thou" displaces the concreteness of specific or realized revelation (as Grisebach in philosophy and Gogarten

[11] Bonhoeffer, *Act and Being*, p. 80. In the English translations of *Act and Being*, "entity" stands for "being" in contrast to "Being." English translations of Heidegger often use both "entity" and "being" in rendering *das Seiende*.

in theology both emphasized). To Bonhoeffer the weakness of this stress on act lies in the fact that it emphasizes a "possibility" that is always imminent, but which cannot break into the reality that alone can destroy the loneliness of an existence "curved in upon itself" (cf. Luther's *cor curvum in se*, the importance of which Karl Holl had taught Bonhoeffer, and to which he frequently refers). "Man must have *been* placed in reality by God if there is to be a place for reality in his thought."[12]

Now it must be asked how real is a God who exists in "eternal non-objectivity" in such a way that his Word is unavailable, and who remains freer *of* man than he is free *for* man. The theological stress on act, which corresponds to philosophical transcendentalism, neglects the place of the church in time and space, a church that is neither pure "instant" in Kierkegaard's sense nor utopian (a word whose root means "no place"), a church in which God reaches out to encounter man by Word and Sacrament, i.e. substantially and materially, and not just potentially and formally. Bonhoeffer seems to fear (in Tillich's thought, for example) that one who experiences "ultimate concern" will feel that the event-centered encounter with the neighbor is enough to dislodge human self-sufficiency, whereas it takes the givenness of the reality of divine revelation to accomplish that.

Furthermore, to think only in terms of act makes any systematic knowledge of God nearly impossible, and reduces theology to existential knowledge. To be sure, the approach manages to avoid three kinds of false knowledge, i.e. the "verbal inspiration" theory of fundamentalism, the inspiration of the human consciousness in liberalism, and the infallible inspiration of the church in Catholicism. But it escapes the Scylla of such errors only to fall into the Charybdis of a nearly total rift between revelation as the act in which God as "the subject of the knowing of revelation" understands himself quite apart from my consciousness, and the always-inadequate images of God that I develop out of my own consciousness. There is a fundamental rift between God and the conceptual reality of him that I formulate. God's ongoing protection against being objectified thus runs the risk of being turned into speech that is always so closely identified with the human speaker that the

[12] Bonhoeffer, *Act and Being*, p. 89.

central affirmation of theological realism, which says that God is closer to me than I am to myself, loses all meaning. Bonhoeffer thus concludes, against the early Barth but even more vigorously against Bultmann, that a theological science must be "passionately interested in concepts of being." For while Barth wants to protect the freedom of God's action, Bultmann wants even more to protect the freedom of man's faith as an act of his own obedient decision.

This brings us to the third characteristic of theologies based on the transcendental category of act, for in addition to their stress on the "pure act" of freedom and their dislike of systematizing, we must notice the dualism of their anthropology. In opposition to theologies of nature or substance,[13] they want to protect the interplay between God and man, as one based on the initiatives of relationship, and not on truths known in themselves. Barth and Bultmann are certainly right on this point, but Bonhoeffer asks them how the continuity of the human "I" can be maintained in the midst of discontinuous acts. Heidegger clearly understood the continuity achieved through the existential and ontological "fallenness" (*Verfallen*) of man's creaturely-existence, as one who is continually being "thrown" into the world. However, as we have already seen, this formalistic understanding of human finitude cannot be utilized theologically to talk about the act of sin and faith. Barth speaks of a new self dialectically described as:

the non-being of the first world which is the being of the second, just as the second has its basis-of-being (*Seinsgrund*) in the non-being of the first.[14]

---

[13] "We ourselves are the accomplishers of our lives." Barth, *Dogmatik* I, p. 72. Man is the question put to God, "whether we know it or not" (Bultmann, "Die Frage der dialektischen Theologie," *Zwischen den Zeiten*, 1926, No. 1, p. 43). "Man's being is not concerned as a nature or substance, but accomplishes itself in its comportment toward God's claim, hence in its ... decision and responsible behavior" (Bultmann, *Theologische Blätter*, 1928, No. 3, p. 66). (All the above are cited in Bonhoeffer, *Act and Being*, p. 98.) Bonhoeffer also prefers the Barthian category of the reality of the completed act to the Bultmannian category of the possibility of completing it.

[14] Barth, *Römerbrief*, 3rd ed., p. 142; cited as above in Bonhoeffer, *Act and Being*, p. 101. The translator notes that "*Seinsgrund* may mean *raison d'être*, which would modify the apparent tautology." The context of this difficult passage is an exegesis of Romans 5.12–21, in which there is not only a transition to "the new man" but also to "the new world." Cf. the English translation: "What is non-existent in the first world forms the very existence of the second; and what constitutes the

But, demands Bonhoeffer, pressing the question, isn't this a matter of some Platonic "heavenly double" that has really replaced the empirical and historical self? Similarly, when Bultmann stresses the continuity of the human self which always remains under the divine claim as well as the fall into sin,[15] does he not jeopardize any real encounter, let alone any potential encounter, between our life and the historic presence of Christ? The dualism in Bultmann's analysis is between potentiality and reality, while with Barth it is between a salvation that has already been completed and man's ongoing life.

2. As a necessary counterpoint to this understanding of theology exclusively in terms of the category of act (where Barth is close to Bultmann just as in philosophy Kant was close to Fichte!) Bonhoeffer next develops his Lutheran understanding in terms of the category of *being*.[16] More quickly than in the refutations preceding this section, he now affirms that revelation demands a being that transcends consciousness because it is independent of the act of faith. Such a being exists in doctrinal teaching, religious experience,[17] and the institution, e.g. the reality of grace in the church. However, scarcely has Bonhoeffer mentioned these possibilities of "revelation in terms of being," than he says that in all three cases man is "unaffected."[18] For in them all God remains an "entity" or being *outside* of his act of grasping men or being grasped by man. Therefore if one is going to think ontologically, this can be done only by distinguishing between revelation as an act

---

existence of the first is non-existent in the second" (*The Epistle to the Romans*, p. 165).

[15] "We are always on trial to see how we will seize the possibilities of our historical existence" (Bultmann, "Zur Frage der Christologie," *Zwischen den Zeiten*, 1928, pp. 67ff.; cited in Bonhoeffer, *Act and Being*, p. 104).

[16] I have called this understanding "Lutheran," formally because Luther is referred to most frequently in *Act and Being*, just ahead of Heidegger, but more substantively because this book was written against what Reformed dogmatics called the *extra-Calvinisticum*, i.e. "the clearest distinction possible between the humanity and the divinity of the person of Christ" (cf. François Wendel, *Calvin*, Presses Universitaires de France, Paris 1950, pp. 166ff.). Bonhoeffer finds fault with revelation based solely on act, which allows for no *communicatio idiomatum*.

[17] The English translation of *Act and Being* renders this as "psychic experience", cf. p. 108. The same term is used in *Life Together*, cf. Ch. V below.

[18] Cf. *Act and Being*, pp. 109–11.

and its various "entities" or beings, just as one can think transcendentally only by moving toward a true ontology of being, the only proper limit on the act, and being unwilling to accept its permanent non-objectification. Bonhoeffer is thus on the lookout for a being who can both "affect" man in contemporary personal and existential terms, and yet with whom such an encounter can be "in continuity" – a being, in other words, who calls men to decision and yet dwells in their midst. It is crystal-clear that Bonhoeffer would not have sought this strange mixture of "pure act" and "given being" if he did not think he had already found it in the church, which he goes on to describe as "the unity of act and being."

The nature of the act of revelation in the church is that it is first of all a contingent event "from outside," which no analysis of the possibilities of human creaturely-existence could possibly reach. As a theological-sociological category, the church is thus the impingement of the future upon man, rather than a journey into the dead past of the original being of his creaturely-existence. The church starts from what actually happens when Jesus Christ takes form as community. But the event of Jesus Christ is also the advent of a communal being and not simply an individual existential encounter. Revelation does not only come *to* the community; it takes place *within* the community. So the being of revelation is neither a past "entity" nor the "pure act" of faith, but the being that has become embodied in the community of persons; it *is* the being of this community. For this reason, Bonhoeffer goes on, there is a possibility of conceiving of the being of revelation in a continuity that is both "ecclesiastical" and trans-subjective, in which preaching is heard by the community and not just the individual self. Such being includes an existential outreach on man's part, since it is Christ "existing as community" who is the permanent foundation, and since Christ by virtue of his communal and representative aspect is already acknowledged as both the *act* of summoning and as the *being* of a new creation. Man can yield to that being only by responding to that act, but it is the act itself that leads him to the being. All of which leads Bonhoeffer to affirm, in a statement that is admittedly abstract and compressed:

If here faith were understood wholly as an act, the continuity of being would be disrupted by the discontinuity of acts. Since however faith as an act knows itself as the mode of being of its being in the Church, the continuity [of the human being] is indeed only "in the believing" but thereby is really preserved as being in the Church.[19]

This is how Bonhoeffer assures the unity between justification which is always an *act*, and the perseverance of the saints, which he describes as a matter of *being*.

This rediscovery of the church as a structure of revelation, made with the help of sociology, avoids both the solidifying of man's being into an "entity," and his evaporation into non-being. The being of the believer is not an abstraction, "a heavenly double," but a reality who participates in time and space, within the church. Belief and unbelief are thus not only decisions and acts, but characteristics and modes of being. In the same way God is not only the one who makes a claim upon me, always behind me (like the Kantian transcendental), but the one who fulfills his being in the world through the structure of the church, and is therefore always ahead of me. Once again we are close to the christology and ecclesiology of Hegel, whose name recurs frequently in *Act and Being* as it had in *Communion of Saints* – although Bonhoeffer continually blames him for setting human creaturely-existence within the historical process of the unfolding of Absolute Spirit, thereby running the risk that the act will finally be dissolved in some amorphous being that will be a strange mixture of idealism and materialism.[20]

Theology finally becomes possible once more as ongoing knowledge, as "the memory of the Church,"[21] as the presupposition more than the aim of preaching, which continually renews it. Theology receives the humble and dangerous task of reflecting about the "entity" of the being of God in the church. This is a humble task since theology can deal only with the "entity" and not the reality itself, and it is a dangerous task since if it is separated from its being in the church (for example in a purely academic kind of theology), the "entity"

[19] *Act and Being*, p. 128.
[20] Cf. particularly *Act and Being*, pp. 26f., but also Bonhoeffer's dismissal of a dialectical system that is always in process of transition, without concrete or decisive acts, neither good nor evil, pp. 41f. and 178.
[21] *Act and Being*, p. 143.

can shrivel up into mere information that no longer affects man. In contrast to the preacher who works productively *within* the community, the theologian will thus be the individual who reflects *for* the community. But the theologian is for the sake of the preacher, not to correct him in his *act* but to serve him by understanding the content of his memory, which is the *being* of his faith. Bonhoeffer concludes this section of his book by revising Luther's famous epigram on sin and faith to read, *Reflecte fortiter, sed fortius fide et gaude in Christo* (Think boldly, but believe and rejoice in Christ more boldly still).[22]

Following the philosophical introduction and the theological debate with its ecclesiological solution, the third part of *Act and Being* deals with the being of man "in Adam" and "in Christ." The "act" of sin is easy enough to understand, but the "being" of sin is another matter. Bonhoeffer speedily rejects attempts to understand it by its "historicization, psychologization or naturalization" in the doctrine of original sin.[23] The "being" of sin, he insists, must be found in the collective nature of its "act." Humanity, to which all men belong, is always turning the good that is offered it into evil. It inverts justice in order to justify itself, truth in order to make God a liar, life in order to deny death, or death in order to complete life.

"Being in Christ" is the opposite of this kind of inversion or curving in upon the self. It opens up a future for man, a future that Bonhoeffer finds beautifully expressed in the gospel parable of the child. For only the child, he says, knows how to let the future create his present. This is the eschatological possibility that is part and parcel of childhood. Thus infant baptism indicates a summons addressed to man to become in Christ the new man of the future,

who no longer looks back on himself but only away from himself to the revelation of God, to Christ, the man who is born out of the narrowness of the world into the breadth of Heaven, who becomes what he was or, it may be, never was: a creature of God – a child.[24]

So *Act and Being* ends with a heavenly vision – a vision that Bonhoeffer certainly did not repeat in the same way in his prison letters.

How has the cultural context changed since 1929? Barth

[22] *Ibid.*, p. 151.   [23] *Ibid.*, p. 163.   [24] *Ibid.*, p. 184.

has moved away from his early stress on act in which revelation was always tangential to the world. He has provided conclusive evidence that systematic theology is possible without having to rely either on the category of "being" in order to speak about God, or on the category of "institution" in order to speak about the church. Bultmann, on the other hand, has remained absolutely faithful to his original stress on eschatological decision as both permanent and existential. Traditional neo-Thomism has virtually faded from the scene. Heidegger's thought (if we adopt the inviting suggestion of Mikel Dufrenne) has developed in two directions: on the one hand, "the dismissal of being or reality, which is exemplified in the procedure of 'formalization,' " and on the other hand "the dehumanizing of man, who is devalued in the name of Being, or such equivalents of Being as logos, meaning and language."[25] In this double direction, contemporary culture oscillates between the neo-positivism of the human sciences and a non-positivistic openness that assumes overtones that are either tragic or ontological, depending on whether the influence of Nietzsche or Heidegger predominates.

In such contemporary emphases we see examples that question the validity of man as subject, whereas in 1929 Bonhoeffer was closer to Kant in questioning the validity of God as object. Bonhoeffer struggled with categories that might express both the existential act and the faithful being of God's revelation. Contemporary culture struggles more with questions about man, necessitated by the collapse of classical notions of transcendence. From this perspective, the Bonhoeffer of *Act and Being* has not yet reached the themes of *Letters and Papers from Prison*. The reality of cultural atheism is not yet a central idea in *Act and Being*; the question of God's existence is simply taken for granted whenever ways of understanding him are discussed.

But such differences of perspective do not destroy the real value of this book from Bonhoeffer's youth. Did he reconcile or merely appease the differences between the existentialist perspective of transcendental idealism and the essentialist perspective of ontological realism, or between the church as an event that happens, and the church as an institution that abides? The weakness in all appeasement is the desire to

[25] Dufrenne, "La Philosophie du Néo-positivisme," *Esprit*, May 1967, p. 793.

harmonize two distinct positions in an artificial unity. This is why we must see *Act and Being* as more than an attempt at theological appeasement – between the Barth-Bultmann position on the one hand, and Heideggerian, Thomistic and Lutheran ontology on the other hand – to see it, in other words, as the book where Bonhoeffer's own method is first made explicit. Let us now turn to an examination of that method.

3. *Ontology without metaphysics?*

A phrase like "ontology without metaphysics" seems at least as difficult to interpret as a phrase like "the non-religious interpretation of Christianity." How indeed, to take the latter case, can faith be denied expression when it is embodied (however equivocally) in religion, without being reduced to absolute silence? Similarly, how can ontology fail to involve some sort of metaphysics, granting all the risks of misunderstanding that the latter entails? Let us hold over the first question on the "non-religious interpretation of Christianity" until Chapter VII. But we can pave the way for it by dealing with the latter question, which is similar to it and is treated in *Act and Being*.

Bonhoeffer's quarrel with the proponents of a theology stressing *act* is clearly over their temptation to fall back on a metaphysical dualism.[26] He is afraid that Barth ends with a Christ who is only a copy or "double" of empirical man, and that Bultmann cannot get beyond a "potential" man of faith who is only a copy or "double" of the man who is really a new man in Christ. The metaphysical temptation is the temptation to divide existence into two worlds, either by emphasizing with Barth the primacy of God's saving act of grace which is virtually independent of man, or by emphasizing with Bultmann the primacy of man's act of faith which is virtually independent of God's reality. The characteristic of metaphysics is to create a division between appearance and reality, living and believing, earth and heaven, this world and the

---

[26] In the Index of *Act and Being*, "metaphysics" appears only twice, and the term is used pejoratively by Bonhoeffer to designate the "illusory transcendence" of a world that only succeeds in extending itself into another world beyond it (cf. pp. 69, 71). Metaphysics is characterized as the systematic illusion of an "unattainable" transcendence.

beyond, the natural and the supernatural. The root meaning of the word itself implies a dualism, for the preposition *meta* ("beyond") carries great weight – even though initially it was only a way of classifying the place in Aristotle's works where his writings on the "first philosophy" followed those on "physics" and nature. So metaphysical transcendence becomes reflection on the above, the beyond, the within, or the other-worldly – all understood as some place *other* than the here and now. Seen in this way, metaphysical theology turns aside from understanding God in his incarnation, and sets itself against the condescension and love of God toward an everyday world that metaphysics considers "deceiving, misleading and evil."[27] But metaphysics survives and is perhaps even strengthened in systems of transcendental thought, whenever they emphasize the act of "grasping" but minimize the being of presence. For example, although Kant criticized the claim of metaphysical reason to discern the Absolute and to claim some kind of control over Being, he gave powerful reinforcement to metaphysics by his separation of the noumenal from the phenomenal, and the thing-in-itself from man's experience of it. Bonhoeffer sees the same process at work in the theologians who stress God's transcendent *act*, for if they deny man the right to control an objectified God whom they might "grasp," they nevertheless reinforce the division between the act of a God who is "totally Other" and man himself who lives in the everyday world. Can this emphasis on act, helpful in describing God's intervention and summoning, take sufficient account of Christ present in the reality of this world? Is not the ecclesiology of such theologians based too much on the *limits* of God's grace and man's faith, without giving sufficient attention to the accomplished work of the covenant and the incarnation?

In contrast to metaphysics thus understood, ontology tries to describe the openness of human reality to the question of *being*. It is directed toward an analytical clarification of the fundamental question of being. Bonhoeffer's position in 1929 concerning the displacement of metaphysics and the revival of the ontological question in Heidegger's work is not always clear. He often speaks of such ontology as a realism of being that

[27] Jean Granier, *Le Problème de la Vérité dans la Philosophie de Nietzsche*, Ch. I, "Métaphysique et vérité," Seuil, Paris 1966, p. 40.

precedes consciousness, which finally leads back to a meta-physical dualism. But Bonhoeffer's attraction to ontological openness and discernment, correcting the gaps and distances of an overemphasis on each, reveals his intention clearly enough: to be able to speak of God not *above* reality, but at the point of his hidden presence *in* reality, remembering that the incarnation is the one place where the Christian can understand God's transcendence, and that as a result such transcendence does not create a Platonic division between earthly appearances and heavenly essences, but that it establishes, in this world, the upholding of a claim that structures its own reality. Understood in this way, ontology is an analysis of the creaturely-existence (*Dasein*) of the present Christ.

The word "ontology" is a forbidding one, and it has rarely been used in the Protestant theological tradition. "Being" is always in danger of becoming a catch-all category, something in which both God and man participate in varying degrees, and Protestantism's aversion to an ontological kind of theology results from such questions as the following: If one proceeds in this fashion, what becomes of the biblical notions of God's intervening in history, of his questioning, of his summons to men – notions that are very different from the Greek categories of manifestation, reappropriation, and a common nature shared by men and gods alike?[28] Is it possible to speak ontologically of the creative personality of God? Where do we learn that Being speaks to man's being in any language other than the closed analysis of man's being in terms of the double dimension of his finitude and openness? And how can we be sure that the ontological difference between Being and being will be maintained, without absorbing Being or emptying being of all content? Bonhoeffer is never unaware of such problems, since he keeps his distance in relation to phenomenological method, which according to Heidegger is the royal road to ontological awakening: "With regard to its subject matter, phenomenology is the science of the Being of entities – ontology."[29]

[28] Cf. A. Dumas, "Loi naturelle et irruption évangélique," supplement to *Vie spirituelle*, May 1967, pp. 233ff.

[29] Heidegger, *Being and Time*, Harper and Row, New York 1962, p. 61. In the above paragraph "l'étant" (*das Seiende*) is variously rendered "man's being," "being" and "entity," depending on the context.

Bonhoeffer endeavors to distinguish an "authentic" ontology from the "phenomenological-ontological" approach and the "transcendental" approach. An "authentic" ontology would presuppose a Being already known as the presupposition of understanding in the pure act of man's "grasping." It would make clear that God does not encounter men only at his limit and theirs, but that he enables them to understand his reality *in the midst of their reality*, so that men can claim not only to exist "before Christ" but also "in Christ." As for eschatology, which always represents the barrier between the transcendent hope of faith and the ontology of sight, Bonhoeffer interprets it as a shift from viewing the present in the light of the past into viewing the present in the light of the future. He suggests that the normative theological problem of the child is not the expectancy of an unfettered future but the way in which his future defines his present. The faith of the child is the ontological act by which his recognition of what lies ahead gives meaning to his daily existence.[30]

In order to describe the epistemology of the incarnation, Bonhoeffer used three conceptual approaches during his lifetime: in *Act and Being* (1929) it was ontology; in *Christ the Center* (1932) it was structuralism, and in *Ethics* (1940–43) it was reality. Each of these approaches has its own inherent risks: ontology can turn into immanentism, structuralism into formalism, and reality into pragmatism. And even the incarnation, if it becomes "ongoing incarnation," may come to mean no more than truth becoming spatial – or temporal, as Hegel's panentheism would suggest. Consequently in each instance Bonhoeffer corrects the possible confusion of the present Christ (the hidden structure of reality) with the empirical world (a self-contained totality). And he does so by the dialectical precaution of an element in tension with itself. In *Act and Being* (1929), the transcendental category of act is not abolished, but is corrected by the category of being from the danger of turning into metaphysical dualism. In *Christ the Center* (1932), the category of structure is given the content of deputyship, and finally, in *Letters and Papers from Prison*, reality is preserved from the triviality of pragmatism by the "secret discipline," as illustrated by Bethge's striking epigram:

[30] Cf. *Act and Being*, pp. 119f., 184.

Secret discipline without worldliness becomes pure ghetto; worldliness without the secret discipline pure boulevard.[31]

By each of these three attempts Bonhoeffer is trying to
protect a very specific and concrete understanding of the
incarnation from either dualism or immanentism, so that
Christ may be known as the present Christ who assures God's
presence to reality and reality's presence before God.

At the beginning of his intellectual life in 1929, and at the
end of his embattled existence in 1944, Bonhoeffer was intensely
concerned with the theory of knowledge, both in theology and
philosophy.[32] During the period of the Confessing Church,
theology thought that it could bypass such crucial questions.
But the decision left theology threatened by a divorce between
its affirmations and the cultural problems of human reality
around it. This is why Bonhoeffer's attitude at the beginning
and end of his life remains so important for us. He recognized
that neither life in the church, i.e. piety, nor action in the
world, i.e. politics, can exempt us from a rigorous pursuit of
the knowledge of God, nor from the attempt to describe him in
categories that are never either adequate or superfluous –
categories that are always subject to the strange nature of the
Christian revelation that affirms the free transcendence of
God *vis-à-vis* the world, and yet his active presence through
the incarnation *in* the world. This means a transcendence that
does not become dualistic and an ontology that does not become
pantheistic; which in turn means that God is not "beyond"
(in an other-worldly transcendence) or "within" (in an
anthropological ontology), but "in the midst" of the world
around us – a world whose true structure is established by
Jesus Christ in the church for the sake of the world.

Transcendence runs the risk of exiling God outside of
reality, and of debasing the worth of creation as a second-rate
imitation of the true realm of essences. Ontology runs the risk
of suppressing the basic human act of "grasping" in favor

---

[31] As cited in M. Bosanquet, *The Life and Death of Dietrich Bonhoeffer*, 1968, p. 280.
[32] In one of the last prison letters, Bonhoeffer writes to Bethge, "It is as you say:
'knowing' is the most thrilling thing in the world, and that is why I am finding
the work so fascinating" (*LPP*, 10 August 1944, p. 212). "Everything tires man
except knowledge" (Virgil).

of an analysis of the identity of the given. Theology must be able to speak of God both as the one who is always coming and as the one who is always present.

What is most striking about Bonhoeffer, compared to the predominance of theologies of the Word as event (represented by Barth and particularly Bultmann), is the way he emphasizes the presence of this Word in reality but without mistaking the penultimate reality itself for the ultimate Word. To anticipate a bit, we discover that after 1929 Bonhoeffer analyzes Christ as the "center" or the median structure in the givenness of this world, and looks for the presence of God in the "godforsaken-ness" of the world. *Act and Being* thus puts us on the track of the one interpretation that provides a continuity in Bonhoeffer's work: Christ present in this world as the ontology of an incarnate transcendence.

V

The Immediacy of Obedience and the Mediation of the Word

The writings of the second period of Bonhoeffer's life are markedly different in tone from those of the first. No longer is he writing university theses intended to describe the christological characteristics of the church, or its revelatory "act" and its revealed "being," in sociological and philosophical language. Instead he is preaching to church people about confessional obedience in the Nazi era. Nazism could easily put up with a harmless "being" of faith so long as it was not expressed in the "act" of obedience. So the tone of these later writings is hortatory and meditative. The Bible remains the basic point of reference, since all cultural analogies had become dubious, and all values could be co-opted by a fence-sitting kind of speculation that destroys the simplicity and directness of obedience. It was no longer a question of knowing how to understand, but of daring to live what one already understood.

Those who have been struck by this shift of emphasis have called it the "pietism" of a man concentrating on the relationship between the call of Jesus Christ in the Scriptures and his personal situation as a disciple, contrasting it with the earlier and later Bonhoeffer who reflected more extensively on the relationship between God and the whole of the reality that we call the world. It is true that Bonhoeffer is a pietist in these writings in the same way that Kierkegaard is a pietist in the *Edifying Discourses* and in *Training in Christianity*. Both Kierkegaard and Bonhoeffer are fully committed Lutherans. In relation to Luther's rediscoveries, they challenge neither salvation by faith alone nor the "monastic" life within the world; i.e. neither extrinsic justification nor the "incognito" of sanctification in the midst of secular life, an incognito such that the true knight of faith can appear as a comfortable and limited member of the middle class. But they both wonder whether this "appearance" has not in fact become the "reality," and whether the extraordinary hiddenness of the vocation of disciple has not evaporated into the ordinary situation of the believer. For faith, no matter how evangelically correct it may be, is only an abstract belief when it is cut off from the immediacy[1] of obedience. Bonhoeffer observes that in the face of the Nazi challenge the churches have certainly seen to it that neither their creeds nor their structures were threatened. But if they are not willing to respond unquestioningly to the call of Jesus Christ, have they not made faith a matter of words rather than deeds? Their faith may be doctrinally unassailable, but are they *disciples*, bearing responsibility along with Christ for witnessing in the world? They may know all about the history of redemption, but are they agents of redemption now?

This reduction of obedience to an abstraction – the same thing for which Kierkegaard had previously criticized Hegel and even more the established church of his time – is what Bonhoeffer is attacking in his treatise on "cheap grace," grace that pays no costly price for its fulfillment. *The Cost of Discipleship* (in German simply *Nachfolge*, "discipleship" or "following after") is centered on this immediacy of the act. Bonhoeffer believes that faith is possible only when two things are simultaneously true: *"Only he who believes is obedient, and only he who is obedient believes."*[2] Only he who is obedient truly believes, for one cannot believe with both sanity and sanctity when one is at a distance. There must be immediacy. Justification by faith in Christ does not excuse one from "watching with Christ," but demands it.

However, immediacy can also become an open door to the

---

[1] "Immediacy" in this chapter is always contrasted to "mediation." "Immediacy" involves the urgency of belief, the need for decisive action now. But it also involves the direct relation between the individual believer and God. "Mediation," on the other hand, emphasizes the corporate nature of Christian life involving both the mediation of Jesus Christ between God and man and the mediation of Christians one with another in their corporate "life together."

[2] Bonhoeffer, *The Cost of Discipleship*, p. 54, italics in text.

pretensions and illusions of "good works." The disciple may be only a humanly motivated fanatic, concerned about his own decision and his own sacrifice. In radicalizing his own obedience, he can surrender to the loneliness of perfectionism and the vanity of legalism. He is then by his very immediacy made a captive of the heights and depths of his own experience, eager or downcast as the case may be. Furthermore, it must be remembered from a Christian perspective that we have access to reality only through the mediation of the Word. Outside of this specific mediation, immediacy falls into capriciousness. *Life Together* issues a strong reminder about mediation to disciples who have followed the way of immediacy. So Bonhoeffer also insists that only he who believes is truly obedient, for one can obey, with sanity and sanctity, only when one is at a distance. There must be mediation. The vocation of discipleship with Christ can only be appropriated through the hearing of his Word, which delivers us from ourselves and from concern about our obedience.

Seen in terms of their complementary emphases, *The Cost of Discipleship* and *Life Together* are thus very close to Bonhoeffer's ongoing concerns, even though their individual emphases are quite different, the former seeking to discover God in the structure of reality (which in these writings is called the immediacy of obedience), the latter seeking to approach reality in a deeper and truer way than any pragmatism or activism, through the mediation of God and his transcendent claim (which in these writings is described as the Word and power of the Spirit). The unity-in-tension of God and reality in Christ is expressed both by the costly obligation of obedience, and by the healthy "distance" of faith. It will be noticed that in *The Cost of Discipleship* Bonhoeffer first launches the call to immediacy, where in true Kierkegaardian fashion he exalts the radical leap of the individual. The book is written *against* the church of the crowd, against a visible Christendom, against any kind of spectator-attitude, and it is written *for* the church of the disciple, for the secret companionship of those who take seriously the "extraordinariness" of the Sermon on the Mount, for those called to follow Christ.

Two years later, in *Life Together*, Bonhoeffer reflects on the value of mediation. This work, which is the report of his experience at the seminary in Finkenwalde in the midst of a small community of disciples, is a reminder of the distance which Jesus Christ maintains between us to establish us in the church of faith, a church that is different from the visible community of our own desires, no matter how pious and committed they may be. Thanks to the ongoing mediation of the Word, individuals can live in the community of the church. In differentiation from Kierkegaard at this point, the individual is not alone before God like Abraham on Mount Moriah, in permanent protest against the institution that offers cheap grace. The church has new possibilities as a community in which one can dwell because of the Word which is both summons and distance, obligation and freedom, involvement and deference. In this context *Life Together* can be seen as the necessary counterpart to *The Cost of Discipleship*. It corrects what is likely to be forgotten in the immediacy of obedience – the ongoing mediation of the One who calls us to obedience.

Let us now look in more detail at each work in terms of an approach to reality in which God is present in Jesus Christ without losing his own identity.

1. *The immediacy of obedience*

Many objections have been raised against the immediacy that is so clearly characteristic of the gospel accounts of Jesus' call to men who hardly knew him. Lutheranism in particular has been fearful of anything that would make immediacy visible, such as knowledge of the boundaries of the true church, works as a means of proving the genuineness of faith, or separation from the world whether by greater ethical perfectionism, stronger ecclesiastical discipline, or stricter application of the law. In all these attempts to provide outward signs of the condition of the disciple, Lutheranism feared that justification by works would be smuggled back in, and that the sheer gift of the gospel would be overcome by the demands of the law. Nevertheless, at the risk of seeming in the eyes of his own Lutheran church to be an "enthusiast" (*Schwärmer*), a Calvinist or a legalist, Bonhoeffer challenged the outcome of this kind of Lutheranism. Luther, he said, had paid the price of the monastery in order to trust in "faith alone." But what price is Luther's follower willing to pay, who would make justification by faith alone into permission to enjoy the world without changing it? By omitting the tension that transforms justification into a liberating force, such a person reduces justification to no more than an uncritical acceptance of things as they are. The word-play on "justify" is most instructive. According to Bonhoeffer, it expresses the disastrous evolution which has led from the justification of the *sinner* by costly grace, to the justification of *sin* by the cheap grace that *excuses* the sinner.

The recognition of grace was [Luther's] final radical breach with his besetting sin, but it was never the justification of that sin. By laying hold of God's forgiveness, he made the final, radical renunciation of a self-willed life, and this breach was such that it led inevitably to a serious following of Christ. He always looked upon it as the answer to a sum, but an answer which had been arrived at by God, not by man. But then his followers changed the "answer" into the data for a calculation of their own. That was the root of the trouble . . . Grace as the data for our calculations means grace at the cheapest price, but grace as the answer to the sum means costly grace.[3]

In 1847, Kierkegaard had made the identical point:

If anyone refuses to understand that forgiveness is nevertheless also a burden which is to be borne, even if an easy burden, then he takes the forgiveness in vain. The forgiveness is not deserved, it is not so heavy; but neither is it to be taken in vain, for neither is it so light. Forgiveness is not to be repaid, it is not so costly – it cannot be repaid; but neither is it to be regarded as nothing, it is too dearly bought for that.[4]

Indeed, there is an even more explicit historical parallel in Kierkegaard:

Present-day Christendom (that at least of which I am talking) attaches itself to Luther; it is another question whether Luther could subscribe to it, whether the turn which Luther took may not only too easily lead into a wrong path when Luther is not at hand to make truth of the true turn he took . . .

  The erroneous path from which Luther turned off was exaggeration with respect to works. And quite rightly, he was not at fault: a man is justified solely and only by faith. So he talked and taught . . .

[3] Bonhoeffer, *The Cost of Discipleship*, p. 42.
[4] Kierkegaard, *The Gospel of Suffering*, Augsburg, Minneapolis 1948, pp. 41f.

and believed. And this was not taking grace in vain, his whole life was testimony to this. So far so good.

But already the next generation slackened; it did not turn in horror from exaggeration in respect to works (of which Luther had had personal experience) into the path of faith. No, they transformed the Lutheran passion into a doctrine, and with this they diminished also the vital power of faith. In this way it was diminished from generation to generation . . .

It is no wonder that this much tried man witnessed so strongly against building one's blessedness upon works, not witnessing against works – it was only the sly world which thus misinterpreted him.[5]

In order to foil such sly attempts and do battle against watering life down by faith in the doctrine of salvation by faith, Bonhoeffer, like Kierkegaard, wrote "edifying discourses,"[6] i.e. sermons in the form of biblical commentary. In them the speaker now holds the prompter's script, the members of the audience are called on stage and the Word of God becomes a call to action. *The Cost of Discipleship* is made up of two parts:[7] first, a long commentary on the Sermon on the Mount, in which Jesus summons men and sends them forth, and second, a briefer treatment of St Paul's notion of the church, in order to discover whether the church is summoned and sent forth in the same way the disciples were. To be called or summoned is to be confronted by a concrete commandment that cannot be divided into knowing versus doing, dogmatics versus ethics, or eternal principles versus worldly compromises. The call frees one from such alternatives and anxieties. In this sense it is an easy yoke and a light burden (Matt. 11.30). When the call sounds forth in reality, the field of possibilities is reduced to the immediacy of obedience. From abstract necessity, reality becomes concrete freedom.

The disciple is dragged out of . . . the realm of the finite (which is in

---

[5] Kierkegaard, *For Self-Examination and Judge for Yourselves*, Oxford University Press, London 1941, Princeton University Press, Princeton 1944, pp. 202f.

[6] "*July 10 [1840]* Hegel's hatred of everything edifying, which crops up everywhere, is very strange: for after all something edifying is not an opiate which lulls to sleep, it is the finite spirit's Amen and is an aspect of knowledge which ought not to be overlooked" (Kierkegaard, *The Journals*, Oxford University Press, 1938, p. 81).

[7] English readers should note that this important division is not clearly distinguished in the Table of Contents of most editions of *The Cost of Discipleship*.

truth infinite) [and thrust] into the realm of infinite possibilities (which is the one liberating reality).[8]

Suppose someone insists that the call presupposes faith, and that in the absence of faith the call can be ignored. Bonhoeffer rejects any such line of argument. He tells the pastor to say to such a person, "You cannot hear Christ because you are willfully disobedient. Somewhere in your heart you are refusing to listen to his call. Your difficulty is in your sins." He then continues:

Our sinner has drugged himself with cheap and easy grace by accepting the proposition that only those who believe can obey. He persists in disobedience, and seeks consolation by absolving himself. This only serves to deaden his ears to the Word of God. We cannot breach the fortress so long as we merely repeat the proposition which affords him his self-defense. So we must make for the turning point without further ado, and exhort him to obedience – "Only those who obey can believe."[9]

In other words, Bonhoeffer wants to make it impossible for us to escape from the immediacy of obedience by taking cover under any excuse, whether it be our own special circumstances, doctrinally justified of course, or "mediation" and religious practices. All that must go. He feels as strongly about this as Schleiermacher did about "absolute dependence," save that where Schleiermacher sought to persuade in the name of the immediacy of the religious consciousness within man, Bonhoeffer appeals in the name of the immediacy of the call of Jesus Christ, present in the reality outside of man. His presence breaks through the division that is so characteristic of the whole phenomenon of consciousness and thought, and restores the simplicity that characterizes risk and action. Jesus abolishes the luxury of weighing ethical alternatives by indicating the immediacy of the commandments. He reunites divided reality around the structure of his call. The role of faith is thus not to erect delaying and hesitant preconditions but to simplify the ambiguity of circumstances so that they can highlight the unambiguous nature of obedience. When this happens, faith is no longer a religious excuse (in the present case, the inadequacy of knowledge) for doing nothing. It becomes a positive

---

[8] Bonhoeffer, *The Cost of Discipleship*, p. 49.   [9] Bonhoeffer, *ibid.*, p. 60.

response. And the hermeneutical circle between word and faith is closed: Christ gives faith only to those who obey, and it is only to those who obey that he gives faith.[10]

When mediation (in philosophy) and paradox (in theology)[11] are introduced they always run the risk of suppressing immediacy, and of dissolving the unity of the call into fragmented alternatives. "From two things one," which according to Kierkegaard is the mark of the ethical and religious "stages," we return to the "either/or" of the aesthetic stage. But Jesus Christ is not "a principle of mediation" that can delay decision or excuse indecision. He is "the mediator,"[12] who unifies reality in the very act of calling it. In him God shares in reality and reality becomes his personal commandment. To go through Christ is to regain immediate access to the world around us, and in the multiplicity of possibilities to see the emergence of the structure of the one thing needful which provides the freedom to obey it. The Sermon on the Mount (Matt. 5–7) along with Jesus' discourse at the sending forth of the twelve apostles (Matt. 9.35–10.42) is interpreted by Bonhoeffer as the basis of this structure; the task is to become a disciple drawn from the world of "possibilities" that the crowd represents, a crowd that is frequently astonished by Jesus but not committed to him.

Two characteristics distinguish the disciples who obey and thus believe. They embody an "extraordinary" visible obedience (Matt. 5) and their obedience is hidden (Matt. 6). They are visible followers of what Jesus Christ does, and invisible companions of his faith in God.

1. Let us look first at the "extraordinary" *visibility* of the disciples. The beatitudes are in the present tense. They describe

---

[10] Cf. *The Cost of Discipleship*, pp. 69–75, where the theme of "Single-Minded Obedience" is developed.

[11] "The idea of philosophy is mediation – Christianity's is the paradox" (Kierkegaard, *Journals*, Oxford University Press, London 1938, p. 89).

[12] "[Christ] is the Mediator, not only between God and man, but between man and man, between man and reality" (*The Cost of Discipleship*, p. 85). The whole section on "Discipleship and the Individual" (pp. 84–91) develops this theme of Christ the Mediator, who replaces the arbitrary immediacy of our pretensions by the true immediacy of his call. It would therefore be false to over-schematize, as was done at the beginning of the chapter, the opposition between the immediacy of obedience (*The Cost of Discipleship*) and the mediation of the Word (*Life Together*). What is really involved is a kind of complementary counterpoint that runs throughout the two works, although their major themes seem to be decidedly different.

a realm here on earth that becomes visible in the life of Jesus Christ right up to Golgotha. Men see the good works of the church, which is thus the salt of the earth and the light of the world. Its righteousness surpasses that of the scribes and Pharisees, for it is a righteousness that is not only professed but carried out, without however turning into a smug legalism, since its justification is bestowed rather than earned. Jesus Christ is thus the only non-legalist who fully keeps the law. True love for the brother, the purity of looking at a woman without lust, the sincerity of life lived in the open, the renunciation of vengeance in pursuit of my own rights, love for the enemies who speak evil of me and persecute me – all such actions are visible repetitions of the "extraordinary" quality of Jesus Christ, whose manner of death showed that he was not simply an ideal from another world, but an actual event in this one. Christ proclaims the Sermon on the Mount as something he and his disciples must actually live, in a life that combines acting and suffering, accepting reality with the kind of acceptance in which resistance and submission are inextricably intertwined.

The "extraordinary" – and this is the supreme scandal – is something which the followers of Jesus *do*. It must be *done* like the better righteousness, and done so that all men can see it. It is not strict Puritanism, not some eccentric pattern of Christian living, but simple, unreflecting obedience to the will of Christ.[13]

The "extraordinary" is therefore neither the extreme nor the exception, but part of the world around us, even though not "natural."

2. We now turn to the second characteristic of discipleship, its *hidden* character. The cross itself exhibits the double character of visibility and hiddenness. On the one hand, it is an event that all can see. It takes place at the conclusion of a public trial, on the top of a hill, before a much larger crowd than listened to the Sermon on the Mount. In relation to men, the crucifixion is an official execution, a most unusual place to discover outgoing love for the enemy. But in relation to God, the crucifixion is a hidden suffering. It is the invisible daily portion of an obedience that gives no inkling of its divine character.

[13] Bonhoeffer, *The Cost of Discipleship*, p. 138.

It is the expression of a practice that is invisible to those in whose midst it is performed. The "extraordinariness" of Christ thus retains the character of a secret, similar to the "incognito" in Kierkegaard. Otherwise, Bonhoeffer explains, Jesus Christ would be only an "enthusiast" and Christianity would be only a messianism dedicated, like all messianisms, to the inevitable sequence of enthusiasm and failure. If there had not been this hiddenness, the spectators at the crucifixion would indeed have had their revenge.

Here at last, they would say, the fanatic, the enthusiastic revolutionary, has come out in his true colors. Now we know he wants to turn the whole world upside down and bid his disciples leave the world and build a new one ... Does it not prove him a victim of spiritual pride, always the first sign of fanaticism? No, they would say, genuine obedience and humility are only to be found in the ordinary, the commonplace and the hidden.[14]

The dialectical turning inside out does not diminish the "extraordinary." It saves it from calculation and from the danger of being expressed in such a way that the urgency of obedience is lost in "distracting" concern about how other people will react.[15]

Jesus insists that his disciples live the hiddenness of a righteousness that is unaware of its righteousness; the hiddenness of prayer in which men "have ceased to know themselves and know only God whom they call upon"[16] and who therefore do not listen to themselves complacently since they know how to pray; the hiddenness of the devout life which would rather "anoint the head and wash the face" than engage in ostentatious asceticism. The hiddenness of ongoing discipleship is for

[14] Bonhoeffer, *The Cost of Discipleship*, p. 140.

[15] Pascal knew best of all how to speak to the necessity of hiddenness in the appearance of truth, to guard against the "distractions" of spiritual worldliness. "Noble deeds are most estimable when hidden. When I see some of these in history, they please me greatly. But after all they have not been quite hidden, since they have been known; and though people have done what they could to hide them, the little publication of them spoils all, for what was best in them was the wish to hide them" (Pascal, *Pensées*, §159, as cited in Pascal, *Pensées*, *The Provincial Letters*, Modern Library, New York 1941, p. 38). "Here is not the country of truth. She wanders unknown amongst men. God has covered her with a veil, which leaves her unrecognized by those who do not hear her voice. Room is opened for blasphemy ..." (*ibid.*, §842). Cf. A. Dumas, "L'Apologétique du Dieu Caché chez Pascal," *Revue d'Histoire et de Philosophie religieuses*, 1962.4.

[16] Bonhoeffer, *The Cost of Discipleship*, p. 146.

the sake of maintaining the unity of the immediacy of obedience. The simplicity of the obedient life is a protection against the divisiveness of anxious perfectionism and the scrupulousness of doing twice as much as is demanded. He who believes by obeying can ignore the anxiety of the one who is always asking himself whether he believes enough to obey, or if he is obedient enough to do justice to his faith. By keeping the matter of his obedience hidden from himself and from others, he becomes a true disciple who is content that all visibility should belong to God alone and his kingdom.

These two characteristics, then, "extraordinary" visibility and hiddenness, distinguish the church of the disciples. Throughout the discussion Bonhoeffer is obviously thinking of things that distinguish the German Confessing Church in the bosom of the state church. But he makes clear that they also serve to distinguish those within the very bosom of the Confessing Church itself, for men will not be saved simply by the fact of their membership in a church that has a proper confession of faith.

God will not ask us ... whether we were good Protestants, but whether we have done his will. We shall be asked the same question as everybody else.[17]

The Sermon on the Mount concludes with a reminder of the unity between word and deed: "Everyone then who hears these words of mine and does them ..." (Matt. 7.24). This unity establishes Jesus' authority and the truthfulness of his disciples. Interpretation can multiply possible courses of action, but only obedience can create and comprehend immediacy. All behavior in relation to the Word that does not issue in action thereby dissolves the unity of obedience into the destructive alternative of preferring either God or the world. But the disciple who responds to Jesus' call discovers "the honor, the power and the strength" of the Word of God in the midst of the world's reality.

Jesus' discourse at the sending forth of the twelve apostles (Matt. 9.35–10.42) actually establishes the church of disciples that the Sermon on the Mount had called for. The apostles are sent forth into the crowd, that mass of people who have

[17] *Ibid.*, p. 173.

"possibilities" and weigh ethical alternatives, among whom Jesus looks for disciples and to whom he wants to bring help and compassion. The sending forth of the apostles entails, as did Jesus' own life, an emphasis on immediacy. It is expressed in terms of such limits as geography, money, and time.

Go nowhere among the Gentiles, and enter no town of the Samaritans . . . Take no gold, nor silver, nor copper in your belts . . . and if any one will not receive you to listen to your words, shake off the dust from your feet as you leave that house or town.[18]

The omnipotence of the Word becomes concrete in the specific discipline of an action. Speculation can wait and dream, but it does not act, whereas faith is active obedience.

[The disciples'] commission is not a heroic struggle, a fanatical pursuit of a grand idea or a good cause. That is why they stay only where the Word stays.[19]

When "they stay only where the Word stays," the disciples experience the same hostility that Jesus does. Like him, they are accused of "undermining family life, [of] leading the nation astray; they will be called crazy fanatics and disturbers of the peace."[20] But they are still to persevere with him who is on the same level with them, for their reward, like his, is not their own achievement but the objective of all their work together, the salvation of the church.

The whole of this long commentary on the urgency of obedience is influenced by the context in which Bonhoeffer wrote it. He was not trying to know or understand or appreciate the world, but to create a church of disciples. He did not want to spread out the infinite possible choices of what one "might" do, but to narrow down to the finite choice of what one "must" do. He who lives as a contemporary of Jesus knows that this narrowing down is the price of action, just as obedience is the price of grace.

But then comes the question: can the church that exists after Jesus' life on earth be just like the one that was contemporaneous with his own life and mission? In Paul's writing,

18 Matt. 10.5, 9, 14.
19 Bonhoeffer, *The Cost of Discipleship*, p. 189.
20 Bonhoeffer, *op. cit.*, p. 192.

for example, does not faith in the cross and the resurrection
become more central than the immediacy of obedience that the
synoptic gospels describe in Jesus' encounters with his disciples?
Bonhoeffer briefly challenges this apparent dissimilarity
between obedience to Jesus and faith in Christ. To believe in
Jesus Christ always consists, he says, in walking in his way, as
his follower. Baptism is the entrance into this way by an act
of visible obedience, with the irrevocable nature of a free
decision.[21] As the body of Christ, the church is the place
where Jesus' bodily presence continues to be real for us. In
entering into this body, Christians are marked off from the
world, as in Jesus' time the disciples were marked off from the
crowd. Their sanctification consists in an "extraordinary"
visibility – such, according to Bonhoeffer, is the "political"
ethic, the universal Word addressed by the church to the
World – but it also consists in a hidden expectation, for only
God knows when our good works are *his* good work. However,
at the end of the book, Bonhoeffer puts more stress on visibility
than on hiddenness. During this period of the German Church
struggle, he hopes for the restoration of a church discipline
that has power "to point out concrete sins, and to punish and
condemn them." Without this discipline "it is an unholy
church, squandering the precious treasure of the Lord's
forgiveness."[22] To bear the name of Jesus Christ means to
follow his way, to live in obedience to his likeness, to take his
nature as crucified man in order to receive his transformed
nature as resurrected man. Here again immediacy turns our
gaze away from our own likeness. Whereas looking in a mirror

[21] The Bonhoeffer of this passage in *The Cost of Discipleship* is close to Barth's
position on the ethical and "imitative" character of Jesus' baptism by John the
Baptist at the beginning of his ministry, and thus the non-sacramental nature of the
baptism. Cf. Barth, "Baptism as the Foundation of the Christian Life," in *Church
Dogmatics* IV/4, T. and T. Clark, Edinburgh 1969. However, Bonhoeffer grants in
distinction from Barth that the baptism of infants preserves an important truth,
i.e. the community is able to remind them of the act. "As far as infant baptism is
concerned, it must be insisted that the sacrament should be administered only
where there is firm faith present which remembers Christ's deed of salvation
wrought for us once and for all. That can only happen in a living Christian
community. To baptize infants without a Church is not only an abuse of the
sacrament, it betokens a disgusting frivolity in dealing with the souls of the
children themselves" (*The Cost of Discipleship*, p. 210). Barth appears to be more
rigorously logical in this discussion than Bonhoeffer.
[22] Bonhoeffer, *The Cost of Discipleship*, p. 260.

is a human reminder of our theoretical dividedness, looking toward Christ is a christological affirmation of our practical unity:

And we all, with unveiled face, beholding the glory of the Lord, are being changed into his likeness, from one degree of glory to another.[23]

2. *The mediation of the Word*

Bonhoeffer later criticized the perfectionist tone of *The Cost of Discipleship*, though without denying its central theme of the call to obedience. On 21 July 1944, he wrote to Bethge:

I remember a conversation that I had in America thirteen years ago with a young French pastor. We were asking ourselves quite simply what we wanted to do with our lives. He said he would like to become a saint (and I think it is quite likely that he did become one). At the time I was very impressed, but I disagreed with him, and said, in effect, that I should like to learn to have faith. For a long time I did not realize the depth of the contrast. I thought I could acquire faith by trying to live a holy life, or something like it. I suppose I wrote *The Cost of Discipleship* as the end of that path. Today I can see the dangers of that book, though I still stand by what I wrote.[24]

However, it seems clear that, as far back as the drafting of *Life Together* in 1938, Bonhoeffer was moving away from the pressing immediacy of *The Cost of Discipleship*. To be sure, he who does not obey in a spirit of immediacy is no longer obedient to Jesus. But only Christ as the true mediator among men can make such immediacy possible. Hitler himself demanded unconditional obedience, which is precisely why he finally led the German people to disaster. The thirst for immediacy in every community (whether Christian or not, but especially if it is Christian) can be the open door to the destruction of those who exploit it as well as those who desire it. For we have no direct access to the reality of other people, or to the reality of the world. Only the mediation of the Word can protect us from the degeneration either of reduction or seduction that is involved in the quest for human immediacy. The danger is

[23] II Cor. 3.18.
[24] Bonhoeffer, *LPP*, 21 July 1944, p. 201. The young French pastor to whom Bonhoeffer refers is Jean Lasserre, until recently the secretary of the Fellowship of Reconciliation, and author of *La Guerre et l'Évangile* (War and the Gospel), La Réconciliation, Paris 1953.

even more pressing when the disciples are united by common convictions, involvements and emotions, as were Bonhoeffer and the future young pastors of the Confessing Church in the seminary at Finkenwalde. The danger in immediacy is like the danger in desire: once it has been fulfilled it is no longer strong and compelling. An unsuccessful blending actually leads to solitude if the communion is not continually aware that it must be grounded in objective love. Therefore the more there is a stress on immediacy, no matter how sensitive, the clearer and stronger must be the emphasis on creative mediation. The relationship between two people is a real threat without the presence of the One whose mediation is not a barrier but a foundation for each of the partners. *The Cost of Discipleship* called for the creation of a church of disciples. It demanded saints. In describing the church as it is experienced by the disciples, *Life Together* put human beings back into it.

The book does not describe the program of some ideal community, but offers a practical and glowing report of the actual experience at Finkenwalde. However, as in all of Bonhoeffer's works, the specific circumstances of that experience are never referred to, and what is read is a carefully constructed statement, rather than the intimate outpouring of a subjective experience. This emotional restraint makes it one of the most solid works that has been written about brotherly communion.

Bonhoeffer speaks of community life as a gift of grace, that moment of repose "among roses and lilies, of which Luther speaks,"[25] but to which Kierkegaard scarcely refers in his *Edifying Discourses* for the individual, addressed simply as "my reader" or "my brother." Christian life together is based on a grace that always comes to us from a reality beyond us, and not from some romanticism within us. By insisting on this "alien righteousness"[26] that comes to us from beyond ourselves, Bonhoeffer finds himself in full accord with the preaching of the Reformation on justification by faith alone through grace, which we recall that *The Cost of Discipleship* feared would be watered down into the doctrine of "cheap grace." Faith in a Word beyond man provides the "distance" that prevents obedience from getting confused with intersubjective immediacy. The major theme of *Life Together* is thus the recovery of

[25] Bonhoeffer, *Life Together*, p. 17.   [26] Bonhoeffer, *op. cit.*, p. 22.

the distinction, very Pauline in character, between a "psychic"[27] or human view of things that is idealist in nature, and a "spiritual" view of things that is realist. Bonhoeffer contrasts them in such ways as the following:

The basis of the community of the Spirit is truth; the basis of the human community of spirit is desire. The essence of the community of the Spirit is light ... The essence of the human community of spirit is darkness ... In the former there is ordered brotherly service, in the latter disordered desire for pleasure; in the former humble subjection to the brethren, in the latter humble yet haughty subjection of a brother to one's own desire.[28]

These contrasts can be further described by Bonhoeffer's rather schematic distinction between *eros* and *agape*. *Eros*, or "human love," is overbearing and weak. It destroys the structures of the real world around it which it despises, for the sake of the ideal world which it covets. *Agape*, however, builds true community by enabling us to recognize what comes to us from the Holy Spirit, from beyond our desires, virtues and natural possibilities. The spiritual sets boundaries and builds, while the human has no boundaries and destroys. According to Bonhoeffer, the opposition between *eros* and *agape* is not, as one so often hears, between the supposedly carnal and egocentric nature of *eros* and the spiritual and self-sacrificing nature of *agape*, but rather between their respective relationships to reality.[29] *Eros* shuns and avoids the reality of the neighbor:

Here is where the humanly strong person is in his element, securing for himself the admiration, the love, or the fear of the weak.[30]

Agape does not desire to destroy the other person but to serve his true needs. In recognizing Christ between myself and my neighbor, *agape* does not reduce this neighbor to a being who is

---

[27] Bonhoeffer defines "psychic" as "that which comes from the natural urges, powers, and capacities of the human spirit" (*Life Together*, p. 31).

[28] Bonhoeffer, *Life Together*, pp. 31f.

[29] The comment seems to me important, for some have wrongly inferred from certain passages of *Life Together* that Bonhoeffer, as a "spiritual" theologian, is scornful, for example, of the "human" psychoanalyst. But if Bonhoeffer gives too little attention here to the legitimacy of desire, he nevertheless struggles for a creative understanding of reality.

[30] Bonhoeffer, *op. cit.*, p. 33.

only a pale reflection of Christ, but preserves him from my human and religious desire to "use" him, in order to establish him in the reality of his own identity.

The other person needs to retain his independence of me; to be loved for what he is, as one for whom Christ became man, died, and rose again, for whom Christ bought forgiveness of sins and eternal life.[31]

In this way Christ as the mediator between men builds up their community and saves it from the damage of sheerly human immediacy.

After this general introduction to the theme of community living, Bonhoeffer deals with the daily life of the community under four headings: the day with others, the day alone, ministry, and confession and communion. These very down-to-earth reflections are discussed in terms of the creative boundaries that must be placed around them. He who does not approach the other through Christ, for example, descends to the level of human gossip that kills the spiritual word. Also it is more fitting to talk with Christ about others than to talk endlessly with others about Christ. Prayer is thus the appropriate boundary to the desire for an immediate outpouring of sentiment. This discipline provided by mediation has even greater importance in spiritual communities than in "human" ones such as marriage, family and friendship. Bonhoeffer therefore finds more help than hindrance, in view of the nature of community life, in the objectivity and non-utilitarian character of the biblical words and liturgical texts. Their external appropriation is a protection against intersubjective influence. Reading aloud helps to create the "we" of the community. In the same way, unison singing drives out those common enemies, the soloist who sings too loudly and the unmusical who are afraid to sing at all. Finally, a collective discipline diminishes the role of envy or personal aversion, so that each can help to bear the burdens of the others.

In all of this, the spiritual life of the community and its structure of mediation are preparing for a creative approach to the outer world of work:

Work plunges men into the world of things. The Christian steps out

[31] Bonhoeffer, *op. cit.*, p. 36.

of the world of brotherly encounter into the world of impersonal things, the "it," and this new encounter frees him for objectivity . . . The passions of the flesh die in the world of things. But this can happen only where the Christian breaks through the "it" to the "Thou," which is God, who bids him work and makes that work a means of liberation from himself.[32]

The external world is thus a means God uses to free believers from themselves, from preoccupation with self.

"Life together" is therefore communion through spiritual mediation and not the confusion of human immediacy. It is balanced around a double phrase: *Let him who cannot be alone beware of community . . . Let him who is not in community beware of being alone.*[33]

With similar parallelism, Bonhoeffer suggests periods of silence, so that speech may become more creative:

Silence does not mean dumbness, as speech does not mean chatter. Dumbness does not create solitude and chatter does not create fellowship.[34]

Receptivity is the real force that creates community. But receptivity implies being alone without being lonely, whereas one can be lonely even though surrounded by people, by communicating in undisciplined fashion.[35] The acceptance of being alone is the basis of the common life of those who are called, for the call of God that establishes community life also sets us apart as individuals and as disciples before life and death. Our reality thus includes both closeness and distance, a power that bestows community in the midst of loneliness and likewise bestows on the community a capacity for being alone.

[32] Bonhoeffer, *op. cit.*, p. 70.
[33] Bonhoeffer, *op. cit.*, p. 77, italics in original.
[34] Bonhoeffer, *op. cit.*, p. 78.
[35] Bonhoeffer here rediscovers certain classical experiences of monastic communal life. Compare this with the rough, almost inflexible language of Georges Bernanos against expressing human feeling in *The Carmelites*, in which the prioress speaks to Blanche as follows: "Do not let yourself imagine that the first duty of our condition is to help one another, the better to be more pleasing to our Master, like the young women who change their powder and their rouge before going to a ball. Our function is to pray, as the function of a lamp is to give light . . . You have been dreaming of this House as a frightened child, when the nurse has put it to bed, dreams, in the darkness, of the living-room where all is light and warmth. You know nothing of the solitude in which a true Religious has to live and die" (Fontana Books, Collins, London 1961, p. 38). Bonhoeffer's tone, however, is never as intentionally harsh as this.

The criterion of true spirituality is its power to strengthen and purify us for participation in God's world. Its bankruptcy would be the creation of a spiritual realm that would weaken it for encounter with everyday, prosaic and secular life. It would produce only the blossoms of religious irrelevance and not the fruits of faith in the midst of reality.

Thus perfectionism is the last thing Bonhoeffer is interested in. With sensitive psychological insight, he acknowledges that the weak play a decisive role, for their elimination would spell the death of the community. However,

The weak must not judge the strong, the strong must not despise the weak. The weak must guard against pride, the strong against indifference. None must seek his own rights. If the strong person falls, the weak one must guard against malicious joy at his downfall.[36]

Thus to serve is to let oneself be interrupted by the other and also to bear the burdens of the other, since it is true that Jesus Christ saves the world by bearing its burdens and accepting responsibility for it, a point Bonhoeffer later makes in *Ethics*. There is consequently no place in the church for the cult of "personalities" or for their powerful authority or unusual gifts, for it is, on the contrary, the possibility of being able to acknowledge one's sin in the church that creates the community in the first place. While God hates sin, he loves the sinner. Confession, which Bonhoeffer feels is more fitting between two brothers than before the entire community, achieves this "permission" to acknowledge sin, without the loneliness that sin normally entails, nor the illusion that can deceive us if we confess only to ourselves. It is necessary, however, to guard against designating a single individual to become confessor for all the rest, and even more to guard against letting confession degenerate into a "pious work," for if the confessant does so,

it will become the final, most abominable, vicious and impure prostitution of the heart: the act becomes an idle, lustful babbling.[37]

Holy Communion, "the joyful sacrament," illustrates in the form of a feast the true existence of the community that lives out of the bonds created between each member by the mediator of them all.

*   *   *

[36] Bonhoeffer, *op. cit.*, p. 102.   [37] Bonhoeffer, *op. cit.*, p. 120.

The two words "immediacy" and "mediation" illustrate the approach to personal and communal reality that Bonhoeffer preached and experienced during the struggle of the Confessing Church against Nazism. Two other words, "act" and "being," have already been used to characterize his university research on the theology of the church. Two more words, "ultimate" and "penultimate," will form the basis of *Ethics*. Two other words, finally, "godforsakenness" and the "secret discipline" with God, will express the message of his prison letters. But it would be wrong to suppose that these different words are simply dialectical aspects of the same reality, aspects which could complete and correct and thus lessen the differences between them. Bonhoeffer lives rather in the midst of a logical and passionate tension, in light of the radical nature of each of these terms. This is why the terms do not lead one from the other to successively higher levels. Dialectic does not move toward an all-inclusive view in which the earlier expressions are all synthesized.[38] The words do not bring about their own negation by a method of creative antagonism, as though in terms of the present subject matter the "immediacy of obedience" were to generate by antithesis the "mediation of the Word." In non-dialectical fashion, Bonhoeffer observes certain partial truths in reality, each of which he discusses in depth. And when he has done so, he virtually forgets them in his concern for what comes next. When he re-reads what he wrote earlier, his words sometimes seem to him to be truths with dangerous consequences, without however ceasing to have been, and in a real sense to remain, necessary truths. It is therefore not appropriate to call Bonhoeffer a "dialectical theologian,"[39]

[38] Such will be the case, as we will see, in Barth's treatment of religion. He thus deserves to be called a "dialectical theologian." Cf. Barth, *The Word of God and the Word of Man*, Hodder and Stoughton, 1928, reprinted Harper Torchbooks, New York 1957, pp. 206–12.

[39] This is an appropriate place to comment briefly on James W. Woelfel's book, *Bonhoeffer's Theology: Classical and Revolutionary*, Abingdon Press, Nashville 1970, 350pp. Woelfel offers very full documentation on the sources of Bonhoeffer's thought, moving from the openmindedness of Harnack, the personalistic approach of Karl Heim and the dialectic of sin and grace in Luther, to the theological objectivity of Karl Barth. He then examines several of the central and ongoing problems in Bonhoeffer's work (the relationship between revelation and religion, christology, ecclesiology, biblical hermeneutics, and ethics) before locating Bonhoeffer's work in relation to three currents which he describes as conservative (Barth), radical (theologians of the death of God) and liberal (Bultmann and Tillich). With real

for these diverse truths about reality are seldom uttered in the same breath, and at the very most in a kind of continuing counterpoint. It is more appropriate to call him, in Kierkegaardian fashion, a theologian of the "stages on life's way," provided one notes that Bonhoeffer travels in the opposite direction from Kierkegaard. He begins with the leap and the radical obedience of the "religious" stage, he continues with the seriousness and discernment of the "ethical" stage, and he concludes with the confident freedom of the "aesthetic" stage, which risks before God the absence of the experience of God. At each stage he responds with Kierkegaardian passion to God's call to understand and to live in the immediate reality of his own situation.

---

insight, Woelfel shows that Bonhoeffer is neither a reductionist like the radical theologians, nor secretly "religious" as the liberals so often are, and that his opposition to Barth, to whom he stands closest in the "classical" tradition, is based in large measure on the different emphases of their two traditions: in Barth a Reformed emphasis on God's transcendence (*finitum non capax infiniti*), and in Bonhoeffer a Lutheran emphasis on his condescension (*finitum capax infiniti*). In all respects the book, which is attempting to show the continuity of Bonhoeffer's theological concerns rather than to stress the shifts as Hanfried Müller and John Phillips do, seems to me well-informed and carefully done. However, we may ask whether Woelfel's conclusion is sufficiently strong and clear. He concludes that Bonhoeffer, a "classical and revolutionary" thinker, practised an "all-embracing dialectic, so expressive of his totally theological mind ... too intense even for *Christian* man 'come of age'" (p. 301). I am afraid that such warm approbation makes it difficult to grasp the basic shape of Bonhoeffer's theological approach, and in particular that the word "dialectic" – most appropriate in describing the balance of Barth's systematic approach – is inappropriate to a work as fragmented, compressed and paradoxically unified as Bonhoeffer's work remains. I fear that the fairly extensive description of influences on Bonhoeffer leads to an overly-syncretistic resolution, combining a "classically" evangelical inspiration with a "revolutionary" desire to speak to the secular world. The book is really more an example of extensive documentation than of interpretation. Woelfel's suggestion that Bonhoeffer "'out-theologized' the theologians and 'out-secularized' the secularists" (p. 50) continues to remain obscure. But such comments take nothing away from the incisiveness of Woelfel's analysis, to which attention has already been called, of the relationship between Bonhoeffer and the theologians who both preceded and followed him.

VI

The Concrete Commandment

Bonhoeffer considered *Ethics* his most important book. In it he tried to describe how God and reality are united in Jesus Christ, a unity that overcomes the distance created by idealism between the concrete reality of this world and the absolute of the world beyond. God must be understood as one who appears in the midst of the world rather than at its edges, whether metaphysical or interiorized. In this way the responsible restructuring of the actual world is fulfilled – which is a better way to describe the work accomplished by Jesus Christ, and the work Christians are to carry on in following him, than such terms as "redemption," which can lead to escapism, or "justification," which can justify letting things remain as they are.

Unfortunately, the circumstances of World War II prevented Bonhoeffer from completing *Ethics*. All we have are fragments written between 1940 and 1943 that were never arranged by him in logical sequence. One section that had been hidden was later found. Another section was seized at the time of Bonhoeffer's arrest. In Eberhard Bethge's two prefaces to the book, one written in 1948 and the other in 1962, Bonhoeffer's hesitations about the basic organization and title of the book are described. His overall theme being "the foundations and structure of a world which is reconciled with God," should he call it "the foundations and structure of a united west," or "the foundations and structure of a future world"?[1] Should he emphasize the past inheritance that was rediscovering its center in Christianity, or the future of Christianity in a world

[1] Cf. *Ethics*, Editor's Preface, p. 12.

that had moved beyond its earlier forms? Bonhoeffer had thought of still another title, one that would correspond with his division of the book into penultimate and ultimate realities. This was "The preparing of the way and the entry into possession." He foresaw two sections, one dealing with "The Foundations," and describing the task of ethics in the inheritance and decay of the world, and the other dealing with "The Structures," treating in succession the structures of personal life, classes and "offices," communities, the church, and Christian life in the world – all from the perspective of a reconciled reality.

In the 1948 edition, Bethge tried to organize the materials systematically. But in the 1962 edition he gave up this attempt, and re-arranged the fragments according to their time of writing. As a result the present arrangement begins with two sections, "The Love of God and the Decay of the World," and "The Church and the World," which were clearly written in 1939–40, and which recall the general tone of *The Cost of Discipleship*. In the following section, "Ethics and Formation," we find a description of the triumph of nihilism over idealism. This portion was written in 1940, when Bonhoeffer was entering into contact with the German resistance and Hitler was scoring his greatest military successes. Next come the most fully elaborated sections, dealing with "The Natural" as the foundation of the ultimate word of grace, and with the concept of "Reality." These date from 1941, the period when Bonhoeffer still hoped to complete the entire work. They are followed by the most political chapter, dealing with the structure of responsible life, called "History and the Good," written during the time of Bonhoeffer's most active work with the underground in 1941–2. Finally there is a collection of fragments, uncompleted due to his arrest, in which Bonhoeffer elaborated his concept of the mandates, as a way of insisting on the need for Christian involvement in the world.

The common thread that unifies the whole is Bonhoeffer's search for the concrete character of the divine commandment, understood as the structure of *this* world rather than the ideal possibility of some other world. But Bonhoeffer attempts to deal with this theme in many ways, sometimes turning to the Christian inheritance from the past, and other times to the future of a post-Christian world; sometimes using an ordered vertical structure of divine mandates, and other times using an open horizontal approach based on the secularity of the world about him. The development of the fragments, as they have here been described, does not permit us, it seems to me, to impose an evolutionary pattern on Bonhoeffer's thought in which, for example, he would be presumed to have given up an initial pietistic, institutional and even aristocratic approach, for the sake of a second "secularized" approach (a word, incidentally, that he never used) that was more existential and democratic. We must of course allow for the complexity of Bonhoeffer's own situation during this period when for the first time in his life he was working essentially outside the context of the church, and where he was forced, as one working in ethics, to acknowledge simultaneously the "present reality" of the divine order within the natural realities, i.e. the "penulti-mates" of the world, and also to take account of the increasing realization of that same divine order – as dogmatics becomes ethics, faith becomes commandment and grace becomes the structure of the actual world. The task of making God's commandment concrete – it might even be better to say the task of its realization[2] – is thus both an acknowledgement of its ontological presence *in* the world, in the "natural" realities of the world as openings to the encounter with Jesus Christ, and also a recognition of its vertical transcendent coming *to* the world to structure it in reality before God. These two approaches – by "ontological" responsibility from below and by "transcendent" mandates from above – are both found in *Ethics*, just as they were both found in *Act and Being* in connec-tion with the discussion about the knowledge of God. But the emphasis is always on the fact that the divine reality has entered into the reality of the world. The place where they are unified is in Jesus Christ, where God is both "correspondence with reality" in responsible living, and also a call or summons to move toward the Christ of that same reality.

Participation in the indivisible whole of the divine reality – this is the sense and the purpose of the Christian enquiry concerning good.[3]

[2] In Hegelian terminology, reality is always "realization" and not mere "factuality."

[3] Bonhoeffer, *Ethics*, p. 193.

In being himself a summons into reality, God discloses that reality is itself a summons. Thus ethics is not a Kantian or Platonic dualism between what is and what ought to be, but rather the simultaneity of the reality of God and the reality of the world, of God in the world and of the world for God.

Before looking in more detail at the concepts Bonhoeffer uses to hold together what God has united, we must understand more clearly how it is possible to speak of God in the midst of the world. For this purpose Bonhoeffer's exegetical studies of the Bible, particularly those dealing with the Old Testament, are an indispensable introduction to an understanding of his ethics.

1. *God in the midst of the world*

Bonhoeffer was increasingly drawn to the Old Testament, because the living God within it becomes known only in the here-and-now of human life. The absence in the Bible of any speculation about the beyond, about the abode of the dead, about inner feelings, or about the world of the soul, strongly differentiates the faith and anthropology of Israel from the various religions that surround it. For Israel, God can only be encountered in the reality of this world. To withdraw from it is to find oneself beyond his reach. It is this conviction that leads to the surprising emphasis of the Old Testament, which is neither speculative nor spiritual, on earth, flesh, land, family and life itself. With all his strength, the believer desires to live and remain in the midst of these things, not so that he can make them into the false gods of nation, race or instinct, but because in them and in them alone his faith both seeks and finds the living God. For Israel, in distinction from the origin of other religions, God is not the God of the dead but of the living,[4] located not beyond the world but in its midst. He

---

[4] In the non-biblical religions, on the other hand, one of the main sources for the appearance of the gods is reflection on what happens after death. Edgar Morin has clearly described the various steps: horror in the face of death; to overcome it the creation of counterparts, e.g. the spirits of the dead; when these become too real and threatening to the living, they in their turn are overcome by the creation of gods, who are either perpetually reborn in the cyclic fashion of the stars and the seasons, or better still, are immortal, and beyond the cycle of birth and death. (Cf. E. Morin, *L'Homme et la Mort dans l'Histoire*, Correa, Paris 1951). Here we undoubtedly find one of the clearest distinctions between the "holy" (*le sacré*) of religions and the faith of the Bible.

cannot properly be associated with either other-worldly transcendence or this-worldly immanence. He is the creator of one as well as of the other, of heaven as well as of earth, neither of which can contain him. In declaring himself the partner and ally of man rather than of celestial hierarchies or cosmic powers, God chooses in the freedom of his love to grant a privilege to this world and to man in its midst, making man his sole partner at the heart of the whole creation, heavenly as well as earthly. Therefore God is not immanent in either nature or history. His personal freedom is not confused with the necessities of either. But neither is God transcendent in relation to nature or history, at least not in the sense of a metaphysical transcendence that separates into dualism. God is present for man only in this world, the unique setting for his freely-given activity on man's behalf. To say of God (as Bonhoeffer does following the language of the Old Testament) that he is in the midst of the world if only one will listen to him, does not mean confusing God with a closed system or some earth-bound empirical reality, but even more it means refusing to locate him in the unreality of some other world. In Ronald Gregor Smith's apt phrase, God is "this-worldly transcendence."[5]

But does this not mean that the New Testament surpasses the Old? Specifically does not the new fact of the resurrection of Jesus Christ transform all these perspectives by enlarging hope to include a beyond – a hope of breaking through the boundaries of this world that had been denied Israel since it clung, for example, to the perpetuating of one's name by means of genealogies and to the permanence of an historical "promised land"? It is true that the New Covenant does not bother with detailed genealogies, since the Messiah has already come, and that it universalizes the promise of Canaan to include the entire human race and the whole expanse of the universe.[6] In this sense the New Testament does extend the scope of Israel's particularized faith. But in another sense it would be utterly wrong to transform Christianity into an other-worldly religion and thereby separate it from Israel's faith in this world.

---

[5] R. Gregor Smith, "Diesseitige Transzendenz," *Die Mündige Welt* II, pp. 104–16.

[6] Thus I Tim. 1.4 and Titus 3.9 take issue, as far as Christians of Jewish origin are concerned, with the notion of genealogies. Since Pentecost, the promise is to the nations of the entire world, far beyond Israel and Jerusalem.

According to Bonhoeffer, it is the Old Testament that protects Christianity from becoming identified with countless other-worldly religions. Without the Old Testament, Christian faith tends to become a religion that initiates its followers into the mysteries of the soul's destiny after death. Without its Hebraic rootage, Christianity is subtly transformed – initially into gnosticism, and more recently into idealism. When this happens, God is no longer in the midst of the world. He returns to a mythical heaven that soon becomes metaphysical. He ceases to be the God of the living and dwells in eternity and immortality,[7] to which man hopes to return once he has (as Socrates said in the *Phaedo*) secured "the release of the soul from the chains of the body."[8]

So the New Testament does not surpass the Old, even though it changes it. It extends it, but always remains in faithful continuity with it. Bonhoeffer never swerved from this insight. It was there in 1932, when he expounded the theological meaning of Genesis 1–3 in *Creation and Fall*, and it was there at the end of his life, when he wrote on 27 June 1944:

Unlike the other oriental religions, the faith of the Old Testament is not a religion of redemption. It is true that Christianity has always been regarded as a religion of redemption. But is not this a cardinal error, which separates Christ from the Old Testament and interprets him on the lines of the myths of redemption? To the objection that a crucial importance is given in the Old Testament to redemption (from Egypt, and later from Babylon – cf. Deutero-Isaiah) it may be answered that the redemptions referred to here are *historical*, i.e. on *this* side of death, whereas everywhere else the myths about redemption are concerned to overcome the barrier of death . . .

The decisive factor is said to be that in Christianity the hope of resurrection is proclaimed, and that that means the emergence of a genuine religion of redemption, the main emphasis now being on the far side of the boundary drawn by death. But it seems to me that this is just where the mistake and the danger lie . . . The difference between the Christian hope of resurrection and the mythological hope is that the former sends a man back to his life on earth in a

[7] We must remember that both the Hebrew and Greek scriptures have the same word to designate time and eternity, *olam* in Hebrew, *aion* in Greek. Here the emphasis is placed on the present which passes away and on the new which always comes in *this* world, rather than on a metaphysical dualism between what is transitory and what is permanent.

[8] Plato, *Phaedo*, 67e.

wholly new way which is even more sharply defined than it is in the Old Testament.[9]

The Christian, unlike the devotees of the redemption myths, has no last line of escape available from earthly tasks and difficulties into the eternal, but, like Christ himself ("My God, why hast thou forsaken me?"), he must drink the earthly cup to the lees, and only in his doing so is the crucified and risen Lord with him, and he crucified and risen with Christ. This world must not be prematurely written off; in this the Old and New Testaments are at one. Redemption myths arise from human boundary experiences, but Christ takes hold of a man at the centre of his life.[10]

Creation and Fall,[11] a series of lectures given at the University of Berlin during the winter semester of 1932–3, was an early expression of one of Bonhoeffer's central convictions, that God is not at the edges of the world but at its center. He does not reveal himself to man through experiences limited to special "religious" times, such as birth, death, mystical awareness or anxiety, but at the center of his life. *Creation and Fall* is a commentary that is philosophical in its formulation, as were *Communion of Saints* and *Act and Being* which preceded it, and biblical in its subject matter, as are *The Cost of Discipleship* and *Life Together* which follow it. It is a description of the work of God the creator in the midst of the reality of the world.

The very notion of a "beginning" is itself something we cannot think and therefore cannot talk about. As Hegel saw clearly, if philosophy wants to be more than a Kantian critique, it must begin by "arbitrarily enthroning reason," which would also entail the impossible claim that reason and creation were contemporaneous events. And theology is placed under the

---

[9] This theme is also found in *Ethics*, where ultimate reality, the resurrection, refers to the penultimate realities (nature and culture) instead of destroying them in process of completing them. It is based on the resurrection appearances in the gospels. The risen Christ does not appear as the ghostly apparition of a living person who has departed, nor as an immortal spirit that has rediscovered its original heavenly dwelling place, but *as a man living a brand-new earthly existence*, preserving the marks of his mortal body in the place where he began his ministry, i.e. Galilee, once again eating and drinking, able to be touched, and utterly "earthly." While to the eyes of non-believers this will surely seem a myth, it is at least the myth of the raising up of a *body*, and not the myth of a dualism of being or of the immortality of the soul.

[10] Bonhoeffer, *LPP*, 27 June 1944, pp. 185f.

[11] Cited from Bonhoeffer, *Creation and Fall/Temptation, Two Biblical Studies*, Macmillan, New York 1965, 128pp.

same impasse here as philosophy, unless the beginning is already a "middle". Bonhoeffer then remarks that the words with which the Bible begins, "In the beginning . . .," do not describe the first instant when being arises out of non-being, or time is born at the edge of eternity, but rather what happens "in the 'middle' of beginning," which would be a better way to translate the phrase. These words describe how God structures the everyday world, or (to use the terminology with which Barth expounds his doctrine of creation) how God refuses the impossible possibility of non-being which rises up like a shadow, always present and yet always denied, from the divine work in the midst of the world.[12]

It may be therefore that "Genesis" (the beginning) is a Greek concept that does not correctly describe this Hebraic book on the creative and sustaining work of God in the midst of reality. It does not make us witnesses of what preceded "the beginning," but rather of what is accomplished in creation when God creates, and when in the midst of our own lives we take account of what he has done.[13] Thus the aim of the creation stories is not to satisfy our curiosity about beginnings and origins, but rather to help us understand and be obedient to the structure and shape of the world around us. Much contemporary philosophy asserts that being is based on nothingness; such a claim seems to establish man as the true creator of values, opposing the creativity of his nothingness to the opacity and massivity of being. But theology does not accept this creative intrusion of nothingness between God and man as redounding to man's favor. It sees nothingness as part of the very inwardness of God's free act, both affirmed and negated by it. Similarly, the cross is part of the re-creative act of the

---

[12] Barth generously recognizes his debt to Bonhoeffer's *Creation and Fall* (1932–3) in his own doctrine of creation (1942–3). Cf. Barth, *Church Dogmatics* III/1, T. and T. Clark, Edinburgh 1958, pp. 194–7.

[13] Bonhoeffer's commentary, like Barth's, is much more theological than it is historical-critical. However, Bonhoeffer emphasizes the situation of the biblical editors more than Barth does. To him, no matter how pious they may be, they are fully part of their own culture and language, not observers of creation. Their situation "in the middle" is thus similar to their message about God, who "is in the beginning" only because he is already "in the middle" of the world. G. von Rad, *Old Testament Theology* I, Oliver and Boyd, Edinburgh, and Harper and Row, New York 1962, esp. pp. 128–53, gives historical confirmation to Bonhoeffer's theological interpretation, linking the creation stories to Israel's reflections about its own historical existence in the accounts of Abraham's election and the exodus.

resurrection, likewise affirmed and negated, which God shares with men, in which he now repels nothingness in himself after having repelled it in the world at the time of creation. The "middle" of time, which is the meaning of redemption, is identical with creation. In these two moments of his ongoing work, God struggles in the "middle" of the world so that in both instances the world will be seen as the place of his love for man. The cross shows us God as the center of life, but so do the books of Genesis and Revelation. The "middle" is also first and last.

After this introduction, in which God the creator has already been established as the God who is in the midst of creatures and things, Bonhoeffer underlines the voluntary and structural, or we might even say the ethical and non-metaphysical, nature of the creative Word. The Word does not show us God's nature or essence, but acquaints us with his commandment. In expressing himself as Word, God shows his creation what he is like. The omnipotence of this Word assures its realization. It links the imperative to the indicative, without the category of causality, so characteristic of the human descriptions that thwart its realization. According to Bonhoeffer, the decisive impact of the word is the appearance of structure or form (*Gestalt*).

That God speaks, and speaking, creates, the Bible strangely only mentions first where it is concerned with the creation of form, the wresting of form out of the formless. Form corresponds to the Word ... As the formless night becomes form by the light of the morning, as the light creates and unveils form, so that primeval light had to order the chaos, create and unveil form.[14]

Structure and not intention constitutes the goodness of the created work. By his work, by what he realizes and not by a spirit or an ideal, God reveals himself in the midst of his creation. Bonhoeffer's commentary on Genesis 1 is an analysis of the various structures by which the unstructured, unformed world is transformed into God's creation for man. The *first* of these, day, establishes the natural dialectic of repose and movement (vv. 1–3). The *second*, "the fixed," consists of the

[14] Bonhoeffer, *Creation and Fall*, p. 24. Note that in the English translation of *Creation and Fall*, the German word *Gestalt* is rendered as "form," whereas in the present volume "structure" is used throughout.

impersonal law of stars and numbers (vv. 6–10, 14–19). The *third*, the living, which is expressed in fertility, is like the fixed but complementary to it, a structure that is dependent on the divine freedom, for neither number nor life could forget that they are both creatures of God (vv. 11–13, 20–25).

But it is to the *fourth* structure that Bonhoeffer devotes most of his commentary on creation, not speculating about its beginning and its edges, but analyzing its structuring and its "middle." Only this fourth structure is the image of God on earth. It is not an analogy of being (*analogia entis*) but an analogy of relation (*analogia relationis*). It is freedom, understood not as some idealized form of lonely autonomy, but as the actual reality of relationship with another. "God created man in his own image, in the image of God he created him; male and female he created them." (Gen. 1.27) Bonhoeffer's initial comment on this theme, which later becomes very important to him and many other thinkers, is as follows:

Being free means "being free for the other," because the other has bound me to him. Only in relationship with the other am I free.

No substantial or individualistic concept of freedom can conceive of freedom. I have no control over freedom as over a property. It is simply the event that happens to me through the other.[15]

This fourth structure, which is the freedom described in the above quotation, fulfills the earlier structures that are grounded in necessity. In the other structures, God manifests himself. But in the structure of freedom he can be truly seen. Freedom-as-relationship is the other side of necessity, which is not a structure opposing it but reality still waiting for the image of the One who has created it with and for freedom. In none of this are we speculating about some first man, of whom we are totally ignorant. Instead, we are analyzing before God the "middle" of the reality in which we ourselves are involved, for with this fourth structure of relational freedom, God's uncreated freedom enters into the world through man who bears God's image. The creator dwells in the creature.

This is what Bonhoeffer means by "mandate" – a notion later developed in *Ethics*:

By the term "mandate" we understand the concrete divine com-

[15] Bonhoeffer, *Creation and Fall*, p. 37.

mission which has its foundation in the revelation of Christ and which is evidenced by Scripture; it is the legitimation and warrant for the execution of a definite divine commandment, the conferment of divine authority on an earthly agent. The term "mandate" must also be taken to imply the claiming, the seizure and the formation of a definite earthly domain by the divine commandment.[16]

A mandate is not an initial and impersonal "order of creation" that has remained unaffected by human development and has served either as the criterion for natural goodness or as a means of holding a sinful world together. Rather, a mandate is a structure in the "middle" of earthly reality that summons the human will and shows it right here and now what the creator demands of his creatures. To recognize a structure and to obey a mandate are one and the same thing. "Freedom from" necessity is realized only in "freedom for" the neighbor. This is how the structuring of the world around us takes place – a task that God entrusts to us both as a blessing and a duty.

The effect of sin is to "de-create" the world, which means to "de-structure" it. Bonhoeffer analyzes this in terms of the second creation story in Genesis, chronologically earlier than the first, in which man plays a central role, whereas in the first account God alone is at work.[17] The human response to the divine structures now begins. Man is described as living in the middle of the world (Gen. 2.8–17) and the presence of God is indicated by the tree of life "in the midst [middle] of the garden" (Gen. 2.9). God does not issue any jealous prohibition about what is done at the edges of his domain, but he does place a curious restriction around what is to happen in the middle. If Prometheus "falls" by stealing fire from the gods (fire representing the power and technical ability reserved for the gods alone), things are utterly different with Adam, who destroys the structures of the world by refusing to accept freedom-in-relationship, even though God had given him all

---

[16] Bonhoeffer, *Ethics*, p. 287.

[17] The fundamental difference between the priestly account (Gen. 1.1–2.4a) and the Yahwist account (Gen. 2.4bff.) is not only that the first emphasizes a vast cosmos ("the generations of the *heavens* and the earth," 2.4a) while the second emphasizes what is close at hand ("the Lord God made the *earth* and the heavens," 2.4b), but above all that man speaks immediately in the Yahwist source to uphold (Gen. 2.33) and then to destroy (Gen. 3.1–13) the structures of the world around him, while according to the priestly source, it is not until Genesis 17.17 that a human word is spoken in response to God's great structuring works.

power and domination over nature, without setting any external limits to the work of his knowledge, his power or his will.

Man's limit is in the middle of his existence, not on the edge. The limit which we look for on the edge is the limit of his condition, of his technology, of his possibilities. The limit in the middle is the limit of his reality, of his true existence.[18]

This limit is grace, because it is the acceptance of living freely for the other, for God, and for man.

But man, after having assented to all this in joyful greeting to the other whom God gives him – woman for man, man for woman – then refuses the gift. So instead of being grace, the limit becomes an obstacle that is refused, overcome, hated and feared. Using life for the sake of the other is turned around and becomes a matter of using life for the destruction of the other. Living before the other ceases to be the goodness of desire, and becomes inhibition, aggressiveness and shame at seeing and being seen. The relational structure of freedom is obscured. The impersonal structures of necessity, which were useful to man, are themselves transformed into hostile fates. Thus the "fall" (which as we have already seen is too neo-Platonic a word) really ought to be called the tearing apart, or the destructuring, of the reality given by God. All this happens because the category of the possible and of alternative choices (e.g. the knowledge of good and evil, "did God *really* say . . . ?") is substituted for the category of realization. As early as 1932, Bonhoeffer was describing this introduction of possibility as the introduction of the "religious" question, the pious question, which prefers the "unreal" world of human temptation to the reality God himself has provided, and which thinks it can improve upon reality and penetrate more deeply than his commandment.

[The serpent] is evil only as the religious serpent . . . With the first religious question in the world evil has come upon the scene. Where evil appears in its godlessness, it is powerless . . . When man proceeds against the concrete Word of God with the weapon of a principle, with an idea of God, he is in the right from the first, he becomes God's master, he has left the path of obedience, he has withdrawn from God's addressing him. In other words, in this question the

[18] Bonhoeffer, *Creation and Fall*, p. 32.

possibility is played off against the reality, and the possibility undermines the reality. However, in man's relationship to God there are no possibilities, there is only reality. There is no "... allow me ...," there is only command and obedience.[19]

Man refuses to live according to the image of God, which is freedom-in-relationship, because he wants to become God himself, an omnipotent lord over all things and creatures, without entering into relationship with them. And what he wants becomes what he is. The world of his experience falls to pieces when separated from the concrete reality that God offers him. Man *is* in the "middle" of everything, and he is all alone. Man is a false god. He has moved from the center of life to the outer limits of anxiety. Grace has turned to envy, work to alienation, and sexuality to insatiable evil desire, a hatred of all boundaries and an unattainable ideal that destroys the immediate relationship. Bonhoeffer interprets sexual modesty as a kind of recollection of this structure in the "middle" of reality which enables one to express that reality without wanting to destroy it by the covetousness for what is beyond reach. Man after the "fall" (or better, after the de-structuring of created reality) thus refuses to respond affirmatively to the here-and-now that God offers him. He "piously" wants to substitute another world for it, e.g. to "be like God." His desire to be divine himself causes him to forsake God who is in the midst of the world. His appetite for the infinite causes him to desert the structures of the finite, which are the very stuff of creation. Locating the god of his desire outside of reality, he is henceforth in a world where God is not.

There is only one thing God can do, and that is to make sure that the world man has destroyed does not appear to him as the true reality God created. This is the creative significance of the words of malediction spoken to man, which record the downfall and the destruction of his world. This speech, not so much from the beginnings as from the "middle" of the world (which is the proper meaning of "Genesis"), describes man as being chased from the "middle" of the earth toward its evil edges, the soil as adversity, the partner as adversary, death as no longer an acceptable finitude but a destructive obstacle, the structures of necessity as forbidding powers, and the structure

19 *Ibid.*, pp. 67f.

of freedom as leading to reciprocal murder. By desiring the tree at the edge of the garden, the tree of the knowledge of good and evil, man is prohibited from eating the tree in the middle of the garden, the tree of life. God himself states the prohibition to man, which is the consequence of his refusal to embody the co-humanity that had been given him in the middle of the garden, and of his covetousness for the unreality of the edge of the garden, where he got only what he was looking for, the false divinity of solitary power, far from God who is not solitary.

Creation and Fall concludes with a reference to the *second* tree of life planted in the "middle" of reality, in the middle of that strange Garden of Eden which is the garden of the Mount of Olives and the Place of the Skull. Here Jesus Christ, the second Adam, re-structured the world by refusing to covet the edges as the first Adam had done, so that he could give men back the knowledge of reality that God had originally given them:

Who, though he was in the form of God, did not count equality with God a thing to be grasped, . . . and being found in human form, he humbled himself, and became obedient unto death, even death on a cross. Therefore, God has highly exalted him . . .[20]

The new Adam, being himself conformed to the world around him, re-created that world by re-structuring it in the midst of time and space.

The christological reading of Genesis thus clarifies its meaning. God is in the "middle" of the world, in the structures that starting from chaos and nothingness constitute the creation, in the relationship with the other, which is the true lost name of freedom. The rejection of this given world for some coveted other world is called the "fall" – if we can use this "religious" word without misunderstanding to characterize a situation that is the opposite of that in other religions. In closing himself off from relationship to this world, man who is able to "see" the meaning of creation plunges himself into darkness. Redemption – if we can use a word that is also tainted by other-worldly imagery – consists of Jesus Christ giving man's vision back to him, and loving the neighbor in the midst of reality without wishing to surpass him. The fall

----

[20] Phil. 2.6–9.

is thus the destruction of the world by the "religious" desire to covet equality with God (Phil. 2.6). And the re-creation in Christ is the re-structuring of reality around him, thanks to the impersonal structures of the day, the "fixed" and the living, and the personal structure of human partnership. Biblical ontology is expressed not by using religion to go beyond reality, or using metaphysics to divide it in two, but by the acknowledgement of the created order of things and persons, by the appropriate love of the "middle" of reality. "Ontology without metaphysics"[21] here signifies a relational openness that does not compartmentalize life.

It was a near catastrophe for Christianity when it became more closely related to neo-Platonic idealism than to Old Testament realism, when it appeared mainly as the religion of another world and no longer as the affirmation of the God who is hidden in the midst of *this* world, when creation became a way of talking about a lost heaven, and the fall a way of describing a destroyed earth. Without the continuing influence of the Old Testament upon it, Christianity would have become one of the religions initiating its followers into the mysteries of the beyond, and redemption would have been changed into escape instead of being re-creation and re-structuring of the reality given by God. It is certain that without Jesus Christ we run the risk of "platonizing"[22] the book of Genesis, but it is just as certain that without the Old Testament we run even more risk of "platonizing" Jesus Christ. Consequently, the Old Testament is important to us, less as a way toward the demythologization of Christianity, than as a way toward the proclamation of God's presence in the here-and-now. Bonhoeffer thinks that Christianity, rooted in the Old Testament, interprets the presence of God in the midst of the actual world in a "worldly fashion." For God is not so much an event

---

[21] Cf. Ch. IV above for an elaboration of this phrase.

[22] "Platonizing" is used here in the way that Nietzsche interprets Plato, out of his dislike of dualism which he thinks is Christian. Plato himself, in creating a rational and mythical idealism, appears to have been more involved in the search for appropriate ontological structures to recreate the empirical world than he is attracted by metaphysical dualism to remove himself from it. "The philosopher is the substitute for God. He is the witness to a lost transparency and the trustee of that way, inadequate but with indefinite possibilities, which has been left to humanity and which we call Reason" (François Châtelet, *Platon*, Gallimard, Paris 1965, p. 239).

coming from another world to this world as he is the very
structure of this world, offered to Adam, rejected because of
the latter's "religious" preference for the edges, and then
revealed and realized in Jesus Christ in the "middle" of human
existence, history and things.[23]

2. *Themes of* Ethics: *the mandates, responsibility, ultimate and penultimate*

This full summary of *Creation and Fall* has been presented to
illustrate the point that the *Ethics* of a decade later could have
been written immediately afterwards. The continuities in
Bonhoeffer's thought, as indicated by the crystallization of his
vocabulary, are stronger than the discontinuities brought about
by rapid shifts in his external fortunes. To stress the discontinuities for the sake of contriving a decisive evolution in his
theological thought is to miss the significance of the continuities.
In particular, if one does not see that the "worldliness"
(*Weltlichkeit*) of God, of which Bonhoeffer speaks, is rooted in
his understanding of the Old Testament, one runs the risk of
conceiving of it as the encounter of faith with secularization –
catastrophic for some, salutary for others – and not as what it
is in Bonhoeffer's vocabulary, the presence of God in the
midst of this world. Worldliness is the characteristic of the God
of the Bible, as opposed to the other-worldliness of the gods of
religion. "Secularization," on the other hand, describes the
gradual disappearance of "Christendom" as an historical
reality. The phenomenon of "secularization" thus poses a
problem that is less theological than apologetic (e.g. how do I
preach and live the Christian faith without either the supports
or the obstacles of the visibility of the faith in a so-called
"Christian culture"?), whereas "worldliness" designates the
permanent characteristic of biblical speech about God, namely
that his Word is a concrete commandment to be recognized
in the midst of reality.

From this perspective, the word "ethics" has two very
different meanings. It can designate either the dilemmas of

[23] The theme of "Christ as structure" will be developed in Ch. VIII below,
treating Bonhoeffer's christology. In it we find the key to his entire work, much
more so than in such themes as "the world come of age," or "the non-religious
interpretation of Christianity."

conscience in the knowledge of good and evil, or it can designate the recognition of reality re-unified by God's commandment. To shift the discussion of ethics from the former meaning to the latter is the task Bonhoeffer sets himself. In the first part of *Ethics* we are in the everyday world, "the world of conflicts," where idealism enlarges the alternatives in such a way that nihilism ultimately triumphs. But at the end of this section we discover that reality is unity, a unity that God gives us in his commandment.

Not man's falling apart from God, from men, from things and from himself, but rather the rediscovered unity, reconciliation, is now the basis of discussion and the point of decision of the specifically ethical experience.[24]

The notion of "reality" thus stands for the abolition of life in two spheres: either God or the world, either sublimation or secularity, either being or appearance, either norms or life itself. Bonhoeffer rejects such ethical alternatives, just as in *The Communion of Saints* he had rejected the opposition between a spiritual church on high and an empirical church here below. At that time he had affirmed the ecclesiological reality of Christ present on earth, "existing in the form of community." He now affirms the ethical reality of the commandment of God on earth, existing in the form of structures and mandates. Ordinary ethical systems make a practice of opposing duty and inclination, idea and reality, intention and deed, individual and collective, person and work. In contrast to this, Christian ethics binds the reality of God to its realization by man.

The question of good becomes the question of participation in the divine reality which is revealed in Christ ... Only if we share in reality can we share in good.[25]

However, such affirmations would be nothing but obscure claims if Jesus Christ had not effected the concretizing of God in the world, the entrance of God into reality, to bring about the

[24] Bonhoeffer, *Ethics*, p. 26.
[25] Bonhoeffer, *Ethics*, pp. 190f. The whole section, "Christ, Reality and Good," contains the heart of the fragments of *Ethics* (pp. 188–213). Bethge describes Bonhoeffer's understanding of reality as follows: "Reality is always the acceptance of the world by the one who has become man. Here Bonhoeffer seeks to avoid the positivist and idealistic understanding, as he regards both as abstractions" (*Dietrich Bonhoeffer*, p. 621).

simultaneity of man's participation with God and with the world. For Jesus Christ does away with any metaphysical duality. He destroys the possibility of existence on two levels, or in two spheres, by the realization of God in the world and the world in God. He does away with the problem of boundaries between God and the world by structuring the world in the midst of the world itself rather than elsewhere. With a kind of inspired logic, Bonhoeffer continues:

A world which stands by itself, in isolation from the law of Christ, falls victim to license and self-will. A Christianity which withdraws from the world falls victim to the unnatural and the irrational, to presumption and self-will.[26]

The task of ethics is not to launch appeals to overcome the divorce between ideal and real, but to describe God's concrete commandment in the midst of reality. Ethics is the ontological description of the world God controls, rather than the metaphysical proclamation of a God exterior to the world: "God and the world are thus at one in Christ [without] a static, spatial borderline between them."[27]

Once this affirmation of an ethic based on God's presence in reality has been proposed, there remains the difficult task of finding ways to recognize God's presence in the midst of a world that Bonhoeffer himself knew very well – a world that was no longer the reality first given in creation, and not yet the reality re-given in reconciliation, but the ambiguous and contorted everyday world where good and evil exist side by side.

There are at least three attempts in *Ethics* to describe how this can be done: the doctrine of the four mandates, the structures of responsible life, and the relationship between the ultimate and the penultimate.[28]

1. The *mandates* are not institutions in themselves, subsisting by themselves like the "orders of creation," but, as the personalistic etymology of the word suggests, they are vocations from God which take the concrete form of earthly demands that have the force of divine commandments. Bonhoeffer distinguishes four

---

[26] *Ethics*, p. 200.   [27] *Ibid.*, pp. 206f.

[28] The latter phrase is used here in preference to "the last things and the things before the last," as being less cumbersome. Both terms are used in the English translation of *Ethics*, and in most secondary source materials.

such mandates: labor, marriage, government, and the church.[29] The curious addition of the fourth "non-natural" mandate indicates that the first three already constitute neither states of being nor separate spheres, but the places where the unity of reality before God is achieved. The divine mandates express the ethics of an ontology of reality based on christology. They manifest Christ existing in the world in the form of community and commandment. They are clearly an attempt to clarify the Lutheran doctrine of the "orders of creation" and the statutes, personalizing them by their continuing relationship to God who is in control of them, and unifying them against the heteronomy of the different "realms."[30]

But even though the doctrine of the mandates had been drafted last, in 1943, it remained too closely allied to a theological heritage that was not moving in the direction Bonhoeffer sought, namely toward a reality re-united by the christological realization of God within it. While he was in prison Bonhoeffer saw the failure of this way of dividing things, which gave so much authority to certain human realities that it ran the risk of destroying freedom in the name of obedience to those divinized demands.[31]

2. Bonhoeffer's second way of recognizing the reality ordained by God in the midst of the everyday world seems much better than the first for it is linked more clearly to the way that Jesus Christ has brought reality into being. Bonhoeffer offers what he calls *the structures of responsible life* which are likewise four in number: (a) correspondence with reality, which the incarnation makes effective; (b) responsibility for others, which is most fully expressed in deputyship (*Stellvertretung*) as Jesus binds himself fully to the destiny of humanity, and to things as well in so far as the world of things is directed toward mankind; (c) the acceptance of guilt, which means that when Jesus acts

[29] Bonhoeffer, *Ethics*, pp. 207–13. In a later discussion Bonhoeffer lists the first of the above mandates as "culture," cf. *Ethics*, pp. 286ff.

[30] Cf. J. Moltmann, "The Lordship of Christ and Human Society," in J. Moltmann and J. Weissbach, *Two Studies in the Theology of Bonhoeffer*, Scribners, New York 1967, pp. 19–94.

[31] "Our 'Protestant' (not Lutheran) Prussian world has been so dominated by the four mandates that the sphere of freedom has receded into the background" (*LPP*, 23 January 1944, p. 120). Later on, in much the same fashion, Barth criticized the arbitrariness of Bonhoeffer's four mandates. Cf. his letter to Landessuperintendent W. Herrenbrück, in R. Gregor Smith, ed., *World Come of Age*, p. 90.

responsibly he becomes guilty although without sin; and finally, (*d*), freedom, understood not as autonomy preserved in the Kantian sense, but as responsibility that is assumed without any reservations whatever, so that the contorted everyday world can once again become a truly unified reality. Freedom is the surrender of oneself and all that one does to God, a submission that is the opposite of resignation and the achievement of resistance.[32] Bonhoeffer's descriptions of these differing structures of responsible life are exceptionally well done. In each case, Jesus re-creates the structures in the "middle" of the world that *Creation and Fall* had described.

3. But the third way of discerning the commandment of the God of reality is the most fruitful of all, for here Bonhoeffer tackles the vast problem of the relationship between "natural" life and the life of faith, which the christological emphasis on the structures of responsible life virtually ignores, and which the doctrine of the mandates hardens too arbitrarily. This third way is the relationship between *the ultimate and the penultimate*. Catholic theology usually deals with the penultimate (e.g. nature and culture) in the light of the ultimate (the supernatural) which perfects it, while in the Protestant tradition the ultimate (grace) frequently repudiates the penultimate as insignificant or even sinful. But Bonhoeffer, with an approach quite original in ethical theory, begins with the ultimate, which undergirds and safeguards the penultimate, in the same way that the New Testament and the resurrection send us back to the Old Testament and to life here on earth. The last word, the ultimate word, which is justification, turns the believer toward the penultimate, which is natural life and the whole cultural enterprise, since the God of grace commands us not to look for him on the edges but to meet him in the "middle" of the world. Therefore the ultimate does not destroy the penultimate, which is always the pietistic temptation of Protestantism, nor does the ultimate simply follow along after the penultimate, which is always the naturalistic temptation of Catholicism. Instead, the ultimate precedes the penulti-

[32] The little volume *Temptation*, containing some biblical studies Bonhoeffer gave at Finkenwalde in the latter part of June 1938, is an attempt to distinguish between the necessary resistance to the accuser, Satan, and legitimate submission to the giver, God. (Cited from *Creation and Fall/Temptation*, Macmillan, New York 1965, pp. 95–128.)

mate and gives it direction. Salvation invests nature and culture with value; it neither scorns nor enthrones them. The ultimate is not found at the edge of the world, but in its "middle" as a way of structuring the penultimate. Just as Jesus Christ, responsible even unto death, raised up from the heart of the earth, discourages his disciples from the temptation to seek him in the heavens (Acts 1.11), so those who follow him are to turn themselves from the ultimate toward the penultimate, where they will find their ultimate justification.

This is Bonhoeffer's route to an interest in *the natural*, which he prefers to the substantive "nature," a word so charged with traditional meanings that it suggests a second way of immanent knowledge of the will of God the creator, parallel to revelation.

The concept of the natural must, therefore, be recovered on the basis of the gospel. We speak of the natural, as distinct from the creaturely, in order to take into account the fact of the Fall; and we speak of the natural rather than of the sinful so that we may include in it the creaturely. The natural is that which, after the Fall, is directed towards the coming of Christ. The unnatural is that which, after the Fall, closes its doors against the coming of Christ. There is indeed only a relative difference between that which is directed towards Christ and that which closes its doors to Christ; for the natural does not compel the coming of Christ, and the unnatural does not render it impossible. In both cases the real coming is an event of grace. And it is only through the coming of Christ that the natural is confirmed in its character as a penultimate, and that the unnatural is exposed once and for all as destruction of the penultimate. Thus, even in the sight of Christ, there is a distinction between the natural and the unnatural, a distinction which cannot be obliterated without doing grave harm.[33]

All the time he was writing the *Ethics*, Bonhoeffer was confronted by the way Nazi nihilism was devouring the best things in idealism, which were turned around and used by their enemy, who lived off their shortsighted virtue. He seeks, not over against reality, but in the midst of it, to discern the concrete commandment of God. The task is extremely difficult, for if idealism sins by its distance from the everyday world,

[33] Bonhoeffer, *Ethics*, pp. 144f. The natural is here clearly christological and not "naturalistic." It is not opposed to the artificial. Cf. Roger Mehl, "La Notion du Naturel dans l'Éthique de Bonhoeffer," in *L'Évangile, hier et aujourd'hui, Mélanges offerts à Franz Leenhardt*, Labor et Fides, Geneva 1970, pp. 205–16.

realism can sin even more when it affirms that the everyday world itself is the expression of the divine will and providence – which was precisely the language the Nazis used to claim nature and culture as their own. Bonhoeffer's *Ethics*, therefore, never deifies the everyday world. Quite the contrary, whatever in the everyday world destroys the reality given by God *Ethics* denounces by means of its three major touchstones; the vocational mandates, responsibility freely undertaken for all men, and the ultimate that validates and directs the penultimate. The very multiplicity of these touchstones shows clearly enough that while writing *Ethics* Bonhoeffer had not yet developed a system. He borrows from the Lutheran heritage as well as from the Catholic tradition. He creates his own approach, according to his understanding of the Old Testament, where God speaks the ultimate word in the midst of the realities of the penultimate. The good ethic is our participation in the reality that God structures on earth for the service of man. The bad ethic, on the contrary, is our willingness to destroy the structures of the world (nihilism), or the irresponsible disengaged judgments we make for the destroying of such structures (metaphysical idealism).

If the word "structure" seems too formal in this connection, all we need to do is look at christology, where the responsibility of Jesus Christ in structuring reality does not stop with a logical analysis of the world, but takes upon itself the sin of the world in order to manifest the reality of the world by means of the true reality of God. For the ultimate word of *Ethics* is that the sinner is finally reconciled with grace, and the existence of man with the reality of God. Edmond Grin has seen clearly what is unique about Bonhoeffer's *Ethics* in relation to other systems of ethics: instead of emphasizing the dilemmas and conflicts between the ideal and what exists, Bonhoeffer emphasizes the will to work toward the unity of reconciliation that Christ has already achieved, in all walks of life, both natural and cultural.

What can and must be said is not what is good once and for all, but the way in which Christ takes form among us here and now.[34]

---

[34] Bonhoeffer, *Ethics*, p. 85. Grin's incisive and careful analysis can be highly recommended: "Une Morale pas comme les autres: Introduction à l'Éthique de Bonhoeffer," *Études théologiques et religieuses*, Montpellier 1965.3, pp. 192–208; 1965.4, pp. 255–76.

Nietzsche likewise sought a reality that would be beyond the knowledge of good and evil, and he did so feeling strongly that allegiance to values had only managed to tear life apart:

There may even be puritanical fanatics of conscience, who prefer to put their last trust in a sure nothing, rather than in an uncertain something.[35]

Nietzsche feels that by stressing the dilemmas and scruples of conscience, idealist and Platonized Christianity has been mainly responsible for the morbid conscience that afflicts western man:

The Christian faith from the beginning is sacrifice: the sacrifice of all freedom, all pride, all self-confidence of spirit; it is at the same time subjection, self-derision, and self-mutilation.[36]

But Nietzsche's view of reality cannot get beyond the terrible ambiguity of loneliness in the world, against which Bonhoeffer rightly affirms the reality of co-humanity, willed by God in his structuring of the world, and embodied by Christ in his life and death for others.

Bonhoeffer thus agrees with Nietzsche on the primacy of reality in his own battle against a false interpretation of a Christianity that has become an inaccessible other-worldly ideal. But Bonhoeffer disagrees with Nietzsche about the nature of that reality. For Nietzsche it is the courage of frozen solitude, while for Bonhoeffer it is the acceptance of the givenness of co-humanity. While Nietzschian freedom is a total protest against the deceptions of idealism, it is still without doubt a hatred of the reality of the neighbor.

We are something else than *"libres-penseurs," "liberi pensatori,"* "free-thinkers," and whatever these honest advocates of "modern ideas" like to call themselves . . . sometimes night-owls of work even in full day: yea, if necessary, even scarecrows – and it is necessary nowadays, that is to say, inasmuch as we are the born, sworn, jealous friends of solitude of our own profoundest midnight and mid-day solitude: such kind of men are we, we free spirits: And perhaps *ye* are

---

[35] Nietzsche, *Beyond Good and Evil*, para. 10, cited in *The Philosophy of Nietzsche*, Modern Library, New York, p. 9.
[36] Nietzsche, *op. cit.*, para. 45, p. 53.

also something of the same kind, ye coming ones? ye *new* philosophers?[37]

What, then, is reality? Nietzsche replied that it is the superman protesting against the deception of ideas, whereas Bonhoeffer maintained that it is Christ with man in the midst of the world. And what is the concrete commandment? Not ideal against existence, but the reality given by God and embodied in Christ for the restructuring of the world, to be followed by all in order that our penultimate realities may be protected by his ultimate grace. Bonhoeffer's *Ethics*, incomplete and many-sided as it is, is important because of its agreement with Nietzsche on the primacy of the concrete, as well as because of the basic disagreement between the two men about the nature of reality.

[37] Nietzsche, *op. cit.*, para. 44. In this passage Nietzsche is scoffing at Feuerbach's humanitarianism. Karl Barth characterizes Nietzsche as basically "the prophet of ... humanity without the fellow-man" (*Church Dogmatics* III/2, p. 232).

VII

Christianity without "Religion"?

1. *Text and context*

Bonhoeffer's *Letters and Papers from Prison* were published in 1951. Not only are they a moving testimony to the last years of his life, but they have also become one of the most provocative resources for theological thought in the middle of the twentieth century. They are even more fragmentary than *Ethics*, consisting of letters to his parents, his close friend Bethge and his fiancée, Maria von Wedemeyer,[1] as well as a number of poems, prayers and brief essays.

Bonhoeffer remained in the Tegel military prison in Berlin for eighteen months, from 5 April 1943 to 8 October 1944. He received permission to write letters through the prison censor. But very soon, thanks to one of the prison guards, Corporal Knobloch, he was able to get letters smuggled out. While he was in prison, Bonhoeffer read incessantly, and in the last letter to be delivered, dated 17 January 1945, we find him asking his father to send him works of Pestalozzi, Natorp and Plutarch.

Until the failure of the plot against Hitler on 20 July 1944, Bonhoeffer believed that the case against him would be dropped. Both he and his brother-in-law, Hans von Dohnanyi, had

---

[1] The letters to his fiancée are not included in *Letters and Papers from Prison*. They have been deposited in the Houghton Library at Harvard University, but are not available to the public. They will not be published. Maria von Wedemeyer-Weller, however, has published some extracts from them in her article "The Other Letters from Prison," in Vorkink, ed., *Bonhoeffer in a World Come of Age*, 1968, pp. 103–43. Several excerpts from these are included below to supplement material from the more readily available *Letters and Papers*.

originally been arrested only for having violated certain rules of the counter-espionage agency (*Abwehr*) to which they were attached, and which served as a camouflage for their anti-Nazi activities. Even before his arrest Bonhoeffer had refused to flee, fearing that reprisals would be taken against one of his brothers who had already been arrested. On 13 July 1943, Keitel dismissed the charge of "high treason" against Bonhoeffer, and retained only that of "subversion of the armed forces." From that time on the problem was to safeguard the camouflage, to present his various trips to foreign countries as undertaken in the interest of the unity of the church and of peace, to learn how to be silent in order to cover up what he was actually doing – in a word to play the political game of telling lies for the sake of truth as well as he could. Bonhoeffer proved extremely adroit at this. The letters give no hint of this background of political shrewdness and delicate manoeuvering that he was engaging in to lull the authorities to sleep. It is not hard to tell why! But these experiences played a hidden yet fundamental role in Bonhoeffer's thinking about man's "coming of age," his "godforsakenness" before God, and his obligation to respond to Jesus' commandment in sending forth the disciples (with which Bonhoeffer had also dealt in *The Cost of Discipleship*), "Be wise as serpents and innocent as doves. Beware of men . . ." (Matt. 10.16).

There is a direct echo of all this in Bonhoeffer's essay, 'What Is Meant by 'Telling the Truth'?", which is printed in *Ethics*, but which was actually written while Bonhoeffer was in Tegel. In it, Bonhoeffer explains why "telling the truth" has different implications according to the situations in which we find ourselves. He disagrees with Kant who pushed the categorical imperative of truthfulness to absurd lengths, saying that "he would feel himself obliged to give truthful information even to a criminal looking for a friend of his who had concealed himself in his house."[2] One does not serve the truth, Bonhoeffer insists, by throwing it about carelessly, either candidly or cynically. One must learn to speak it in relation to the reality of the questioner, the context and the circumstances. The word only seems to be true if it is spoken without taking account of the one to whom it is spoken. Truth apart from reality is the

[2] Cf. Bonhoeffer, *Ethics*, pp. 363–72, quotation on p. 369.

delusion of idealism. To be sure, the realism of truth is dangerous. It can even lead to the destruction of truth itself. It is dangerous to live in such a way that one is finally answerable only to the living God. Here we confront the "exceptional situation" that results from Bonhoeffer's solitude in prison. Again and again he comments to Bethge about his need to be checked by the opinions of others, and his thirst for communal sharing. But that is what reality has become. For in the final analysis, responsibility, like death, must be faced alone.

With such considerations we are already into the well-known problem of the prison letters: how to live paradoxically before God without God, with God though apart from God; how to identify oneself with the reality of the world while still holding on to the identity of faith in the reality of God; how to be faithful, with God, to the reality of the world without God. The letter of 1943 that Bethge places at the end of "What Is Meant by 'Telling the Truth'?" is relevant here:

Nietzsche says that "every profound mind has need of a mask." In my view "telling the truth" means saying how something is in reality, i.e. respect for secrecy, confidence and concealment. "Betrayal," for example, is not truth, nor are frivolity, cynicism, etc. What is concealed must be disclosed only at confession, i.e. before God.[3]

Attention has been given to this example of the truth as hidden in reality without God, and confessed in reality before God, for the same problem is present both in the *Ethics* where Bonhoeffer refines his concepts, and in the prison letters where he embodies them. The example supports the thesis I wish to defend here, namely that the later Bonhoeffer thought in perfect continuity with all of his preceding work although in a much more radically confined context. Until he entered Tegel, Bonhoeffer continually examined the unity-in-tension between God and reality that is found in Jesus Christ, under-stood both as the structure of reality and the one crucified

[3] Bonhoeffer, *Ethics*, p. 372. The letter is dated "Advent II" in *LPP*, pp. 104f., but the paragraph here quoted is omitted, and can be found only in *Ethics*. Note that when Bethge published the fragments of the *Ethics* in 1948, he did not hesitate to conclude them with a letter written from prison in 1943. The problem of a possible shift of position between the Bonhoeffer of the *Ethics* and the Bonhoeffer of *LPP* is only raised later, after the publication of the letters in 1951.

within it. But in Tegel, Bonhoeffer affirmed that unity, by living out the tension of being faithful before God in this life no matter what the cost. The prison letters deal with the claim that God is in the midst of a "godless" world, in order that the believer may sustain before God the reality abandoned by God. This is surely a paradox. But the same thing is in *Ethics*:

There are, therefore, not two spheres, but only the one sphere of the realization of Christ, in which the reality of God and the reality of the world are united.[4]

In Tegel, the reality of the world is perceived more clearly than before as "non-religious" and even "without God." But the underlying principles of Bonhoeffer's thought are unchanging, as is the paradox that runs through all his work.

Such, however, is not the usual judgment of Bonhoeffer's interpreters. Intrigued by the spirit of discovery that begins with his long letter of 30 April 1944,[5] they believe in the existence of a real "epistemological shift," to use the expression of Bachelard that Louis Althusser has popularized.[6] A new Bonhoeffer then comes into view – of the highest importance or else extremely disconcerting, depending on who is talking. On the positive side, this is where Hanfried Müller approvingly locates the break that enlarged Bonhoeffer's vision from the community of the church to that of the global society. According to him, whereas *Ethics* still looks to Christendom's past, the prison letters from April 1944 on finally relate the hidden Word of the cross directly to the self-sufficient secularity of the world. On the negative side, however, John Godsey characterizes Bonhoeffer's third period as one of "theological fragmentation." Even more negatively, René Marlé is alarmed by what he calls the "disturbing vision" of "the dissolution of

---

[4] *Ethics*, p. 197.

[5] William Hamilton has most strongly emphasized the rupture that is introduced by the appearance of "non-religious Christianity" in a "world come of age." He feels that the theme of the letter of 30 April 1944 is begun in the letters of 18 December 1943 and 23 January 1944. Cf. "'The Letters are a Particular Thorn'; Some Themes in Bonhoeffer's Prison Writings," R. Gregor Smith, ed., *World Come of Age*, pp. 131–60.

[6] L. Althusser, *For Marx*, Pantheon, New York, 1970. If, as Althusser believes, Marx did not really become a "Marxist" until 1845, then surely Bonhoeffer did not really become a "Bonhoefferian" until April 1944.

Christianity" although he stresses the difference between Bonhoeffer's inspiration, "mystical in the best sense of the word," and the "mistaken or destructive theories" into which future generations may distort mystical ideas.[7] Bethge himself takes account of a "new start" in April 1944, before the failure of the plot against Hitler on 20 July and independently of it.[8] He feels that Bonhoeffer entered a new period of theological creativity at this time, turned away in large part from reading about the past (novels and history), began once again to do basic work in the philosophy of knowledge, wrote the lost book about which the prison letters give us only a smattering of information, and overflowed with new ideas that kept appearing right up to the final letters that have survived.[9]

That there is a final burst of creative energy is an undeniable and fascinating fact. But is it appropriate to describe it as a period of transformation and contradiction as Müller does, of "fragmentation" as Godsey does, of a "disturbing vision" as Marlé does, or even of "a new start" as Bethge does? I do not believe so. To call Bonhoeffer's writings paradoxical, as I prefer to do, is to describe certain inner contradictions in each of them taken by itself, not to compare successive stages of development from text to text. Bonhoeffer's central conviction remains unchanged throughout: in Jesus Christ God is present in the midst of the reality of the world. The truth of this reality is expressed in different ways in different periods of Bonhoeffer's life, depending on the question, the context and the place. These vary. The early context is the university, during the period of *Communion of Saints* and *Act and Being*; next comes the Confessing Church, at the time of *The Cost of Discipleship* and *Life Together*; and finally, of course, there is the world – ambiguous, penultimate, disguised, abandoned, and yet

---

[7] Marlé, *Bonhoeffer*, pp. 119f.   [8] Bethge, *op. cit.*, pp. 762f.

[9] In his biography, Bethge stresses two inner shifts in Bonhoeffer's development. The first of these in January 1935 is the conversion from "theologian" to "Christian," the second in April 1944 from "Christian" to "contemporary." Paul Lehmann, however, seems to me rightly to challenge this notion of shifts, which in themselves challenge the overall theme of Bethge's biography, with its emphasis on the organic continuity of Bonhoeffer's thought. "If there is an organic development in Bonhoeffer's thought, why does Bethge admit to a shift? If there is nevertheless a shift (in 1944) what is it precisely? Is it a shift of position or of accent? Bethge leaves the question unsatisfactorily open" (*Union Seminary Quarterly Review*, Autumn 1967, p. 104).

accountable, already visible in the theoretical presentation of
Ethics, and even more in its living embodiment in the *Letters
and Papers from Prison*. The place where Bonhoeffer sets forth
the truth about reality may change, but not its content. God's
"space" is the world and the secret of the world is the hidden
presence of God. Jesus Christ is the structure of that "space"
and the name of that secret.

There is a larger question that can provide another test
of our thesis that there is a logical continuity in Bonhoeffer's
thought throughout his trying but triumphant confinement in
prison. If *Letters and Papers from Prison* is full of paradoxes,
sometimes so obscure as to seem equivocal, is it not also the
case that long before those letters, as far back as the beginning
of his work, Bonhoeffer had been wrestling with basic questions:
can the God of reality, in the midst of the world, be called an
immanent (even if hidden) structure of the everyday empirical
world? Can the ontology of the creaturely-existence (*Dasein*) of
Jesus Christ be called an "anonymous" ontology of global
reality? Can the christological transcendence of this world
be expressed, without reduction, by the transcendence of the
love of neighbor, as William Hamilton believed, twenty years
later, it could be understood?

Faith has almost collapsed into love, and the Protestant is no longer
defined as the forgiven sinner . . . but as the one beside the neighbor,
beside the enemy, at the disposal of the man in need.[10]

To sum up – and Bonhoeffer never gave up grappling with his
own question – what kind of relationship is possible between a
theology of the Word and a theology of ontological presence?
What happens is simply that this discussion becomes more
apparent, more challenging, more unsettling and more
absorbing when Bonhoeffer, in his prison letters, goes on to
speak of the ontological presence in a world visibly without
God.

But we must come back to the letters of 1943–4 and explore
more fully the context out of which they came. Their well-known

[10] Hamilton, "The Death of God Theologies Today," in T. J. J. Altizer and
W. Hamilton, *Radical Theology and the Death of God*, Bobbs-Merrill, New York
1966, pp. 36f. I reserve my own comments on these questions for the final chapter
below, "The God of Reality and the Reality of God."

theme, "the non-religious interpretation of Christianity in a world come of age," arises out of Bonhoeffer's continual reflection on the reality of daily life. In this particular situation, it is the absence of an experience of God that spurs Bonhoeffer to reflect theologically on the presence of God in the world that lies ahead. Although he is in prison, Bonhoeffer does not lose touch with reality. He does not lose his footing either in the nostalgia of idealism or in the destructiveness of nihilism. He leaves yesterday to those who are shocked by events and to-morrow to those who take refuge in prophecies. He shows a strong preference for nineteenth-century writers, theologians, historians and particularly novelists, for, as he puts it, "they treat the most delicate matters without flippancy, and they express their convictions without pathos."[11] He expresses his gratitude for the bourgeois heritage in which he grew up. He never stops preparing for the things he hopes to do when he is released. He works out a paper on prison reform. In letters to his fiancée he foresees their home and what they will do, learning to dance and taking up riding! He urges Maria to practice the violin and to study English. On 12 August 1943, he wrote her:

Jeremiah says at the moment of his people's great need, "still one shall buy houses and acres in this land," as a sign of trust in the future. This is where faith belongs. May God give it to us daily. And I do not mean the faith which flees the world, but the one that endures the world and which loves and remains true to the world in spite of all the suffering which it contains for us. Our marriage shall be a yes to God's earth; it shall strengthen our courage to act and accomplish something on the earth. I fear that Christians who stand with only one leg on earth also stand with only one leg in heaven.[12]

This time of reading and writing was also a time of suffering. Bonhoeffer sometimes described the sadness that came over him in waves, the *acedia* of heart that made him long for those he loved. He asked to be given as much advance notice as possible of family visits so that he could live in anticipation of them. He had met his fiancée for the first time when she was only twelve years old, on the estate of her grandmother Frau Ruth von Kleist-Retzow. She was now nineteen years old.

[11] Bonhoeffer, *LPP*, 25 July 1943, p. 60.
[12] Cited in Vorkink, ed., *Bonhoeffer in a World Come of Age*, pp. 107f.

Their engagement was announced the day after Bonhoeffer's arrest. She came to see him regularly at Tegel and even brought him a Christmas tree. She did her best to convert him to her enthusiasm for Rilke, Bergengruen, Binding and Ernst Wiechert, but Bonhoeffer remained reticent about what he called the "insipid" quality of recent literature, "the thin lemonade ... with no insight, no ideas, no clarity, no substance, and almost always the language is bad and restricted."[13] With all the ardor of her nineteen years, Maria valiantly started reading *The Communion of Saints*, but became frustrated by its abstract language, to the great amusement of her fiancé. Twenty-five years later she wrote, recalling the visiting room in the prison:

He was able to convert painful longing into gratitude for the fact that there was something to anticipate; he was able to convert self-reproach for the suffering he may have caused others into a joy that those relationships existed at all. He was able to transform the fumbling and erratic emotions of a young girl into the assured certainty that this was an addition of strength to his own life.[14]

But the naturalness of these meetings did not remove the reality of the situation. "Man," Bonhoeffer wrote to Maria, "is created from earth, and does not consist of air or thoughts."[15] It was to Maria also that he confided his melancholy comments about the inability of the middle class to act responsibly in times of decision:

I believe that the weakness of our class is based on its justified or unjustified scruples. Simple people are different. They make more mistakes, but they also do more good, because their road to action does not lead through scruple.[16]

He explained to her why his own family was so unexpressive in contrast to hers, particularly where religious matters were concerned. He also wrote her about the pain of life:

Isn't it so that even when we are laughing, we are a bit sad? ... It would be better if I succeeded in writing to you only of my gratitude, my joy, and my happiness in having you and in keeping the pressure and the impatience of this long imprisonment out of

---

[13] Cited in Bethge, *op. cit.*, p. 747.   [14] Vorkink, ed., *op. cit.*, pp. 103f.
[15] Vorkink, ed., *op. cit.*, p. 110.   [16] Vorkink, ed., *op. cit.*, p. 107.

sight. But that would not be truthful, and it would appear to me as an injustice to you. You must know how I really feel, and not take me for a pillar saint (*Saeulenheiligen*).[17]

Your life would have been quite different, easier, clearer, simpler had not our path crossed a year ago . . . I believe that happiness lies for both of us at a different and hidden place which is incomprehensible to many . . . Only in this work will we grow completely together when God gives us the time for it.[18]

Stifter once said, "pain is a holy angel, who shows treasures to men which otherwise remain forever hidden; through him men have become greater than through all joys of the world." It must be so and I tell this to myself in my present position over and over again – the pain of longing which often can be felt even physically, must be there, and we shall not and need not talk it away. But it needs to be overcome every time, and thus there is an even holier angel than the one of pain, that is the one of joy in God.[19]

After Bonhoeffer was transferred to the Gestapo prison in October 1944 his fiancée could no longer visit him. It is unlikely that he received any more of her letters. After February 1945 he simply disappeared from sight, and Maria sought him in vain in the camps at Dachau, Buchenwald and Flossenburg. It was not until several months later that the circumstances surrounding his execution on 9 April 1945 became known. The last letter that Maria received was written on 19 December 1944:

In solitude the soul develops senses which we hardly know in everyday life. Therefore I have not felt lonely or abandoned for one moment. You, the parents, all of you, the friends and students of mine at the front, all are constantly present to me. Your prayers and good thoughts, words from the Bible, discussions long past, pieces of music, and books – [all these] gain life and reality as never before. It is a great invisible sphere in which one lives and in whose reality there is no doubt. If it says in the old children's song about the angels: "Two to cover me, two to wake me," so is this guardianship (*Bewahrung*), by good invisible powers in the morning and at night, something which grown-ups need today no less than children. Therefore you must not think that I am unhappy. What is happiness

[17] *Ibid.*, pp. 109, 111.　　　[18] *Ibid.*, p. 112, 20 September 1943.
[19] *Ibid.*, p. 112, 21 November 1943.

and unhappiness? It depends so little on the circumstances; it depends really only on that which happens inside a person. I am grateful every day that I have you, and that makes me happy.[20]

Such was Bonhoeffer's personal life during the time he was thinking through the question, "Who is Jesus Christ today for a world of adults who no longer believe in angels ...?" and working out his ideas on the death of metaphysics and inwardness. We must now fill in the rest of the picture. In prison Bonhoeffer lived with men who never seemed to turn to God when life was falling apart, when fear was uppermost or even when death was imminent – whether the crisis was a court decision against politicians or deserters, the incessant Allied bombardment of Berlin and all of Germany, or the whole upheaval of war, repression and disaster. In distinction from what is usually said about the religious impact of great times of testing, both individual and collective, these men in the midst of danger were not changed into the "religious" creatures that Feuerbach described as "candidates for heaven" and "beggars in the sky." Contemporary man, Bonhoeffer remarks, has no religious inclination whatsoever. He has neither metaphysical concerns nor a pious inner life. He has become finite man, completely at home in this world. He no longer has anything in common with the two great human responses that had been around for centuries and even millennia: the archaic man who lived by myths and divided his life religiously, and his successor, the classical man, who lived by metaphysics and divided his experience intellectually, and who from Plato through Descartes to Kant, affirmed the immortality of the soul and the eternality of reason. Contemporary man simply does not divide life that way any longer. He struggles, endures, submits, resists and dies. And the question is whether Christianity can make any impact whatever on this "third man" who has emerged in our cultural history.

It is precisely to this point that the theological inquiry of Bonhoeffer's final letters is directed. The problem is described in the famous letter of 30 April 1944, at the moment when, as he believes, "great decisions will already be setting things moving on all fronts."

[20] *Ibid.*, p. 113. Note the strong similarity between this letter and Bonhoeffer's last known poem, "Powers of Good," written about the same time (*LPP*, p. 221).

What is bothering me incessantly is the question what Christianity really is, or indeed who Christ really is, for us today. The time when people could be told everything by means of words, whether theological or pious, is over, and so is the time of inwardness and conscience – and that means the time of religion in general. We are moving towards a completely religionless time; people as they are now simply cannot be religious any more. Even those who honestly describe themselves as "religious" do not in the least act up to it, and so they presumably mean something quite different by "religious." Our whole nineteen-hundred-year-old Christian preaching and theology rest on the "religious *a priori*" of mankind. "Christianity" has always been a form – perhaps the true form – of "religion." But if one day it becomes clear that this *a priori* does not exist at all, but was a historically conditioned and transient form of human self-expression and if therefore man becomes radically religionless – ... what does that mean for "Christianity"?[21]

It is important to notice that Bonhoeffer says "we" and not "they." He found that he himself was like the "non-religious" men who surrounded him in prison. Like them he lived a life of finitude and this-worldliness; like them (even though he could write to his fiancée about angels without any sense of contradiction between his ideas and his prayers) he did not feel the need to turn to another world in order to solve the problems of this world in illusory fashion. And yet throughout all of this he continued to believe in Jesus Christ. There is no trace whatever of what might be called a "crisis of faith." Thus his problem was not the problem of "apologetics," i.e. how in this new situation to offer other men a Christianity that would no longer be based on the presupposition of religious need. Basic for Bonhoeffer was a troublesome problem of logical coexistence: how to live out the identity of my faith in Jesus Christ when I also recognize my deep identification with the world of non-religion.[22] In establishing that he himself was both a believer and a non-religious person, Bonhoeffer indicated his simultaneous commitment to God and the world, but he was troubled about what would happen to theology,

[21] Bonhoeffer, *LPP*, pp. 152f.

[22] This dialectic of identity-identification is borrowed from Bethge. It clearly captures the personal course of Bonhoeffer's own self-questioning, the troubling consequences of which he did not deny: "How can Christ become the Lord of the religionless as well? Are there religionless Christians?" (*LPP*, 20 April 1944, p. 153).

church, and liturgy in trying to cope with such a strange and novel situation.

He looked around to see who had already confronted the problem and he mentioned the early Barth of the *Epistle to the Romans*. It is not clear that this reference is much help. Many times in the course of its history Christianity has been presented as different from other religions and even as opposed to the essence of religion. To understand Bonhoeffer's "non-religious interpretation of Christianity," it will be necessary to grasp his specific understanding of "religion" and remove from the word the vagueness with which present discussion surrounds it, so that if today it is venerated by some, it is more often despised. This can be done, it seems to me, only by differentiating Bonhoeffer's understanding of religion from other understandings that may be close in meaning but are differently focussed and motivated. We shall take the two examples of primitive Christianity and Barth's theology, since Bonhoeffer's justification for his own conclusions is limited to these two precedents. (Feuerbach, who is often referred to in discussions of this problem, is mentioned only once in *Letters and Papers from Prison*, in the letter of 16 July 1944, on p. 196.)

2. *Christianity's case against religion*

During the greater part of its history, Christianity has been presented as the true religion of mankind. The Roman Catholic theologian, Fr Bernhard Häring, expresses the usual position in describing everything that is concerned with our relationship to God, the worship offered to God and the community of those who are united among themselves by the same faith and the same worship as possessing the quality of religion. According to Fr Häring, "religion is a filial relationship with God expressed in the worship of his glory."[23] Consistent with this widely accepted understanding, Calvin had no hesitation in writing *The Institutes of the Christian Religion*, and Pascal, even less suspect than Calvin of complacency toward "natural religion," always spoke in the *Pensées* of Christianity as a religion, prefixing the adjective "true," as Barth does in his *Church Dogmatics*. Some experts feel that our word "religion" is derived from

---

[23] Häring, *La Loi du Christ*, Vol. II, Desclée, Paris-Tournai 1957, p. 140.

religare (to bind or fasten), while others feel that it comes from *relegere* (to cultivate or gather again, as opposed to *negligere*, to neglect). But in both cases the word "religion" is a good way to describe the worship rendered to the One to whom we are bound by faith, obedience, hope and love.

Nevertheless, the use of the word "religion" to describe biblical faith has always raised problems, and we shall briefly deal with the two instances of opposition to the term that influenced Bonhoeffer.

1. Let us look first at why early Christianity refused to let itself be called a "religion."[24] From the standpoint of Greek and Latin thought, "religion" sometimes stood for poetic and mythical theogonies, sometimes for the portion of a philosophical system that followed logics and physics, and sometimes for the worship of the emperor. Ordinarily referred to in the plural, the "religions" laid down the sacred obligations that were incumbent upon the head of the household and the ancient city: scrupulous and careful observance of religious ceremonies, pious reverence, venerable beliefs, and, of course, worship and sacred actions. Man bound himself to the gods by vows, oaths and even bandages (cf. *religare*, to bind); he also paid respect to the gods (cf. *relegere* in the sense of to recollect, to recall, almost the equivalent of *colere*, to take pains).

The hesitation, indeed the refusal, of the early Christians to adopt this sort of vocabulary and practice was deep-rooted, as a few examples will show. The word "religion" (Greek *threskeia*) appears only three times in the New Testament, once favorably in an insignificant passage in James 1.26, and twice unfavorably, in Col. 2.18 (a discussion of the gnostic cult of angels) and Acts 26.5 (a treatment of the rigidity of the Pharisees). The Greek word *eusebeia*, which stands for the inner

---

[24] Cf. *Dictionnaire de Théologie catholique*, Letouzey, Paris 1939 and 1956, the article "Religion" by E. Magnin, Vol. XIII, part 2, pp. 218ff., and the article "Théologie" by Fr Yves Congar OP, Vol. XV, part 2, pp. 342ff. The same Christian hesitation that surrounded the word "religion" also surrounded the word "theology." Until the time of Clement of Alexandria, the Greek fathers avoided it. The "theologian" *par excellence* was the pagan poet Orpheus. Until the time of St Augustine, the Latin fathers used the word only in a polemical sense. In the Middle Ages preference was given to such terms as *sacra doctrina* and *scripturae eruditio*. And Luther continued to hear overtones in the word that were more Aristotelian than clearly Christian.

religious life in differentiation from the emphasis of *threskeia* on external ceremonies, appears more frequently, but with the exception of Acts 3.12 (where Peter characterizes the faith of the early Christian community as *eusebeia* in the eyes of the Israelite onlookers since they do not understand its origins), the word is found only in the late New Testament writings, ten times in I and II Timothy and Titus, and four times in II Peter. Finally, *deisidaimonia*, veneration of the supernatural, appears only twice. It is used with flattering irony in Paul's speech on Mars Hill to characterize the excess of Greek religiosity toward the gods known and even unknown (Acts 17.22), and is also used by Festus with the scorn of a high functionary for the strange beliefs of his subordinates (Acts 25.19). Never once is "religion" used to describe the new faith in positive terms.

Thus all along the line the New Testament avoids a vocabulary based on pagan notions of religion. To express its doctrine, ecclesiology and ethics, the New Testament drew its new vocabulary from the non-religious world – psychological, political, domestic, military, athletic, commercial and financial. It spoke not of religion but of grace and faith; not of the priest (*iereus*) but of the overseer (*episcopos*), the elder (*presbyteros*) and the deacon (*diaconos*); not of cultic associations but of a civic assembly (*ekklesia*, ecclesiastical) and of an outlying colony (*paroikia*, parish); not of sacraments but of washing, submersion (*baptisma*) and a meal (*agape*, *eucharistia*).

In this way, the new covenant carried on in its own situation the same struggle as the old. In the Old Testament, faith in the Word of Yahweh was opposed to all the surrounding religions, whether these were cults of earthly fertility, celestial astrology, veneration of the beyond or deification of the king. Yahweh forbade his people to create gods from human mysteries of procreation or mortality, since the true God, Yahweh, is creator rather than procreator. He is a living God rather than one who is re-born on the far side of death as vegetation and planets are, or immortal on this side of death as are the Olympian deities who gradually escape the cycle of birth and decay. Isaiah mocks the gods of the religions that Yahweh has allotted to the other peoples of the earth (Deut. 4.19). The gods, i.e. the "graven images" (*eidolon*, idols, ideas) that men make for themselves, have ears but hear nothing, eyes but see nothing, and hands but do nothing (Isa. 44.9–20). They are visible and powerless, whereas Yahweh alone is invisible and powerful. As Alan Richardson makes the point, "The worship of Jehovah was not *one* of the religions of the Fertile Crescent. It implied the abolition of religion as the ancient world understood it."[25]

During the period of its creative expansion, Christianity continued this struggle of faith against the religions of the time, although this is more difficult for us to trace because of the Christian "religious" history that followed in its wake. For the early Christians, however, "religion" meant idols, false gods, imperial worship, spiritual syncretism, and a false deification of family, city and nature. Consequently Christians in this era are taken for atheists, just as Socrates was. In A.D. 155 Polycarp was condemned and burned in Smyrna for "pulling down our gods" and refusing to repeat in the sense demanded by the proconsul, "Away with the atheists," in the sense of pledging loyalty to Caesar and the state divinities.[26]

The reasons for this Christian and more generally biblical disavowal of religions and "religion" are numerous: the specificity and the newness of the revelation, the rejection of idols as the fruits of human ignorance, fear and desire, and the fact that Yahweh had been encountered as one who was present though invisible on Mount Sinai, rather than as one who was absent though visible in Baal and the golden calf. Hemmed in by a great many very religious men, the biblical believer refused to let his "non-religious" faith become identified with his religious quest for the unknown. It is "when the gods are silent"[27] that man hears the One who says to him simply, "I am who I am" (Ex. 4.14). The One who speaks thus is Yahweh, the founder and partner of the covenant, who sent his Son, not as a religious demi-god but as an ordinary man, to live, work and die, in order to raise him up as the one who had earned the reward of such freely-given obedience, being raised up physically (neither metaphysically nor spiritually) beyond mortality.

[25] Richardson, *Religion in Contemporary Debate*, SCM Press, London, and Westminster Press, Philadelphia 1966, p. 26.

[26] Richardson, *op. cit.*, p. 61.

[27] Cf. the title of an important work by K. H. Miskotte, *When the Gods are Silent*, Harper and Row, Inc., New York, and Collins, London 1967.

Primitive Christianity was not a "religion," because it refused to be part of the idolatrous extension of nature worship or the gnostic preoccupation with the beyond.

2. Let us now turn to the second example that influenced Bonhoeffer as he looked at precedents for his understanding of a "non-religious interpretation of Christianity." This is the early Karl Barth and his commentary on *The Epistle to the Romans*.[28] In the first two editions, those of Berne in 1919 and of Munich in 1922, the discussion of religion was centered on Romans 7, which examined Christian freedom from the law, the role of that law, and the realm of sin that alienated man from himself. In the 1919 edition, Barth attacked both romanticism and pietism. In the 1922 edition, however, religion became the dominant theme, and was treated in a truly dialectical fashion that Barth did not have to modify in his long discussion of religion in paragraph 17 of his *Church Dogmatics*, published in 1939. In three successive sections, Barth deals with the frontier of religion (Rom. 7.1–6), the meaning of religion (Rom. 7.7–13) and the reality of religion (Rom. 7.14–25). As Barth sees it, religion constitutes the impossible effort of man to raise himself up to fellowship with God in a sinful attempt at self-justification. At the very outset, he insists that grace is related to religion "as life is related to death."[29] Religion cannot rescue man from his destructive ambiguity. It simply leaves him caught in all his dualisms between "there" and "here," presupposition and fact, truth and reality. It is a catastrophic pretension on man's part in the face of the freedom of divine grace. The religious need, which Barth insists is present in all mankind, therefore only witnesses, like the ethical alternative, to the destruction of man's immediacy with God. Man's religious experience makes clear that he cannot encounter anyone other than himself. The moment of Jesus' "religious consciousness" at Golgotha was precisely the discovery that he

---

[28] On Barth's understanding of religion, cf. *inter alia* Henri Bouillard sj, *Karl Barth*, Paris 1957, Vol. I, pp. 53–60; Benkt Erik Benkston, *Die Religion bei Barth, Bonhoeffer und Tillich*, Calwer Verlag, 1967; John Baillie, *The Sense of the Presence of God*, Oxford University Press, London, and Scribners, New York 1962, Ch. IX. "Faith and the Faiths"; Emil Brunner, *Revelation and Reason*, Westminster Press, Philadelphia 1946, and SCM Press, London 1947.

[29] Barth, *The Epistle to the Romans*, Oxford University Press, London 1932, p. 229.

was abandoned by God. Religion is nothing but a problem for mankind. Its dream of relationship with God only underlines its separation from the One who is truly God. Thus, like all human passion, religion draws its strength out of human mortality. It is the opium of faith that only serves to stimulate man's spiritual *eros*. Barth praises Feuerbach (who would scarcely have appreciated the reason for the commendation) for having pointed out man's desire to overstep the boundaries, and his failure to do so, in a rude awakening that leaves him worse off than before. That is why Barth identifies the religious impulse with the "thorn" of the law. Christ is the end of the law, the frontier of religion.[30]

At this point we discover that grace, as the antithesis of religion, can become religion's salvation. If there is any meaning to religion, it can only be in the destructive sense that it turns inside out everything that it vainly claims to accomplish. According to Barth's first image, the religion of mankind is the "transgression of the fatal line laid down for us," "the drunken blurring of the distance which separates us from God," "our devotion to some romantic infinity," "our investing of men with the form of God, and of God with the form of man," "the divinisation of man and the humanising of God," the "shameless anticipation" of what can come to us only from God alone. Religious man is "that most obstinate species of the human genus," "a sinner in the most obvious sense of the word." "From the grossest superstition to the most delicate spirituality, from naked rationalism to the most subtle mysticism of the metaphysician," religion remains "on this side of the abyss," scarcely to be differentiated from hunger and the need for sleep and sex. Now unfortunately Christianity and atheism are filled with this kind of religion: "All human activity, from the devotional exercises of a Benedictine monastery to the vigorous and comprehensive programme of the Social Democrats, is enacted on the rungs of one single ladder." And it is very clear that as far as Barth is concerned, this particular ladder leads neither to God nor to heaven.[31]

[30] Barth, *op. cit.*, pp. 236–8. There is a fuller treatment of Feuerbach in Barth, *Theology and Church*, SCM Press, London, and Harper and Row, New York 1962, pp. 217–37.

[31] The above quotations from Barth's *Epistle to the Romans* are collected in H. Zahrnt, *The Question of God*, Collins, London 1969, pp. 34f. Zahrnt goes on to

However, the dialectical movement now begins all over again, for like the law, religion has a positive function: it demonstrates the reality of sin. In showing the impossibility of self-sufficient human pretension, it induces a crisis which is man's judgment. In being the supreme "illusion," just as Freud insisted, in stirring up man's energies destructively, religion entraps him in his own sin. When illusions tumble, the real world is exposed and revealed. By separating truth from reality, religion creates the knowledge of death. Barth here refers to two religious figures, Prometheus, the mythological figure who stole fire from the gods, and Eve, the first religious personality, who "worships" Yahweh (as Michelangelo has shown so powerfully in "The Creation of Eve") at the same time as she is disputing about him from a distance.[32] In neither case does religion signify the harmony of the self with the infinite; instead, it is the revelation of finitude and death within the self. So religion must both judge and destroy. It is needed to implant God's "no" to man in the powerlessness of man's violent religious feeling. Once this limit has been reached, we can see the *positive* meaning of religion in humbling man's incredible pretension.

And when that has happened, the dialectical thrust can be continued until it comes full circle. As early as 1922, Barth had strongly affirmed the reality of religion. As one who is subject to both religion and law, man is caught in his mortality. But Christ lives. And far beyond anything that religious or pious men could do for themselves, there is Jesus Christ, stepping over the boundary line of death itself! God's revelation of himself supplies precisely what man's religious quest lacks. In discovering that he cannot save himself, man receives salvation. It is God above, and not man below, who makes

show that all the supporters of dialectical theology share in this Barthian understanding of religion: "Of all man's presumptions, that which is commonly known as religion is the most monstrous. For it is the presumption of seeking to bridge over from opposite to opposite, from creator to creature, and to do so by starting from the creature" (Gogarten). "Religion in itself is the most untenable of all the manifestations of man's destiny" (Brunner). "The watchword 'Yahweh *or* Baal' has been uttered, and anyone who has heard it can no longer change this 'or' into an 'and'. He may perhaps know these gods, but to him they are non-god, they are demons" (Thurneysen). Cf. *ibid.*, p. 44.
[32] Cf. Barth, *op. cit.*, p. 247.

religion function. Barth can talk about "the reality of religion," as he does in his third dialectical thrust, only when it is the religion of *grace*. Paragraph 17 of his *Church Dogmatics*, written in 1939, develops this dialectical inversion of religion at great length.[33] In it Barth uses Hegelian vocabulary to describe "the revelation of God as the abolition of religion."[34]

The revelation of God in the outpouring of the Holy Spirit is the judging but also reconciling presence of God in the world of human relation, that is, in the realm of man's attempts to justify and to sanctify himself before a capricious and arbitrary picture of God. The Church is the locus of true religion, so far as through grace it lives by grace.[35]

Barth feels that one of theology's most important tasks is to confront the religion of humanity in general, the "new world" that has arisen since the seventeenth and eighteenth centuries. According to Barth, who looks back toward German idealism and modern philosophies of religion, "the revelation of God is actually the presence of God and therefore the hiddenness of God in the world of human religion."[36]

But this is possible only on condition that the proper relationship between revelation and religion is carefully maintained. Contrary to the belief of modern Protestantism and its most illustrious spokesman Schleiermacher, theology must explain religion from the stance of revelation, and not vice versa. Once that stance has been secured, Barth says, theology can rediscover the way of St Thomas and John Calvin. By giving up any attempt to raise itself from "natural religion" or religion-in-general to the "special instance" of Christian revelation, theology can speak of *true* religion, which is embodied in Christian faith. Barth continues to maintain in 1939 as he had in 1922 that in the natural order of things religion is unbelief, the being of man without God, the sign of presumption and arbitrariness, i.e. the sign of man's basic weakness. Mysticism and atheism are the two aspects of that weakness, the first a

[33] Barth, *Church Dogmatics* I/2, T. and T. Clark, Edinburgh 1956, pp. 280–361.
[34] In Hegel's *Phenomenology of Mind*, *Aufhebung* means both abolition (*aufhören lassen*) and fulfillment (*aufbewahren*). The analogy with the law and justification in Barth suggests the same double meaning: revelation is the "abolition" of religion, in abolishing it as the sin of pretension, but also the "fulfillment" of religion as the forerunner of enacted grace.
[35] Barth, *op. cit.*, p. 280.   [36] Barth, *ibid.*, p. 282.

conserving force, the second a critical one, reflected in the double pretension of man's ignorance. However, in 1939 even more fully than in 1922, Barth affirmed that religion can become *true* religion, just as the sinner can become righteous and holy. Looked at from the vantage point of revealed grace, Christian religion accomplishes what the futile religious endeavors of Babel could not. Christianity has the right to call itself the religion of pure grace. When it is bound to God by election, human worship becomes both possible and blessed.

Justification of the Christian religion only by the name of Jesus Christ obviously involves a certain positive relation between the two ... That is why the problems of the nature and form of this religion are serious problems.[37]

Christianity can therefore be described by the word "religion" – not a religion that justifies man, but one that is itself justified by Jesus Christ.

In *Letters and Papers from Prison*, Bonhoeffer indicates surprise and annoyance that Barth had not continued his battle against religion:

Barth, who is the only one to have started along this line of thought, did not carry it to completion, but arrived at a positivism of revelation, which in the last analysis is essentially a restoration. For the religionless working man (or any other man) nothing decisive is gained here.[38]

But Bonhoeffer's critique misses the difference between the Barthian understanding of religion and his own. For Barth, all men are religious. To press the point, modern men since the eighteenth century are even more religious than men of an earlier era. Their religion is a self-justification that is all the more real and formidable since it is no longer a pagan idolatry outside of Christianity, as was true at the beginning of the Christian era, but an idolatry that has been Christianized. Dialectically, therefore, religion is a paradoxical sign of human weakness, a reminder of man's finitude, and the place where he is confronted by sin and death. But it is also true that as sin, religion can be condemned, justified, sanctified, restored, and fulfilled by grace. By itself, religion is impossible and illusory, but through revelation it can express reality. As a good

[37] Barth, *ibid.*, pp. 358, 360.   [38] Bonhoeffer, *LPP*, 30 April 1944, p. 153.

dialectician, therefore, Barth "abolishes" nothing. He attacks, criticizes, examines, turns things around, tests, builds and completes. He remains a Hegelian in the sense that he develops a synthetic approach through negation toward wholeness.

Bonhoeffer, however, works in a very different way. He is a paradoxical rather than a dialectical thinker. His attention is not focussed, like Barth's, on the "religious" eighteenth and nineteenth centuries, but on the "non-religious" twentieth century, and he observes that all twentieth-century men, himself included, manage to live without religion. Where early Christianity saw religion as the spread of idolatry and Barth sees it as spiritual covetousness, Bonhoeffer sees it simply as non-reality. This means that Barth is much closer to Feuerbach, Marx and Freud, who in their actual experience of the religious phenomenon in general and Christianity in particular identified it as a false projection, an imaginary detour and an obsessional phantasy for a lost object. Bonhoeffer himself is much closer to Nietzsche who describes how men have killed God and why the madman provokes such laughter in public places as he continues to look for God with his lantern. While Bonhoeffer feels that religion may have been neither impossible nor illusory, it has now, much more radically, become unreal. All this suggests that Bonhoeffer does not understand the problem Barth is dealing with, and Barth surely fails to understand Bonhoeffer's problem. Barth is upset by some non-systematic obscurities in Bonhoeffer, and Bonhoeffer is disconcerted by the classic and imposing way that Barth fulfills religion in the very process of "abolishing" it. He sees this abolition-fulfillment as a restoration of the non-reality of religion, and Barthianism by consequence as a positivistic orthodoxy that uses revelation to construct a world of theological truths alongside the reality of man and God.

From a certain point of view, therefore, Bonhoeffer's approach is much closer to that of early Christianity than to that of his great theological mentor Barth. He too is trying to find a non-religious vocabulary and mode of expression to speak of a God who is found in the midst of the reality of the world and not in some metaphysical beyond or in the inwardness of a divided reality. This perplexing task is the theological counterpart of what is being asked in contemporary philosophy: if metaphysics is both dead and buried for the same reasons that religion is, how can a sense of ontological openness be conveyed to those who do not want to reduce philosophy to pragmatism? This is the reason for the question marks at the end of the chapter titles "Ontology without Metaphysics?" and "Christianity without 'Religion'?"

On the basis of the above discussion, we are now sufficiently equipped to take up the distinctive themes with which Bonhoeffer examines the future of Christianity in the midst of a reality that no longer acknowledges the need of religion.

3. *Bonhoeffer's understanding of religion and reality*

Bonhoeffer's scattered flashes of insight on the development of faith in a new world that denies both metaphysics and inwardness can be read on three different levels: cultural, biblical and christological. Each level can be characterized by a key phrase: for the cultural level, "the world come of age"; for the biblical level, "this-worldly faith"; and for the christological level, the "godforsakenness of reality." Each level seems more profound, compressed and open to question than its predecessor.[39]

1. On the *cultural* level, Bonhoeffer observed that the world has already passed beyond the need of God. To characterize this new situation he chose the term "come of age" (*mündig*), the same word that Kant had used in his brief essay of 1784, "What is Enlightenment?" in which he said that "The Enlightenment is the emergence of man from immaturity that he himself is responsible for (*aus seiner selbstverschuldeten Unmündigkeit*)."[40] That Bonhoeffer draws the idea from Kant seems to be indicated by the following lines from the letter of 30 June 1944:

Now I will try to go on with the theological reflections that I broke off not long since. I had been saying that God is being increasingly

[39] Paul Ricoeur has published a perceptive commentary on "L'Interprétation non religieuse du Christianisme chez Bonhoeffer," in *Cahiers du Centre protestant de l'Ouest*, November 1966, pp. 3–20. Several of his formulations are used in what follows.

[40] Cited in Bethge, *Dietrich Bonhoeffer*, p. 770.

pushed out of a world that has come of age (*mündig*), out of the spheres of our knowledge and life, and that since Kant he has been relegated to a realm beyond the world of experience.[41]

This Kantian source makes it possible to interpret the meaning of the term correctly: to have "come of age" in Bonhoeffer's thought as well as in Kant's does not mean to be better or happier. It is simply a descriptive term that presupposes nothing about the optimism or the progressivism of its author. Nor does the term "come of age" stand for secularism – a word which, as Bethge has pointed out, Bonhoeffer never used after 1939, since it implied a certain contempt for the new-found reality of the world, or, according to other interpreters, a positive evaluation of it. However, Bonhoeffer was not interested in developing an interpretation of history, or hailing the rise of the Enlightenment at the end of the eighteenth century, as Kant had done. With an astonishing historical casualness, he concedes that the "coming of age" of the world, "the movement ... towards the autonomy of man," can be dated from the thirteenth century just as well as from the eighteenth.[42] Only one thing is of concern in the present discussion: in every realm of life God is ceasing to play the role of confirming or supplementing, in any causal or final sense, an analysis of the world or its functioning. The stop-gap god at the *lacunae* of what we can know, the *deus ex machina* god at the breakdown of what we can will, the hypothetical god at the limits of what we can do – all such gods have withered away. According to Bonhoeffer this withering away means the death of religion, which always lived off the unexplored areas of human experience. God continues to be reduced to just the degree that human knowledge is expanded. Religion decreases as scientific knowledge increases. What Bonhoeffer tells us here has become a commonplace in many

[41] Bonhoeffer, *LPP*, 30 June 1944, p. 188.
[42] Bonhoeffer, *LPP*, 8 June 1944, p. 178. This casualness toward past history seems to me to relieve us from the necessity of discussing the accuracy of Bonhoeffer's analyses of whether man and the contemporary world have really come of age or not. This does not seem to me any more useful than a discussion of Bultmann's description of the non-mythological character of modern man. Even if we concede that Bonhoeffer and Bultmann sin by oversimplification, their questions, which do not depend on their cultural appraisals, remain: what does faith become in the modern world?

quarters. Gabriel Marcel has also said that the application of the category of causality to God is the major contemporary reason for atheism (and the same thing has been true in relation to finality, notwithstanding Teilhard de Chardin). But the impassioned reaction that Bonhoeffer's pages have provoked shows how deeply rooted in the most "adult" minds is the identification of the creator God with the notion of the first cause or first principle of the phenomenal world – to such a degree that any attempt to separate them always causes scandal, either shaking people up or freeing them.

As Bonhoeffer sees it, this God who has become an unnecessary hypothesis, who has lost his usefulness and been relieved of his functions, takes refuge in two privileged places (similar to Kant's retreat into ideas that are regulative but not constitutive): metaphysics and inwardness. First of all, metaphysics:

We are in a cultural situation where "God" has been relegated to the edges of the world. In the final phase of this process men try to retain him as an answer to unanswerable questions. They have recourse to him to clear up an unresolved intellectual situation and such a "God," consigned to the outer reaches of life, on an increasingly narrow fringe, seems far off and insignificant.[43]

So much for the kingdom of ends. Next comes the appeal to inwardness:

When God was consigned to a place outside the world and the public sphere of life, he was retained in the personal, inward, private sphere of life . . . The God who simply fills up the gaps in our knowledge of the world is also the God who is experienced only at the edges of human life, i.e. in death, sin and suffering.[44]

So much for the legislator and consoler of human hearts.

Bonhoeffer insists that God is neither a refugee fleeing toward vanishing metaphysical frontiers, nor one who is painted into the corner of solitary inwardness:

I should like to speak of God not on the boundaries but at the centre, not in weakness but in strength; and therefore not in death and guilt but in man's life and goodness.[45]

[43] Ricoeur, *op. cit.*   [44] Ricoeur, *op. cit.*
[45] Bonhoeffer, *LPP*, 30 April 1944, p. 155.

When Christian apologetics speculates about the immaturity, weakness and failure of man, when (as Ricoeur puts it) "it sniffs out man's sins in order to capture the sinner," it receives harsh treatment from Bonhoeffer:

I consider [it] to be in the first place pointless, in the second place ignoble, and in the third place unchristian. Pointless, because it seems to me like an attempt to put a grown-up man back into adolescence, i.e. to make him dependent . . ., and thrusting him into problems that are, in fact, no longer problems to him. Ignoble, because it amounts to an attempt to exploit man's weakness for purposes that are alien to him and to which he has not freely assented. Unchristian, because it confuses Christ with one particular stage in man's religiousness, i.e. with a human law.[46]

"Nothing," to quote Ricoeur again, "is more debased than the type of bargaining that insists: either Christ or despair." God will therefore not be saved for man either by some metaphysical proposal or by the device of making man feel anguish. The "world come of age" signifies the emancipation of the human enterprise with respect to what remains unknown of either sky or soul. It is the presupposition of human responsibility. From this point of view, no matter how chaotic and suffering and de-structured the world was for Bonhoeffer in 1944 (and as it likewise is for us today), it is a mature world, a world "come of age." If one concedes that "religion" is not idolatry (as it was for the early Christians) and not covetousness (as it was for Barth), but rather a kind of childish nostalgia for a supernatural protector, then it is clear that the present world has become non-religious. To be more precise, wherever man extends his understanding, he discovers that this world can manage quite well without any outside interference.

This first level of cultural interpretation impresses Bonhoeffer, because Christianity is so often confused with the religious task of providing the world with a mysterious kind of spiritual "plus."

In the eyes of most of our contemporaries, Christian faith appears to be a gateway into mysteries, an introduction to wonders, an access beyond the veil of secret initiation. In other words, Christianity is seen as one of the "religions of salvation"

---

[46] Bonhoeffer, *op. cit.*, 8 June 1944, p. 179.

that puts us in touch with the world beyond.[47] There is therefore a tremendous job to be done in distinguishing biblical
faith from metaphysical speculation and individualistic inwardness. Bonhoeffer anticipates that this will be a more radical
task than Bultmann's program of demythologizing, for it not
only challenges the rationalistic formulation (primitively
mythological in character) of the events of grace and faith,
but also the whole attitude of "religious" man who speaks so
easily of transcendence, a world beyond this one, eschatological
events, the Word, and the acts of God.[48] (In this respect
Bonhoeffer feels that Bultmann is still a "religious" man.)
In comparison to a non-religious interpretation that is neither
metaphysical nor "spiritual," demythologizing appears as a
quite limited dispute about language, which does not move
toward a radical purification of thought, since it continues to
operate in the dualistic framework of this world and the
beyond.

2. However, we know enough about Bonhoeffer's ongoing
concerns to be sure that the cultural interpretation of the
collapse of the religious groundwork based on metaphysics
and inwardness did not deeply trouble the inmate of Tegel
prison. His second and *biblical* level of interpretation, although
much earlier than his cultural analysis, comes immediately to
view. And it is this second solid groundwork that makes the
destructive cheerfulness of the first one possible. The God of the
Bible is indeed neither metaphysical nor inward, neither
religious nor individualistic. Only since the Renaissance –
probably only since Petrarch, says Bonhoeffer even more
specifically[49] – has Christianity become popular Platonism to
such a degree that Nietzsche could use Plato as a means of

[47] Here are two examples from among many others:
   1. "Spiritual power in our time is divided in two ways: the spiritual power of
tradition (i.e. the churches of the religions of salvation) and a new spiritual power,
found in the intellectuals and the ideologists of the parties of the masses" (R. Aron,
Dix-huit Leçons sur la Société industrielle, Gallimard, Paris 1962, p. 360).
   2. "Christianity is the basic religion of salvation, the last which shall be the
first, the one which expresses with the greatest force, the greatest simplicity and the
greatest universality, the summons to individual immortality and aversion to
death" (Edgar Morin, *L'Homme et la Mort dans l'Histoire*, Corréa, Paris 1951, p. 199).
[48] Cf. Ricoeur's preface to Bultmann's *Jesus*, Seuil, Paris 1968, p. 22.
[49] Bonhoeffer, *LPP*, 8 July 1944, p. 192.

attacking Christianity. It is the God of the Bible himself who confronts the whole man in the midst of the world. He is the living God, the Lord of the earth, quite apart from any speculation about another world, any cosmological or teleological proofs of his existence, any belief in the immortality of the soul or an inner spiritual preserve in man. What really distinguishes man in the Bible (as well as in Augustine, Luther, Pascal and Kierkegaard) is not the "inner" man, but everyday man, concrete and whole, in relation to God. The Bible expresses psychological insights by the metaphorical use of the parts of the human body,[50] and the biblical writers do not hesitate to use the same kind of bodily language when talking about the invisible God, for the body is always the vehicle through which any presence is communicated. Bonhoeffer's preference for the Old Testament is clear in his prison letters and is interwoven with his cultural interpretation of non-religious modernity. Bonhoeffer identifies the place where God lives and works, in the very process of describing the metaphysical inward heaven that God has vacated. Man is thus able to remain and once again become a believer, when he stops being religious. In the etymological meaning of apologetics set forth so well in I Peter 3.15 – not to prove or reduce or seduce but to "be prepared to make a defense to anyone who calls you to account for the hope that is in you" – true apologetics consists in moving directly from the reality of the God of the Bible to the non-religious reality of the world, without going through the unreal preliminaries of religion. Bonhoeffer compares this approach to that of St Paul, who repudiated the notion that circumcision was the necessary preliminary for the admission of pagans into the church.

This second biblical interpretation constitutes the *cantus firmus*, as Bonhoeffer calls it, the ground bass part that is sung through the prison letters:

God wants us to love him eternally with our whole hearts – not in such a way as to injure or weaken our earthly love, but to provide a kind of *cantus firmus* to which the other melodies in life provide the

---

[50] Cf. E. Dhorme, "L'Emploi métaphorique des noms de parties du corps en hébreu et en accadien," *Revue biblique*, 1920, pp. 470ff.; F. Michaeli, *Dieu à l'Image de l'Homme*, Delachaux, 1950; Claude Tresmontant, *Essai sur la Pensée hébraïque*, Cerf, 1953.

counterpoint ... The two are "undivided and yet distinct," in the words of the Chalcedonian Definition, like Christ in his divine and human natures. May not the attraction and importance of polyphony in music consist in its being a musical reflection of this Christological fact and therefore of our *vita christiana?*[51]

As God in the midst of the world, Jesus Christ is the ultimate reality who causes, continues and completes the natural and cultural polyphony of the penultimate. No longer the God of an inward metaphysical world, but rather of the all-embracing physical world, God encounters reality directly. There is only one world; the world in which God, according to the Old Testament perspective, becomes a "body" rather than a "soul," a living presence rather than an ideal, and a reality rather than a Kantian transcendental regulation.

3. But what happens when God enters into the reality of this world? After the cultural and biblical levels of interpretation we come to the *christological* level, which is by far the most compressed and enigmatic. God's encounter-in-tension with reality in Jesus Christ is neither a victory nor an abolition, but the humiliation and annihilation of the cross. This is the opposite of Feuerbach's religious position, where God's enrichment represents man's impoverishment, but it closely resembles Hegel's analysis of Christ as the historical embodiment of negation.

[God] is weak and powerless in the world, and that is precisely the way, the only way, in which he is with us and helps us ... The God who is with us is the God who forsakes us (Mark 15.34). The God who lets us live in the world without the working hypothesis of God is the God before whom we stand continually. Before God and with God we live without God. God lets himself be pushed out of the world on to the cross.[52]

The world's secret, which is its forsakenness (*Verlassenheit*), becomes the secret of God in Christ. Atheism about the God of metaphysics becomes concretely the godforsakenness of Christ crucified – to such a degree that atheism and faith cannot be outwardly distinguished from one another. Henceforth

[51] Bonhoeffer, *LPP*, 20 May 1944, p. 162.
[52] Bonhoeffer, *LPP*, 16 July 1944, p. 196.

the statement "God is dead,"[53] has an import totally different from the dogmatic affirmation, "God does not exist." The latter statement concerns the realm of ideas, whereas the first is describing the process of reality itself. If a Kantian perspective illumines our understanding of a world "come of age," a Hegelian perspective can give us further insight into the way Bonhoeffer sees Christ as the weakness of God helping man within the reality of the world. The power of God, to which classical religion usually refers, is no help here, for it challenges man's coming of age, and, by challenging it, shows how out of touch it really is. A "strong" God is never concrete or actualized in the midst of the world; he remains abstract and ephemeral. But from a christological perspective, the "godlessness" of responsible resistance overlaps with the "before God" of believing submission.[54] The cross expresses the full meaning of incarnation and is the place where the mutual disparities between God and reality are overcome. Because God is willing to alienate himself, man need no longer be alienated. Theology becomes christology because in Christ God himself is present. And because God is present, christology is more than a matter of example, more than providing a model to imitate. It becomes concrete. It effects reconciliation. In this sense it helps man in a way that an ideal does not help, since an ideal remains law and is remote. A reality, on the other hand, does help. It becomes the grace and structure of this world. To take part in the sufferings of God in this world is henceforth more than a moral act of solidarity with the poor and the weak; it is, as Bonhoeffer puts it in *Ethics*, "participation in the indivisible whole of the divine reality."[55] Such suffering, he goes on to say, becomes a reconciliation and blessing that is not destroyed by the kind

[53] The expression "the death of God" does not occur as such in Bonhoeffer's writings. He speaks of the world "without God," *etsi Deus non daretur*, using Anselm's expression, where the *etsi* (as though God were not given) is combined with the *coram Deo* (before God) of Lutheran faith. He also speaks of a suffering, powerless God being "pushed out" of the world while preserving the act of his presence in God's annihilation on the cross. If "the death of God" is meant to signify simply his effacement, his withdrawal and his absence, it does not do justice to the fullness of Bonhoeffer's paradoxes, since it would lead either to secularization or mystical silence, both of which are foreign to the Old Testament and therefore to Bonhoeffer himself.

[54] Cf. the German and French title of Bonhoeffer's prison letters, *Resistance and Submission*.

[55] Bonhoeffer, *Ethics*, p. 193.

of romanticism about God's brotherly powerlessness that Camus describes in *The Rebel*:

For as long as the Western world has been Christian, the Gospels have been the interpreter between heaven and earth. Each time a solitary cry of rebellion was uttered, the answer came in the form of an even more terrible suffering. In that Christ had suffered, and had suffered voluntarily, suffering was no longer unjust and all pain was necessary. In one sense, Christianity's bitter intuition and legitimate pessimism concerning human behavior is based on the assumption that over-all injustice is as satisfying to man as total justice. Only the sacrifice of an innocent god could justify the endless and universal torture of innocence. Only the most abject suffering by God could assuage man's agony. If everything without exception, in heaven and earth is doomed to pain and suffering, then a strange form of happiness is possible.[56]

✓ Once again it is the Old Testament that offers protection against such a consoling and interiorized religion of the distress and bitterness of the cross. For very paradoxically and very acutely as Bonhoeffer sees it, the Old Testament is both the reminder and the announcement, at the heart of the cross, of the joy of the rediscovered earth, i.e. of the resurrection, of which the Old Testament almost never speaks directly. The Old Covenant protects the New from reducing the cross to a sorrowful spectacle, and from escape into other-worldliness or pious inwardness.[57]

In the Old Testament the person who receives the blessing has to endure a great deal of suffering (e.g. Abraham, Isaac, Jacob and Joseph), but this never leads to the idea that fortune and suffering, blessing and cross, are mutually exclusive and contradictory – nor does it in the New Testament. Indeed, the *only* difference between the Old and New Testaments in this respect is that in the Old the blessing includes the cross, and in the New the cross includes the blessing.[58]

---

[56] Camus, *The Rebel*, Vintage Books, New York 1956, p. 34.

[57] I prefer "inwardness" to express Bonhoeffer's opposition, not, to be sure, against personal meditation, but against a spiritualizing isolation and withdrawal. Bonhoeffer maintains a position which is the exact opposite of that held by Herbert Braun: "When we move from the Old Testament to the New, the representation of God undeniably shifts from objectivity (*Gegenstandlichkeit*) to spiritualization" ("Gottes Existenz und meine Geschichtlichkeit im Neuen Testament," in *Zeit und Geschichte: Dankesgabe zum Rudolf Bultmann zum 80. Geburtstag*, Mohr, Tübingen 1964, p. 403).   [58] Bonhoeffer, *LPP*, 28 July 1944, pp. 205f.

The christology of the suffering God, which is the atheism of the metaphysical God, is also the theology of earthly blessing, the divine "yes" to the earth. Such blessing remains a transcendent idea and utopian expectation unless the resurrection brings it into being – both concretely and invisibly, both in reality and in the hidden divine incognito, in the same way that Yahweh is the invisible Lord of the visible earth.

This third level of a christological interpretation of the prison letters seems to me to raise two questions. The first can be directed more to Bonhoeffer and Hegel, the second to Bonhoeffer and Bultmann.

(*a*) Within a single sentence Bonhoeffer can use the single word "God" in confusing fashion. Sometimes he is speaking of a conceptual hypothesis that has now become superfluous through the functioning of understanding and technique; at other times he is speaking of Jesus Christ, who has been crucified because of man's refusal to live in the obedience of faith. In the same breath he can describe the dying out of the unused and unusable God of metaphysics, and the putting to death of the rejected God of the covenant. In so doing he equates in quick succession a cultural emancipation and a spiritual abandonment. Sometimes God stands for a principle of causation no longer needed for responsible decision in the world come of age, and sometimes for the participant who agonizes in the obedient sufferings of life on earth. This mixture of the two meanings of God is most evident in the well-known words:

Our coming of age leads us to a true recognition of our situation before God. God would have us know that we must live as men who manage our lives without him. The God who is with us is the God who forsakes us (Mark 15.34). The God who lets us live in the world without the working hypothesis of God is the God before whom we stand continually. Before God and with God we live without God. God lets himself be pushed out of the world on to the cross.[59]

Now unless theology is to be reduced to a word game, it must be pointed out that in speaking this way Bonhoeffer short-circuits the two previous interpretations we have examined, the cultural interpretation of modern man's non-religious coming of age, and the biblical interpretation of the God who

[59] Bonhoeffer, *LPP*, 16 July 1944, p. 196.

comes, lives, suffers and blesses in the midst of the world. My
question does not center on the fact of this short-circuiting,
but on the obscurity that it can let loose.

If there had not been this short-circuit, Bonhoeffer would
not have related his theological speech about God to the
human experience of God's cultural disappearance. He would
have made no impact and attracted no attention. In this
sense it is quite legitimate that the biblical God should be
affected by the consequence of the cultural disappearance of the
concept of the God who was the keystone of classical metaphysics and early mythologies. "God" remains a common
name open to all kinds of meanings and lack of meanings. In
the Old Testament, *Yahweh*, which is a proper name, is also
referred to by two common names, *El* in the singular and
Adonai in the plural. Bonhoeffer's boldness is therefore legitimate when in his third interpretation he rejects a complacent
separation between the first two interpretations that would
allow one to say that even if the God of metaphysics and
inwardness should collapse, the biblical God in the midst of the
earth would in no way be affected by the collapse. Such a
separation would be pure abstraction. It would not take
sufficient account of what the human community hears when
the believing community speaks. It would utterly remove
God from cultural and intellectual reality. But theology is
always affected by what happens philosophically.[60] Whatever
happens to the God of the philosophers has bearing on the
meaning of the God of Abraham, Isaac and Jacob. But it is
just this closeness that calls for special rigor. And Bonhoeffer
seems at this point to have opened up an obscure crevice in
which many of his disciples can be swallowed up, particularly
if they only hold onto this third precarious interpretation.
They may actually be far from Bonhoeffer's position but not
without a certain initial justification they got from him.

We can now refine the question. On the one hand, the death
of the hypothetical God is clearly a *gain* for men, who are
freed from the obscurity of transcendent explanations. The
living God can only approve such a death, since he wants man
to enter into relationship with him as a free partner, which

[60] Cf. A. Dumas, "De l'Objectivité de Dieu," *Revue d'Histoire et de Philosophie
religieuses*, 1966.4.

means always as one who has come of age. When Yahweh called Adam, he did not limit him or overwhelm him, as though he were Zeus and Adam were Prometheus. On the other hand, the death of Jesus Christ upon the cross is clearly a *loss* for man, since it demonstrates earth's repudiation of the living God who is in its midst. Now let us take these two deaths, the one a cultural gain, and the other a cultural loss, and superimpose them, i.e. place them in the same context without considering their divergences. When we do this, Bonhoeffer's statements suggest both that the living God would have regretted finding himself removed from his exalted position as the normative God-concept, and also that the crucified Jesus Christ would have achieved the actual liberation of man from the excessive otherness of an oppressive God and an omnipotent Father. Such suggestions distort both the human liberation that appears to be vaguely regretted by the biblical God, and the crucifixion of the Son that appears to be vaguely acclaimed as the decisive step in man's liberation from the sovereign God (or, to put it in Hegel's terms, man's liberation from the abstract and a-historical God of the Old Testament).[61]

This is Hegelianism pure and simple, in which the death of God does not signify man's guilt before God but rather the logical and dialectical richness of the principle of negation. Hegel thinks on the conceptual level of the separation and reconciliation of reality and not on the existential level of sin and grace, as Kierkegaard never tired of pointing out.

We are thus a long way from Bonhoeffer, who always saw the Old Testament as the place where God's manifestation in the world was most apparent, who never in the prison letters spoke of God in Freudian fashion as a jealous Father, challenged, put to death and disposed of, and who never worked out a positive cultural interpretation of the contemporary pheno-menon of secularization starting from the cross.[62] I am afraid,

[61] One of the most striking examples of this interpretation of Jesus' crucifixion as liberation from the God of the Old Testament, as the condition of our becoming free men, is the book by François Jeanson, *La Foi d'un Incroyant*, Seuil, Paris 1963. Jeanson is quite logical with respect to his unbelief, even though his faith in Jesus is often surprising and unexpected.

[62] Gabriel Vahanian rightly points out that the "secularization of the world" is a redundancy, and that we must speak instead of "desacralization." Although Bonhoeffer never uses the latter word (perhaps because of his emphasis on the "secret [sacred] discipline" he would have seen it, I believe, as a synonym for

however, that Bonhoeffer opened the door here for such theological-cultural speculation, not so much by his ambiguous use of the word "God" as by his simultaneous reference to a positive death (the abandonment of the God of hypotheses), and a negative death (the rejection of the man Jesus by guilty humanity). But to destroy a useless hypothesis and to destroy the crucified Christ are by no means the same thing. So the question once again is: did not Bonhoeffer like Hegel use christology to describe the ongoing journey of the individual consciousness and universal history, employing unlikely analogies between the development of conceptual understanding and the development of the history of salvation, thereby increasing the confusion between the act of incarnation and the movement of immanence?

(*b*) My second question concerns the christology of the suffering and crucified God. Like Bultmann, Bonhoeffer follows Paul closely in wishing to preach nothing but Christ crucified. But unlike Paul, such preaching shifts every now and then from scandal to explanation, and from folly to a system. Bonhoeffer is engaging in an inversion of religion: the strong man is helped by the weak God. But every inversion runs the risk of preserving the initial position it was trying to challenge. From an apologetic of divine triumphalism there is the risk of moving toward an apologetic of divine self-emptying. In many respects the theologies of the death of God appear in this time of non-religious consciousness and secularization as inversions of the theologies of religious consciousness that appeared in a time of romanticism and idealism. Thus natural or cultural theologies join forces in interpreting God by examining the state of the world.

To be sure, from a biblical standpoint God comes to man's aid through the suffering of his Son, which does away with the objection to the changeless and far-off omnipotence of a good creator. But God also comes to man's aid through the power

---

"religionlessness." Instead of talking about the antibiblical sacralization of the world, Vahanian suggests talking about sacramentality, according to which "the world is not able to attest the presence of God but can only do so charismatically, in spite of itself (Gen. 28.16f.). The sacral world is hostile to man. The sacramental world depends on man and offers itself to him as the theatre of his activity, even while reminding him of his finitude" (Vahanian, *No Other God*, Braziller, New York 1966, p. 19).

of the resurrection of that same Son, which does away with the
contrary objection to the changeless and far-off omnipotence
of an evil Satan. If one speaks only of the weakness of God,
does this not render incomprehensible the claim that the
strength of God also loves the earth in the weakness of its
rejection, inertia and forsakenness? Too little is said about
God's actual reconciliation with reality for fear that the
resurrection will reintroduce the distance between God and
the world that had been overcome by his identification with
the world in the crucifixion. This leads to the danger that the
resurrection will not be affirmed in its proper incognito as a
reality accessible only to faith, but rather as a dubious kind of
secret that may appear to separate God from humanity. The
full sweep of Bonhoeffer's work rules out such an interpretation
even though some of his statements occasionally suggest it,
particularly those that are too apologetic in their exact reversal
of Feuerbach's notions about weak and poor man confronting
a powerful and rich God.

Christology is thus at the heart of Bonhoeffer's theological
thought, and we will examine it in detail in the next chapter.
With wonderful simplicity and directness, the prison letters
witness to God present in Jesus Christ in the midst of the world,
a world come of age and forsaken. Here Christianity is no
longer an other-worldly or interiorized religion of salvation,
but is redirected toward the future, a faith responsible in
the world without God – before God. This responsibility
expresses itself simultaneously as public action in politics, and
as hidden action in the life of the "secret discipline" and
prayer.

4. *The "secret discipline," prayer and suffering in the life of man come of age*

Consequently the Christian is called to follow the reality of
Jesus Christ in his godforsakenness in the midst of the world
come of age, so that the world can be "re-structured" – a word
preferable to the religiously-colored word "saved." This
fellowship of christological obedience and trust transforms
Letters and Papers from Prison from simply a provocative theological essay into a book of profound spiritual insight. Bonhoeffer

followed up *The Cost of Discipleship* with *Life Together* in order
to describe the background of discipline and prayer that
prevents discipleship from slipping into activist revivalism and
"enthusiasm." In the same way, *Letters and Papers from Prison*,
which could be called "solitary life in the invisible community,"
follows *Ethics* in order to analyze and clarify the task of the
Christian as he lives his life so close to reality without God that
his life before God takes the form of a secret life.

1. As a means of describing this experience and manner of
living, Bonhoeffer chose an unusual term, "the secret discipline"
(*arcani disciplina*). It appears for the first time in the important
letter of 30 April 1944, usually looked upon as the crucial
turning point of his thought:

Christ is no longer an object of religion, but something quite different,
really the Lord of the world. But what does that mean? What is the
place of worship and prayer in a religionless situation? Does the
secret discipline, or alternatively the difference (which I have
suggested to you before) between penultimate and ultimate take on a
new importance here?[63]

The theme reappeared in the next letter not in opposition to a
positivistic and atheistic secularity, but to Barth's theology,
which in Bonhoeffer's view was too positivist and all-inclusive:

Barth was the first theologian to begin the criticism of religion, and
that remains his really great merit; but he puts in its place a positivist
doctrine of revelation which says, in effect, "Like it or lump it":
virgin birth, Trinity, or anything else; each is an equally significant
and necessary part of the whole, which must simply be swallowed
as a whole or not at all. That is not biblical. There are degrees of
knowledge and degrees of significance; that means that a secret
discipline must be restored whereby the *mysteries* of the Christian
faith are protected against profanation.[64]

In subsequent letters the idea, if not the term, frequently
occurs. Around it can be grouped the sections on the secret
shared with God in his sorrowful struggles in the midst of the
world, on the mystery of freedom received in the midst of
discipline, action and suffering, and on prayer as "breaking

[63] Bonhoeffer, *LPP*, 30 April 1944, pp. 153f.
[64] *Ibid.*, 5 May 1944, pp. 156f.

the circle of anxious hesitations" and as "confrontation with the stormy events of life."

The "secret discipline" is a hidden certainty, which does not thrust itself coercively on others, but offers them the fully human and available presence of the believer. Thanks to it, the relationship with Jesus Christ does not divide life into compartments, either metaphysical or inward. It is the source of an existence that is free, concrete and transcendent in the sense of a life turned toward the neighbor, rather than a life separated from the neighbor and turned toward the other-worldliness of the omnipotence, omniscience and omnipresence of a remote God. The "secret discipline," one could say, maintains relationship with God while disengaging mankind from the ponderously objective or falsely supernatural character that often marks such a relationship. It avoids banal irrelevance and self-destructive inwardness. It safeguards man's existence without heaping unnecessary things upon it. It is not a tactic of silence, as though the times were not felt to be propitious for a more ample witness, for every tactic is able to sniff out the apologetic that manipulates it. It is a costly discipline. It knows that form and style are always as important as content and message. Its ultimate assurance is that in Jesus Christ on the cross, God and reality form a unity that is both indivisible and in creative tension. Human conduct must be based on maintaining this hidden reality, without letting the indivisibility relapse into bland immanentism, or the creative tension lead to remote transcendental dualism. Harmless as the dove, wise as the serpent, both the conduct and the style that comprise the secret discipline protect the ultimate certainty from a double "profanation" which could be either an uncritical celebration of the secular order (as though God had not been crucified in it), or a triumphalistic affirmation of the divine victory (as though God were outside of the world he had forsaken). The secret discipline is the only adequate form for a faith held before God in a world without God. It is the discipline of the Christian as he struggles not to betray the incarnation to either of the two positivisms that deny it: reality apart from the gospel or the gospel apart from reality. It is the way in which the Christian pursues or "follows after" (*Nachfolge*) the Messianic secret of Jesus Christ, who repeated again and again that the Kingdom of heaven comes quietly and without fanfare and that his disciples must take care not to cheapen the secret of the Kingdom as pearls trampled under foot by swine (Matt. 7.6), i.e. by offering misleading securities for believers that appear as religious banalities to non-believers. The secret discipline protects the costliness and the savor of grace just when life is immersed in the non-religious world. It is, as Bethge puts it, the "guarantee of an identity," the identity of faith, as the Christian, in terms of a non-religious interpretation, lives out his identification in a godless world.[65]

As we have already seen, Bonhoeffer uses this first of all against a dogmatics so preoccupied with the truth of its doctrines that it ignores the kind of critical, careful and discriminating presentation by which its doctrines might gradually convince someone, instead of simply being stated and affirmed outright. Theologians and Christians who are no longer bound by a secret discipline of thought and life become absorbed in the chatter, the "careless words" (Matt. 12.36), the "empty phrases" (Matt. 6.7) that Jesus describes before teaching his disciples the costly restraint of the Lord's Prayer, and which are the major pagan enemies of prayer offered to God. So the secret discipline is the opponent of dogmatic glibness – that religious wine that intoxicates theological speech by releasing it from the need to verify its conclusions in terms of the unique reality of a God involved in the world. The secret discipline weighs the value of a word in relation to the cost of its communicability.

But it is also the opponent of platitudes about the everyday world, emptied of the reality of Christ's presence in that world. It thus refuses to let incarnation be confused with secularization, religionlessness with immanence, forsakenness with non-existence, reality with ordinary life, or man's coming of age with a complacent acceptance of man as one who has finally become aware of the inconsistency of his childish dreams. I suggest, borrowing my terms from Nietzsche, that the secret discipline distinguishes between the banalities of "the last man," the ordinary man informed by his ordinary mind, and the new claims of the "superman," if we may purge the latter notion of its contemptuous and frozen solitude in order to

[65] Bethge, *Dietrich Bonhoeffer*, p. 783.

understand it more clearly in the crucified Christ. Bonhoeffer makes use of the secret discipline against a too-simple religionlessness, to maintain the tension which is the heart of God's encounter with reality, an encounter based on crucifixion and resurrection. He speaks as a man of the earth, knowing that in this world Christ does not relinquish responsibility for reality but assumes it, in both life and death. If cultural analogies are needed, we can do better by referring to Hegel's tragic optimism than to the self-sufficiency of the Enlightenment, against which Bonhoeffer speaks explicitly:

The Christian is not a *homo religiosus*, but simply a man, as Jesus was a man – in contrast, shall we say, to John the Baptist. I don't mean the shallow and banal this-worldliness of the enlightened, the busy, the comfortable, or the lascivious, but the profound this-worldliness, characterized by discipline and the constant knowledge of death and resurrection. I think Luther lived a this-worldly life in this sense.[66]

The secret discipline is thus a reminder that man following after Christ is subject to the *whole* of reality, and cannot be content with only a portion of the world around him that has become tolerable and manipulable under his direction. To have come of age, to be religionless, implies this secret discipline of struggle, which for the Christian is the very secret that God shares with man.

2. In the perspective of the secret discipline, *prayer* takes on a new meaning for a humanity come of age that no longer tries to cast the troubles of this world onto another one, when it is relieved of such debased meanings as "religious first aid," magical manipulation or a false and childish dualism. During the Enlightenment Kant called prayer a "superstitious illusion."[67] Now *Letters and Papers from Prison*, seeking a nonreligious interpretation of Christianity for men who are leaving behind the immaturity for which they themselves are responsible, as Kant put it, speaks of prayer as an obvious mode of behavior to enable faith to breathe – much more in evidence in the later Bonhoeffer than all talk about God. Do we have a contradiction or at least an inconsistency here, a

[66] Bonhoeffer, *LPP*, 20 July 1944, p. 201.
[67] Cf. Helmut Gollwitzer, *The Existence of God as Confessed by Faith*, SCM Press London, and Westminster Press, Philadelphia 1965, pp. 67f.

retention of the kind of pietism that reassures some of Bonhoeffer's interpreters and disconcerts others?[68]

It is certainly strange that Bonhoeffer never appears to have
doubted the reality of prayer, as have many of the theologians
more or less inspired by him. The reason for this seems to me
to be found in his relationship to the secret discipline, just as in
the gospels Jesus sees the prayer of the Pharisee as a kind of
non-disciplined display, while the prayer of the publican is
linked to the discipline not of solitude but of hiddenness and
secrecy. Prayer is not man's evasion of God but the sharing
which God himself demands as a result of his own involvement
with the world. It is the work man does to share in the work
God does. It is the way man gives heed to God. It is the
continuation of man's responsibility, giving in without giving
up, in which man offers up to God even his human resistance
to God.

The very title that was given to the German edition of the
prison letters, *Widerstand und Ergebung* (Resistance and Submission), expresses the flexibility that prayer gives to action:

I have often wondered here where we are to draw the line between
necessary resistance to "fate," and equally necessary submission.
Don Quixote is the symbol of resistance carried to the point of
absurdity, even lunacy; and similarly Michael Kohlhaas, insisting
on his rights, puts himself in the wrong ... In both cases resistance
at last defeats its own object, and evaporates in theoretical fantasy.
Sancho Panza is the type of complacent and artful accommodation
to things as they are. I think we must rise to the great demands
that are made on us personally, and yet at the same time fulfil the
commonplace and necessary tasks of daily life. We must confront
"fate" – to me the neuter gender of the word "fate" (*Schicksal*) is
significant – as resolutely as we submit to it at the right time ...
God [meets] us no longer as "Thou", but also "disguised" in the
"It"; so in the last resort my question is how we are to find the
"Thou" in this "It" (i.e. fate), or, in other words, how does "fate"
really become "guidance"? It is therefore impossible to define the

[68] Cf., for example, the discussion between Jean Bauberot and Philippe de
Robert: "Vivre la mort de Dieu: l'Œuvre de Bonhoeffer," *Le Semeur*, 1964, No. 4,
pp. 41–84. Bauberot says, "Bonhoeffer was a pietist and he remained a pietist to
his death. How can one escape his own cultural upbringing?" (p. 66), whereas
Philippe de Robert comments, "For Bonhoeffer, in this world that lives out of the
forsakenness of the cross, the church ought to live out of the secret power of the
cross" (p. 82).

boundary between resistance and submission on abstract principles; but both of them must exist, and both must be practised. Faith demands this elasticity of behaviour.[69]

Bonhoeffer thus seems to understand prayer as the secret breath of action, which saves it from asphyxiation in times of obstinacy (Don Quixote) as well as in times of accommodation (Sancho Panza). Prayer is not speech but action. It exists not to divide man either metaphysically or inwardly, but to unify him in the reality of God here on earth in the midst of an existence that is always destroying him between the suffocating effects of passivity and endless disputes. He who lives prays, and he who prays lives. Prayer thus takes on the meaning of reality, in protecting our "theoretical" lives by its practice. Authenticated in action, "quiet and hidden" prayer is the sign of a coming of age that is not solitary, the presence of the community with him that Christ expects of man. It does not ask God to place himself at man's disposal. It shares God's resistance and submission in the "Thou" and the "It" of the world. If we may follow the explicit reversal that Bonhoeffer uncovers in Christianity, it is the presence of man come of age at the side of God who is struggling and suffering in this world.

3. Along with prayer, *suffering* plays a considerable role in Bonhoeffer's writings, even if one considers it illogical that a world come of age would still be a world in distress, or that a non-religious interpretation of Christianity would be fundamentally focussed on the cross. In prison, Bonhoeffer refused to be described as either a saint or a martyr. He was simply a man who in the midst of reality did not evade the secret discipline of suffering. In suffering as in prayer man becomes God's companion in the world. As early as 1934, Bonhoeffer had written in a sermon on II Cor. 12.9:

Why is suffering holy? Because God suffers in the world through men . . . Human suffering and weakness is a sharing in God's own suffering and weakness in the world . . . Our God is a suffering God. Suffering forms man into the image of God. The suffering man is in the likeness of God.[70]

[69] Bonhoeffer, *LPP*, 21 February 1944, pp. 133–4.
[70] Bonhoeffer, *GS* IV, p. 182.

In a sermon at Finkenwalde in 1935, Bonhoeffer made the point that Jesus Christ experienced his own suffering as a "secret discipline" that created the human community.

He suffered without saying a word. Suffering that sought to justify itself and interpret itself would not be true suffering. But since he suffered without saying a word, faith in him becomes mandatory.[71]

This suffering of Christ, to which Bonhoeffer constantly returns, lacks all the nobility, honor and splendor usually associated with the suffering of tragic heroes. But it is a necessary suffering, linked to Christ's participation in man's destiny in reality. It is neither glorious nor accidental, but obscure and unavoidable. It results from confronting the world. It is experienced not as a more or less arbitrary private ascetic act, but as companionship with those who cannot escape it.

It remains an experience of incomparable worth that we were able to look at the important events of world history from below – from the perspective of those who are left out, suspect, abused, powerless, oppressed and mocked, in brief, those who are suffering. If only bitterness and envy have not corroded our hearts during this time, so that we may look upon stinginess and greatness, happiness and unhappiness, strength and weakness, with new eyes; that our vision of greatness and humaneness, of right and mercy, may have become clearer and less corruptible; that our personal suffering may be a more suitable key, a more fruitful principle, a more contemplative and active opening to the world, than personal happiness would have been.[72]

Thus the suffering of Christ is itself a costly apprenticeship both for him and for his own who follow him:

It is infinitely easier to suffer in obedience to a human command than in the freedom of one's own responsibility. It is infinitely easier to suffer with others than to suffer alone. It is infinitely easier to suffer publicly and honourably than apart and ignominiously. It is infinitely easier to suffer through staking one's life than to suffer spiritually. Christ suffered as a free man alone, apart and in ignomy, in body and spirit; and since then many Christians have suffered with him.[73]

However, this suffering in companionship with Christ is

---

[71] Bonhoeffer, *GS* IV, pp. 212f.   [72] Bonhoeffer, *GS* II, p. 441.
[73] Bonhoeffer, *LPP*, "After Ten Years," p. 37.

rightly understood only within the secret discipline. Without the secret discipline it would be transformed into a "religion of suffering," a one-sided statement of costly sorrow as something redemptive and purifying in itself. Suffering comes to Christ because of his involvement in reality, not as some privilege of tragedy or misfortune. Bonhoeffer does not forget the ongoing lesson of the Old Testament that God desires happiness for man:

> The intermediate theological category between God and human fortune is, as far as I can see, that of blessing ... which includes in itself all earthly good ... It would be natural to suppose that, as usual, the New Testament spiritualizes the teaching of the Old Testament here, and therefore to regard the Old Testament blessing as superseded in the New ... Now, is it right to set the Old Testament blessing against the cross? That is what Kierkegaard did. That makes the cross, or at least suffering, an abstract principle; and that is just what gives rise to an unhealthy methodism, which deprives suffering of its element of contingency on a divine ordinance ... In suffering, the deliverance consists in our being allowed to put the matter out of our own hands into God's hands ... Whether the human deed is a matter of faith or not depends on whether we understand our suffering as an extension of our action and a completion of freedom.[74]

Like prayer, such suffering is the hidden assurance that submission does not negate resistance, but advances it. Such actions must find their meaning within the secret discipline. Let loose without precaution to the ordinary light of everyday life, they can only by their very frankness be misunderstood by men, leading them, for example, to believe that God delights in suffering, and is thus masochistic to himself and sadistic toward mankind; or again that all suffering is creative, as is implied by the frequently-used analogy of the grain that dies in the ground and brings forth much fruit; or finally that Christianity speaks too glibly of what is intolerable simply by sublimating it. Bonhoeffer's comments on suffering can therefore only be understood in terms of the secret discipline which protects them against the misunderstandings of profanation:

> When people suggest in their letters ... that I am "suffering" here, I reject the thought, for it seems to me a profanation. These things

[74] Bonhoeffer, *LPP*, 28 July 1944, pp. 205f.

must not be dramatized. I doubt very much whether I am "suffering" any more than you, or most people, are suffering today . . . I believe, for instance, that physical sufferings, actual pain and so on, are certainly to be classed as "suffering." We so like to stress spiritual suffering; and yet that is just what Christ is supposed to have taken from us . . . Now that's enough for today. When shall we be able to talk together again? Keep well, enjoy the beautiful country, spread *hilaritas* around you, and keep it yourself, too![75]

The discipline of suffering thus denies Bonhoeffer the right to make a weak display of himself. *A propos* of a cellmate who whimpered at every little sign of danger, Bonhoeffer describes his harsh reaction:

I would throw any such specimens out of the party for making it look ridiculous, and so on . . . I don't really think I find it easy to "despise" anyone in trouble . . . But there is a kind of weakness that Christianity does not hold with, but which people insist on claiming as Christian, and then sling mud at it. So we must take care that the contours do not get blurred.[76]

In other respects, both before and during his imprisonment, Bonhoeffer exercised a ministry of compassion, strength and hope during the war years, especially toward the many families whose sons, former students of Bonhoeffer, were killed at the front.[77]

In these times when our thoughts are turned to the passion of our Lord Jesus Christ, when we try to bring all the widespread sorrow that we cannot ignore to the foot of his cross, God has sent you, and all of us, a great personal sorrow in the death of your dear son.[78]

An entire section of the balance-sheet, "After Ten Years," written by Bonhoeffer as a Christmas gift for certain of his friends in 1942, is devoted to sympathy:

We can share in other people's sufferings only in a very limited degree. We are not Christ, but if we want to be Christians, we must have some share in Christ's large-heartedness by acting with

---

[75] Bonhoeffer, *LPP*, 9 March 1944, p. 140.
[76] Bonhoeffer, *LPP*, 2 February 1944, pp. 126f.
[77] "When the cell door closed behind Bonhoeffer at Tegel in 1943, he had written twenty-five times to the relatives of a fallen brother. He did not live to know that the final total of dead was more than three times that number" (Bethge, *Dietrich Bonhoeffer*, p. 609).
[78] Bonhoeffer, *GS* II, p. 590.

responsibility and in freedom when the hour of danger comes, and by showing a real sympathy that springs, not from fear, but from the liberating and redeeming love of Christ for all who suffer. Mere waiting and looking on is not Christian behaviour.[79]

There is an adjective that constantly recurs in Bonhoeffer's writing – "real" (as in "real sympathy" above) – which means "participating" as opposed to "religious," which in turn is a synonym for the unreal, for pretence, for evasion. God's suffering is "real" in this sense, for it is neither theorized nor sublimated. Christ is a man who really suffers and dies. In him, God defines himself in this world as an executed man. By that act God asks as did Jesus at Gethsemane not to be left alone, without Christians, without his earthly body, without his "collective person" which is the church understood as that portion of the world that shares his secret. It is in this context that we can best appreciate the famous words that are the only ones in *Letters and Papers from Prison* concerned with the identity of the Christian, not at the level of doctrinal definitions and confessions, but at the level of acknowledged and active participation:

"Christians stand by God in his hour of grieving"; that is what distinguishes Christians from pagans. Jesus asked in Gethsemane, "Could you not watch with me one hour?" That is the reversal of what the religious man expects from God. Man is summoned to share in God's sufferings at the hands of a godless world.

He must therefore really live in the godless world, without attempting to gloss over or explain its ungodliness in some religious way or other. He must live a "secular" life, and thereby share in God's sufferings ... It is not the religious act that makes the Christian, but participation in the sufferings of God in the secular life.[80]

The question is often asked, and by Bonhoeffer first of all, what becomes of "religious" acts such as worship and prayer if Christianity is interpreted in a "non-religious" way? How does one live before God when he identifies himself with the godlessness of the world? If Barth is wrong, and religion cannot dialectically become "true religion," transformed from its covetous grasping by the gift of grace, then does not the non-religious interpretation of Christianity lead to a total impasse at the level of

[79] Bonhoeffer, *LPP*, p. 37.   [80] Bonhoeffer, *LPP*, 18 July 1944, p. 198.

expression? Is it not reduced to an endless protest against religion, always being dislodged and denounced by its own critique? Is it not nourished only by protest? If religion and the Christian religion specifically were to disappear would not Christianity disappear with it, like the ivy firmly attached to the tree from which it draws nourishment? Surely such a Christianity, whose vigor consists only in being non-religious, would have no staying power of its own. The one who is only an anti-religious protester cannot talk about faith.

It seems clear that the response Bonhoeffer had already worked out goes far beyond such a denial of religion. The secret discipline is the affirmative part of the polemic against religion. It binds one to God here on earth, whereas religion first unbinds one from this world and then re-binds him to another world. The secret discipline is the understanding and practice of the incarnation, whereas religion becomes disincarnation from human responsibility. The radical revision that is sought by Bonhoeffer for a Christianity come of age is based on this shift from irresponsible evasion to responsible participation. In the latter, man no longer makes use of an omnipotent, absolute and eternal God to repair the breakdown of man's knowledge, power and will. Rather, God in Jesus Christ, crucified, relative and contingent, asks man for companionship in his discipline, prayer and suffering. God needs man here in the world. The prayer and suffering that are encountered in action bear witness to the human willingness to share in this companionship. They are the acts that within the secret discipline bear witness to God of man's believing presence, and that make possible a totally free presence of believers alongside non-Christians.

I do not believe that Bonhoeffer ever gave up the search for a clear ecclesiology, even though we are only familiar with the elaborations of his first two periods, *The Communion of Saints* during the period of the state church (*Volkskirche*), and *The Cost of Discipleship* during the period of the Confessing Church (*Bekenntniskirche*). We can only offer some suggestions and warnings concerning what a non-religious church ought to be in the present time, i.e. a lay, secular, and worldly church, a church that is neither the church of institutional Christendom nor the church of the persecuted community, but rather the church in which Christians participate in the work of God in a world without God. To his godson, baptized in May 1944, Bonhoeffer wrote:

Reconciliation and redemption, regeneration and the Holy Ghost, love of our enemies, cross and resurrection, life in Christ and Christian discipleship – all these things are so difficult and so remote that we hardly venture any more to speak of them ... Our earlier words are therefore bound to lose their force and cease, and our being Christians today will be limited to two things: prayer and righteous action among men.

As he looks ahead, all he can see is the need for

a new language, perhaps quite non-religious, but liberating and redeeming – as was Jesus' language ... Till then the Christian cause will be a silent and hidden affair, but there will be those who pray and do right and wait for God's own time.[81]

A new non-religious church will then rediscover a language which in speaking of God will not release one from the earth, but which, open toward the earth, will not superimpose God upon it. The resurrection will not re-establish the distance between God and man that was overcome by the cross. The discipline of prayer and suffering will not be the mystifying and anticipating dream of another world but the companionship of God in this world. Worship will not be a means of evasion away from the earth but will awaken everyday life to the dimensions of its own reality,[82] which is the unknown God in the midst of the world. The community will not sit at the foot of a raised pulpit listening to a learned discourse so high-flown that one has to take off for the stratosphere in order to follow it. Instead it will be nourished by its participation here on earth in the task of restructuring everyday life, just as Jesus Christ did earlier on its behalf, a task he pursued extensively and concretely while on earth. The non-religious church will

[81] Bonhoeffer, *LPP*, "Thoughts on the Baptism of D.W.R.," May 1944, p. 172.
[82] Throughout these pages I have consistently used such terms as "everyday life," "the everyday world," "our empirical situation" (*réel*) in opposition to "reality" (*réalité*). This is a linguistic device to indicate the difference between the ordinary quality of facticity, *de facto* experience (*faktisch*), and reality, in which God is both present and hidden, both concrete and realizing, both effective and effectual, both working things out and the one through whom things have been worked out (*wirklich*).

work out a style of life and conduct that will not betray its understanding of the incarnation, namely that God is in the world doing whatever is necessary to transform disjointed everyday life into the reality he has promised it. All this, however, Bonhoeffer only hints at between questions and ellipses. Compared to the *Ethics*, which traced various proposals for the christological restructuring of reality, the prison letters, with their secret discipline, remain very reserved – letters to a friend who is invited to share in a creative but difficult secret.

Bonhoeffer was seized by Hitler's emissaries on Low Sunday, 8 April 1945, after having conducted his final service during which he preached on Isa. 53.5 and I Peter 1.3. He was hanged at daybreak the next day. As we reflect on this, let us not forget that this final "religious" act was virtually wrung forth from Bonhoeffer and insisted upon by his fellow prisoners, who included both Catholics and atheists. Until the very end, Bonhoeffer, the man of the secret discipline, wanted to avoid imposing his faith on anyone else.

There is a final question we must raise. Is this phrase, "the secret discipline," which was Bonhoeffer's own choice, really a good choice? Does it clarify things and does it possess a convincing logic of its own? Let us recall the origin of this phrase in the history of the church.[83] At the beginning of the fourth century, the conversion of Constantine and then the Theodosian government abruptly transformed Christianity into the religion of the state.

The church grew into an essential element of public life, an element forming part of the very world which she had combated obstinately up to that point.[84]

During this time, under the pressure of masses of pagans who were suddenly thrust into the church, an element originally drawn from the older mystery cults also made its way into the Christian community, casting a veil of mystery over the two sacraments of baptism and the Lord's Supper. Only the bap-

[83] The following information is taken from the interesting article by Gisela Meuss, "Arkandisziplin und Weltlichkeit bei Dietrich Bonhoeffer," in *Die Mündige Welt* III, 1961, pp. 70–115.

[84] H. Lietzmann, *History of the Early Church*, Vol. IV, Lutterworth Press, London 1961, p. 98.

tized could participate in the Lord's Supper. Even the Lord's Prayer was offered only by the participants in the eucharistic meal. The baptismal formula was never written down, but had to be learned by heart and kept secret. Its content was made known to the catechumens only a few moments before their baptism. The custom also grew up of postponing baptism, which in and of itself was believed to have purifying power, until as close to the moment of death as possible.

All phenomena of this kind are to be understood partly by reference to the prevailing air which favoured mysticism; and, more importantly, as a device of the church when seeking a means of self-defence against the incoming floods of people who wished for nothing more than a formal conversion to Christianity.[85]

In this way, the church preserved the mysteries of the faith against their profanation in the face of mass conversions. The congregation was divided into two groups, the non-baptized auditors and the baptized or initiated, who were admitted to the Lord's Supper. And it was this strict separation that was called "the secret discipline." Theology in the seventeenth century developed a theory about the secret discipline, linked to the disappearance of ancient paganism in the middle of the fifth century, characterized by a retreat into the secret discipline of the two sacraments, the creed, the Lord's Prayer and the liturgy of the eucharist.[86]

The meaning of a word is certainly not determined by the historical usage that created it. Bonhoeffer surely had the right to pick up the notion of the secret discipline that was elaborated during the establishment of Christendom under the influence of the mystery religions to preserve a "religious" secret from secular profanation, and use it to express an opposite meaning during the breakup of Christendom – namely a passionate protest against confusing Christianity with the mystery religions, with secret information (*gnosis*) about another world, and with evasions leading to metaphysics and pious inwardness. And Bonhoeffer was able to bring about just as complete a change of meaning as that. But it would have helped if he had described his own purpose more clearly, since the secret discipline has a

---

[85] Lietzmann, *op. cit.*, p. 99.
[86] Cf. *Religion in Geschichte und Gegenwart* II, col. 530.

meaning that is so heavily charged with "religious" meaning. Bonhoeffer does not seem to have been aware that he had both a linguistic and a theological problem on his hands. This is why his "secret discipline" is handicapped by the fact that its meaning is not clear.

Why should there be such a secret discipline? Let us look at three possible answers. (*a*) Is it because men cannot understand the language of faith – unable to do so in the fifth century because of an excess of religious longing, and unable to do so in the twentieth century because of the loss of metaphysical interest and inward anxiety and a consequent limitation to immanentistic ways of thinking? But if that is the case, faith will never find a humanity capable of understanding it, and the secret discipline will always be a sociological presupposition making theological speech impossible. (*b*) Or does Bonhoeffer talk about a secret discipline because prayer, suffering and the sacraments are more significant means of expressing the presence of God in the world than, for example, preaching – in which case preaching will be the only act of the church that is exposed to non-religious criticism and suspicion?[87] But if that is the case, why give such a privileged position to prayer and sacramental life to the detriment of the sermon, as though the being of God could never be present except through his Word, the same Word which, to be sure, is prayed, lived, encountered and confirmed in the sacraments, but which is also spoken, announced, secretly heard and publicly proclaimed? Every difference created here by the secret discipline between preaching and sacrament helps to establish the false notion of an unjustified sacred realm. (*c*) Or, to suggest a final reason, does Bonhoeffer speak of a secret discipline because the times might not yet be ripe for a new language purged of its religious, evasive and pious overtones by the quiet practice, over a sufficiently long period of time, of Christians working in the world? I think this third reason is closest to those actually given by Bonhoeffer, for example in the statement of his hopes for his godson quoted above. It is similar to the opinion

---

[87] Even in *The Communion of Saints*, as we have already seen, the early Bonhoeffer had gone astray in my opinion, in the direction of a highly debatable theological sociology, dividing the concrete community into three increasingly secret circles, e.g. the baptized, those who hear the sermon, and finally the participants in the Lord's Supper.

of the *Jeunesse de l'Église* in France immediately after World War II, who characterized their own time as the time of John the Baptist and of "preparing the way,"[88] so that, tomorrow perhaps, a Word given new life by their silent waiting might be reborn.

But why and how are we to disguise the Word to conform to our fatally "apologetic" evaluations? Just as in his comments on the godlessness of the world, Bonhoeffer seems to have left an ambiguity hanging over the meaning of the secret discipline. Either it is directly related to the true mystery of the presence of God in this world, in which case it is the power of the companionship to which God calls his children in obedience and freedom, in resistance and submission, in prayer, suffering and blessing; or it is conditioned by the state of the world, which seemed overly eager to engulf Christendom in the fifth century, and seems inclined to become the "post-Christian" world of the twentieth century. The secret discipline thus runs the risk of enclosing the Word in a questionable kind of secret – as questionable when the early church believed that it was a good thing to transform the baptized into the initiated and the sacraments into mysteries, as it is today when certain Christians speak of "anonymous Christianity," the "incognito" of faith, a silent worship, a theology of silence and a theology of death, a tacit creed and an unexpressed identity. The first type of secret discipline binds the Christian to the secret of God, while the second makes God into a secret for man to possess. The first speaks within the incognito, while the second keeps silent and goes underground. I believe that Bonhoeffer basically wanted the first kind of understanding, but that some of his statements suggest the second. In a later chapter we will see certain of his followers pursuing just the opposite path.

However that may be, *Letters and Papers from Prison* is clearly

---

[88] The idea of "preparing the way" (*Wegbereitung*) is often found in *Ethics*, where it characterizes life in the penultimate. The secret discipline would thus be the unexpressed preservation of the knowledge of the ultimate in the midst of the worldly penultimate. "The secret discipline" is action in the penultimate for the sake of and by the power of the ultimate, "preparing the way" for the coming of Christ, undertaken in responsibility . . . The penultimate is the realm of the world, into which the ultimate, the eschaton, what we are indeed able to call the secret discipline, enters" (Meuss, in *Die Mündige Welt* III, p. 89).

the place where Bonhoeffer is testing his discovery. Bonhoeffer lived before God in the godless world. He prayed in a secular fashion and joined in God's struggles in this world. This attitude was not one of duplicity either toward God, as though Bonhoeffer had denied him while still obeying him totally,[89] or toward reality, as though he had adapted to it while still pretending to be responsible for it. It was the report of an experience for which christology provided the logic and furnished the key. And it is with Bonhoeffer's christology that we must therefore conclude this attempt to get inside his thought.

[89] This is Mascall's simplistic criticism of Bonhoeffer: "To believe that there was a God and then to live as if one believed that there was not, whatever else it might be called, could hardly be called honest." E. L. Mascall, *The Secularisation of Christianity*, Darton, Longman and Todd, London 1965, p. 42.

VIII

Jesus Christ as Structure and as Place

The statement that God and reality are united has no meaning in itself, although it can imply some incorrect meanings, such as the belief that reality is an empty area that God has now seized for his own benefit, or that God has been diminished and depersonalized in the unfolding process that was supposed to manifest him. Each way leads to an impasse. Either we have the transcendence of a distant world and a distant God, or we have the immanence of this world alone, a world that aspires to divinity.

The incarnation of Jesus Christ is the historic doctrine that challenges this kind of transcendence or immanence. It claims to unite God and reality in one living and indivisible whole, not speculatively but concretely. The real test of a theology of reality, therefore, is its christology. It has an obligation not to separate what is united, but to unite it in the way that Jesus Christ has done. Bonhoeffer's central theme – Christ present – thus stands for the presence of God in reality and the presence of reality to God. If it can make good its claim, then instead of seeing (or even better *not* seeing) how the previously established concepts of the divine and the human, the absolute and the relative, could possibly be joined together, we would learn from christology, in reverse fashion, something about the two unknowns of which we are so ignorant: who is God, and, at the same time, who is man? The question is not *"How* can Jesus Christ, in his own unique being, reconcile the contradictory characteristics that human speech attributes to the terms 'divine' and 'human'?", but rather, *"Who* is Jesus Christ?" By starting from this concrete manifestation we can be more precise about the concepts of "God" and "reality," which are otherwise so poorly defined and behind which we hide our ignorance. So christology is not only that portion of theology devoted to the study of redemption. It is also the description of what can give meaning to the word "God" as well as the word "reality," since the work of Jesus Christ consists in making each evident to the other in the unified relationship that reveals them both. Consequently, christology will not only describe a past event, to which religiously-inclined people attach special emotion and meaning. In addition it will now claim to interpret the fundamental structuring of what is, thus becoming the interpretive center of theology, ontology, anthropology and cosmology. It will be normative because it is descriptive, relevant because it deals with everyday life, able to question because it is firmly based, understandable because it is logical, non-religious because it is active in this world.

Bonhoeffer's systematic writings on christology date from 1932 to 1933. They include a course on "The Nature of the Church," given during the summer semester of 1932,[1] another course on "Christology,"[2] and a third on "Hegel's Philosophy of Religion,"[3] the latter two given during the summer semester

[1] There is a helpful summary of these lectures, compiled from students' notes, in Bethge, *Dietrich Bonhoeffer*, Appendix A, pp. 1057–72. Unfortunately this material is not included in the English translation.

[2] Reconstructed by Bethge in *GS* III, pp. 166–242, and translated into English as *Christ the Center* (=*Christology*), 1966, 126pp. All quotations below are taken from this translation.

[3] Unfortunately it has not been possible to reconstruct Bonhoeffer's lectures on Hegel, the announcement of which surprised Barth's students in Bonn. In Bonhoeffer's own library the books by Hegel are full of notations. Bethge has preserved a typical comment:
"Aim: to overcome the Enlightenment. Reconciliation of reason with religion. The knowledge of God.
1. The question of truth ... dogma, doctrine, church, faith.
2. The question of reality ... world history ... a total abstraction!
3. Theologically = the question of the church. God in the community ... Salvation, Rebuke: Intellectualism? Disposing of God? Hegel says God disposes of man from on high. Grace? Sin? Pardon? All three are central for Hegel. But – the dialectic stops at one place, namely with the concept of Becoming itself ... It is done.
Not 'thy will be done' but *it* is done.
The devil is let out to play, and that is why the final accounting is really so good. Each isolated concept (sin, etc.) is seen clearly in itself, but it is understood in the total scheme only as a moment of becoming. To overcome understanding by reason. But, to overcome reason by faith, faith that drives out the devil" (Bethge, *Dietrich Bonhoeffer*, German edition, pp. 266f.).

of 1933, with which Bonhoeffer must have concluded his university teaching. By dealing with them last, we are of course interpreting Bonhoeffer's works in reverse order. This decision is based on the clear convictions that have guided our interpretation: namely, that christology is as normative for Bonhoeffer's interpretation of God as it is for his interpretation of reality; that Hegel gave Bonhoeffer his basic stimulus when he was a student (during the writing of *Communion of Saints* and *Act and Being*) and when he was a young professor, after which he went on to work out his own point of view;[4] and finally that Bonhoeffer's limitations may center around an understanding of the incarnation that overemphasizes ecclesiology as well as secularization, and says far too little about eschatology, so that the relationship between a theology of the Word and an ontology of presence remains unclear.

Even if these convictions are wrong, it is better not to end with *Letters and Papers from Prison*, as though the whole of Bonhoeffer's thought were summed up in those final flashes of insight from his prison cell. The continuity of his thought is too apparent, as can be shown by the stability of his vocabulary. Words like reality (*Wirklichkeit*), deputyship (*Stellvertretung*) and structuring (*Gestaltung*), for example, run through all his works, and nowhere are they more clearly defined than in the texts of 1932–3, when Bonhoeffer was reflecting on the development of Christianity, the church and reality, at the very moment when Hitler was coming to power.

1. *Jesus Christ as concrete "spatiality"*

Bonhoeffer speaks of Jesus Christ both as a place and as a structure of the world around us, and almost never refers to him as an event in history. *Christ the Center* was planned as three parts: "The Present Christ," and his existence for me (*pro me*); "The Historical Christ," where Bonhoeffer deals with various christological approaches in the history of the church; and "The Eternal Christ," a portion that was never

---

[4] It should be noted that Martin Luther King, Jr, was also profoundly influenced by Hegel in the course of his studies from 1948 to 1953 at Crozer Theological Seminary in Chester, Pennsylvania, and later as a graduate student in philosophy at Boston University.

written. The first part is divided into two sections, one called "The Figure [or Structure] of Christ"[5] (Christ as Word, Sacrament and Community), and the other called "The Place of Christ" (Christ as the center of human existence, the center of history and as the mediator – and thus also "center" – between God and nature). In the course Bonhoeffer had given the preceding summer on "The Nature of the Church," we find the same kind of vocabulary being used for the church: part one is called "The Place of the Church," and part two, "The Structure of the Church" (the active community, the worldliness of the church, the Christlike nature of the church and the boundaries of the church).

This vocabulary based on spatial imagery seems to me fundamental to a correct interpretation of Bonhoeffer. While a vocabulary based on events suggests that history brings to existence such things as openness, possibility, conversion, decision, progress and eschatology, i.e. things that change its course (but perhaps only seem to), a vocabulary based on structural imagery aims at revealing what in reality is determinative, already present and discoverable in the here-and-now, logical and providing a foundation both in abstraction and concreteness. Most contemporary theology, particularly the dialectical theology represented by Barth's early writings and Bultmann's ongoing work, uses a vocabulary based on events and vertical imagery; such words as event, advent, tangent, encounter, leap and decision are common. Structural and horizontal vocabulary seems, in fact, less suited for speaking about revelation, which is indeed an amazing historical event, constantly renewed eschatologically. But a doubt soon arises about whether an outside event can ever fully make its way into reality, and whether it does not remain tangential to reality and finally insignificant. By adopting a forthrightly spatial vocabulary, drawn from both sociology and logic,[6] Bonhoeffer is trying to overcome this suspicion that the revelation of God in Jesus Christ might be only tangentially related to the ongoingness of the world, without being

[5] The German word is *Gestalt*, translated as "figure" in *Christ the Center*, but in the present work as "structure." Cf. further n. 7 below.

[6] In *The Communion of Saints*, Bonhoeffer never enters into dialogue with the sociologists of history, who are the most interesting, such as Marx, but with the logicians of social existence, who are necessarily conservative.

understood for what it truly is, the central structure of all reality.

Consequently, in the 1932-3 lectures, Bonhoeffer adopts the word "structure,"[7] and uses it to describe what Jesus Christ means in reality. Let us use this word as the key to Bonhoeffer's lectures on christology. He begins by reminding us that dogmatic teaching comes to birth in silence before the absolute, not because the teaching is a "mystical" introduction to the contemplation of silence as in the mystery religions, but because Christ, the spoken word of God, is himself inexpressible. The natural sciences examine causes, the arts examine meanings. Both are works of reason, of *logos*, imminent in things and in beings. Christ comes into conflict with both of them, as the unassimilable anti-Logos, even though Hegel, more cunning in this regard than the Enlightenment, thought he could assimilate him under the transitory form of negativity. Christ is the anti-Logos, the death of the human *logos* and the life of the divine *logos*. To ask *how* he is what he claims to be indicates a desire to reassimilate his anti-*logos* into the arrangement of the *logos* in a system of atheistic immanence. But to understand *who* he is, is to recognize in him the transcendence of the anti-*logos* as the boundary of our own *logos*. The church is the place and the space where the question "Who are you?" is asked and heard. Christology is the study of the "ontological structure of this 'Who are you?' ", when it claims to be the unknown and hidden center of reality, "without coming to grief on the Scylla of the question 'How?' or the Charybdis of the question of the 'fact' of revelation."[8] By this cryptic phrase Bonhoeffer locates his christological research outside the early church's creedal controversies over nature and substance (the "how"), and those of modern theology since the Enlightenment and Schleiermacher on the inner experience of Christ (the "what"

---

[7] Throughout this work, *Gestalt* is translated as "structure," even though the word "form" is often used elsewhere. Cf., for example, the fullest work on Bonhoeffer's christology, John A. Phillips, *The Form of Christ in the World, A Study of Bonhoeffer's Christology*, 1967, 302pp. However, the word "form" preserves, in Aristotelian terminology, an external meaning that is inappropriate, I believe, in relation to Bonhoeffer. "Form is defined by its relation to matter that is foreign to it; while structure does not have a separate content; it is the same content understood in a logical relationship conceived as a property of reality" (Claude Lévi-Strauss, "La Structure et la Forme," *Recherches et Dial. phil. et écon.* 7, p. 3).

[8] Bonhoeffer, *Christ the Center*, p. 33.

or the "fact"). *Who*, therefore, is it who comes to destroy man's *logos*, and is destroyed in man's place? Bonhoeffer comments that the unique kind of question that Jesus asks about himself, in distinction for example from Socrates or Goethe, is often heard better by those who know little than by those who believe they know a great deal.

When [the worker] says, "Jesus was a good man," he is at any rate saying more than when the bourgeois says, "Jesus is God."[9]

Jesus is always being betrayed by kisses, particularly theological ones. He is encountered by those who remain firm under the ambiguity of his questions. Can this ambiguity be overcome by referring to his works? But his works, like all works, remain ambiguous. Either they are only very human works, or they are unable, as works of human history, to lift us to God. Therefore, the person has priority over the work, and christology over soteriology. It is the task of christology to analyze the structure of this personal being defined in the history that Bonhoeffer describes as "the present Christ."

We encounter him in the sphere or "space" of the Church, concretely, spatially and temporally, not as immanent energy, not as an inspiring personality, but as a person who continually questions us about himself.

Ever since his resurrection Christ has been everywhere all the time, Bonhoeffer states as a good Lutheran believing in ubiquity. "When he was on earth, he was far from us. And now that he is far from us, he is near to us" (Luther). Thus the present Christ is he who today is the pioneer, deputy and initiating structure of our reality. Three actions help to identify this structure:

1. Christ as *the structure of the Word* sets me free by establishing me as one who speaks, in distinction from animals or stones. However, I do not offer this word to myself, as German idealism believes. Nor am I in control of it, in analogical relationship to God, as Catholic natural theology would allow me to believe. On the contrary, I am established by it when it is addressed to me. Christ, the structure of the Word, creates me as word because there is the possibility of response.

2. Christ as *the structure of sacrament* reaches my reality not at

[9] Bonhoeffer, *Christ the Center*, p. 35.

the level of my *logos* but at that of my very nature. Thus the sacraments do not merely "represent," they *are*, as Bonhoeffer declares with vigorous Lutheran positivism. This does not mean that the sacraments are a second incarnation, but that they are the presence of the "divine majesty" in the humiliation of the flesh, revelatory actions that locate the divine incognito both in nature and in history – although Bonhoeffer worries about the depersonalization of the Lutheran doctrine of ubiquity, which he sees as an unfortunate response to the even more unfortunate question asked by the Reformers about the "how" of Christ's presence.

3. Finally, Christ as *the structure of community* is known in the church, which is the extension of his body in time and space. Both he and the church are the "communion of saints," revealing God on earth, for Bonhoeffer rejects as not originally Pauline the separation that Ephesians makes between the head of the church and its members.

Christ as structure finds his place in reality. He who is the founding Word, the present sacrament and the ongoing community, becomes (to refer again to Lévi-Strauss) the "property of reality." Here, indeed, the two most central words in Bonhoeffer's vocabulary take shape: the deputyship (*Stellvertretung*) of Christ becomes the structuring (*Gestaltung*) of reality. What he is becomes the place where we are.

If this structure [here, *Struktur*] can be demonstrated to be existential, and not a chance accidental one, then we shall have theological proof that the mode of the existence of the person of the Risen One is in time and space.[10]

Christ stands in my place, both on the boundary of my existence in order to cross over the impassable boundary that separates me from my new being, and in the rediscovered center of that existence. He leaps over the wall of judgment that imprisons me, in order that he may be the center or "middle" of the reality inhabited by God, like the tree of life in the middle of the garden where God walked with man.

Christ is at the same time my own boundary and my rediscovered centre, the centre lying both between "I" and "I" and between "I" and God. The boundary can only be known as a boundary from

[10] Bonhoeffer, *op. cit.*, p. 61.

beyond the boundary. In Christ man knows it and thus at the same time finds his new centre.[11]

Three spatial images help Bonhoeffer describe the structural sphere in which the person of Christ is understood:

1. He is the center of *human existence*, not in the psychological sense of personalities being inspired by him, but in the onto-logical sense of our being persons before God. Such an ontology cannot be demonstrably confirmed and can only be accepted by faith. Christ's fulfillment of the law that separates me from myself, is in itself a creative act that is both the judgment and justification of man.

2. Christ is also the center of *history*, not in the demonstrable sense that he is well known in sacred and secular history, always a relative matter, but in the ontological sense of his messianic reality, which leaps over the boundary never before overcome in history between promise and fulfillment. As the center of history, at that place of real and yet hidden messianism which is Israel, Christ simultaneously destroys and fulfills all the expectations of human history. There history is forced to recognize its own insurmountable limit, as man had previously done, and find a new center in Christ. Bonhoeffer adds to this affirmation a very Lutheran conclusion about the church (*Christus prolongatus*) as the boundary and center of the state – a boundary that announces the crossing over of all human orders by the cross, and a hidden center, not in the sense of a visible state church, but of a church that realizes on behalf of the state that the real order is God's and not its own. From this we get statements that clearly reflect the Lutheran doctrine of the two realms:

As long as Christ was on earth he was the rule of God. When he was crucified, the rule broke in two, one by his right hand and one by the left hand of God. Now his rule can only be known as twofold, as church and as state. But the whole Christ is present to his church. And this church is the hidden center of the state . . . Christ is the centre of history as the mediator between the state and God, in the form of the church.[12]

3. Finally, Christ is the center between God and *nature*.[13]

[11] Bonhoeffer, *op. cit.*, pp. 61f.   [12] Bonhoeffer, *op. cit.*, p. 66.

[13] At this point, for linguistic reasons the English translation of *Christ the Center* breaks the parallelism of structure in the German text, and here translates *Mitte* as "mediator" rather than "center."

As the new creature, he does not reconcile nature to God, but delivers it from its enslaved and senseless silence (cf. Rom. 8). For nature is not under guilt, but under the curse. It is no longer free. In the sacraments, where "elements of the old creation have become elements of the new creation," Bonhoeffer sees one of the signs of the promised deliverance:

Enslaved nature does not utter the Word of creation directly to us. But the sacraments speak. In the sacrament, Christ is the mediator between nature and God, and stands for all creatures before God.[14]

Christ is the liberating structure of these three "places" – human existence, world history, and the created order – in that he marks off the boundaries of their power (which offer a false salvation, a false messiah, a false dominion and a false lord) and also becomes their rediscovered center.

The second part of *Christ the Center*, "The Historical [*Geschichtlich*] Christ," is a long study of attempts in the early and contemporary church to describe the risen Christ as the center of reality. Bonhoeffer notes that all of the early christological definitions were negative, critical and anti-heretical. They established a point of view by excluding other points of view. They rejected the Docetic heresy in which Christ only seemed (*dokein*) to have a human body; the Ebionite heresy of the elevation of a man to divine status; the Monophysite and Nestorian heresies, the former a speculation about the identity of the incarnate one, and the latter a speculation about the unreality of the incarnation itself (during which discussion Bonhoeffer recalls at great length the Lutheran position against the Calvinists: *finitum capax infiniti, non per se sed per infinitum*);[15] and finally the Subordinationist and Modalistic heresies, which sought to reconcile God and reality at the price of sacrificing either the unity of God or the fulness of his revelation. According to Bonhoeffer, these early christologies, although overly-influenced by Greek emphasis concentrating on the concept of substance, had the negative value of showing that the question "How?" could *not* be asked about the incarnation. As a result they leave the way open for the question "Who?"

Out of this question Bonhoeffer develops a positive christology in two brief sections:

---

[14] Bonhoeffer, *op. cit.*, p. 67.   [15] Cf. *Christ the Center*, p. 96.

1. *Christ is he who became man.* His divinity adds nothing to his humanity. It qualifies it from above by saying, God is this weak man, born in a manger, whose baptism ratifies his freely chosen weakness until the cross, just as freely chosen, ratifies his baptism. Bonhoeffer states here that the virgin birth ought not to be used to describe the "how" of the incarnation, but to express "who" this God is who has become weak and challenged. For the glory of God is expressed in the fact that he himself becomes contingent, free and hidden.

2. *Christ is the humiliated and exalted one.* These two modes of being describe him better than the "two natures" theory of the early Greek fathers. Christ is fully God in his humiliation and fully man in his exaltation. His miracles do not destroy the incognito of the humiliated God within him, for where the non-believer sees only magic, which does not bring him out of his unbelief, the believer sees in them the foreshadowing of the divine action at the end of the world. Not even the resurrection, the miracle of miracles,[16] penetrates the incognito, for it too remains ambiguous, accessible only to the faith of the disciples who followed Jesus and believed without seeing, whereas those who saw did not believe. Here Bonhoeffer discusses the empty tomb in the same way he had early discussed the virgin birth. The empty tomb likewise remains ambiguous. "Empty or not empty, it remains a stumbling block (*ärgerlich*),"[17] and does not destroy the incognito.

This is why the church continues to live as the humiliated body of Christ, even after the resurrection. It is not good if the church boasts of its lowliness too hastily. It is equally bad if it boasts of its power and influence too hastily. It is only good if the church humbly acknowledges its sins, allows itself to be forgiven and acknowledges its Lord.[18]

It is on this note that the 1933 lectures on christology end. There was to have been a third part on "The Eternal Christ," but Bonhoeffer did not have time to complete the lectures.

His lectures in 1932 were on "The Nature of the Church," and thus preceded by a year those on the nature of christology.

[16] Bonhoeffer, like Bultmann, always uses the term *Wunder*, a marvel, rather than *Mirakel*, with its overtones of magic.

[17] Bonhoeffer, *op. cit.*, p. 117.   [18] Bonhoeffer, *op. cit.*, p. 118.

In these lectures also Bonhoeffer used structural categories of concrete spatiality and not the event-centered categories of historical questioning.

The church is not a postulate. Man has no "need" of it. It is the place where God speaks. The church and theology have nothing to do with postulates but only with concrete realities (*Tatsächlichkeiten*). Barth emphasizes the character of revelation as "act," and speaks only of the demands of the church, not of its "being." Catholicism, on the other hand, stresses only the "being" or nature of the church. When speaking about the "place" of the church, Bonhoeffer would like to think at the same time of both the demands and the nature (the act and being) of the church. It is from rationalism and mysticism that we have inherited the idea of the "non-spatiality (*Ortlosigkeit*) of God."[19]

The initial place of the church is the world. When the church has no location in space, it becomes

intangible and unassailable. It lives in the midst of flight from itself, it becomes the world without the world becoming the church. It leads the existence of Cain – always a fugitive.[20]

Another danger is that the church will be found only in certain privileged places. Today it is likely to be among the bourgeois and the conservatives:

Its worship deals only with the needs of the middle classes. It is no longer able to deal with the difficulties of economic questions, the intellectuals, the atheists or the revolutionaries.[21]

But God alone can choose his place and transform it by his gracious presence, so that the church can witness to that portion of the world that God alone creates. "Christendom" localized the church in certain activities that were peripheral to reality. Religion thus became something apart from the main stream of life – which is not true of God. Consequently the church, in contrast to "Christendom," ought not to locate itself outside the secular world, nor (on the principle that it is a "special light") separate itself from the world. Furthermore, dogmatic

[19] Bethge, *Dietrich Bonhoeffer*, German edition, p. 1057.
[20] *Ibid.*, p. 1058. [21] *Ibid.*, p. 1058.

theology must have a central and not peripheral place in its work for the church as the "given revelation" with a concrete spatiality that saves it from metaphysical speculation. Instead of asking about the place of the church in theology, one must turn the question around and study the place of theology in the community of faith. "The empirical church is the presupposition and the object of theology." Theological method must therefore be "neither analytic, nor synthetic, but descriptive."[22]

So we see that, in differentiation from his course on christology, Bonhoeffer began his lectures on the church by putting "place" before "structure," since Christ is the structure that determines the place of the church understood as the extension of his body, while the church is the place where the new structuring of the world by Jesus Christ is understood and interpreted. Having dealt with the place of the church, Bonhoeffer then moves on to deal with its structure. The church's structure is given to it by God.

Structure signifies unity and totality. Inauthentic structures are synthetic and fragmented.[23]

Thus instead of speculative religious syntheses, Bonhoeffer prefers a description of revealed reality. In this connection he picks up the parallel, first developed in *Communion of Saints*, between Christ and Adam, both seen as recapitulations of reality – Adam as a recapitulation of its rupture, and Christ as its communal restoration. The church is the place where the christological foundation of the reciprocal relationship between submission and deputyship is developed. In the life of the church the Holy Spirit interprets the meaning of Christ, who is present only through such interpretation. This is why Bonhoeffer fears using a confession of faith in an overly-objective way when it is needed as a "means of propaganda and combat," forgetting that only the Holy Spirit understands the "secret discipline" – a theme to which Bonhoeffer had given much attention even by 1932 – as something that is thought and lived, and not only spoken and proclaimed. He recalls that the early church had engaged only in negative definitions against heresy, i.e. the "places" that faith did *not* occupy, letting faith remain as an immediate and inner jewel, not unexpressed to be sure, but nevertheless far removed from the public propaganda of the community. Picking up also certain themes of "life together," Bonhoeffer insists on sacrifice, intercession and mutual forgiveness, "a daily repetition of the sacrifice on Golgotha, but without the shedding of blood," as well as the confession of sin, which does not turn men individualistically toward their own problems but toward God in the midst of reality, and toward Christ as every man's deputy, present within the community.

Bonhoeffer next attacks the unreality of the notion of a perfect church. Just as Christ became a worldly creature, the church is not docetic, but worldly also. Only an acknowledgement by the church of its worldliness can free it for service to all men. This worldly church, however, will recognize the need for self-discipline:

It has to limit the arbitrariness of individuals. It has to prevent its ministers from becoming moralists and demagogues. It must not surrender its worship to politics or aesthetics. A forced worldliness and conscious lack of discipline does not overcome the world, but stems from secret anxiety. The church must even be able to ex-communicate.[24]

Finally, Bonhoeffer quickly indicates two limits for the church: first, the Kingdom of God, within which God alone knows the elect (and in describing which Bonhoeffer unleashes a Lutheran broadside against the too-precise information Calvinists have about predestination); and secondly, the state, which alone has received the judgmental sword of power from God. "The office of the state is neither Christian nor godless, but responsible and objective (*sachlich*)."[25] Only the word of the present Christ enables the church to see in the state the limit of its own competence in relation to the state, and to be the state's critical and hidden center.

These early lectures on a spatial and structural approach to christology and ecclesiology suggest two comments:

1. Bonhoeffer describes the presence of Christ as a reality in so far as he is an object of faith. But a vocabulary based on

[24] *Ibid.*, p. 1070.   [25] *Ibid.*, pp. 1071 f.

structure is no more able than a vocabulary based on events to claim that the reality of Christ's presence – in the world, the church, human existence, history and the natural order – is a reality available to those outside of faith. I encounter only what I believe. But what I believe is in the midst of reality itself: it is not a metaphysical idea that is postulated from outside itself, not a privileged inner experience, not an event that takes place outside its own foundation. To describe Jesus Christ as the unifying structure of mankind and the world must appear to non-faith to be a postulate as absurd as to call the cross and resurrection the events which are the bearers of decisive meaning for history. Indeed the former may seem even more absurd, in that the desire to define a theological object on the level of structure, and not be content to leave it as one of a number of possible interpretations (about which philosophies, ideologies and religions could then dispute endlessly), appears to be an abuse of language – as though by formalizing the language of "structure" one had communicated the message of "deputyship." This difficulty is insurmountable outside of faith.

It should be noted, however, that Bonhoeffer always qualifies the structuring of reality by the notion of deputyship, and that reality is therefore never either formal or abstract, but always concrete and active. Since Christ is the reconciler of the world, Christ as structure is the one qualified to give reality a dynamic quality. The very fact that he is this structure is itself reconciliation. Christ is God in his deputy-role as "the man for others," to quote the famous phrase so often picked up since by Bonhoeffer's followers – a phrase that has been avoided in the present discussion since it is later than the 1933 lectures on christology, and since it can imply a humanistic reduction of christology quite out of keeping with the classical emphases of the texts we have been discussing.

2. The second comment can be put in the form of a question: did not Bonhoeffer's christology and ecclesiology change so much that these early writings have become "dated" by what came later? This is the thesis of most of the commentators on Bonhoeffer's christology. John Phillips, who has made the most careful study of the matter, bases his own interpretation on a progression in Bonhoeffer's thought. According to Phillips,

Bonhoeffer began with Christ existing in the form of the church, a theme represented by his two university dissertations; made this more specific as Christ present in the secret discipline of discipleship during the period of the Confessing Church; and finally discovered the hidden presence of Christ beyond the boundaries of the church in the whole world, the secular "world come of age" inhabited by the this-worldly transcendence which is Christ "the man for others." Although agreeing with E. H. Robertson that christology is the key to Bonhoeffer's thought in each period of his life, Phillips stresses the difference between the periods. In particular, he sees Bonhoeffer gradually breaking through the ecclesiological limitations of Christ existing as community, toward "an emerging Christology of the person and work of Christ, separate from and in some opposition to his 'Christ existing as the church.' "[26] On this reading, *The Cost of Discipleship* marked the stage of freedom in facing the world, while *Letters and Papers from Prison* represented freedom for the world. Whereas during the period of the Confessing Church the presence of Christ was limited to the boundaries of the church, the later Bonhoeffer could finally cross over those boundaries and discover the church as being "nothing but a section of humanity in which Christ has really taken form."[27] And from this Phillips states the conclusion which traces the supposed evolution in Bonhoeffer's christology and ecclesiology:

We have followed the path of Bonhoeffer's theology from his early "Christ existing as the church" to the breaking down of the limitations of his ecclesiological doctrine of revelation and of Christ in the *Ethics*, and to the final affirmation of the this-sidedness of Christ and the Christian life in a world come of age.[28]

There are several reasons why this interpretation of various stages in Bonhoeffer's christology is not convincing. For one

---

[26] Phillips, *The Form of Christ in the World*, p. 74. In a review of this work, Robert Hartman notes the coexistence of what Phillips calls Bonhoeffer's two christologies throughout the whole of his work. One of them is the "classical" christology of the person of Christ, the other an "historical" approach that stresses Christ's being with men in their historicity. But when Hartman reproaches Bonhoeffer for his lack of historicity, does he not misunderstand the originality of Bonhoeffer's notion of the structuring of space? Cf. *Union Seminary Quarterly Review*, Autumn 1967, pp. 108–13.

[27] Bonhoeffer, *Ethics*, p. 83.   [28] Phillips, *op. cit.*, p. 245.

thing such themes as the non-religious character of faith,[29] and the "secret discipline," which are said to characterize the later Bonhoeffer, appear very early in his writings. Conversely, his vocabulary, in any case particularly in *Ethics*, remains spatial and structural.[30]

Behind these critical details lies an important question: did Bonhoeffer give up an attempt to interpret Christ and the church in concrete terms, and was he convinced that only an "anonymous Christianity" (immersed in the secularity of the world and living a sort of double life between existence for others in a godless world and the "secret discipline" before God and with God) could now correspond to the form that the presence of Christ in reality ought to take? Did he feel that the concretizing of the church was a hindrance to the human freedom of Christ, understood as this-worldly transcendence?

These questions must be left open. Only Bonhoeffer himself could say what he was seeking. But it would be most surprising if this interpretation corresponded to his ongoing task, namely to unite God and reality. Indeed, "anonymous Christianity," a church not acknowledging the secret discipline or the incognito, but a church of silence and waiting, would appear to be just like the modern forms of that duality between the visible and invisible church, between idea and fact, between God and reality, against which Bonhoeffer never stopped fighting. Without concretizing the church, how could there be a concrete commandment, and furthermore how could there be a real coming to grips with the concrete world? Naturally, the church must do battle against "religious" evasion, provincialism and shortsightedness, on behalf of the incarnation and the fulness of the faith in the midst of reality, but how can this be done concretely, if the church does not have a "place," and a concrete embodiment? The recoil from spatial and concrete

---

[29] According to Bethge, the word "religious" is criticized by Bonhoeffer as early as 1927 – from *Act and Being* right through *Letters and Papers from Prison*.

[30] I do not see on what basis Phillips can say, in tones of commendation, that Bonhoeffer's christology and ecclesiology finally cease being spatial: "A non-religious Christianity seems necessarily bound to a decisive and final rejection of 'spatial' descriptions of Christ as the Church or any other limited spaces ... In their present form the prison letters reflect the final separation of Bonhoeffer's Christology and his conception of revelation from ecclesiology and the search for a *spatial* 'concretion'" (Phillips, *op. cit.*, pp. 141f.).

modes of thinking always runs the risk of becoming a gnostic and docetic attraction to an abstract idea, once described in religious, metaphysical and inward terms, but currently in immanentist, secular and anonymous terms. Thus instead of being afraid to give a place to the church for fear of the limitations implied in all concepts of place, should we not on the contrary want to give a place to it, so that in just that place the "non-religious" nature of faith could be developed and made concrete? Who if not the church can carry out this work? What would the idea of the church amount to without a place where the reality of Christ as the representative structure of this world could be embodied? Consequently, there must be a place – a place that is neither a ghetto nor merely an idea, a place in the very center of reality, neither a retreat at the edge of things nor an ivory tower of piety, theology or liturgy. Possibly all of this is no more than a quarrel over words. But it is words that constitute things, and there is a danger that from a supposed evolution in Bonhoeffer's thought one might infer the surrender of spatial christology, concrete ecclesiology, and the identity of faith, as having become contradictory to identification with the world. In that case Bonhoeffer's battle for God in the midst of reality would finally emerge as a diminution of God's reality, i.e. as a new dualism between the visibility of the world and the invisibility of faith.

More significant, therefore, than any such evolution would seem to be Bonhoeffer's constant emphasis on the concrete. He discovered it first of all in the empirical state church that refused, for conservative reasons, to succumb to the temptations of perfectionist separatism. As a young man, Bonhoeffer was a defender of "Christendom" in a way that was most disconcerting to his later readers. In *Ethics*, he was still trying to preserve the heritage of the "Christian west"! He next embodied this emphasis on the concrete in relation to the Confessing Church, making a specific decision in its favor the crucial test of truth in the midst of reality, both in Nazi Germany and in the ecumenical movement. And at this point, according to those who recall the conservative emphases of his earlier life, he himself became a separatist. But concrete faith went through the rejection of heresy and the acceptance of what was not schism but salvation, for Bonhoeffer was convinced that unity without truth was an illusion. Finally, Bonhoeffer was seeking this same sense of the concrete when, in prison, he foresaw a Christianity and a church no longer in real contact with the mental, technological and political evolution of humanity. What would be the point of a church that had preserved its soul at the cost of losing the world? What would be the point of a place for a church that manifested Christ not in the center but at the edges and backward corners of reality? The "non-religious interpretation of Christianity" and the "secret discipline" are Bonhoeffer's attempt to establish some concrete structures throughout this third part of his life. Therefore, far from acclaiming them as the crossing of anachronistic frontiers of the church, or as a way of becoming free of structure, place and concreteness by means of an indefinable anonymity and an involvement without identity, we must, it seems to me, understand them as the pursuit of a single quest, that of maintaining the unity between God and reality which the incarnation of Jesus Christ has established as the recreated structure of the world.[31]

2. *Incarnation and Eschatology*

An overall question remains: might not Bonhoeffer's christology, and particularly his ecclesiology, actually be *too* concrete? This is a question that applies as much to the formulation of the church of "Christ the man for others" in Bonhoeffer's final period, as to his "Christ existing in the form of community" in the first period, or to the imitation and "following after" Christ in the second period. To put the question more sharply: when Bonhoeffer says that in Christ God enters fully into reality, and that the church is the place where God's penetration of the world is centered, does not the realism of his position

---

[31] Bethge has described this basic quest admirably: "Bonhoeffer's concern in 1944 was not merely an hermeneutical device for interpreting old Biblical documents, nor an outline for a program of 'religionless Christianity', nor a phenomenological study of 'man coming of age.' This kind of perspective would turn Bonhoeffer into the reductionist he never wanted to be." ("Bonhoeffer's Christology," in Vorkink, ed., *op. cit.*, pp. 49f.) He goes on to note that in 1944, even more clearly than in 1932, Bonhoeffer said, "What is bothering me incessantly is the question what Christianity really is, or indeed who Christ really is, for us today." (Cf. *LPP*, 30 April 1944, p. 152.)

transform the theology of the Word into an ontology of the divine presence? The incarnation of Jesus Christ is the real[32] mystery of the revelation of the Creator in the created order, and of the struggle of the reconciler, so that the crossed arms of destiny now take the form of arms summoning men from the cross. The incarnation is the moment of the specific understanding of God's activity that changes both man and reality. Thus when Bonhoeffer speaks of it as a structure of reality, does he not come dangerously close to a Hegelian ontology in which the incarnation is above all the point at which God ceases to be external to the world? In this case the incarnation is in danger of becoming one of the ongoing structures of becoming, and of being universalized as it is depersonalized.

The charge may seem strange when one remembers how Bonhoeffer insists on the person of Christ by his repeated question, "Who are you for us today?" But his thought continually veers toward the specific and tangible presence of God in the church – whether it be the state church, the Confessing Church or the "non-religious" community of the prison letters – as though the incarnation had brought about an irrevocable presence, instead of revealing an irrevocable summons to reality. Between God, Christ, the church and the world a consistency is established that is almost ontological in character, and which makes it hard to understand the "without God" of the tangible world and the "before God" of reality grasped by faith. Pushed to its logical conclusion, we get the following sequence: Christ is God become man; the church is Christ prolonged in the world, the extension of the Incarnation; the world is the church determined by that presence of Christ, i.e. of God, in reality – from all of which follows a unity between reality and God that is established in christological, ecclesiological and worldly terms. All this sounds very Hegelian, and is a far cry from the Kantian transcendentalism that so strongly characterized the early Barth and all the post-Bultmannians. In this view, God is himself involved in the development of the world. He does not sit in another world of unchanging lordship

[32] Recall again that *wirklich*, particularly in Hegel's use of the word, points not so much to something that is less objective in its meaning as to something realized and being realized. Cf. the root *werken* meaning "to bring about" or "effect," and the noun *Werk*, meaning work, act or deed.

undiscernible to us on earth. He becomes man, flesh and world so that we can only speak of him in worldly terms, as the inner secret of the only intelligible worldly mode of speech, which is its own mode of speech. Worldliness is thus the only theological language that is really possible, just as divinity is the only real but hidden key to worldliness.[33]

No matter how intriguing may be this attempt to take seriously God's involvement with the world, in Christ and in the community, we must ask ourselves whether this is the real meaning of incarnation, and whether it is really talking about God being transformed into reality and reality being transformed into God. Kierkegaard objected to Hegel's lack of a true eschatology, since it meant that the last judgment became history's verdict upon itself. To be sure, Bonhoeffer always has a place for eschatology, and he makes a clear distinction between the church and the Kingdom of God – although this is less clear in 1932 between Christ and the church, and even less clear in 1944 between the church and the world. But he often gives the impression of having pressed the similarities too strongly (even with the hidden tension of the "secret discipline"), just as others press the differences too strongly. Now it is both the good fortune and the distinction of reality not to be God and vice versa, just as it is the good fortune and distinction of the church not to be Christ, and vice versa. It is their good fortune and distinction, in other words, to be themselves, united and not confused, personal and not anonymous. The finite is capable of the infinite, reality is capable of God, as the Lutherans like to say. But man is not God, and reality cannot contain him, as the Calvinists like to add. So we must say that there is a Lutheran emphasis in Bonhoeffer (similar to that found in Hegel) that troubles us here, in which the incarnation is in danger of ceasing to be the word of revelation *to* reality

---

[33] A single sentence from Altizer, one of the radical followers of Bonhoeffer in the United States, will illustrate the point: "It is only the language of the radical profane that can give witness to the fullest advent of the Incarnation." To which may be added the final sentences of his article, so odd in a bold manifesto on "Christian atheism," but so indicative also of the double reversal, divine-profane, profane-divine: "When faith is open to the most terrible darkness, it will be receptive to the most redemptive light. What can the Christian fear of darkness, when he knows that Christ has conquered darkness, that God will be all in all?" (T. J. J. Altizer and W. Hamilton, *Radical Theology and the Death of God*, Bobbs-Merrill, New York 1966, pp. 20f.)

and of being transformed into the ongoing structure *of* reality. Only in an eschatological sense can it be claimed that theology is a patent ontology. Until the end comes, we live by faith in a Word that has come to structure reality, but has not yet become the actual structure itself. I am thus less aware of the evolution that led Bonhoeffer, according to the title of Hanfried Müller's book, "from the church to the world," than of the permanence of his ontological realism, which in 1927 led him to believe too much in the presence of Christ being continued in the church, just as in 1944 it led him to believe too much in the presence of Christ hidden in the secular world come of age.

But the Protestant tradition has insisted so strongly, with Kant, Kierkegaard, Bultmann and Barth, on God's transcendence over the world, that when Bonhoeffer comes speaking and living God's involvement *in* the world, he sets on fire the thoughts and lives of our generation.

IX

Interpretations of Bonhoeffer

The currents of thought that witness to Bonhoeffer are many and varied. It has become unusual in our century of intellectual specialization and unbroken careers for the same person to be an intellectual, a churchman and an activist. It is even more unusual for a body of thought, continually chopped up by outside events in the course of a life prematurely ended at thirty-nine, to stand the test of time, once the spotlight of current interest has been dimmed by passing years and the myth of a "precocious genius" has been punctured by critical study.

It was well over a decade before extensive commentaries on Bonhoeffer began to appear, beginning with Gerhard Ebeling, who was a young pastor at Finkenwalde, as far back as 1956; Hanfried Müller in 1961; the team of Thomas J. J. Altizer and William Hamilton from 1963 to 1966; and Heinrich Ott in 1966. There is no doubt that the publication of Bethge's monumental biography in 1967, with all of its previously unpublished material, also contributed to this discovery in reverse – the discovery of a point of view that came into full flower through a private correspondence from prison about the future of Christianity in the era of the death of religions and ideologies, but was rooted in the era of great intellectual debates about the transcendental or ontological nature of the knowledge of God, and grew its branches when the Confessing Church rediscovered the theological dimension of political struggle and the political dimension of "theological existence today."[1] To

[1] *Theologische Existenz heute*, the name of a journal founded in Germany in the early '30's to carry on the theological struggle against Nazism.

everyone – theologian, Christian, and contemporary man alike – Bonhoeffer offers strong and creative nourishment for dealing with the world around him.

There is a twofold difficulty in interpreting Bonhoeffer: (1) as far as Bonhoeffer himself is concerned there is a wide variety of material in his fragmentary writings, whereas (2) after his death the harvest of what he sowed grew up in a variety of ways, depending on the kind of soil where his legacy bore fruit. As in all interpretation, we must first of all understand the author on his own terms, taking account of possible ambiguities of meaning, and only then see him through the eyes of his readers, taking account of their possible misunderstandings or their creative responses. Previous chapters have already suggested places where Bonhoeffer seems unclear in his own terms. In the present chapter, therefore, our task will be to listen to the interpreters on their own terms, naturally paying attention to how accurately they interpret Bonhoeffer, but also noting where they come out after starting with him. It would not be particularly interesting to establish an orthodox interpretation of Bonhoeffer, and all the less so since he criticized himself as his thought was developing, and since no one can claim to know where his theology of reality would place him on the theological spectrum today. On the other hand, the impulses which he has generated are important elements in the situation of the faith, thought and action of Christianity today. To speak of the development of Bonhoeffer's legacy is to deal with a part of the Christian quest in order that faith may have worth and weight.

We will begin by recalling the perplexing many-sidedness of the man, what could even be called his apparent discontinuities. He was a man for whom even the undeniable continuity of his vocabulary did not offer clear indication of the basic consistency of his thought. Karl Barth, whose most independent disciple Bonhoeffer surely was, can serve to express the perplexity of systematic minds when confronted by the Bonhoefferian fragments. Following that, three main interpretations of Bonhoeffer will be classified, in full recognition that such categorizing is itself an interpretation, and that it means taking a position on the accuracy of these expositions and the truth in what they propose.

The preface to *Bonhoeffer in A World Come of Age*, a series of papers first presented at Union Theological Seminary, describes the many-sidedness in striking fashion:

Interpretations of the life and thought of Dietrich Bonhoeffer are like the answers elicited by a Rorschach test – no two commentators see the same things. Bultmannians view his work as the creative application of demythologization; Tillichians discover that "the world come of age" has affinities to a "theonomous culture"; Barthians, despite Bonhoeffer's criticism of "revelational positivism," find in his thought the extension of the master's critique of "religion"; radical theology locates its *textus classicus* in the *Letters and Papers from Prison*; secularists rejoice in his anti-clericalism; and mass culture finds in his life and death its needed martyr.[2]

It is not hard to extend this catalogue of contrasting impressions and contradictory effects. Bonhoeffer centered his work on the church – and yet he has become the inspiration of those who attack the church. He was nourished on Barth – and yet he is one of the most prominent figures of the post-Barthian era. In politics he was undoubtedly a right-wing Hegelian – and yet there are new left-wing Hegelians who admire him tremendously. He lived and contemplated suffering – and yet he is hailed today for having made an end to the gloom and masochism of sin. He was both a Lutheran and a German – and yet it is not in German Lutheranism that he is most seriously heard. He committed himself wholeheartedly to ecumenism and was open to many aspects of Roman Catholicism – and yet his followers today are less interested in ecumenism and Catholicism than in atheism and secularism, looking not toward Rome (or Geneva or Moscow) but toward Cuba, Latin America and Vietnam. He was a man whose sentences were strained, abstract and always heavy – and yet he has given birth to a multitude of slogans. But none of this is really important, since he himself preferred to speak controversially rather than to repeat sterile platitudes. Like Georges Bernanos, his favorite novelist, he vowed to "disturb" people out of love or anger, and for him to "disturb" meant making people think and act.

Let us look at some of the ideas Bonhoeffer engendered, first of all among those who feared that alongside his amazing

[2] Vorkink, ed., *Bonhoeffer in a World Come of Age*, p. ix.

degree of involvement there was a lack of systematization and balance which, while providing an intriguing stimulus to thought, was also a disconcerting invitation to talk nonsense. As early as 1952, Karl Barth had expressed reservations about the later Bonhoeffer, all the while using the pages of his *Church Dogmatics* to express his appreciative debt to the younger Bonhoeffer of *The Communion of Saints, Creation and Fall*, and *The Cost of Discipleship*. Some extracts from a letter Barth wrote in 1952 will communicate his mood:

One cannot read [Bonhoeffer's letters] without having the impression that there might be something in them ... But as always with Bonhoeffer one is faced by a peculiar difficulty. He was – how shall I put it? – an impulsive, visionary thinker who was suddenly seized by an idea to which he gave lively form, and then after a time he called a halt (one never knew whether it was final or temporary) with some provisional last point or other ... Do we not always expect him to be clearer and more concise in some other context, either by withdrawing what he said, or by going even further? Now he has left us alone with the enigmatic utterances of his letters – at more than one point clearly showing that he sensed, without really knowing, how the story should continue – for example, what exactly he meant by the "positivism of revelation" he found in me, and especially how the program of unreligious speech was to be realized.[3]

In the remainder of the letter Barth asks himself, with a slightly troubled sense of humor, about the import of the criticism Bonhoeffer makes of him. He also minimizes the importance of Bonhoeffer's project of a "non-religious interpretation of Christianity," as no more than an attempt to guard against "unthought-out repetition ... without searching for a deeper meaning which he himself did not offer us, and perhaps had not even thought of himself."[4]

Finally, in relation to Bonhoeffer's spirituality and his theme of sharing in the suffering of God, Barth evokes the image of "the melancholy theology of the North German plain," a theology that seemed to him to have marked Bultmann as well. But he ends with the comment, "A lessening of the offence he has provided for us would be the last thing I should wish ..."[5]

[3] "From a letter of Karl Barth to Landessuperintendent P. W. Herrenbrück, 21 December 1952," in R. Gregor Smith, ed., *World Come of Age*, pp. 89f.
[4] *Ibid.*, p. 91.   [5] *Ibid.*, p 92.

Fifteen years later Barth resumed his reflection on the later Bonhoeffer, in a letter sent to Bethge after reading the latter's huge biography which had just been published. This letter also includes praise and perplexity:

I was surprised to learn that Bonhoeffer had arrived specifically during one of his early visits to Rome at a fresh view of what *the Church* (and within the Church the institution of confession) could really be, and that he was thus called to part company with the school of Seeberg, Harnack and Holl.

I was even more surprised to learn that in the years following 1933 Bonhoeffer was the first and practically the only one who came to grips with the *Jewish Question* in a central and vigorous way. For a long time I have considered myself somewhat guilty for not having brought out that same question publicly in the German Church (for instance in the two Barmen Declarations of 1934 that I helped to write), even though a text containing this would not have been, because of the mood of that time, acceptable either to the "confessors" in the Reformed Synod or in the general Synod. This does not however excuse the fact that at that time – because of my other interests – I did not at least come out strongly for that cause and in the proper form. Only through your book did I become fully conscious of the fact that Bonhoeffer had done just that from the very beginning . . .

More important for me than these discoveries was the fact that through reading your book I was stimulated to rethink in its totality the unfinished path that was trod by your brother-in-law and friend. It seems to me that there are three perspectives to be distinguished that form a unity for him, even if they are not seen by him as a unity and do not quite come out that way in your presentation.

1. First there is what Andreas Lindt in his essay in *Reformatio* called "the way from Christian faith to political action." This was also my theme after I had left theological liberalism. It took the form of "Religious Socialism" in its specifically Swiss form. By the way, did Bonhoeffer ever concern himself with Blumhardt, Kutter and Ragaz, who were at the time my "fathers"?[6] In Germany,

---

[6] It is clear that many of Bonhoeffer's most important ideas are found in the writings of Ragaz. A number of Bonhoeffer's later emphases can already be found in these writings, such as the work of God moving from the church to the world, recognizing however that the theology of the cross saves faith in the Kingdom of God from being confused with earthly progress or messianic movements; faith in the "ultimate" as nourishing the "penultimate" of culture; the need to unite positive socialism with the hidden cross; emphasis on the Kingdom of God as standing against "religion"; the praise of secularization; "following after" Christ; true worldliness, etc. Surely no author has shared so much in common with

which was still burdened by its Lutheran tradition, there was a true "need for catching up" in this direction, a need which I had either taken for granted or only mentioned on the side: ethics – human relations – the servant Church – discipleship – socialism – the peace movement – and along with all this: politics. Bonhoeffer felt this lack and the need to remedy it very strongly from the start and even more intensely later on when he was bringing it out for discussion on a broad basis. It was and still is – we hope in a definite way – this long overdue addition, so vigorously defended by him, that creates the secret of his enormous impact in this respect, particularly after he had also become a martyr.

2. Side by side with this, he seems to have pursued the renewal of private and public worship. I can sense what he intended and I would like to express it by the term "discipline." If that is indeed what he had in mind, I could only agree, but must confess, even after having read your book, that the answer is still not complete and clear to me. Apparently this was the "secret discipline" of which he spoke toward the end of his life. It is clearly different from the one of Berneuchen or Taizé.[7] But beyond that, what? . . . I would like to have been present and active at Finkenwalde, as you were, in order to understand better. In this matter did Bonhoeffer arouse as much interest, find as many followers (*disciples!*) and create as much of a "school" as in the matter I shall deal with now?

3. Even after having read your book, I still remain in the dark about the point upon which the discussion focussed from so many sides in

---

Bonhoeffer as Ragaz. He is certainly closer than the more mystical Blumhardt and the more pragmatic American, Walter Rauschenbusch.

However, certain basic differences remain. Ragaz was consistently anti-ecclesiastical in a way that Bonhoeffer never was. Ragaz was a socialist who was doctrinally committed to non-violence. Bonhoeffer's "state-controlled" Lutheranism was quite different from such an orientation, even when he was close to Gandhi, when he was unwilling to undertake military service, and when he talked about a new society. Ragaz developed his position before Barth, Bonhoeffer after Barth. Ragaz worked in the political-cultural context of the Social Democratic Party, Bonhoeffer in the context of Nazi nihilism. And above all, Bonhoeffer was clearly not well acquainted with the thought of Kutter, Rauschenbusch or Ragaz, and had only a slight knowledge of the two Blumhardts, each of whom is cited only once in Bethge's biography.

This is why I am more impressed with the affinity of Bonhoeffer's thought to Hegelianism, which is more explicit, decisive and fairly continuous, even if it is less clearly expressed from 1940–3 than from 1927–32. The interesting relationship between Bonhoeffer and "religious socialism" is a similarity, but never a true affinity or influence.

[7] Berneuchen is a movement in Germany for the restoration of liturgical piety. The French Protestant monastic community of Taizé has, of course, grown up since Bonhoeffer's time.

Letters and Papers from Prison, i.e. his intended renewal of theology both in the narrower and in the wider sense of the term. What is the "world come of age"? What does "non-religious interpretation" mean? What am I to understand by "positivism of revelation"? I know everything, or at least a great deal of what the experts make of it up to Heinrich Ott. But to this day I do not know what Bonhoeffer himself meant or wanted by it, and I am even inclined to doubt a little whether Systematic Theology (I am also thinking of his *Ethics*) was his strongest field ... Even if I should be mistaken, I should still re-affirm that his letters from prison represent only one (in this case the last) of the stations in his intellectual and spiritual journey, a journey that was very turbulent from the beginning even though that was not its aim; that he might have been capable of the most astonishing evolution in quite a different direction; and that we do him an injustice when we suddenly place him in some line with Tillich and Bultmann and interpret him in relation to those passages (or as his own prophet based on these passages), whether in the sense of a very bourgeois liberalism or, as H. Müller sees it, as the precursor of the ideology of the D.D.R., or, in R. Prenter's interpretation, as a new Lutheran Church Father.

Barth concludes by speculating how he would be remembered if he had died early in his own theological life – after the publication of his *Epistle to the Romans* or even after the 1927 edition of *Christliche Dogmatik*, totally scrapped a few years later in favor of the new approach expanded in the twelve volumes of *Church Dogmatics*. He feels that Bonhoeffer enthusiasts are in danger of subjecting their hero to a similar and undesirable fate.

Such is Barth's final appraisal in trying to understand the last thoughts of the one of whom he had said in the field of ecclesiology, "I openly confess that I have misgivings whether I can even maintain the high level reached by Bonhoeffer, saying no less in my own words and context, and saying it no less forcefully than did this young man so many years ago."[8]

We shall now listen to those to whom the later Bonhoeffer spoke in a significant way, which if not always fully clear was nevertheless indispensable, provocative and fruitful. These interpretations will be classed under three headings: Lutheran, atheist, and ontological, and will be limited to the main emphases the interpreters themselves choose. Over and above the convenience of using certain headings to sort out a complex

[8] Barth, *Church Dogmatics* IV/2, p. 641, T. and T. Clark, Edinburgh 1958.

problem, these three particular currents of interpretation also correspond to certain areas of theological influence and represent a kind of chronological progression. It should be clear from the start that I personally feel that there is a growing value in these three kinds of interpretation.

1. *Lutheran interpretations*

Like Kierkegaard, Bonhoeffer was a Lutheran who challenged established Lutheranism's application of sound doctrine to the world around it, but who was deeply committed to the main emphases of Luther's discoveries. Thus it is only natural that some of his interpreters try to explain all his work on the basis of these great discoveries. This seems to be the case with Gerhard Ebeling, who interprets Bonhoeffer in the light of Luther's contrast between law and gospel, and with Hanfried Müller, who does the same thing from the Lutheran doctrine of the "two realms." In support of their interpretations, both can point to Bonhoeffer's deep rootage in the Lutheran tradition. But against such interpretations one can ask whether the similarity between Bonhoeffer's twentieth-century concerns and Luther's sixteenth-century concerns is as great as either interpreter assumes it to be.

Ebeling's interpretation of Bonhoeffer is found in a speech he gave in 1955 on "The Non-Religious Interpretation of Biblical Concepts," and in an article, "Dietrich Bonhoeffer," first published in 1958.[9]

Ebeling clearly recognizes Bonhoeffer's three great concerns: the concrete structure of the church, the relationship of faith to the world's reality and the secular mind, and "the question of the concrete demand, that is, of bringing to expression what is commanded here and now, and not just general ethical principles."[10] Now, he says, the later Bonhoeffer expressed these three concerns by setting up a radical opposition between faith and religion, consistent in so doing with a similar opposition he had expressed as far back as 1928, when as a young assistant pastor in Barcelona he had written:

[9] Both are reprinted in Ebeling, *Word and Faith*, SCM Press, London, and Fortress Press, Philadelphia 1963, pp. 98–191, and 282–7 respectively.

[10] Ebeling, *op. cit.*, p. 286.

Here one meets people as they are, away from the masquerade of the "Christian world," people with passions, criminal types, little people with little ambitions, little desires and little sins, all in all people who feel homeless in both senses of the word, who loosen up if one talks to them in a friendly way, real people; I can only say that I have gained the impression that it is just these people who are much more under grace than under wrath, and that it is the Christian world which is more under wrath than under grace.[11]

The "Christian world" in a religious sense is here synonymous with the unreal world, ultimately incapable of encountering God, who did not come to fulfill reality in a "religious" sense, but in order that this reality itself might be held before him in faith.

Ebeling next enters into a systematic discussion of the opposition between religion and faith, and in so doing uncovers some fundamental roots that go beyond a sociological understanding of the gains or losses of the religiosity that is either explicit or latent in the outlook of contemporary man. (This is an issue to which, rightly in my opinion, he attaches only relative importance, just as among our contemporaries an appreciation of the importance of mythology in understanding Bultmann is only of relative importance.)

It is here that the Lutheran opposition between law and gospel becomes the crucial issue. For did not Bonhoeffer himself, for illustrative purposes, set up an analogy between the contemporary presupposition of religion and the Pauline presupposition of circumcision – neither of which is of any value in coming to faith in Jesus Christ? And what was circumcision except a form of legalism from which the gospel frees us? It follows from this that the theological principle with which to think through the opposition between religion and faith would be provided by the relationship between law and gospel. While we cannot simplistically identify religion with law, we can think through the opposition between religion and non-religion within the problem of law, since it is here that the legalistic opposition between what must be believed and what cannot be believed is played out, whereas faith is based on what one truly and freely believes, without any division between duty and remorse, which is the distinctive characteristic of the rule of law. Ebeling is quite explicit on this point.

[11] Bonhoeffer, *No Rusty Swords*, p. 37, cf. *GS* I, p. 51.

Religious interpretation is legalistic interpretation. Non-religious interpretation means interpretation that distinguishes law from gospel.[12]

From this starting point Ebeling explains how, in distinguishing gospel from law, one must avoid making the gospel into "a special religious law" that is added to reality and divides man once more between two spheres – the ordinary world around him and the oppressive and unreal world of religion. However, as a good Lutheran Ebeling does not deny the necessity of law as an expression of our captive situation. His intention is to distinguish the gospel from it – a gospel that never leads man back into bondage. But a difficulty arises from the fact that men in our time, unlike men in Luther's time, no longer understand their situation as one of being in bondage to the law. So Ebeling, with many nuances, virtually equates religion and non-religion, i.e. supernatural answers or consolations and atheism, as implicit bondage. Both these forms of bondage are confronted by the gospel, i.e. faith, which is anti-legalistic because it is neither religious nor anti-religious, but which challenges both forms of bondage in the name of the Word of grace that frees men from all judgment. So religion, which is one of Bonhoeffer's major themes (and even though Ebeling always places it alongside its brother enemy, atheism), exercises an authority over man similar to that of the law. When religion insists on the question, "What *must* I believe?" it transforms faith into the law of reason, as happened in the Middle Ages. When it insists on the question, "What *can* I believe?" it transforms reason into the law of faith, as happened in the Enlightenment. Religion is thus a foreign category, incapable of embodying the spontaneity of grace which alone can say what it believes from within its own reality – living out the autonomy of reason in the bosom of a man dependent on God by faith, achieving that "arrival at the language" of the Word of God that is one of Ebeling's central themes.

Now Ebeling's interpretation of religion (and atheism) as a problem of law surpassed by faith certainly strikes a responsive chord in Bonhoeffer who, indeed, opposes the church, understood as Christ's creation, to religion understood as man's anxiety (or indifference).

[12] Ebeling, *Word and Faith*, p. 142.

What matters in the church is not religion but the form of Christ, and its taking form amidst a band of men.[13]

In this sense Ebeling helps us to understand religion as the captive aspect of reality, and faith as the liberated aspect of that same reality, and his clarification shows how deeply rooted Bonhoeffer is in the soil of orthodox Lutheranism. But Ebeling appears to stumble over three difficulties:

1. In reintroducing *atheism* as an equal partner of religion when confronting law, Ebeling is stressing something that is not present in Bonhoeffer, whose interest centers on the encounter of faith with atheism and not on a "religious" (though anti-religious) definition of atheism. Hence the point of Bonhoeffer's discussion fades away, and is replaced by a classical discourse on the opposition between what comes from man (non-religion as religion) and what comes from God (faith).

2. Ebeling emphasizes the battle against *legalism*, which he sees as the real mainspring of religion (as well as non-religion). But did this ever characterize Bonhoeffer's thought? Was he not by contrast passionately concerned to discover the concrete commandment, i.e. the law of obedience created by faith? By reorientating Bonhoeffer in the Lutheran perspective of gospel versus law, Ebeling seems to me to lose sight of Bonhoeffer's own emphasis, the transition from faith in the gospel to concrete ethics and politics, whatever else he may say, often very well, about the medieval side of Bonhoeffer's work that is more attached to reality than to abstract truth or freedom.

It is not surprising under these circumstances that Ebeling should do all he can to draw Bonhoeffer and Bultmann together, something that not only goes against Bonhoeffer's own statements (judged by Ebeling to be erroneous) but also fails to grasp the basic difference between the two positions. Bultmann and the Bultmannians operate within the framework of a transcendental Kantianism that prohibits any objectivization of God, more or less reduces the values of the Old Testament to the level of an imagery that has been destroyed by over-objectification, and thinks in the categories of act, event, individual summons and vertical eschatology. Bonhoeffer and the Bonhoefferians, on the other hand, operate within the framework of an incarnational Hegelianism that forbids any

[13] Bonhoeffer, *Ethics*, p. 84.

"spiritualizing" of God, emphasizes the value of the Old Testament as protecting a "this-worldly" Christianity from the constant temptation to gnostic irrelevance, and thinks in the categories of being, communal deputyship, structure and spatiality indwelt by the presence of Christ. Any interpreter of Bonhoeffer (and this would include Bishop Robinson as well as Ebeling) who fails to take account of the profoundly different ethos between these two theological currents (without pre-judging the similarities they might still have) does not help us understand what is at stake, and runs the risk of a kind of triviality, flatly opposing new theologies worried about the confrontation with modernity, with so-called traditional theologies. The content of Bonhoeffer's thought, as well as Bultmann's, deserves better treatment than this.

3. The final question to Ebeling is the most difficult. He remarks that according to Luther the law describes man's true situation before faith delivers him from it. He adds that today *twentieth-century man* ignores the law, thus making it difficult to preach to him about grace, and then goes on to raise the whole question of the contemporary irrelevance of the gospel of Jesus Christ for a humanity that no longer looks for salvation in sixteenth-century terms. I have the feeling that Ebeling raises the question courageously, but that he lacks the innovative power of a Bonhoeffer, who, when confronted by the same issue, speaks of responsibility rather than salvation, of dislocation rather than sin, and of restructuring life rather than redeeming it. In this way he creates new "non-religious" concepts, just as the Old and New Testament writers did in their time, so that the living God could speak not in the outmoded language of the gods and pious practices that were dying out, but in the day-to-day language of men living in the reality of the world. So by interpreting religion (and non-religion) as the present-day equivalents of legalism, Ebeling seems to fall into the trap Bonhoeffer wanted to avoid, of expressing himself as though we were still in the sixteenth century, as though we had to reassure ourselves from the stance of classical theology, instead of listening to the question: what does Jesus Christ become today for non-religious men who feel themselves neither in bondage to the law nor looking for salvation, men who on the contrary feel, much more than men of the sixteenth century, the grandeur and

the difficulty of living with the responsibilities of earth, technology, psychology and outer space?

For such reasons as these, Ebeling's interpretation of Bonhoeffer, so full of insight in its details, seems to me more an attempt to fit Bonhoeffer into a Lutheran framework than a creative pursuit of his heritage.

It seems to me that the same thing happens with Hanfried Müller's interpretation.[14] Although both Ebeling and Müller are Lutherans, their context and concerns are totally different. Ebeling lives in West Germany and is particularly concerned about hermeneutics and the relation of being to language. Müller lives in East Germany and is particularly concerned about politics and the development of the evangelical church in an atheistic socialist regime. However, both of them hear in Bonhoeffer what they had already learned from Luther, Ebeling that the gospel frees one from the law, the law of the sufficiency of atheism as much as the law of the fulfillment of religion; and Müller that God's governance is expressed through the "two realms" – the hidden realm of grace, and the visible realm formerly ruled by the prince but today ruled by rationality. Ebeling stresses the development from law to faith in individual understanding, while Müller stresses the fundamental duality that makes up reality, e.g. full acceptance of the secular (and atheistic) coming-of-age of man's corporate life, combined with the "secret discipline" of those who live by the hiddenness of the cross in the midst of that world.

Müller's book is very large, and it is impossible to do full justice to its learning and impact in a few pages. He stresses the development in Bonhoeffer's thought, which evolved from a Word of God limited to the community of the church, during the first period of his life, toward a Word of God directly related to the whole of human society, during the third period. He puts

---

[14] Hanfried Müller, *Von der Kirche zur Welt. Ein Betrag zu der Beziehung des Wortes Gottes auf die Societas in Dietrich Bonhoeffers theologischer Entwickelung*, 1961, 575pp. A shorter version of Müller's basic thesis is found in "Concerning the Reception and Interpretation of Dietrich Bonhoeffer," in R. Gregor Smith, ed., *World Come of Age*, pp. 182–214, translated from *Die Mündige Welt* IV, pp. 52–79. Two assessments of Müller's position are J. M. Lochman, "From the Church to the World," in Marty and Peerman, eds., *New Theology*, No. 1, Macmillan, New York 1964, and Bethge, "Bespreschung Müllers *Von der Kirche zur Welt*," in *Die Mündige Welt* IV, pp. 169–74.

little stress on the second period of Bonhoeffer's life, that of the struggle of the Confessing Church, which he tends to judge rather severely as a necessary response made within the bosom of the confessional family. Thus the "clerical" Christianity with which Bonhoeffer started became "societal" – a term that is preferable to "social" which is too liberal, or "socialist" which is too ideological. Bonhoeffer had groped for a long time before arriving at his recognition of a world fully "come of age" joined to life under the cross alongside the suffering of God. The decisive turn takes place between *Ethics*, which is still characterized by a Christian nostalgia for the fading order, and the prison letters that are open to the future of Christianity in a rational atheistic society. Müller finds this shift characteristic of the radical alternative that he sees running through the history of the church, between a position that is clerical and bourgeois, exemplified by "early Catholicism, the apologists, the scholastics and orthodoxy, the romantics and their ideology of the Christian west," and another position that is worldly and free, exemplified by "Paul . . . the early Luther and the later Bonhoeffer."[15] The latter position refuses to clericalize society. It stresses the importance of this world by living the *theologia crucis* within it, conformed to the life of Jesus Christ on earth. This is the non-religious word of the forsakenness of God that has truly overcome the world. Contemporary preaching must retain the messianic secret of the New Testament about the presence of God in this world, for "the condescension of God is the true fulfillment of his transcendence."[16]

Thus christology opens up toward a humanism instead of getting lost in metaphysics. Bonhoeffer's truly unique greatness is seen in his ability to break the fatal liaison between the debasing of man by the doctrine of sin and the necessity of grace, and the equally fatal liaison between an authentic humanism and atheism. Bonhoeffer's solution draws its power not from an awkward compromise that either gets rid of the cross or surreptitiously limits the possibilities of the world, but from a hidden unity between an affirmation of man and the "christological" suffering of that same man, between a "yes" to the world and the basic struggle that is involved for Jesus

---

[15] Müller, in *World Come of Age*, p. 211; cf. *Die Mündige Welt* IV, p. 75.
[16] Müller, *Von der Kirche zur Welt*, p. 421.

Christ and those who follow him when that "yes" is lived out. As Müller puts it:

What is qualitatively new is that Bonhoeffer is eliminating the pessimistic elements from his world view, and strongly emphasizing the optimistic ones, and at the same time committing himself fully to a *theologia crucis* and eliminating all the elements of a *theologia gloriae*. This liaison between a *theologia crucis* and immanentist optimism seems to be the new way that Bonhoeffer opens up to us in his last letters. It seems to me that this is the first time that a Protestant theologian has witnessed to Christian freedom in the world, not only by the desecularization of the church and the declericalization of the world but, beyond that, by a positive, optimistic, immanentistic and progressive use of this freedom, instead of avoiding the tasks of this world by conservatism or this-worldly resignation.[17]

Bonhoeffer would thus be a witness to the transition from "Christendom" (so clearly evident from *The Communion of Saints* to *Ethics*) to a type of Christianity that gave up trying to remain a social structure, in order to become a pure word of pardon in a secular world come of age. Indeed, he helped to bring this transition about. According to Müller, Bonhoeffer was a bourgeois youth who learned the hard way to leave the maternal womb of his class and church so that he might live out the future of faith in a world in which God could no longer lay claim to a "place" for his hidden presence. During the time of the Confessing Church, Bonhoeffer had been tempted to move to pure condemnation of the evil world for the sake of a doctrinal and pious other-worldliness. Thus Müller views *Life Together* as a "program" of inward response, coincident with the threatened breakup of the Confessing Church after the Synod of Oeynhausen.[18] But Bonhoeffer recovered from this temptation and separated a *theologia crucis* from "social irrationalism." Without equating them he joined together human "sociality" and the reality of God become man – a man who suffered because he felt responsibility for the world around him.

---

[17] Müller, *op. cit.*, p. 356.

[18] Bethge, incidentally, takes issue with this interpretation. He points out that *Life Together* was not a "program" but the account of the actual experience shared during the years at Finkenwalde in the course of the Confessing Church's continued struggles against Nazism. Cf. Bethge's review of Müller in *Die Mündige Welt* IV, pp. 171ff.

Bonhoeffer clearly saw the real duality, which is not between the religious and the secular, between this world and the beyond, but *within* this world, between the two dissimilar realms of the same God, i.e. rational positivism and the secret discipline of the cross. Bonhoeffer thus carried on the struggle that Luther waged in his own lifetime against a metaphysical dualism that abolished the incarnation; against a clericalism that corrupted both the church and the world; and equally strongly against the "enthusiasm" of the sect groups who abandoned the penultimate realm of culture and reason for a pietistic withdrawal into the ultimate realm of grace. But God rules in both realms. *Absconditio Dei sub contrario* (Luther).

Thus Bonhoeffer helps us confront the future by extending the old concern about Christendom and the relation between church and state into the new concern about a society in which Christendom has disappeared, and the relationship between the Kingdom of God and the whole of humanity.

What matters is no longer the old question that has been "solved" so often, of the relation between church and state, nor even the more alarming theme of the relation between "justification and justice" (*Rechtfertigung und Recht*), but a much more general question: How can God's first creation and his second, i.e. human society and the Kingdom of God, meet in the church in such a way that the church can give to each the rights that belong to it: rights to the world come of age, i.e. to a society that realizes its autonomy in free responsibility, and rights to a new humanity which in distinction from the other is given to us only by faith and not by sight? It is a question of the freedom of the church to understand itself as part of "the world come of age" – not contemptuous of it but sharing its existence – that part which believes for the rest of the world in the justification of the sinner.[19]

Müller's whole book is thus dominated by the search for ways in which Christianity can relate to a society that offers it no "place," and a society in which Müller does not want the church to defend its past privileges in a reactionary manner, since we are not going to return to the situation before the "coming of age" of the world – before the eighteenth century, before Lessing and (quite clearly as far as Müller is concerned) before the 1917 revolution, let alone before the communist government

[19] Müller, *op. cit.*, p. 155.

in East Germany. This is why Müller's large book ends with a small quotation from Bonhoeffer:

It may be that on us in particular, midway between East and West, there will fall a heavy responsibility.[20]

Müller's attempt to interpret Bonhoeffer as favoring a Christian acceptance of atheist society is a powerful one, particularly in the context in which he develops it:

Today it seems that the religionless world hears the gospel in Bonhoeffer's controversy with the religion of a false church. Might the open and public attack of the sovereign Word of God upon his church – which is fleeing to religiosity, restoration, and the past, or is itself attacking and ruling the world from this fortress – be the secret of non-religious proclamation, or, more correctly, the secret of the non-legalistic preaching of the gospel for the religionless?[21]

But two questions remain, particularly pressing to those who are aware how hard it is for the church freely to be the church when its past and perhaps even its present influence all its public activity in a reactionary, bourgeois and anachronistic fashion.

1. In relation to society, what happens to the church's *prophetic* ministry if its existence is reduced to the secret discipline of hidden suffering? In that case, is it not society's turn to complain when the church becomes silent? If one is not entitled to infer a "social irrationalism" from the *theologia crucis*, even less can one infer an unconditional approval of the secular world, as though it were rational and legitimate in and of itself. A Christian apologetic built on loyalty to the established order is just as dubious as one built on clericalism. Truth and freedom are indivisible, and Müller's book seems too conditioned by the context to which it is addressed to remain convincing.

2. How can the church give up a structural embodiment without becoming unduly "spiritualized"? If it is that portion of the non-religious world that believes on behalf of the rest of the world in the justification of sinners, how can it make clear that

---

[20] Bonhoeffer, *LPP*, 30 April 1944, p. 155; cited in Müller, *op. cit.*, p. 421.

[21] Müller, in *World Come of Age*, p. 212. This is an appropriate place to recommend the excellent book by Daniel Cornu, *Karl Barth et la Politique*, Labor et Fides, Geneva 1968, as an example of a kind of freely political proclamation to both the religious and non-religious world.

this justification really exists in the reality of human experience, without having some structure of its own? Can an invisible church (or more precisely one whose existence is hidden within the secret discipline) make plain to a secularized society that God is present in its midst – which was certainly Bonhoeffer's intention – and not only at the borders of inwardness and metaphysics? If the visible church can be guilty of a "triumphalism" that lords it over the world and denies the cross, an invisible "spiritualized" church might be guilty of denying its own tangible existence in the world and replace proclamation of the cross with an introverted mysticism.

Thus when Müller, in line with the Lutheran doctrine of the two realms, stresses a separation between the world come of age and the "secret discipline," does he not fall into the very separation between God and reality against which Bonhoeffer was always struggling, no longer seen as a separation between this world and the beyond but now as a separation within this world? As with Ebeling's interpretation we must ask if Müller's stress on the Lutheran heritage does not also lead him further and further from Bonhoeffer. We must also ask if the twentieth-century task can be summed up in terms identical with the sixteenth-century task, e.g. "to declericalize the world and desecularize the church," as Müller puts it. Today we are not the inheritors of the great medieval confusions, but live in a world that acquired its full autonomy long ago. It is a time when the church is no longer threatened by religious or clerical omnipotence but rather by its marginal impact, its insignificance and its fleeting importance in the world. Müller's title, "from the church to the world," i.e. from the cloister to the streets, had a creative ring to it in the sixteenth century. But does it not sound like a plea for reductive conformism in the twentieth century?

Like Kierkegaard, Bonhoeffer admired Luther without simply repeating him. Kierkegaard did battle for faith against the "Christendom" of Danish Lutheranism. Bonhoeffer perceived his own battle for faith in other terms: to embody in himself, before God, the "non-Christendom" character of the world. Neither Bonhoeffer nor Kierkegaard sought to return directly to Luther; both sought to discover what Luther would have said in their situations. Thus Bonhoeffer's question does not seem to center on being delivered from the bondage of law by faith, nor on the purifying corrective of a doctrine of the two realms, but rather on how existence with Jesus Christ can restructure a "secular" world come of age – a world with a high degree of technical organization, but without any protection against "the menace of organization."[22]

Bonhoeffer's whole project, to the very end of the prison letters, seems to me to combine his intuitions about existence with Jesus Christ (developed in *The Cost of Discipleship*) and the structuring of reality (developed in *Ethics*), with a clear recognition of the "godforsakenness" of Christ and of the "coming of age" of that reality without God. This is certainly a "new" Bonhoeffer, but not a "different" Bonhoeffer.

2. *Atheistic interpretations*

The interpreters of Bonhoeffer who are included under this heading are the ones who have attracted the most attention. Most of them come from North America, with some European counterparts to the degree that part of the American cultural situation is reflected in Europe as well. They have developed a movement called "the death of God theology,"[23] although as

---

[22] Bonhoeffer, *LPP*, "Outline for a Book," following the letter of 3 August 1944, p. 209. Attention should be called to the whole outline of the book on which Bonhoeffer worked while in prison, pp. 208–11. It is surprising that the commentators make so little use of this outline, in which Bonhoeffer describes this new world by its secularity, its security, its over-organization, its constraints and its spiritual emptiness, as much as by the words that have become so well known, i.e. the world "come of age," and the "religionless" world. Bonhoeffer wrote in Germany where there was no separation of church and state. The "peoples' democracies", such as the one in which Müller writes, have not achieved that separation either. The United States, where Hamilton and Altizer live, although having always legally had separation, is however accustomed to a "secular" church as well as to a state that is more or less "religious"! A large part of the message of Bonhoeffer and his followers is thus explained by the discovery of a secularity that has been common currency in France for a long time. It is less important in opening doors, already long open, to the world's coming of age or the non-religious nature of the church, than to the restructuring with Jesus Christ of the emancipated, over-organized and forsaken world which to Bonhoeffer is what our world has become.

[23] On the "death of God" theologians cf. Gabriel Vahanian, *The Death of God*, Braziller, New York 1961; Paul van Buren, *The Secular Meaning of the Gospel*, Macmillan, New York, and SCM Press, London 1963; William Hamilton, *The New Essence of Christianity*, Association Press, New York, and Longmans, London 1963; Thomas J. J. Altizer, *The Gospel of Christian Atheism*, Westminster, Philadelphia 1966; and especially the closest thing to a manifesto for the movement, a collection

we shall see, the two main proponents of this movement seem to differ strongly with one another, even more than Barth, Bultmann and Gogarten did at the beginning of the movement of dialectical theology in Europe. Within the scope and purpose of the present chapter, no attempt will be made to give a detailed account of their position. From an examination of their writings we will assess the recurring themes and the conclusions drawn from them. They are theologically motivated by the later Bonhoeffer, particularly his themes of the "forsakenness" of Jesus Christ and the "non-religious" world come of age, and culturally motivated by Nietzsche, particularly his themes of the "death of God" and the affirmative acceptance of "eternal return." However, Bonhoeffer is only the evening star in their sky, which is filled with many other heavenly bodies, modern planets and contemporary comets.[24] After looking at their

---

of articles by Altizer and Hamilton, *Radical Theology and the Death of God*, Bobbs-Merrill, Indianapolis 1966, 202pp. Except where indicated all of the following quotations are from this last book, with the page number cited in parentheses within the text. Thomas W. Ogletree, *The Death of God Controversy*, Abingdon, Nashville 1966, treats the thought of Altizer, Hamilton and van Buren. C. N. Bent, *The Death of God Movement*, Paulist Press, Westminster, Md. 1967, and Robert L. Richard, *Secularization Theology*, Herder and Herder, New York 1967, Burns and Oates, London 1968, are Roman Catholic treatments. A variety of critiques is contained in Bernard Murchland, ed., *The Meaning of the Death of God*, Vintage Press, New York 1967. Materials on the historical background are collected in Altizer, ed., *Toward a New Christianity*, Harcourt, Brace and World, New York 1967.

[24] The bibliography which Hamilton has added to *Radical Theology and the Death of God* is perhaps the most interesting part of the entire book. It groups the main catalysts by chapters. The beginnings are found in Enlightenment theology and the French revolution. These are followed by nineteenth-century materials, with particular emphasis on the Hegelian left, Nietzsche and William Blake, but also the early Schleiermacher, Heinrich Heine, Dostoievsky, Tolstoy, and Matthew Arnold, as well as such Americans as Melville and Mark Twain. These are followed by various examples of modern radical religious thought, such as Dewey, Santayana and Huxley; Catholics who have concerned themselves with the theological interpretation of atheism (Borne, Chenu, Lacroix, Lepp, Rahner, von Balthasar); literary figures from André Gide to D. H. Lawrence; modern drama (Brecht, Büchner, O'Neill); existentialism (Camus and Sartre); psychoanalysis (Freud, Jung, Fromm, Marcuse); Jewish thinkers (Buber, Fackenheim, Jacob Taubes and particularly Richard Rubenstein). This leads to the thinkers who are described as "Preparation for radical theology in Protestant neo-orthodoxy," Bonhoeffer, Bultmann and Tillich. Among European exponents of radical theology are John Wren Lewis, J. Moltmann, J. A. T. Robinson, R. G. Smith and Dorothee Sölle. Alongside of them are thinkers who have studied the problem of "secularization" (Harvey Cox, Gogarten, Hoekendijk, Larry Shiner, Van Leeuwen, von Weizsäcker), men of letters (Ingmar Bergman, Lucien Goldmann, Hubert Fingarette), and finally five thinkers who are held to be representative of radical theology:

positions, we will try to assess whether Bonhoeffer is better understood in this American cultural perspective than in the return to German Lutheranism we have just examined.

The present theological situation seems to Altizer and Hamilton to be dominated by the awareness of an event, the fact that God has died in our time, our history and our existence. When these authors speak of the "death of God" they are not just referring to the God of Greek metaphysics, or the inadequate imagery that has characterized Christian attempts to speak of God, or the false gods of pagan idolatry; they are speaking of the death of the Christian God himself. Any theological reflection today that tries to skirt around this reality is nothing but neo-orthodox irrelevance. However, even in this situation the theologian still has a job to do, for having been deprived of his former subject matter – God – he must now, according to Altizer, deal with God's absence, and according to Hamilton with man's freedom. Thus atheism has a positive meaning: it becomes a creative possibility within Christian thought itself, the chance for a new lease on life out of sterility, and for a reawakening from sleep – in short, the chance for a brand-new theological adventure. The movement calls itself "radical" because it tries to go beyond the halfway measures that seem to it to be typified by Bultmann's willingness to demythologize the New Testament world-view but not the New Testament *kerygma*, and by Tillich's subsuming of supernaturalistic categories in the Ground of Being – in a word to go beyond such non-renunciation to a transcendence that is always hidden behind the adaptations that total immanence makes to modernity. This theology radicalizes as its message that one must will the Nietzschian observation of the death of God, as the madman relates it in *The Gay Science*:

Herbert Braun, David Miller, Gabriel Vahanian, Richard Underwood and Paul Van Buren (to which list should naturally be added the names of Altizer and Hamilton themselves).

As one can see, the panorama is virtually all-inclusive. The whole span of modern thought appears here to whatever degree it represents an awareness first of the non-objectivity of God, next of his eclipse, and finally of his present non-existence in reality. There is no doubt that if this bibliography had been prepared by Altizer rather than Hamilton it would have given special attention to Kierkegaard, Mircea Eliade and eastern mysticism as the gnostic and ancient counterpart of the western, secular and eschatological approach to the death of God.

"Where is God gone?" [the madman] called out. "I mean to tell you! *We have killed him,* – you and I! We are all his murderers! But how have we done it? How were we able to drink up the sea? Who gave us the sponge to wipe away the whole horizon? What did we do when we loosened this earth from its sun? Whither does it now move? Whither do we move?

Away from all suns? Do we not dash on unceasingly? Backwards, sideways, forwards, in all directions? Is there still an above and below? Do we not stray, as through infinite nothingness? Does not empty space breathe upon us? Has it not become colder? ... Do we not smell the divine putrefaction? – for even gods putrefy! How shall we console ourselves, the most murderous of all murders? The holiest and the mightiest that the world has hitherto possessed, has bled to death under our knife.[25]

Such a putting to death, where so many things are interspersed – the loss of any sense of cosmic identity which dooms the earth to a contingent and erratic existence, a more or less christocentric guilt about the crucifixion, the courage to be without God as either a father or center for one's existence – all this is clearly hard for Christian theologians to swallow in one mouthful even when they call themselves radical. Indeed, Hamilton and Altizer have uncovered no less than ten possible meanings for the event of the "death of God": traditional atheism, claiming that there is no God and never has been; the awareness that although there once was a God who was adored and praised, now there is no such God; a recognition of the need to reformulate the idea of God[26] and even the word "God," and that in the meantime a "decent silence" about God is called for; the search for new liturgical and theological language; Christianity understood as something other than redemption; the purification of the Christian doctrine of God from its confusion with metaphysical notions of a first cause, necessary being and absolute power; the temporary experience of God only in his absence, silence, retreat and eclipse; the putting to death of false gods so that there can be a rebirth of the true God; the medieval and Lutheran mystical meaning of the exchange that took place on the cross, God dying in the

[25] Nietzsche, *The Gay Science*, No. 125, as cited in Altizer and Hamilton, *op. cit.*, pp. 26f.

[26] Cf. the comment by André Gide, "God, the dumping-ground for all ill-defined concepts . . ."

world in order to be born in men; and finally the recognition that our language will always be inadequate to speak truly of God (pp. x–xi). In the book itself many of these meanings are used interchangeably, and the idea of the "death of God" resembles a nebula that is both powerful and diffuse, but even so the authors explicitly claim the second meaning as their own: our Christian God is no more.

Three perspectives follow from this affirmative declaration. The first is common to both authors, the second particularly to Hamilton, the third to Altizer.

1. There is a relationship that unfortunately is never clarified between the incarnation and crucifixion of Jesus Christ on the one hand, and modern secularization on the other:

> Only the Christian can celebrate an Incarnation in which God has actually become flesh, and radical theology must finally understand the Incarnation itself as effecting the death of God. Although the death of God may not have been historically actualized or realized until the nineteenth century, the radical theologians cannot dissociate this event from Jesus and his original proclamation (p. xii).

By lumping several deaths together, the authors are able to speak of a widespread "collapse": there is the death on Golgotha; the death of Christendom as a deceptive objectification, a non-paradoxical understanding, in the language of Kierkegaard, of Christ incarnate, incognito and "emptied";[27] the death of theology as speech that separates man from reality; the death of whatever may be summed up under the name of tradition (archaic conceptions, immobility, and unproductiveness) for the sake of openness, risk and new directions; and finally the death of theology for the sake of ethics:

> Faith has almost collapsed into love, and the Protestant is no longer defined as the forgiven sinner, the *simul justus et peccator*, but as the one beside the neighbor, beside the enemy, at the disposal of the man in need (Hamilton, pp. 36f.).

This theological current affirms such "collapses." It is

---

[27] The notion of "emptying" (*kenosis*) refers to the passage in Phil. 2.6–7: "Christ Jesus, who though he was in the form of God, did not count equality with God a thing to be grasped, but emptied himself (*ekenōsen*), taking the form of a servant, being born in the likeness of men." From which Altizer concludes: "We know that the Word becomes kenotically incarnate in its own other" (p. 132), and "Theology is now called to a radically kenotic Christology" (pp. 135f.).

therefore not surprising to find it full of psychoanalytic overtones. Hamilton tells us that we must abandon "oedipal"
theology, in which the believer is always unconsciously seeking
his father, and adopt "Orestian" theology, in which man
voluntarily makes himself responsible for the *polis* (the city,
politics and the neighbor), a theology that will evolve (to use
Shakespearian imagery rather than Freudian imagery) from
Hamlet to Prospero (pp. 43–5). In these writings, "God"
nearly always stands for security and fatherly protection. By
contrast, Jesus as a contemporary word raised up against the
traditional Christian image of God, represents the future, the
way things can actually go. Altizer says that we must celebrate
the death of God as the epiphany of the eschatological Christ:

A recognition that the Christian God is a creation of Christian
history – of the coming together of Word and history in a particular
time and space – can lead to an openness of faith to a new and
radical epiphany of the Word in a future beyond the history of
Christendom (p. 137).

Thus a secularization that destroys the images of God in reality
would be a creative response to Jesus as the prophet of the
future. The celebration of this kind of death of God would be
the affirmation of life in the midst of history.

Nevertheless, although Hamilton and Altizer are at one in
their critical celebration, the inner emphases that move them
seem fundamentally different, no doubt because each is carrying
a different Nietzschian torch, Hamilton one of jubilation and
Altizer one of anguish.

2. Hamilton is a secular and optimistic Anglo-Saxon. His
interests are ethical rather than mystical, and political rather
than inward. He disavows the disastrous linking of sin and grace
with its implication of guilt and dependence. He likes to point
out, against Augustine, that the godless can also have their
hearts at rest, that they can lead capable and creative lives
without hopelessness or guilt, and that they no longer fear God.
Among the various interpretations of the Reformation, ranging
from the liberal and psychological interpretation of the nineteenth century (in which Luther embodied the revolt of the
individual conscience against external power), to the dogmatic
interpretation of recent "neo-orthodox" theology (in which the

sinner is justified by the free gift of grace), Hamilton prefers an ethical interpretation, teaching us to leave the secure and protected cloister of the church, and walk the secular and dangerous streets. We have to learn the uselessness of God in order to discover his fruitfulness – borrowing the old Augustinian distinction that Hamilton approves of in this instance, between *uti* (make use of) and *frui* (to delight in). Hamilton turns out to be neither anguished nor perplexed, neither proud nor guilty, to be, in short, simply a man loving life and his neighbor, taking part in the political struggle against racism, convinced that man can improve and change most of the things that discourage and limit him. He celebrates the death of tragedy in vigorous fashion, not only as a way of rejecting a faith that builds on human misfortune, but one that also hesitates to offer a radically triumphant "yes."

> We are the non-havers, whose undialectical *yes* to the world is balanced by a *no* to God. This is not an optimism of grace, but a worldly optimism I am defending (p. 169).[28]

This affirmation of the earth brings Hamilton close to contemporary Jewish thinkers in a relationship he describes as follows:

> The believing Jew is the man with God and without the Messiah; the death of God Protestant is the man without God but not without something like the Messiah (p. 7).

We can say, to use an expression that does not appear in the book, that Hamilton wants to be a "christological atheist."

3. Altizer appears to be at the farthest remove from this non-dialectical optimism. He is a disciple of Mircea Eliade, an admirer of William Blake, interested in and attracted by the eastern religious mystics, and yet convinced that only the death of the western God can open a way toward life in the world that avoids gnosticism. Altizer thinks by anticipations and dialectical

---

[28] I cannot resist citing the date that Hamilton offers "for the fun of it," to locate this change of sensibility from the pessimism of crisis (theologically illustrated by Karl Barth and Reinhold Niebuhr) to the new optimism of the great society as both just and possible. His date is 4 January 1965, the day T. S. Eliot, poet of the wasteland, died, and also the day President Johnson gave a "State of the Union" message on the revolutionary possibilities of the twentieth century.

However, Hamilton also prefers Ivan to Alyosha in Dostoievsky's *The Brothers Karamazov*, because Ivan remains scandalized by the injustice of the world whereas Alyosha tries to evade it by turning to God.

returns. He views America, his intellectual home, as the most spiritually barren place possible. This is why America may have the chance to develop a more radically creative kind of thought than the deeply entrenched European heritage. It may be that out of the American chaos a future can be forged that will be different from the dead cosmos of classical metaphysics, which was so tied in with the Christian God that both of them inevitably died at the same time. The world can no longer be understood as a "creation," at least as theology has traditionally understood that doctrine. This is why in a world devoid of meaning, a faith that is truly open to tomorrow can be born again without nostalgia for yesterday's lost center of meaning. The Nietzschian doctrine of eternal return is the absolute dialectical antithesis to the Christian God. This means that from the perspective of the eternal return we can listen again to Jesus as the one who has abolished and will continue to abolish the whole distance between man's reality and God's plenitude.

As has been indicated, Altizer is attracted by gnosticism, which is the eastern way of avoiding history. He overcomes it only by his constant reaffirmation of the "coincidence of opposites" between sacred and profane, speech and silence, time and eternity. He sees Kierkegaard as the real founder of modern theology and its only significant exponent, because Kierkegaard held tenaciously to both ends of the chain, to the absolute non-objectivity of God *and* the historicity of Christ, to eternity *and* incarnation. However, Altizer believes that our situation is more complicated than Kierkegaard's, for whom subjectivity could still make room for God. But this is no more the case with us, who no longer identify authentic existence with life in faith. So even though Altizer's phrases sound Kierkegaardian – paradox, faith by virtue of the absurd, and so forth – he seems in fact to end up as a Hegelian, hovering between politics and mysticism:

An authentically kenotic movement of "Incarnation" must be a continued process of Spirit becoming flesh, of eternity becoming time, or of the sacred becoming profane (p. 152). Christianity invariably becomes religious at precisely those points where it refuses to become incarnate (p. 153). "God is dead" are words that may only truly be spoken by the . . . radical Christian who speaks in response to an Incarnate Word that empties itself of Spirit so as to appear and exist as flesh [in such a way that] flesh negates itself as flesh so as to become Spirit (p. 154). Hegel and Nietzsche were Christian thinkers who grasped the necessity of a theological atheism (p. 134).

By following Hegel and Nietzsche we learn that God is present for us only in his absence. For the death of God, in which God loses his transcendence entirely in immanence, is an act of grace by which he becomes incarnate in order to transform our being. The realm of the profane thus becomes the epiphany of the sacred which occurs within it.

Before raising questions about these conclusions we must remember that the death of God theologians give central attention to the later Bonhoeffer. Hamilton asserts that *Letters and Papers from Prison* is playing and will continue to play the same decisive role for the younger American theologians of the sixties and seventies that Reinhold Niebuhr's *Nature and Destiny of Man* played for the theologians of the forties and fifties (p. 114). For both Altizer and Hamilton, Bonhoeffer has placed at the center of theological life and reflection a recognition that "We are not talking about the absence of the experience of God, but about the experience of the absence of God" (p. 28). This "experience of the absence of God" is the experience of the presence of Jesus, not as a savior who has come from the beyond to lead us there, but as one who lives his transcendence in this world as co-humanity with all men. According to Hamilton, Bonhoeffer above all teaches us about worldly optimism understood as a sharing with God in his sufferings – a more secularized version of Müller's position, though without being based on the Lutheran doctrine of the two realms. This is the Bonhoeffer who talks of Jesus as being in the midst of the world. According to Altizer, Bonhoeffer teaches us all not to start talking too quickly again about the God who has disappeared: "For a time [theology] must dwell in darkness, existing on this side of the resurrection." It must "cultivate the silence of death," and "consequently the theologian must exist outside the Church" (p. 15). It must *will* its present destiny, which is to be silent, under pain of rejecting its real identity and existence. The possibility of a new epiphany will be at the cost of its willingness to wait in the darkness:

A faith which is not open to the loss of faith is not a true form of faith . . . When the Christian bets that God is dead, he is betting upon the real and actual presence of the fully incarnate Christ.[29]

In France, apparently without knowing about the work of these American theologians, Jean Bauberot has developed a similar interpretation of Bonhoeffer that combines Hamilton's world-affirmation with Altizer's non-knowing.[30] Along with them, Bauberot emphasizes the later Bonhoeffer. He feels that treatments of Bonhoeffer that emphasize the continuity within his writings are conservative and culturally pietistic. Bauberot begins with two quotations about Jesus' forsakenness: "God fails at the altar where I am the victim. There is no God! God is no more" (Gérard de Nerval, "Le Christ aux Oliviers," 1844) and "The dead cry out, 'O Christ, is there no God at all?' He replies, 'There is no God'" (Jean-Paul Richter). Taking his lead from a book by Yann Roullet[31] Bauberot sees Jesus' forsakenness as the center of Christian faith. The scandal is not Jesus' humanity but his utter abasement, his loss of all possessions, his ignorance on Golgotha, his death as perdition, the human failure of his claim to be the Christ, his revelation "under the contrary aspect," as Luther put it.

Bauberot next turns to Jesus' "worldly" activity.

If Jesus is forsaken, there is no one left facing him, not even God. Jesus without God is then the only God. But God does not exist any longer. God dies when Jesus dies. Jesus dies an orphan, without a Father, one who has come of age.[32]

A "religious" Christianity complete with God wants to go back behind this forsakenness, which is a coming of age, behind this loss of meaning, which is the nature of the new reality. But the world come of age is based upon a void, without any eschatological "Hollywood ending." It is not necessarily a world without idols – idols are always threatening it – but there is nothing to guarantee "an ongoing relationship between the

---

[29] Altizer, *The Gospel of Christian Atheism*, pp. 28, 145.

[30] Cf. his articles in *Le Semeur*, "Un Christianisme a-religieux? Vivre la mort de Dieu," "Calder et Bonhoeffer," and "Note sur une récupération centriste: Dietrich Bonhoeffer, piétiste tentant d'être irréligieux," 1965.5, 1966.1, and 1966–7.6.

[31] Roullet, *Mon Dieu, mon dieu, pourquoi m'as-tu abandonné?*, Plon, Paris 1946.

[32] Bauberot, *Le Semeur*, 1965.5, p. 51.

universe and those who inhabit it."[33] In any case, "God is of no use to anyone, he is no help at all, he can never be recovered as a help in our tasks as men."[34] Life without the hypothesis of God will be honest:

Bonhoeffer's religionlessness is a search for an unachievable faithfulness and communion; a desire not to stop thinking because of fear, dread of nothingness or horror of the void.[35]

By way of illustrating this himself, Bauberot gives up any attempt to describe in positive terms what a non-religious interpretation of Christianity would be. But he does draw a fascinating analogy from the world of art:

Religionless Christianity will be related to traditional Christianity in the same way that the mobiles of Calder or Tinguely are related to traditional sculpture ... The truth communicated by a mobile is true only as the original form dies ... The creator of the mobile gives up any attempt to maintain control over the shape it will have at any given moment ... There is a complete antinomy rather than a synthesis, for as Proudhon pointed out, "A synthesis can always be kept under control."[36]

A non-religious interpretation of Christianity would abandon speculative interpretation. It would begin to think and to live "from below," open to the fulness of life without asceticism, open also to the sorrows of life, "without seeking to believe that the sorrow is either significant or absurd," "keeping its eyes open without minimizing the resultant dizziness," being willing to let others interpret such a version of Christianity as equivocal and questionable, accepting "the religionlessness of language as a preliminary to dialogue"[37] – living dangerously with a kind of stern joy, in a manner reminiscent of Nietzsche but also of the Bonhoeffer who could comment from prison:

I shall be writing next time about Christians' "egoism" ("selfless self-love"). I think we agree about it. Too much altruism is oppressive and pretentious: "egoism" can be less selfish and less demanding.[38]

---

[33] Robbe Grillet, *Nature, Humanisme, Tragédie*, 1958, cited by Bauberot, *op. cit.*, p. 59.
[34] Bauberot, *op. cit.*, p. 60.   [35] *Ibid.*, p. 61.   [36] *Le Semeur*, 1966.1, p. 45.
[37] Bauberot, *op. cit.*, pp. 65f.
[38] Bonhoeffer, *LPP*, 6 May 1944, pp. 157f., modifying the English translation to render *Anspruchvoll* as "pretentious" rather than "exacting."

In brief, Bauberot feels that life without the hypothesis of God will be free, costly and dangerous, always ready to sacrifice "the security of its consciousness and its reputation" for necessary action, knowing nothing of the "universal good" or "the meaning of history," no longer clear about the place of the church,[39] and coming finally to the point where only silence is appropriate, and where everything vanishes, "taking upon itself the aspect of death without claiming that this death possesses any meaning that goes beyond it (and yet nevertheless wishing to live)."[40]

Bauberot's article is particularly interesting because of its clear call to a non-religious style of life lived without God, a life that is fragmentary, lacking any center, free, clear, resolute, human, ready to act whenever necessary, attempting to live both with and for the neighbor, "the only truly vital relationship – particularly with a weak person – one that proceeds from love, i.e. from a desire to be in communion with the other" – a life, in short, in which the hypothesis of God is no longer a barrier to love.

Of the various interpretations of Bonhoeffer, the "atheistic" interpretations have struck the most responsive chords. Their proponents do not pose as being themselves absolutely faithful to Bonhoeffer. They pose either as believers or rationalists. They credit Bonhoeffer with raising important questions and answers, for which he is both the source and difficulty. They reflect the situation of people who express such concerns more frequently than they follow the one who formulated them. Consequently the three questions to be raised are really directed more to them than to Bonhoeffer.

1. I have already pointed out in dealing with the "non-religious interpretation of Christianity" that Bonhoeffer himself seems to have confused two meanings of the word "God" and thus to have made talk about the "death of God" more difficult.

---

[39] Bonhoeffer, not knowing how to reply to Bethge's question, writes: "Now for your question whether there is any 'room' left for the Church, or whether that room has gone for good; and the other question, whether Jesus did not use men's 'distress' as a point of contact with them ..." (*LPP*, 8 June 1944, p. 182). But although the questions are asked, they are never answered in the prison letters.

[40] Bauberot, *Le Semeur*, 1965.5, p. 71. Another characteristic French example of this news of the death of God is the article by Ennio Floris, "L'Abandon de Jesus et la Mort de Dieu," *Études théologiques et religieuses*, 1967.4, Montpellier.

Does he mean the "God concept," as the keystone of the cosmos and of transcendental reason, or does he mean the living God crucified in Jesus Christ? Getting rid of the first meaning is *not* the same thing as removing the second! The sense of adulthood one attains through disposing of the hypothetical God is a far cry from revolting against truth, justice and love – which is what it means theologically to put the living God to death. To lose a sense of transcendence, understood cosmologically, need not destroy the possible reality of a God who questions man, and as a result of that questioning gives a meaning to nature and the cosmos that is based on creation rather than necessity. Such things should be possible no matter what the earlier connections between metaphysics and biblical faith out of which Christian theology has so often emerged as an illegitimate offspring. In my opinion, the whole current of the death of God theology is hampered by a lack of clarity between these two meanings, a difficulty that goes back to certain passages in Bonhoeffer himself, and is likewise characteristic of many passages in Nietzsche. The confused state of mind of "the world come of age" follows from this difficulty: is it affirmative, as Hamilton insists, or ephemeral, waiting for a dialectical recurrence to the sacred (actually God) as Altizer suggests? In short, are we adults or murderers? – a question Nietzsche's madman had already asked.[41]

2. There is a more pressing problem: the expression "death of God" never appears in Bonhoeffer's writings. He speaks instead of life "before God" in a world without the hypothesis of God, and by means of the "secret discipline" (which Hamilton scarcely mentions and which Altizer interprets as a need for silence) he maintains a typically Lutheran tension between a view of the world forsaken by God and faith in the God whom the world forsakes. Nor does Bonhoeffer ever speak of God from

[41] Fr Duquoc comments in this connection, rightly I believe, on the lack of a doctrine of the Trinity in the American death of God theologians. In violent opposition to theism, opposing to an omnipotent God a Christ who challenges him, they cannot conceive of a God who gives himself by the Son through the Holy Spirit. Kenotic christology, reducing the Trinity to a movement of divine self-negation, thus brings about, in Hegel's terms, an infusion of the absolute into history, without the freedom of the incarnation, and following that without true freedom for the Word in that history. Struggle disappears in the mingling of God with the historical phenomenon of his epiphanies. (Cf. C. Duquoc, *Christologie*, Cerf, Paris 1968, pp. 329–36.)

a psychoanalytic point of view as a father who both renders the son impotent and yet is irremediably lost, i.e. of God as a rival to man's autonomy or the fulfillment of human desires. From his own father, a non-Freudian psychiatrist, Bonhoeffer seems to have inherited certain reservations about psychoanalysis, reservations that are clearly evident in *Life Together* and the prison letters where he vigorously resists all apologetic approaches that build on anxiety, distress, conflict, insufficiency or inadequacy. For this reason (without rasing the question of the relationship between psychoanalysis, religion as obsessional neurosis, and faith) it is regrettable that the American death of God theologians have so indiscriminately mixed up Hegel, Nietzsche, Freud and Bonhoeffer. An insatiable hunger for cultural inclusiveness finally leads to theological indigestion.

3. Finally we may ask why those who call themselves atheists also want to be Christian theologians. Could it be that they have a cultural need to support their argument from those who have attacked and alienated them? Could it be that their kenotic christology forces them to attribute a unique quality to Jesus as revealer of the truly human in his freedom and his unconditional love? Could it be that they still hope that Bonhoeffer offers the drastic remedy that can purge Christian existence of its introverted blandness and metaphysical abstraction, and that one day might even purge the church of its stifling smugness and tiresome isolation?

Unfortunately these writings, in spite of being remarkably intelligent and full of genuine commitment, are very self-assured and frequently seem more like the fruits of anti-religious, anti-ecclesiastical and anti-pietistic resentment than like a real contact with the atheistic world of which they speak so much. There is often more anti-religious introversion in them than real secular outreach. As in the case of Hanfried Müller, the obviousness of their context raises questions about their credibility. Müller wants to be part of a country that is avowedly atheistic, while Hamilton and Altizer want to renounce a country that is avowedly religious. Thus we have Bonhoeffer transplanted to the east and then to the west, but in neither case "midway between East and West,"[42] which is where he felt himself to be. Do we not see here an accommodation of theology

[42] Bonhoeffer, *LPP*, 30 April 1944, p. 155.

to the religionless world of existentialism, psychoanalysis and the destruction of ideologies and metaphysics, similar to what happened in reverse fashion a hundred and fifty years ago with the accommodation of theology to the religious world of romanticism, idealism and the burgeoning of ideologies and world-views? In both cases, do not the proximity and immediacy of the surrounding culture risk destroying the prophetic mediation of the Word in its approval as well as in its criticism of the emphases of culture and the world? Such a theology depends on action and silence, and runs the risk of becoming a mystical doctrine of the destitution of the cross in a world of unbelief.[43]

We are emerging from an era in which theology was content to gaze from afar at the cultural situation because it thought it had achieved an overarching dogmatic truth, an acceptance of the church's centrality, and even an easily grasped "christo-logical concentration." Consequently it is a great relief to encounter theologians who have begun writing in secular magazines instead of shutting themselves off within theological faculties. More is involved than simply a "misunderstanding," when the theologians who want to live out the consequences of the death of God are heard in strange ways by those who have grown accustomed to putting the hypothetical God and reality without God, church and world into two separate

[43] The book by Dorothee Sölle, *Christ the Representative: An Essay in Theology After the Death of God* (SCM Press, London, and Fortress Press, Philadelphia 1967), although formally related to the death of God movement, seems to me to come to different conclusions and to be much closer to Bonhoeffer. According to her, Jesus Christ is the "representative" (*Stellvertreter*, translated in the present work and in Bonhoeffer's *Ethics* as "deputy") of both the dead God and of man before God. He negates neither, but takes their place in an immediate and responsible way. This deputyship is the foundation of dogmatics as well as ethics. Jesus thus offers man a future for his need of an identity in the midst of a world that always tends to equate him with its interchangeable objects. And even though some ambiguity remains about the meaning of the "death of God," Miss Sölle seems to me to have a clear grasp of one of Bonhoeffer's essential themes. It is difficult for men today to understand Jesus Christ as "Savior," with all the overtones the word carries of gnosticism, individualism and anxiety about the beyond, but it may be possible to understand him as a deputy (e.g. a "representative"), as the new Adam, of a responsible humanity, e.g. a *partner* to God as well as to the neighbor. Accordingly, what is the best term for describing the reality of Jesus today? Early Christianity grappled with this problem and tried out various words that it felt might strike a responsive chord for the hearers of its first sermons. (Cf. Oscar Cullmann, *The Christology of the New Testament*, SCM Press, London, and Westminster Press, Philadelphia 1959.) We have to be free to do the same thing.

compartments. Personally, I doubt that Bonhoeffer's reaction would have been alienation or bewilderment, since he himself wrote:

The Church must come out of its stagnation. We must move out again into the open air of intellectual discussion with the world, and risk saying controversial things, if we are to get down to the serious problems of life.[44]

3. *Ontological interpretations*

Heinrich Ott, Karl Barth's successor in the chair of dogmatics at the University of Basel, has devoted a large volume published in 1966 to Bonhoeffer's theological heritage.[45] In my opinion, this book gets closest to the heart of Bonhoeffer's theology of reality and of the credibility of Christian faith in the midst of reality. But by interpreting the theology of the incarnation as an ontology of the everyday world, Ott also accentuates a danger that is always latent in Bonhoeffer's thought.

This large work, often difficult to read, is divided into three sections: "Situation and Method," "Bonhoeffer's Contribution," and "Perspectives." Ott seeks to locate Bonhoeffer's sources of inspiration as clearly as possible. Bonhoeffer seems to him the voice that contemporary Protestantism needs to hear, without the false concessions made by the death of God theologians. For Ott believes that Protestant theology has been caught between Barth's traditional objectivism and Bultmann's individualistic existentialism, and that the impasse has been accentuated even more by each man's disciples: one group isolates itself in a misunderstanding of the problems of contemporary hermeneutics while the other pursues the deobjectivizing of God up to the very negation of his otherness and personality.[46] In this confrontation, which is finally unproductive, Bonhoeffer can act as a catalyst, since as early as *Act and Being* he was open both to the existential truth of the actualists and the essential truth of the ontologists – even though since

---

[44] Bonhoeffer, *LPP*, 3 August 1944, p. 208.
[45] Ott, *Wirklichkeit und Glaube* I, 394pp.
[46] Ott gives a long account of the controversy between Herbert Braun and Helmut Gollwitzer, *op. cit.*, pp. 28-50. I have analyzed this discussion in the symposium *L'Objectivité de Dieu*, Cerf, Paris 1968.

Act and Being Barth appears to Ott to have forsaken the first of these positions for the second, while Bultmann has never budged from his earlier position. Bonhoeffer thus avoids getting trapped within such false alternatives as fact versus interpretation, *extra nos* versus *in nobis*, otherness versus openness, God-in-himself versus God-for-us, objectivity versus subjectivity, givenness versus relationship, "positivism of revelation" versus existential interpretation, cosmology versus anthropology, revelation outside the world versus the world outside revelation, orthodoxy without dialogue versus existentialism without an object, dogmatics versus hermeneutics, the duty of belief versus the possibility of belief – in short, to sum up these contrasts (which are my own): Barth versus Bultmann. Actually, Bonhoeffer like Barth never reduces theology to anthropology, but like Bultmann he always tries to relate the gospel to the actual world around him. He believes that God both speaks to us and is spoken about by us. Bonhoeffer is a Barthian who is sensitive to the questions raised by liberal theology that Bultmann has never stopped asking, and so he is the key man in dealing with the present theological situation. Ott places him in the inner circle of his questioners, where he enters the company of Barth, Bultmann and of course Heidegger, and where it appears that he will soon be followed by Martin Buber, Teilhard de Chardin and Karl Rahner. Later on we will see where this unusual group seems to be heading.

But there is a problem here, for Bonhoeffer did not leave a body of systematic writings. He wrote and thought in a fragmented way, as Nietzsche philosophized only in aphorisms. We thus have to enter into conversation with Bonhoeffer, looking for that "blending of perspectives" which, according to Gadamer, is the true hermeneutical principle. We are both his inheritors and his contemporaries – partners with him by virtue of the common subject matter he pursues with us, and partners with that subject matter by virtue of our dialogue with him. For, Ott insists, the discovery of truth today is a corporate task, in which (in relation to our dialogical partner) it is appropriate for us (1) to find new ways to say what he has said, (2) to contradict what has been said for the sake of new insight, (3) to be more concerned with the subject matter than with the way it is expressed, and finally (4) to weigh seriously the most recent expression of the issue. These four rules constitute the methodology of fruitful dialogue. They can be stated in different ways as different people use them for the ongoing testing of their words to discover whether or not they "verify" reality,[47] since "It is not only occasionally but always that the meaning of a text surpasses its author."[48] Finally and above all they provide a means of grasping what the author really wants to say, since, as Heidegger puts it, "Thinking means reduction to one thought which will some day remain in the sky of the world like a star."[49] Such a concentration of thinking is for Bonhoeffer the basic ontology of reality, i.e. the world around us where God is incarnate and in which he dwells – to anticipate the results of Ott's approach.

After thus locating Bonhoeffer's "Situation and Method" in order to be able to interpret him correctly, Ott turns in the second part of his book to "Bonhoeffer's Contribution." He begins with what Bonhoeffer was working on at the very end of his life, "the non-religious interpretation" of Christianity. He moves from there to christology ("Jesus Christ and Reality") and then to ecclesiology ("The Communion of Saints"), concluding with treatments of ethics and providence. This approach is neither chronological nor systematic. It makes no reference to the part that historical events played in the development of Bonhoeffer's thought. While it has the advantage of challenging theories about the presumed discontinuity of Bonhoeffer's thought, it does not persuade one that Ott has systematized Bonhoeffer's thought any better than Bonhoeffer did himself. Even so, the details of Ott's approach are interesting. At the heart of his work, Ott clearly sees Bonhoeffer's search for an ontological uniting of God with reality. From this perspective, "non-religious interpretation" is the knowledge of God in this-worldly incarnation, not in other-worldly speculation that was originally gnostic, later metaphysical, and most recently

[47] The concept of "verification" seems central to Ott as to Ebeling. It is not a matter of proving the existence of God from an examination of the world about us, but of speaking of God as always related to reality in terms of the incarnation. It is not a matter of "proof" (*Beweis*) but of "showing forth" (*Aufweis*), not declarative statement (*Aussage*) but effective witnessing (*Zeigen*), faith (*Glaube*) in credibility (*Glaubwürdigkeit*).

[48] H. G. Gadamer, *Wahrheit und Methode*, p. 280, cited by Ott, *op. cit.*, p. 77.

[49] Heidegger, *Aus der Erfahrung des Denkens*, Neske, Pfullingen 1954, p. 7, cited by Ott, *op. cit.*, p. 81.

existential. The worldliness of God is opposed to the dualistic "other-worldliness" of religion. Ott emphasizes Bonhoeffer's attachment to a verse in which in the midst of terrible human misfortune God speaks to Jeremiah of his own ongoing presence in the here and now of human experience:

Behold, what I have built up I am breaking down, and what I have planted I am plucking up – that is the whole land . . . And do you seek great things for yourself? Seek them not; for behold, I am bringing evil upon all flesh.[50]

Reality is not deduced speculatively from Christ; Christ is analyzed ontologically in reality. Anthropology does not reproduce christology by way of "reflection and correspondence."[51] Anthropology "verifies" the christology that is present within it. This is why it is fitting to "pose the ontological question in relation to the reality of the world around us," by rejecting a christology that would be imposed from outside man's empirical reality, since the latter has already been "reached, held and penetrated by God in Christ."[52] It is thus taken for granted that reality is already inhabited by Christ's presence in the world, a presence that is the most concrete expression of his being.

Ott points out that Bonhoeffer appreciated the sense in which the Greek divinities were immanent within the world, and that he found nourishment in this fact for his faith in the here and now:

We must keep on trying to find our way through the petty thoughts that irritate us, to the great thoughts that strengthen us – I am at present reading the quite outstanding book by W. F. Otto, the classics man at Königsberg, *Die Götter Griechenlands* [*The Greek Gods*]. To quote from his closing words, it is about "this world of faith, which sprang from the wealth and depth of human existence, not from its cares and longings." Can you understand my finding something very attractive in this theme and its treatment, and also – *horribile dictu* – my finding these gods, when they are so treated, less offensive than

---

[50] Jer. 45.5. This verse is quoted many times by Bonhoeffer in *LPP*, cf. pp. 65, 136 (a reference omitted from the Index of the English translation), 151, 169, 202, just as Pascal had his own favorite verse, "Truly thou art a God who hidest thyself, O God of Israel, the Savior" (Isa. 45.15).

[51] Cf. A. Dumas, "Reflet et Correspondance," in "Mélanges pour Karl Barth," *Foi et Vie*, May 1966.

[52] Ott, *op. cit.*, p. 121 n.8b.

certain brands of Christianity? In fact, that I almost think I could claim these gods for Christ? This book is most helpful for my present theological reflections.[53]

In this allusion to Greece we undoubtedly have what Ott considers the key to an interpretation of Bonhoeffer, and I think also the most assured (and most questionable) side of Bonhoeffer himself; not the tension between law and gospel, between the world come of age and the secret discipline of the cross, between ultimate and penultimate – not even the unfolding of God's self-emptying in godless humanity, but rather the polyphonic presence of Christ in the midst of the world around us in the ontological structures of reality, as though the incarnation had transformed Christ into the Dionysius of the earth. In this view, God is not in exile, but in the many-sided, rich, deep and also hidden presence of reality, for the pragmatism of the empirical world blocks reality's openness toward being.

It is the task of christology to make such openness possible. It does so through the non-religious interpretation of God, who dwells neither in the "other world" of ideas, nor in the depths of consciousness, but in reality itself in its this-worldly expression. As the presence of the word in the structures of the empirical world, christology is the basis of all knowledge. "It remains the unknown and hidden centre of the *universitas litterarum*."[54] Outside of its "Christic" structure, reality is fragmented between the corresponding abstractions of idealism and pragmatism, of spiritual views and empirical views, of fact and interpretation. Christology is the foundation of this-worldly ontology in contrast to other-worldly metaphysics. This ontology is discovered in the risk of responsible action following Christ who restructures the empirical world in reality. Thus even more than justification (which is threatened by the misunderstanding of a dualistic position, e.g. nature versus grace, law versus gospel, the

---

[53] Bonhoeffer, *LPP*, 21 June 1944, pp. 182f.

[54] Bonhoeffer, *Christ the Center*, p. 28. Along with this university assignment in "Christo-logic," written in 1933, note what Bonhoeffer confided in a letter to his friend Rössler on 18 October 1931: "I am now chaplain to the Technical High School: how can one preach such things to these people? Who is there who still believes them? The invisibility kills us ... This eternal desperate fact of being thrown back upon the invisible God Himself – there is not a person who can stand it any longer" (*GS* I, p. 61, as translated in Bosanquet, *The Life and Death of Dietrich Bonhoeffer*, p. 95). Christo-logy of Christ present in the silence of the theo-logy of the invisible God?

world versus the Kingdom), the incarnation becomes the major theme. Redemption dominated the Christian tradition from Augustine to Luther. But today, Christ present in reality is what is at stake in the theological struggle, when men no longer ask questions about whether the divine countenance is one of wrath or grace, as they did in the Middle Ages and the Reformation, but ask instead about the reality or unreality of God himself facing the everyday world. So incarnation, cross and resurrection must all be reinterpreted. They not only point to "salvation-history" outside of or merely tangential to history in general; they structure the world about us and its history. They give substance to human society:

Dogmatic ecclesiology is finally nothing other than the recognition of the structure of the divine-human reality of the church that is given to us through the revelation in Christ.[55]

To the existential categories that make it possible to think about the relationship to God in terms of interpersonal relations, must be added the structural categories that make it possible to enter with God into the relationships of being with things. As a result, Ott interprets the young Bonhoeffer's ecclesiology and epistemology as attempts to bypass an existential stress on act that is too individualistic, without however falling into an ontological stress on being that is too immobile. The solution would be a "societal" understanding of the person, which in addition to the personal emphasis on summoning and questioning would have a structural emphasis on the integration of the individual into the interrelationships that make him what he is – Christ being both the one who summons and the foundation of the interrelationship.

Ott feels that all this brings Bonhoeffer curiously close to Tillich (although "God as the ground of reality" is preferable to "God as the ground of being" in order to retain the personal and ethical side of God's presence), to Teilhard de Chardin (although Teilhard, according to Ott, reasons more from the resurrection and Bonhoeffer more from the cross),[56] and finally to Karl Rahner (who speaks of an "existential supranatural

[55] Ott, *op. cit.*, p. 175.

[56] Cf. Ott, *op. cit.*, pp. 328–40, "Der universale Christus bei Dietrich Bonhoeffer und Pierre Teilhard de Chardin."

Christology" and an "anonymous Christianity"). I see Ott's work coming to a climax in his evoking of an implicit faith, a presence of the universal Christ who can be known outside the visible church, and a "natural piety." Ott rests his case for all this on an isolated and very obscure passage in the prison letters:

The question how there can be a "natural piety" is at the same time the question of "unconscious Christianity," with which I am more and more concerned. Lutheran dogmatists distinguished between a *fides directa* and a *fides reflexa*. They related this to the so-called children's faith, at baptism. I wonder whether this does not raise a far-reaching problem. I hope we shall soon come back to it.[57]

There is a certain logic in this obscure outcome: if God is neither a transcendent, supra-worldly being nor an immanent principle at the foundation of being, he must be understood as a personal voice who comes to us at the foundation of reality – a reality that Ott affirms by faith has Christ as its fundamental structure. Thus there would be an "anonymous Christianity" latent everywhere, and patent in the church that both knew it and affirmed it openly. Christ present and hidden in "the polyphony of life" would be waiting to be discovered in what might better be called (in Greek fashion) his manifestation than his revelation.

Only when man finds himself within the reality of grace is he able to experience the reality in which he stands as a reality of grace.[58]

Against Heidegger, who in *Being and Time* described theology as one of the positive sciences that despite their own ontologies are nevertheless based on the fundamental ontology that *Being and Time* sets forth, Ott affirms that "theology itself is the true fundamental ontology."[59] The "proofs" of God are a reflective experience (*Erfahrung denkerisch*) of reality. Consequently it is not surprising to find Ott singing the praises of Aquinas, even though he feels that the "five ways" are overly metaphysical,

---

[57] Bonhoeffer, *LPP*, 27 July 1944, pp. 204f. This fleeting new thought does not receive any further development in later letters. Ott deals with the theme, *op. cit.*, pp. 167, 232, and 261. Cf. also H. Ott, "Existentiale Interpretation und anonyme Christlichkeit," in *Zeit und Geschichte, Dankesgabe an Bultmann*, Mohr, Tübingen 1964, pp. 367–79.

[58] Ott, *op. cit.*, p. 294.   [59] *Ibid.*, p. 300.

not sufficiently historical, and too indifferent to soteriology, as though sin and grace had not affected the ontological understanding of God that can be drawn from the reality of the world. "It is an act of God's grace when reality becomes transparent for man."[60] Christ is understood as a universal "concept of reconciliation," as "inclusive cosmic process of the new creation, in which basically all men can participate, regardless of their faith (!), speech or race."[61]

Through the coming of Christ, God becomes a structural moment in human existence, not out of necessity, of course, but out of the free divine initiative of the incarnation. "To preach the gospel means to witness to the evidence of Christ in every human situation."[62] One must not claim or proclaim a God who is exterior to man but rather recognize and follow the present and concrete Christ who is already in our midst. Witness counts for more than speech, as Heidegger has said:

True speech is witness. Saying is showing. The showing is not based on any signs, but all signs have their origin in showing in which realm and for what purpose they may be signs.[63]

It is somewhat disconcerting to see what those who enter into conversation with Bonhoeffer make of him, and what strange amalgams result from such encounters, sometimes with Luther, sometimes with Feuerbach, Freud and Nietzsche, and sometimes even with St Thomas Aquinas, Teilhard de Chardin and Karl Rahner! Barth's question is unavoidable: did this "impulsive young thinker" really have a systematic viewpoint if his readers can organize his thought into so many contradictory systems? Even so, I think that Ott has correctly grasped Bonhoeffer's central purpose, which was to understand and follow the structuring presence of God in reality by means of the christology of the incarnation, and to overcome the dualism of metaphysics and inwardness by an ontology of presence and openness. However, rather than questioning Bonhoeffer on the decisive

[60] *Ibid.*, p. 311.
[61] *Ibid.*, p. 354. Ott's summary of the universalism of modern Asiatic christology. It is not clear whether he is approving, criticizing or merely describing.
[62] *Ibid.*, pp. 381f.
[63] Heidegger, *Unterwegs zur Sprache*, Neske, Pfullingen 1959, p. 254, cited by Ott, *op. cit.*, p. 384 n.28.

point of the relationship between a biblical theology of the revelation of the Word of God *to* the world, and a Greek theology of the manifestation of the Logos *through* the world, it seems to me that Ott has chosen the least compelling of the various ambiguities in Bonhoeffer. To say that "theology is basically ontology," as Ott does, is either to make a christological confession, an act of faith identical with Barth's theological stance, or to engage in an analysis of the openness of being to Being, which simply takes for granted, as Heidegger does, that there is a "possible revelation of a God of Being," that corresponds to the listening attention and "attentiveness" of man.[64]

Ott does not seem to want to choose here, sometimes proceeding in Barthian fashion with declarative affirmations and other times by immanent verifications *à la* Heidegger. He does an excellent job with Bonhoeffer's central question of how to know God in the midst of reality. But in interpreting that reality he vacillates between a confession of faith and an explanation of the indeterminate and indeterminable Being on which faith is based and within which it is manifested. Ott seems to be caught in a confusion between a theology of grace and an ontology of the availability of Being, which is widely accepted by one group of contemporary theologians, just as there is a confusion between a kenotic theology and a sociology of secularization and atheism on the part of another group. The first group draws on Greek thought, and we have seen that Bonhoeffer was not less sensitive than Nietzsche to the antidualistic currents of pre-Socratic theology, and thus, in Bonhoeffer's eyes, to the emphasis within it that "inclines" toward an incarnate Christ. The second group is just the opposite, looking for a post-Nietzschian point of view – since Nietzsche, as Heidegger interprets him, is still an inveterate "Cartesian" who places the triumphant, lonely and technical subjectivity of man in the center of the world. Members of this school interpret christology as God's costly affirmation of the world come of age.

But in either case does reality (whether interpreted in

---

[64] Cf. the penetrating analysis by Rouven Guilead, professor at the University of Tel Aviv, on "L'Echec de l'Être chez Heidegger," in *Les Hommes devant l'Echec*, Presses Universitaires de France, Paris 1968, p. 175.

ontological or secular fashion) retain that "unity-in-tension" to which Bonhoeffer was so clearly committed?

It would be a complete and dangerous misunderstanding if [reality] were to be taken in the sense of that "servile conviction in the face of fact" that Nietzsche speaks of, a conviction which yields to every powerful pressure, which on principle justifies success, and which on every occasion chooses what is opportune as "corresponding to reality." "Correspondence with reality" in this case would be the contrary of reality; it would be irresponsibility.[65]

All systems of thought that are inspired by Hegel (and surely Bonhoeffer belongs in such a category),[66] with his Janus-head looking toward both the ontological *and* the historical, the sacred *and* the secular, must confront the question of truth and freedom in relation to reality, the question Plato asked when he was searching for the right and the law of the foundations, a search which wears the mythological clothing of dualism. In the name of what and of whom can one say yes or no? Here the biblical prophets do a better job than the Greek ontologists.

Neither Hegel nor Socrates (no matter how severely the latter is questioned by Callistes) is in a position to respond to the decisive question, which concerns the nature of the power that dwells in reason ... The fact that something develops does not mean that it has a foundation; self-sufficiency does not explain power ... Hegel established the laws of reason – perhaps more surely and fully than Spinoza or Kant – but he only succeeded in doing so by reducing law to fact, by presupposing their fundamental identity. He avoided the question that Spinoza, Kant and also Rousseau formulated very clearly, the question of the foundation and the effective power of the law, of the basis of reason.[67]

Can we presume that reason can provide a concrete commandment to man, or is it necessary to think (as Bonhoeffer had written in his notes on Hegel) that we must surpass reason by faith, i.e. hold as firmly to the reality of a *God* who actively

---

[65] Bonhoeffer, *Ethics*, p. 228.

[66] It seems to me that Ott would have been much more convincing if he had dealt with Bonhoeffer's ontology in terms of Hegel, rather than St Thomas, Paul Tillich, Teilhard de Chardin and Karl Rahner.

[67] François Châtelet, *Hegel*, Seuil, Paris 1968, p. 178.

reveals himself as to the God of *reality* who is present within it?

I am somewhat perturbed that the major interpretations of Bonhoeffer[68] generally lack this prophetic dimension when confronting the everyday world – the dimension that gave his life such distinctiveness.[69] For knowledge of the incarnation

[68] Summaries of other interpretations can be found in the four volumes of *Die Mündige Welt*. Cf. also A. Dumas, "Sociologie et Irréligion, à propos de D. Bonhoeffer," *Archives de Sociologie des Religions*, Paris 1965, 19, pp. 21–5.

[69] One cannot, however, bring such a charge against the excellent small book by Benjamin Reist (*The Promise of Bonhoeffer*, 1969). Refusing to study Bonhoeffer in abstract terms, he relies heavily on Bethge's biography, and he succeeds to a remarkable degree in placing Bonhoeffer's work in the midst of the political responsibility that gradually drew the theologian, trained in the Lutheran doctrine of the two realms, into the midst of a plan that was designed not only to overthrow Hitler, but if possible to rebuild a new Germany. We must not forget that Bonhoeffer's brother-in-law, Hans von Dohnanyi, relied on Bonhoeffer's ethical discernment and on his ability to set out the options clearly. The task was all the more important since Bonhoeffer took the risk at arriving at an ethic deprived of all norms, particularly in his famous essay, "What Is Meant By 'Telling the Truth'?", printed at the conclusion of *Ethics*, but actually written while Bonhoeffer was in Tegel. In dealing with these matters, Reist clearly shows how false is the notion of a radical shift between the later Bonhoeffer and the preceding stages of his thought. Bonhoeffer's *Ethics* is involved in worldliness and not only secularization, as Reist shows with great sensitivity. It has a double character: it is committed to the search for the concrete commandment of God, and at the same time it refuses to erect specific norms. It is utterly demanding and at the same time perfectly fluid. Reist has seen this tension very clearly in stating that to understand Bonhoeffer's legacy consists less in writing about the process of modern secularization in abstract sociological terms, than in re-working all the classical theological concepts in ethical and social terms.

But at this point, it seems to me, we want a bit more than we are given. Is this the result of too uncritical an admiration of Bonhoeffer? I wish there could have been a clearer establishment of the bases of a social ethic in Bonhoeffer's terms, and would like to have heard from Reist (particularly in the light of his great knowledge of both Karl Barth and Ernst Troeltsch) how he views the second of the great shifts in twentieth-century Protestant theology, e.g. after Barth's break with Troeltsch's personalistic liberalism, the later shift from Barth's own reportedly too traditional dogmatics. This would have fulfilled "the promise of Bonhoeffer" even more fully, difficult as it would have been to work out. I would have liked very much to understand how Bonhoeffer learned better from Seeberg than from Barth that "the traditional headings of theological reflection are arbitrary" (p. 109). Does Reist want us to return from Barth to Troeltsch? If it is accepted that christology protects man's social freedom, how do we find concrete direction, if not practical norms, in that christology for subsequent political action? Barth wrote on the theme of "The Christian Community and the Civil Community" (*Against the Stream*, SCM Press, London 1954, and Philosophical Library, New York, pp. 13–50). A corresponding work done in Bonhoeffer's perspective still remains to be written, taking account of the sociological importance of ecclesiology (*The Communion of Saints*), of the anti-cynical realism of *Ethics*, and of the reflection on the world that lives culturally without God (*Letters and Papers from Prison*). Reist's

does not sacralize reality but sanctifies it, departing from reality by the crucifixion in order that it may also bless rather than sacralize this reality in the resurrection.

---

point is well taken that our task in working with Bonhoeffer's fragments is not to use them to draw faulty conclusions from a few ideas, but to incorporate them into systematic research of our own (pp. 116–21).

X

The God of Reality and the Reality of God

1. *"Our mother the earth"*

Dietrich Bonhoeffer's life and work represented a total commitment to the indestructible relationship established by the incarnation between God and reality, a relationship in which God neither engulfs the world nor is the latter separated from God. He wrote:

This participation must be such that I never experience the reality of God without the reality of the world or the reality of the world without the reality of God.[1]

But the more it is possible, along with Hegel and even before him, to think in this way about the mutual reversals of the unfolding of absolute Spirit in secular reality, and about a fully rational understanding of such concrete moments, the more experience teaches us that we do not actually live as rationally as we claim we do.

Bonhoeffer tackled this difficulty in Christian terms. He was well acquainted with it, for it was part of his own upbringing. Although he belonged to a scientifically-oriented family that respected religion but was sceptical about faith, he decided as a young man purely on his own initiative and in a way that was characteristic of all his later decisions, to head toward theological study and the pastorate. Subsequently, the whole of his brief life of thirty-nine years reflected that initial experience: namely to think and choose *in the present moment,* even

---

[1] Bonhoeffer, *Ethics,* p. 195.

though Christianity would seem to encourage us to postpone deliverance until some future time and place – particularly if we understand Christianity as a "religion" in the sense that the word was used in gnosticism and the mystery religions that were the immediate neighbors and competitors of early Christianity. ¶Bonhoeffer himself wondered whether interpreting Christianity as a theology of redemption had not transformed it in the eyes of contemporary man into the gnosticism of a God who has come and gone, who may be present in some invisible other world or in the inner consciousness of certain people, but who is absent from the reality of this world.│At the age of twenty-five, when he was acting as chaplain to students at the Technical High School in Berlin, he confided to one of his friends:

The great dying of Christianity is at hand ... What do you think of the immortality of Christian faith in the face of the world situation and our own way of living? It seems to me more and more incomprehensible that for the sake of one righteous man "the city should be spared." I am now chaplain to the Technical High School: how can one preach such things to these people? Who is there who still believes them? The invisibility kills us ... This eternal desperate fact of being thrown back upon the invisible God Himself – there is not a person that can stand it any longer.[2]

Who is talking in such fashion? A man who cannot understand *how* he believes, and a man who believes in order to understand better *what* he believes. Such questions are sometimes called adolescent. They have not yet opted for either cloistered faith or convinced atheism. Bonhoeffer lived with such questions until his death. But they did not leave him introverted and tormented by a troubled conscience, or so caught up by his quest for God that he ignored history, or increasingly separated from God by his ongoing life in history. It seems to me that without arriving at a neat synthesis, probably without making much headway but also without getting trapped in rigid obscurity, Bonhoeffer managed to live by resources that gave him that conformity to reality and that companionship with God's presence and suffering in the world

[2] *GS* I, p. 61, letter to Helmut Rössler, 18 October 1931, cited in Bosanquet, *The Life and Death of Dietrich Bonhoeffer*, p. 95.

which were finally identical. In an address given in Barcelona on 25 January 1929, he said:

The Christian remains earthbound, even when his desire is toward God; he must go through all the anxiety before the laws of the world; he must learn the paradox that the world offers us a choice, not between good and evil, but between one evil and another, and that nevertheless God leads him to himself even through evil. He must feel the gross contradiction between what he would like to do and what he must do; he must grow mature, through this distress, grow mature through not leaving hold of God's hand, in the words, "Thy will be done." A glimpse of eternity is revealed only through the depths of our earth, only through the storms of a human conscience. The profound old saga tells of the giant Antaeus, who was stronger than any man on earth; no man could overcome him until once in a fight someone lifted him from the ground; then the giant lost all the strength which had flowed into him through his contact with the earth. The man who would leave the earth, who would depart from the present distress, loses the power which still holds him by eternal mysterious forces. The earth remains our mother, just as God remains our father, and our mother will only lay in the Father's arms him who remains true to her. That is the Christian's song of earth and her distress.[3]

Fifteen years later from his Berlin prison Bonhoeffer wrote in similar fashion to his fiancée, from whom death would separate him in April 1945:

Every day I am overcome anew at how undeservedly I received this happiness, and each day I am deeply moved at what a hard school God has led you through during the last year. And now it appears to be his will that I have to bring you sorrow and suffering . . . so that our love for each other may achieve the right foundation and the right endurance. When I also think about the situation of the world, the complete darkness over our personal fate and my present imprisonment, then I believe that our union can only be a sign of God's grace and kindness, which calls us to faith. We would be blind if we did not see it. Jeremiah says at the moment of his people's great need "still one shall buy houses and acres in this land" as a

[3] Bonhoeffer, *No Rusty Swords*. p. 47, cf. *GS* III, pp. 57f. This is not without analogies to Hölderlin's pledge: "And openly I pledged my heart to the grave and suffering land, and often in the consecrated night I promised to love her faithfully until death, unafraid, with her never to despise a single one of her enigmas. Thus did I join myself to her with a mortal cord" (Hölderlin, *The Death of Empedocles*, cited in Camus, *The Rebel*, p. 2).

sign of trust in the future. This is where faith belongs. May God give it to us daily. And I do not mean the faith which flees the world but one which endures the world and which loves and remains true to the world in spite of all the suffering which it contains for us. Our marriage shall be a yes to God's earth; it shall strengthen our courage to act and accomplish something on the earth. I fear that Christians who stand with only one leg upon earth also stand with only one leg in heaven.[4]

And there is a statement in another letter that illustrates the same point:

I have long had a special affection for the season between Easter and Ascension Day. Here is another great tension. How can people stand earthly tensions if they know nothing of the tension between heaven and earth?[5]

Bonhoeffer first of all represents a style, a manner of being silent when speech does not communicate, and of speaking when silence does not communicate, so that the worth and value of Jesus Christ and of every human undertaking will never be covered over by banality, or dissipated by thoughtlessness or hesitation. In a manuscript discovered in 1945, hidden in the tiles of a roof and destined for his comrades in the German resistance, Bonhoeffer wrote a memorandum that contained the following lines:

When we forget what is due to ourselves and to others, when the feeling for human quality and the power to exercise reserve cease to exist, chaos is at the door.[6]

Such a style is typical of all of Bonhoeffer's writing. It is concise, unpretentious and reserved, combining the abstraction of youth, which is creative, with the responsibility of adulthood, which weighs things carefully. This style of writing scarcely changed at all. Those who have read only *Letters and Papers from Prison* would find it much the same as his student writings – full of contrasts and aphorisms, but also very disciplined. Bonhoeffer throws himself totally into the subject under discussion, whether it is a theory of knowledge or a biblical meditation or a cultural analysis, but he almost never

---

[4] "The Other Letters from Prison," in Vorkink, ed., *op. cit.*, pp. 107f.
[5] Bonhoeffer, *LPP*, 11 April 1949, p. 148.
[6] Bonhoeffer, "After Ten Years," in *LPP*, p. 35.

displays his own inner feelings. He writes with a controlled spontaneity, thoughtful yet reserved. The most abstract argument is suddenly illuminated by a very concrete figure of speech. A personal edifying discourse is likely to be expressed in impersonal conceptualized terms.

Bonhoeffer read as widely as the circumstances of his life allowed.[7] However, his writings are not burdened with extensive documentation, and he expressed his ideas in his own words. All of a sudden he will lay hold of an idea and his thought will take wings without having to explore every nook and cranny before becoming airborne. Except in his youth, Bonhoeffer's books and essays were written far from libraries, during some pause in his active life, as a way of continuing to act or of reflecting about action that was temporarily impossible. There are few literary devices, and there is little sparkle to his prose, but there is a detached quality about his writing that is always willing to be corrected by subjection to reality. He has the freedom of daring to say things that will shock atheists (who likewise have their own saints) as much as Christians, for Bonhoeffer is less interested in sparing feelings than in challenging them. As one out of many other possible examples, let us take the following passage, written when Bonhoeffer was twenty-three:

The Christian himself creates his standards of good and evil for himself. Only he can justify his own actions, just as only he can bear the responsibility. The Christian creates new tables, a new Decalogue, as Nietzsche said of the Superman. Nietzsche's Superman is not really, as he supposed, the opposite of the Christian; without knowing it, Nietzsche has here introduced many traits of the Christian made free, as Paul and Luther described him ... Thus the discovery of what is beyond good and evil was not made by Friedrich

---

[7] Bethge, for example, notes all the books that Bonhoeffer received while he was in Tegel prison. The wide range of his interests is thus illustrated to a remarkable degree (cf. Bethge, *op. cit.*, German edition, pp. 1102–4). The same thing can be indicated by sampling the names that appear most frequently in the index to the German edition of Bethge's biography (used here since it is fuller than the English translation). A sampling: Barth, 101; Luther, 46; Bultmann, 20; Schleiermacher, 14; Kant, 10; Hegel, 9; Heidegger, 9; Griesebach, 6; Kierkegaard, 6; Nietzsche, 5; Schlatter, 4; Bernanos, 3; Feuerbach, 3; Blumhardt, 3. Near the bottom of the list are Calvin, 4; Freud, 2; and Marx, 2. Naturally this is only a skimming of the surface of an index that consists of no less than twenty-two pages of double columns.

Nietzsche, who from this standpoint utters polemics against the hypocrisy of Christianity; it belongs to the original material of the Christian message, concealed, of course, as it is.[8]

The style is in large part the man. Bonhoeffer continually had to make decisions, and one is struck by the fact that he nearly always made them alone, without relying on his friends. Indeed, he often went contrary to their advice, even though all of his writing is centered upon the "communion of saints" and the human community all men share. The notion of responsibility is central for Bonhoeffer. He reinterprets Christianity so that it is less a religion of redemption or "salvation" (a circumlocution for Feuerbach's "candidates for heaven"?) and more an acceptance of responsibility for life here and now – an ongoing and active exercise in "resistance and submission" in relation to it.[9] He rarely refers to Jesus Christ as "savior"; instead he uses other words to describe him, which as we have already seen are related to the non-religious character of his vocabulary, words like "the responsible man," "the man for others," "the deputy (*Stellvertreter*)," as well as words like the "structure," the "place" and the "center" of human existence, history and nature. God wants to invest man with responsibility. He gives him impetus and basis for it in what Jesus Christ has done as the head of a restructured humanity.

Toward the end of his life, Bonhoeffer characterized responsible life as a life free from self-preoccupation due to the bonds that tie us to our fellowmen, as a life lived in conformity to reality without which life degenerates into dualism, and as a life continually testing itself in order to risk the concrete decisions that are the hallmark of freedom. The pages of *Ethics* that are devoted to the four structures of responsible life (deputyship, correspondence with reality, the acceptance of guilt, and freedom) are, even in their abstract form, among the most concrete things Bonhoeffer ever wrote. *Life Together* represents Bonhoeffer's reflections on his life in the community of the church, yet its pages are also reflections on responsible life, both solitary and in solidarity, in the world as well.

[8] "What Is a Christian Ethic?" in *No Rusty Swords*, pp. 44, 41, cf. *GS* III, pp. 53, 50.

[9] *Resistance and Submission* is the German and French title of Bonhoeffer's prison letters.

There can be ethics only in the framework of history, in the concrete situation, at the moment of the divine call, the moment of being addressed, of the claim made by the concrete need and the situation for decision, of the claim which I have to answer and for which I have to make myself responsible. Thus there cannot be ethics in a vacuum, as a principle; there cannot be good and evil as general ideas, but only as qualities of will making a decision. There can only be good and evil as done in freedom; principles are binding under the law ... In ethical decisions we are brought into the deepest solitude, the solitude in which a man stands before the living God.[10]

2. *Prophet of the present*

From the vantage point of historical hindsight, Bonhoeffer's decisions appear clearheaded – acts of commitment and realism. But when he was making them, no doubt because they were made in extremely troubled times that permitted neither a retreat into the past nor idle hopes about the future, his decisions were disconcerting to his closest friends. He would have been upset to be remembered as a "prophet." He only wanted to be present in the midst of reality, exercising the freedom which life lived before God gives to man. But is that not precisely the etymological meaning of the word "prophet" (*pro-phanai* – to speak forth), i.e. not one who is a crystal-ball gazer into the future, but one who remains both "in the world" and "before God" all the time?

One must completely abandon any attempt to make something of oneself, whether it be a saint, or a converted sinner, or a churchman (a so-called priestly type!), a righteous man or an unrighteous one, a sick man or a healthy one. By this-worldliness I mean living unreservedly in life's duties, problems, successes and failures, experiences and perplexities. In so doing we throw ourselves completely into the arms of God, taking seriously, not our own sufferings, but those of God in the world – watching with Christ in Gethsemane. That, I think, is faith, that is *metanoia*; and that is how one becomes a man and a Christian (cf. Jer. 45!).[11]

Let us examine this theme by a final review of the three "periods" of Bonhoeffer's life.

(*a*) From 1927 to 1930 Bonhoeffer opposed those who wanted

---

[10] "What Is a Christian Ethic?" in *No Rusty Swords*, pp. 46f., 44, cf. *GS* III, pp. 56f., 44.   [11] Bonhoeffer, *LPP*, 21 July 1944, pp. 201–2.

to break away from the state church on the grounds that it was too sleepy and too structured and start a "voluntary" church – an individualistic and easy sort of reform. He also opposed those who were excited by the existentialism of the new dialectical theology and acknowledged God only as the supernatural "Totally Other" and the "tangential challenger" who challenged all human values – the very values that, however imprudently, nineteenth-century idealism and liberalism had prolonged in the belief that God could be contained within them. This early Bonhoeffer did not succumb to the moods of the moment, when the fashions were critical impatience and laziness of thought. To be sure, Bonhoeffer was a man of his time, a careful reader of Barth and Heidegger, but he kept working on Troeltsch and Lutheran scholasticism as well. Let it never be said that he had to fight for his independence. He was always independent. As a young man, he thus discovered that knowing how to avoid being swept off his feet by a rushing wave of decisions was as important as knowing how to gather momentum when he was down in the trough of indecision.

(*b*) But by 1933 the hour had come. Earlier than Barth, who at first encouraged calm, ongoing theological work,[12] to say nothing of Heidegger, Bonhoeffer saw which way the wind was blowing. Hindenberg called Hitler to the Chancellor's office on 30 January 1933. On the morning of 1 February the Berlin radio broadcast a speech of Bonhoeffer's on "The Younger Generation's Changed View of the Concept of *Führer*," in which he issued the warning:

Should the leader allow himself to succumb to the wishes of those he leads, who will always turn him into their idol, then the image of the leader will gradually become the image of the "misleader." . . . This is the leader who makes an idol of himself and his office, and who thus mocks God.[13]

Bonhoeffer's text had been prepared several days earlier.

[12] In this connection, cf. the excellent book by Daniel Cornu, *Karl Barth et la Politique*, Labor et Fides, 1968. For Barth, the strong temptation of the first months of the Nazi regime was "that because of the strength of other demands we cease to understand the intensity and exclusiveness of the demand of the divine Word, and so we at once cease to understand this Word at all" (Barth, *Theological Existence Today*, Hodder and Stoughton, London, and Musson, Toronto 1933, pp. 5f., as cited in Bosanquet, *op. cit.*, p. 125).

[13] *GS* II, pp. 35, 37; cited in Bethge, *Dietrich Bonhoeffer*, p. 194.

Before it had been read to the end, the broadcast was cut off. Had Goebbels' men already gained control of the radio in one night of power? Bonhoeffer quickly saw what was going on. So did his brother-in-law, Hans von Dohnanyi, who was later hanged just as Bonhoeffer was, for when he came home on the evening of 30 January 1933, he cried out, "This can only mean war!"

From April 1933, Bonhoeffer saw that anti-Semitism was at the heart of Nazism, which got enthusiastic support from the crowds, and sought church support for its "positive Christianity" and its celebration of the "divine providence" that had smiled upon it. Bonhoeffer thought theologically about what the church ought to say and do when "the Jew has been made subject to special laws by the state solely because of the race to which he belongs and quite apart from his religious beliefs."[14] He responded as follows:

There are three possible ways in which the church can act towards the state: in the first place, as has been said, it can ask the state whether its actions are legitimate and in accordance with its character as state, i.e. it can throw the state back on its responsibilities. Secondly, it can aid the victims of state action. The church has an unconditional obligation to the victims of any ordering of society, even if they do not belong to the Christian community. "Do good to all men." In both these courses of action, the church serves the free state in its free way, and at times when laws are changed the church may in no way withdraw itself from these two tasks. The third possibility is not just to bandage the victims under the wheel, but to put a spoke in the wheel itself. Such action would be direct political action, and it is only possible and desirable when the church sees the state fail in its function of creating law and order, i.e. when it sees the state unrestrainedly bring about too much or too little law and order. In both these cases it must see the existence of the state, and with it its own existence, threatened.[15]

As a supporter of the order of the state, as a convinced Lutheran and Hegelian, Bonhoeffer continued his battle against the disorder of Nazism from 1933 until his death in 1945 in the concentration camp at Flossenburg. His active participation in the plot against Hitler's life was only the logical outcome of this conviction. Through times of despondency and resolve, in both

[14] "The Church and the Jewish Question," in *No Rusty Swords*, p. 222, cf. *GS* II, p. 45. [15] *Ibid.*, p. 225.

agony and serenity, he stuck to his decision to follow the third possibility mentioned above, that of direct political action envisaged back in April 1933, since "only he who cries out for the Jews has the right to sing Gregorian chant."[16]

(c) Finally, from 1943 to 1945, when Bonhoeffer was alone in prison, he continued thinking about the contemporary world – not about the old bourgeois society with its state church whose resources had been placed at the service of Nazi totalitarianism; nor about the Nazi society with its persecuted church, a society that wanted to carry everything down to destruction with it, friend and foe alike. Instead, Bonhoeffer was thinking about the world that was coming, a world already present for those who knew how to see it, a world "come of age," "non-religious," where "'God' as a working hypothesis, as a stopgap for our embarrassments, has become superfluous."[17] Bonhoeffer described this world in the outline of a book (unfortunately lost) that he was working on in prison, and about which the letters to Bethge give us only scraps of commentary. Bonhoeffer saw this world "come of age" as an organized world, as "the safeguarding of life against 'accidents' and 'blows of fate.'"

The aim: to be independent of nature. Nature was formerly conquered by spiritual means, with us by technical organization of all kinds. Our immediate environment is not nature, as formerly, but organization. But with this protection from nature's menace there arises a new one – through organization itself.

But the spiritual force is lacking. The question is: what protects us against the menace of organization? Man is thrown back upon himself. He has managed to deal with everything, only not with himself. He can insure against everything, only not against man. In the last resort it all turns on man.[18]

This outline was written in 1944, when the war was coming to an end, when Germany was on the verge of defeat and yet still held on to the Nazi demons, and the allies were close to the intoxicating prospect of liberation and were dreaming about revolution (or restoration). It is full of insight. Surely a mistake is made by those who see Bonhoeffer only as the prophet of the world come of age and of a non-religious humanity – themes

[16] Bethge, ed., *Die Mündige Welt* I, p. 23.
[17] Bonhoeffer, *LPP*, "Outline for a Book," after the letter of 3 August 1944, p. 209.
[18] *Ibid.*, pp. 208f.

that have been popularized by the theologians of the "secular city" as well as those of the "death of God." World come of age, non-religious interpretation, secularity, atheism – such themes are indeed present in Bonhoeffer's writing, but in many respects they are already things that have been experienced in the ordinary situation of the world. However, simply to notice what is going on is not in itself enough to constitute responsible action in the present. From 1944, Bonhoeffer saw that the world of organization, without religion, metaphysics or ideology, was likewise being revealed as an unstructured world, technologically capable but psychologically and spiritually fragile. Its organization might save it from natural disasters, but the same organization was condemning it to an inner emptiness. The abundance of its means was hiding the nihilism of its ends.

What role could the church play in this new world where it would be neither a state church nor a persecuted church, but only marginal? Bonhoeffer offers no agenda for this, and gives only a few brief hints. It would be necessary, he says, to understand Jesus Christ as "the man for others," that is to say, the crucified one, and to ask ourselves personally: "What do we truly believe in such a way that our very life depends on it?"

The Church is the Church only when it exists for others. To make a start, it should give away all its property to those in need. The clergy must live solely on the free-will offerings of their congregations, or possibly engage in some secular calling. The Church must share in the secular problems of ordinary human life, not dominating, but helping and serving. It must tell men of every calling what it means to live in Christ, to exist for others. In particular, our own Church will have to take the field against the vices of *hubris*, power-worship, envy, and humbug, as the roots of all evil. It will have to speak of moderation, purity, trust, loyalty, constancy, patience, discipline, humility, contentment, and modesty. It must not underestimate the importance of human example (which has its origin in the humanity of Jesus and is so important in Paul's teaching); it is not abstract argument, but example, that gives its word emphasis and power.[19]

Anyone who was anticipating a brand-new Christianity in the "religionless" era will probably be disappointed by this call for realism and humility in the life of faith. But here again

[19] *Ibid.*, p. 211. Note that Bonhoeffer is writing out of the situation of the German Church that has traditionally been supported by the state.

Bonhoeffer guards against idle theorizing. The authenticity of the church depends on a hidden coincidence, in the life of each and every member, between faith and the world. Their model is the structure of responsible deputyship, exemplified by Jesus Christ, for whom "transcendence" is the reality of his service to others. Bonhoeffer feels that the "non-religious world come of age" of contemporary organized societies has just as much need (though in a different way) of that lost center who is Jesus Christ, as did the earlier mythic and "religious" worlds of "natural" societies. What must change in Christianity is surely that it must rid itself of its traditional attachment to the earlier position in order to relate itself more truly to the contemporary one. This must be done so that the "organization man" will no longer see God as the phantom of an ultimate assurance and support who disappears when the beyond disappears, but will see him rather as the presence of a structure able to reunite the earth and respond to the concerns, both resistant and submissive, of human responsibility.[20] When a "meta-physical" view loses credibility, a question is raised: can a merely "physical" view, on its own terms, provide a word to which we can make creative response? Who speaks in this new situation of ontological openness?

Bonhoeffer is particularly impressive in his ability to have anticipated the present, and since 1944 to have foreseen, without trying to foretell, that today Christianity is face to face as far as most men are concerned with a latent doubt about the reality of God. During the Enlightenment, religion was attacked particularly for its obscurantism, pessimism and fanaticism. "Destroy these enclosures which obstruct your horizons; liberate God; see Him everywhere He actually is, or else say that He does not exist at all," was Diderot's cry.[21] During the nineteenth century, and into the middle of the twentieth, God was accused instead of infringing human freedom. "Man becomes an atheist when he discovers that he is superior to his God," Proudhon announced, and Sartre echoes the theme in *The Flies* in an exchange between Zeus and Orestes:

[20] Once again, a play on the German and French title of Bonhoeffer's prison letters, *Resistance and Submission*.

[21] Diderot, *Pensées Philosophiques*, cited in E. Cassirer, *The Philosophy of the Enlightenment*, Beacon Press, Boston 1955, p. 166.

Zeus: I gave you freedom so that you might serve me.
Orestes: Perhaps. But now it has turned against its giver and neither
you nor I can undo what has been done.[22]

Today the attacks and accusations are very different – less
aggressive but more radical. They turn on the absence, the
silence, the eclipse, the ineffectiveness, the unreality and the
death of God. Bonhoeffer wrote in terms of this present climate
of opinion. He re-examined his faith in Christianity's development in an empirical world that feels itself without God.

Bonhoeffer's first response to this new situation was to
emphasize responsible action and decision in the present. When
God and reality are separated, nothing can reconcile them
except an actual demonstration that life before God is life in
the world and vice versa, in a unity that one cannot explain but
to which one can witness. This will be a witness that does not
seek to put anything else on trial but is itself on trial, a trial in
which the ethic of behavior understands itself as ontology within
faith.

3. *A paradoxical thinker*

But Bonhoeffer also makes a second response, based on the
specific and concrete nature of God's action in biblical history.
His attachment to the Old Testament is the determining factor
here. In the Old Testament, the reality of God is limited to the
boundaries of the God of reality: God is discerned only within
the boundaries of life and the body, and not in the "beyond" of
death or the "within" of the disembodied soul. Consequently
gnosticism is unthinkable and dualism is ruled out. According to
Christianity, the Old Testament leads toward a God confined
to the reality of a man (the incarnation) and what happened to
him (the crucifixion). The specific nature of such a God is that
he becomes weak for man's sake. In contrast to the classical
religious construct of an all-powerful God giving aid to human
misery, Bonhoeffer offers the construct (which he considers the
only truly biblical one) of an enduring, suffering God, "in
agony" as Pascal said, and of an autonomous mankind,
liberated not for irresponsible self-sufficiency, but for responsible
adulthood.

[22] Sartre, *No Exit and Three Other Plays*, Vintage Books, New York 1949, pp. 120f.

Nietzsche accused Christianity of being only a "Platonism for the people," of falsely dividing the world in dualistic fashion, and of teaching, out of a jealousy born of powerlessness, that men should always sacrifice the truth and tragic beauty of the world around them to the illusion of an ideal world. Feuerbach saw God as a vampire who gained omnipotence by feeding on human weakness. He foresaw the day when man would recoup his losses against God, and by ceasing to continue the futile detour through divinity would finally learn to consider humanity itself as the highest value.

On the face of it, Bonhoeffer seems to be responding to Nietzsche. From the perspective of his realism he sees God not at the edges but at the center of life, not beyond the world but within it, as the Word that structures and unifies the world, as the "this-worldly transcendence" to which Ronald Gregor Smith refers. Basically, however, Bonhoeffer is responding even more to Feuerbach[23] – provided the God of the cross, who wants man to come of age, escapes from the dangers of the alienating and destructive humbug contained in the religious detour, provided faith no longer leads to the revolt of atheism against reducing religion's status, and provided such faith returns man to the world in God's company, when "religion" is understood as a turning away from the world toward a God found elsewhere.

The world has come of age and God is on the cross. And now comes the final question: does not the reality of God disappear by the time he is fully present in reality? Here is where Hegel had difficulty, for according to his logic the death of God does not mean the deliverance of reality by God, but the loss of any distinction between the two. Kierkegaard exults:

The fact that God could create free beings *vis-à-vis* of himself is the cross which philosophy could not carry, but remained hanging from.[24]

Bonhoeffer himself moved so close to a theology of the involvement of God in the world (much closer in this regard to Hegel

[23] On the relationship of Bonhoeffer to Feuerbach, cf. Henri Mottu, "Feuerbach and Bonhoeffer: Criticism of Religion and the Last Period of Bonhoeffer's Thoughts," *Union Seminary Quarterly Review*, Fall 1969, pp. 1–18.

[24] Kierkegaard, *The Journals*, Oxford University Press, London 1938, §204, p. 58.

fusion of transcendence

than to Kierkegaard) that some of his ways of speaking lean toward a reality of presence that is scarcely distinguishable from the presence of reality. This is not to say that God has disappeared from reality or become identical with it. Rather, he unites himself with reality (if one may so dare to put it) not in terms of a theism of divine absence but of an atheism of divine presence.

When all is said and done, the man who wrote *Letters and Papers from Prison* does not talk very much about God. He often talks about the world, and he talks even more about the world *to* God, as though prayer, along with responsible action, was the act of identity with God for one who experiences his own identification with the world. One of the clearest indications that Christianity no longer cuts the "religious" man off from secular reality would be the experience of a prayer in which man found in God the natural partner of his own responsibility in the world. It is true that prayer is more the presupposition than the solution to the problem of the knowledge of God. But prayer itself, like responsible action, is also a kind of behavior in which understanding comes through decision. As Bonhoeffer puts it:

It is a dangerous error, surely very widespread among Christians, to think that the heart can pray by itself. For then we confuse wishes, hopes, sighs, laments, rejoicings – all of which the heart can do by itself – with prayer. And we confuse earth and heaven, man and God. Prayer doesn't mean simply to pour out one's heart. It means rather to find the way to God and to speak with him, whether the heart is full or empty. No man can do that by himself. For that he needs Jesus Christ.[25]

This is the Jesus Christ whom Bonhoeffer called "center" of the world rather than mediator, "structure" rather than norm, "responsible man" rather than divine Savior.

Such, then, was Dietrich Bonhoeffer – a theologian, a Christian, a paradoxical contemporary, who developed at one and the same time a theology of the God of reality and of the reality of God.

[25] Bonhoeffer, *Psalms: The Prayer Book of the Bible*, pp. 9f. What then does becoming a Christian add to becoming a man? Nothing, if one does not try to embody what Jesus Christ did and encountered as a man: love leading to the cross, and hope leading to the resurrection.

BIBLIOGRAPHY

Bibliographical material about Bonhoeffer has gone beyond all compassable bounds. Consequently, the works cited below are limited to (*a*) some basic German materials not otherwise available in English, (*b*) writings of Bonhoeffer himself that are available in English, and (*c*) books about Bonhoeffer in English. Omitted are articles about Bonhoeffer in periodicals, and books that deal only in part with Bonhoeffer. Bibliographies that fill in the latter omissions can be found in John D. Godsey, *Preface to Bonhoeffer*, Fortress Press, Philadelphia 1965, pp. 70–73; William Kuhns, *In Pursuit of Dietrich Bonhoeffer*, Pflaum Press, Dayton 1967, pp. 287–97; and Peter Vorkink, ed., *Bonhoeffer in a World Come of Age*, Fortress Press, Philadelphia 1968, pp. 133–40. Two full German bibliographies are contained in *Die Mündige Welt* II, pp. 204–13, and Hanfried Müller, *Von der Kirche zur Welt*, pp. 552–62.

A. *Basic German materials not available in English*

Eberhard Bethge, *Dietrich Bonhoeffer: Theologe – Christ – Zeitgenosse*, Chr. Kaiser Verlag, München 1967, 1128pp.
    Although this book has been translated into English, the translation is abridged, and the appendices, giving outlines of Bonhoeffer's courses at the University of Berlin, have been omitted.
Eberhard Bethge, ed., *Die Mündige Welt*, Chr. Kaiser Verlag, München, I-V.
    Five volumes of symposia dealing with Bonhoeffer's thought have been published since 1955. A few of the essays have been translated in R. Gregor Smith, ed., *World Come of Age*, Collins, London and Fortress Press, Philadelphia 1967.
Dietrich Bonhoeffer, *Gesammelte Schriften*, Chr. Kaiser Verlag, München, I-IV, 1958–61, edited by Eberhard Bethge.

Along with Bonhoeffer's published books, these four volumes comprise the basic primary source materials. Volume I contains Bonhoeffer's ecumenical writings during 1928–42. Volume II deals with the period of the German "church struggle," and the seminary at Finkenwalde, during 1933–43. Volume III contains lectures, letters and speeches on theological themes during 1927–44. Volume IV contains biblical exegesis and sermons given in Berlin, London and Finkenwalde during 1931–44, including a few writings from Tegel that are omitted from *Letters and Papers from Prison*.

Considerable portions of Volumes I–III, and a few extracts from Volume IV, have been translated into English in *No Rusty Swords*, Collins, London, and Harper and Row, New York 1965, and *The Way to Freedom*, Collins, London, and Harper and Row, New York 1967.

Hanfried Müller, *Von der Kirche zur Welt*, Koehler und Amelang, Leipzig 1966, 561pp.

Heinrich Ott, *Wirklichkeit und Glaube, I, Zum Theologischen Erbe Dietrich Bonhoeffers*, Vandenhoeck und Ruprecht, Zürich 1966, 394pp.

The above two extensive analyses of Bonhoeffer's thought are considered in detail in Chapter IX.

B. *Writings of Bonhoeffer available in English*

The writings listed below are placed as nearly as posssible in the order of their composition, rather than their publication. Only the most recent editions, from which they have been cited, are mentioned. A great many of Bonhoeffer's important writings, particularly during the German Church struggle, are included in the two volumes translated from the *Gesammelte Schriften*, *No Rusty Swords* and *The Way to Freedom*. Three further essays and two sermons from the *Gesammelte Schriften* are also included in the list below, since they appear in that collection in English and furnish further clues to Bonhoeffer's thinking at crucial points in his life.

The Communion of Saints, Collins, London, and Harper and Row, New York 1963, 256 pp., translated by R. Gregor Smith and others. Bonhoeffer's university thesis, defended in 1927, first published in German in 1930.

Act and Being, Collins, London, and Harper and Row, New York 1962, 192 pp., translated by Bernard Noble, introduction by Ernst Wolf. Bonhoeffer's habilitation thesis, defended in 1930, first published in German in 1931.

"The Religious Experience and the Ethical Life," paper at Union Theological Seminary, 1930–31, in *Gesammelte Schriften* III, pp. 91–9.

"Concerning the Christian Idea of God," written in 1931, in *Gesammelte Schriften* III, pp. 100–109, also published in *The Journal of Religion*, April 1932, pp. 177–85.

"Thy Kingdom Come," a lecture given in 1932, first published in German in 1933, available in John D. Godsey, *Preface to Bonhoeffer*, Fortress Press, Philadelphia 1965, pp. 27–47.

Creation and Fall, pp. 9–94 of *Creation and Fall/Temptation*, Macmillan, New York 1965. (*Creation and Temptation*, SCM Press, London 1966, is the same translation but with slightly different pagination.) Translated by John C. Fletcher and others. Lectures given in Berlin in 1932 under the title "Creation and Sin," and first published in German in 1933.

Christ the Center, Harper and Row, New York (= *Christology*, Collins, London) 1966, 126 pp., translated by John Bowden, introduction by Edwin H. Robertson. Lectures given in Berlin in 1933 under the title "Christology," compiled from students' notes by Eberhard Bethge, and first published in German in 1960 in *Gesammelte Schriften* III, pp. 166–242.

No Rusty Swords, Collins, London, and Harper and Row, New York 1965, 384 pp., translated by Edwin H. Robertson and John Bowden, edited and introduced by Edwin H. Robertson. Writings of Bonhoeffer from the years 1928–36, translated from *Gesammelte Schriften* I–IV.

The Way to Freedom, Collins, London, and Harper and Row, New York 1967, 288 pp., translated by Edwin H. Robertson and John Bowden, edited and introduced by Edwin H. Robertson. Various writings of Bonhoeffer from 1935–9, translated from *Gesammelte Schriften* I–IV.

Sermons on Proverbs 16.9 and II Corinthians 12.9, preached in London in 1934, in *Gesammelte Schriften* IV, pp. 174–82.

The Cost of Discipleship, SCM Press, London, and Macmillan, New York 1959, 285pp., translated by R. H. Fuller and Irmgard Booth, with a foreword by G. K. A. Bell and a memoir by G. Leibholz. Lecture materials used at Finkenwalde and Berlin, first published in German in 1937.

Temptation, pp. 95–128 of *Creation and Fall/Temptation* (see above). Translated by Kathleen Downham. Lectures given at a Finkenwalde reunion in June 1938 (not 1937 as stated in the note appended to the text), first published in German in 1953.

Life Together, Harper and Row, New York, and SCM Press, London 1954, 122 pp., translated and with an introduction by John W. Doberstein. An account of the Finkenwalde experiment, written in 1938 and first published in German in 1939.

Psalms: The Prayer Book of the Bible, Augsburg, Minneapolis 1970, 86pp., translated by James H. Burtness, with a biographical sketch by Eberhard Bethge. Brief meditations first published in German in 1940, the last of Bonhoeffer's writings published during his lifetime.

"The Church and the New Order in Europe," comments on a book by William Paton, written in 1941, in *Gesammelte Schriften* I, pp. 362–71.

Ethics, Macmillan, New York 1965, and Collins, London 1968, 382pp., translated by Neville Horton Smith, with an editor's preface by Eberhard Bethge. (The translation is that of the 1955 edition, SCM Press, London, and Macmillan, New York, but the arrangement is that of the sixth German edition of 1963. See Ch. II, n.63, and Ch. VI, p. 140.) The extensive fragments of what Bonhoeffer expected to be his major work, written between 1940 and 1944, first published in German in 1949.

I Loved This People, John Knox Press, Richmond 1965, 62pp., translated by Keith Krim, with an introduction by Hans Rothfels. Very brief fragments from 1941–4.

"The First Table of the Ten Commandments," written in Tegel in 1944, and available in Godsey, *op. cit.*, pp. 49–67.

Letters and Papers from Prison, SCM Press, London, and Macmillan, New York 1967, 240pp., translated by Reginald Fuller and revised by Frank Clarke and others. Materials written in prison, 1943–5, together with "After Ten Years," written in 1942, first published in German in 1951.

c. Books about Bonhoeffer in English

J. M. Bailey and D. Gilbert, *The Steps of Bonhoeffer: A Pictorial Album*, Pilgrim Press, Philadelphia 1969, 128pp.

Eberhard Bethge, *Dietrich Bonhoeffer: Theologian, Christian, Contemporary*, Collins, London, and Harper and Row, New York 1970, 867pp.

Mary Bosanquet, *The Life and Death of Dietrich Bonhoeffer*, Hodder and Stoughton, London 1968; Harper and Row, New York 1969, 287 pp.

Theodore A. Gill, *Memo for a Movie: a Short Life of Dietrich Bonhoeffer*, Macmillan, New York 1970; SCM Press, London 1971, 164pp.

John D. Godsey, *The Theology of Dietrich Bonhoeffer*, Westminster Press, Philadelphia, and SCM Press, London 1960, 209pp.

William B. Gould, *The Worldly Christian: Bonhoeffer on Discipleship*, Fortress Press, Philadelphia 1967, 94pp.

Kenneth Hamilton, *Life in One's Stride: A Short Study in Dietrich Bonhoeffer*, Eerdmans, Grand Rapids 1968, 91pp.

William Kuhns, *In Pursuit of Dietrich Bonhoeffer*, Pflaum Press, Dayton 1967; Burns & Oates, London 1968, 314pp.

René Marlé, *Bonhoeffer: The Man and His Work*, Newman Press, New York 1968, 141pp.

Martin Marty, ed., *The Place of Bonhoeffer*, Association Press, New York 1962; SCM Press, London 1963, 224pp.

Jürgen Moltmann and Jürgen Weissbach, *Two Studies in the Theology of Bonhoeffer*, Scribners, New York 1967, 159pp.

John A. Phillips, *The Form of Christ in the World: A Study of Bonhoeffer's Christology*, Collins, London = *Christ for Us in the Theology of Dietrich Bonhoeffer*, Harper and Row, New York 1967, 303pp.

Benjamin A. Reist, *The Promise of Bonhoeffer*, Lippincott, Philadelphia 1969, 128pp.

Edwin H. Robertson, *Dietrich Bonhoeffer*, Carey Kingsgate Press, London, and John Knox Press, Richmond 1966, 54pp.

R. Gregor Smith, ed., *World Come of Age*, Collins, London, and Fortress Press, Philadelphia 1967, 288pp. (selections from *Die Mündige Welt* I–IV).

Peter Vorkink, ed., *Bonhoeffer in a World Come of Age*, Fortress Press, Philadelphia 1968, 141pp.

J. W. Woelfel, *Bonhoeffer's Theology: Classical and Revolutionary*, Abingdon Press, Nashville 1970, 350pp.

Wolf-Dieter Zimmermann and R. Gregor Smith, eds., *I Knew Dietrich Bonhoeffer*, Collins, London, and Harper and Row, New York 1966, 238pp.

INDEX OF BIBLICAL REFERENCES

INDEX TO WORKS BY
DIETRICH BONHOEFFER

INDEX OF NAMES